THE DEATH OF MONEY

THE DEATH OF MONEY

THE COMING COLLAPSE
OF THE INTERNATIONAL
MONETARY SYSTEM

JAMES RICKARDS

PORTFOLIO / PENGUIN

PORTFOLIO / PENGUIN
Published by the Penguin Group
Penguin Group (USA) LLC
375 Hudson Street
New York, New York 10014

USA I Canada I UK I Ireland I Australia I New Zealand I India I South Africa I China
penguin.com
A Penguin Random House Company

First published by Portfolio / Penguin, a member of Penguin Group (USA) LLC, 2014

ISBN 978-1-59184-670-3
ISBN 978-1-59184-741-0 (Export Edition)

Printed in the United States of America
19 20 18

Set in Sabon LT Std
Designed by Alissa Rose Theodor

For Glen, Wayne, Keith, Diane, and Eric—all best friends since the days we were born

Write down, therefore, what you have seen, and what is happening, and what will happen afterwards.

Revelation 1:19

CONTENTS

THE DEATH OF MONEY

INTRODUCTION

The Death of Money is about the demise of the dollar. By extension, it is also about the potential collapse of the international monetary system because, if confidence in the dollar is lost, no other currency stands ready to take its place as the world's reserve currency. The dollar is the linchpin. If it fails, the entire system fails with it, since the dollar and the system are one and the same. As fearsome a prospect as this dual collapse may be, it looks increasingly inevitable for all the reasons one will find in the pages to come.

A journey to the past is in order first.

Few Americans in our time recall that the dollar nearly ceased to function as the world's reserve currency in 1978. That year the Federal Reserve dollar index declined to a distressingly low level, and the U.S. Treasury was forced to issue government bonds denominated in Swiss francs. Foreign creditors no longer trusted the U.S. dollar as a store of value. The dollar was losing purchasing power, dropping by half from 1977 to 1981; U.S. inflation was over 50 percent during those five years. Starting in 1979, the International Monetary Fund (IMF) had little choice but to mobilize its resources to issue world money (special drawing rights, or SDRs). It flooded the market with 12.1 billion SDRs to provide liquidity as global confidence in the dollar declined.

We would do well to recall those dark days. The price of gold rose 500 percent from 1977 to 1980. What began as a managed dollar devaluation in 1971, with President Richard Nixon's abandonment of gold convertibility, became a full-scale rout by the decade's end. The dollar debacle even seeped into popular culture. The 1981 film *Rollover,* starring Jane Fonda, involved a secret plan by oil-producing nations to dump dollars and buy gold; it ended with a banking collapse, a financial panic, and global riots. That was fiction but indeed was powerful, perhaps prescient.

While the dollar panic reached a crescendo in the late 1970s, lost confidence was felt as early as August 1971, immediately after President Nixon's abandonment of the gold-backed dollar. Author Janet Tavakoli describes what it was like to be an American abroad the day the dollar's death throes became glaringly apparent:

> Suddenly Americans traveling abroad found that restaurants, hotels, and merchants did not want to take the floating rate risk of their dollars. On Ferragosto [mid-August holiday], banks in Rome were closed, and Americans caught short of cash were in a bind.
>
> The manager of the hotel asked departing guests: "Do you have gold? Because look what your American President has done." He was serious about gold; he would accept it as payment. . . .
>
> I immediately asked to pre-pay my hotel bill in lire. . . . The manager clapped his hands in delight. He and the rest of the staff treated me as if I were royalty. I wasn't like those other Americans with their stupid dollars. For the rest of my stay, no merchant or restaurant wanted my business until I demonstrated I could pay in lire.

The subsequent efforts of Fed chairman Paul Volcker and the newly elected Ronald Reagan would save the dollar. Volcker raised interest rates to 19 percent in 1981 to snuff out inflation and make the dollar an attractive choice for foreign capital. Beginning in 1981, Reagan cut taxes and regulation, which restored business confidence and made the United States a magnet for foreign investment. By March 1985, the dollar index had rallied 50 percent from its October 1978 low, and gold prices had dropped 60 percent from their 1980 high. The U.S. inflation rate fell from 13.5 percent in 1980 to 1.9 percent in 1986. The good news was such that Hollywood released no *Rollover 2*. By the mid-1980s, the fire was out, and the age of King Dollar had begun. The dollar had not disappeared as the world's reserve currency after 1978, but it was a near run thing.

Now the world is back to the future.

A similar constellation of symptoms to those of 1978 can be seen in the world economy today. In July 2011 the Federal Reserve dollar index hit an all-time low, over 4 percent below the October 1978 panic level. In August 2009 the IMF once again acted as a monetary first responder and rode to the rescue with a new issuance of SDRs, equivalent to $310 billion, increasing the SDRs in circulation by 850 percent. In early September gold prices reached an all-time high, near $1,900 per ounce, up more than 200 percent from the average price in 2006, just before the new depression began. Twenty-first-century popular culture enjoyed its own version of *Rollover,* a televised tale of financial collapse called *Too Big to Fail.*

The parallels between 1978 and recent events are eerie but imperfect. There was an element ravaging the world then that is not apparent today. It is the dog that didn't bark: inflation. But the fact that we aren't hearing the dog doesn't mean it poses no danger. Widely followed U.S. dollar inflation measures such as the consumer price index have barely budged since 2008; indeed, mild *deflation* has emerged in certain months. Inflation has appeared in China, where the government revalued the currency to dampen it, and in Brazil, where price hikes in basic services such as bus fares triggered riots. Food price inflation was also a contributing factor to protests in the Arab Spring's early stages. Still, U.S. dollar inflation has remained subdued.

Looking more closely, we see a veritable cottage industry that computes U.S. price indexes using pre-1990 methodologies, and alternative baskets of goods and services that are said to be more representative of the inflation actually facing Americans. They offer warning signs, as the alternative methods identify U.S. inflation at more like 9 percent annually, instead of the 2 percent readings of official government measures. Anyone shopping for milk, bread, or gasoline would certainly agree with the higher figure. As telling as these shadow statistics may be, they have little impact on international currency markets or Federal Reserve policy. To understand the threats to the dollar, and potential policy responses by the Federal Reserve, it is necessary to see the dollar through the Fed's eyes. From that perspective, inflation is *not* a threat; indeed, higher inflation is both the Fed's answer to the debt crisis and a policy objective.

This pro-inflation policy is an invitation to disaster, even as baffled Fed critics scratch their heads at the apparent absence of inflation in the face of unprecedented money printing by the Federal Reserve and other major central banks. Many ponder how it is that the Fed has increased the base money supply 400 percent since 2008 with practically no inflation. But two explanations are very much at hand—and they foretell the potential for collapse. The first is that the U.S. economy is structurally damaged, so the easy money cannot be put to good use. The second is that the inflation is coming. Both explanations are true—the economy is broken, and inflation is on its way.

The Death of Money examines these events in a distinctive way. The chapters that follow look critically at standard economic tools such as equilibrium models, so-called value-at-risk metrics, and supposed correlations. You will see that the general equilibrium models in widespread use are meaningless in a state of perturbed equilibrium or dual equilibria. The world economy is not yet in the "new normal." Instead, the world is on a journey from old to new with no compass or chart. Turbulence is now the norm.

Danger comes from within and without. We have a misplaced confidence that central banks can save the day; in fact, they are ruining our markets. The value-at-risk models used by Wall Street and regulators to measure the dangers that derivatives pose are risible; they mask overleveraging, which is shamelessly transformed into grotesque compensation that is throwing our society out of balance. When the hidden costs come home to roost and taxpayers are once again stuck with the bill, the bankers will be comfortably ensconced inside their mansions and aboard their yachts. The titans will explain to credulous reporters and bought-off politicians that the new collapse was nothing they could have foreseen.

While we refuse to face truths about debts and deficits, dozens of countries all over the globe are putting pressure on the dollar. We think the gold standard is a historical relic, but there's a contemporary scramble for gold around the world, and it may signify a move to return to the gold standard. We greatly underestimate the dangers from a cyberfinancial attack and the risks of a financial world war.

Regression analysis and correlations, so beloved by finance quants and economists, are ineffective for navigating the risks ahead. These analyses assume that the future resembles the past to an extent. History is a great teacher, but the quants' suppositions contain fatal flaws. The first is that in looking back, they do not look far enough. Most data used on Wall

Street extend ten, twenty, or thirty years into the past. The more diligent analysts will use hundred-year data series, finding suitable substitutes for instruments that did not exist that far back. But the two greatest civilizational collapses in history, the Bronze Age collapse and the fall of the Roman Empire, occurred sixteen hundred years apart, and the latter was sixteen hundred years ago. This is not to suggest civilization's imminent collapse, merely to point out the severely limited perspective offered by most regressions. The other flaw involves the quants' failures to understand scaling dynamics that place certain risk measurements outside history. Since potential risk is an exponential function of system scale, and since the scale of financial systems measured by derivatives is unprecedented, it follows that the risk too is unprecedented.

While the word *collapse* as applied to the dollar sounds apocalyptic, it has an entirely pragmatic meaning. Collapse is simply the loss of confidence by citizens and central banks in the future purchasing power of the dollar. The result is that holders dump dollars, either through faster spending or through the purchase of hard assets. This rapid behavioral shift leads initially to higher interest rates, higher inflation, and the destruction of capital formation. The end result can be deflation (reminiscent of the 1930s) or inflation (reminiscent of the 1970s), or both.

The coming collapse of the dollar and the international monetary system is entirely foreseeable. This is not a provocative conclusion. The international monetary system has collapsed three times in the past century—in 1914, 1939, and 1971. Each collapse was followed by a tumultuous period. The 1914 collapse was precipitated by the First World War and was followed later by alternating episodes of hyperinflation and depression from 1919 to 1922 before regaining stability in the mid-1920s, albeit with a highly flawed gold standard that contributed to a new collapse in the 1930s. The Second World War caused the 1939 collapse, and stability was restored only with the Bretton Woods system, created in 1944. The 1971 collapse was precipitated by Nixon's abandonment of gold convertibility for the dollar, although this dénouement had been years in the making, and it was followed by confusion, culminating in the near dollar collapse in 1978.

The coming collapse, like those before, may involve war, gold, or chaos, or it could involve all three. This book limns the most imminent threats to the dollar, likely to play out in the next few years, which are financial warfare, deflation, hyperinflation, and market collapse. Only nations and individuals who make provision today will survive the maelstrom to come.

In place of fallacious, if popular, methods, this book considers complexity theory to be the best lens for viewing present risks and likely outcomes. Capital markets are complex systems nonpareil. Complexity theory is relatively new in the history of science, but in its sixty years it has been extensively applied to weather, earthquakes, social networks, and other densely connected systems. The application of complexity theory to capital markets is still in its infancy, but it has already yielded insights into risk metrics and price dynamics that possess greater predictive power than conventional methods.

As you will see in the pages that follow, the next financial collapse will resemble nothing in history. But a more clear-eyed view of opaque financial happenings in our world can help investors think through the best strategies. In this book's conclusion you will find some recommendations, but deciding upon the best course to follow will require comprehending a minefield of risks, while poised at a crossroads, pondering the death of the dollar.

Beyond mere market outcomes, consider financial war.

■ Financial War

Are we prepared to fight a financial war? The conduct of financial war is distinct from normal economic competition among nations because it involves intentional malicious acts rather than solely competitive ones. Financial war entails the use of derivatives and the penetration of exchanges to cause havoc, incite panic, and ultimately disable an enemy's economy. Financial war goes well beyond industrial espionage, which has existed at least since the early 1800s, when an American, Francis Cabot Lowell, memorized the design for the English power loom and recreated one in the United States.

The modern financial war arsenal includes covert hedge funds and cyberattacks that can compromise order-entry systems to mimic a flood of sell orders on stocks like Apple, Google, and IBM. Efficient-market theorists who are skeptical of such tactics fail to fathom the irrational underbelly of markets in full flight. Financial war is not about wealth maximization but victory.

Risks of financial war in the age of dollar hegemony are novel because the United States has never had to coexist in a world where market participants did not depend on it for their national security. Even at the height of dollar flight in 1978, Germany, Japan, and the oil exporters were expected to prop up the dollar because they were utterly dependent on the United States to protect them against Soviet threats. Today powerful nations such as Russia, China, and Iran do not rely on the United States for their national security, and they may even see some benefit in an economically wounded America. Capital markets have moved decisively into the realm of strategic affairs, and Wall Street analysts and Washington policy makers, who most need to understand the implications, are only dimly aware of this new world.

▪ Inflation

Critics from Richard Cantillon in the early eighteenth century to V. I. Lenin and John Maynard Keynes in the twentieth have been unanimous in their view that inflation is the stealth destroyer of savings, capital, and economic growth.

Inflation often begins imperceptibly and gains a foothold before it is recognized. This lag in comprehension, important to central banks, is called *money illusion*, a phrase that refers to a perception that real wealth is being created, so that Keynesian "animal spirits" are aroused. Only later is it discovered that bankers and astute investors captured the wealth, and everyday citizens are left with devalued savings, pensions, and life insurance.

The 1960s and 1970s are a good case study in money illusion. From 1961 through 1965, annual U.S. inflation averaged 1.24 percent. In 1965 President Lyndon Johnson began a massive bout of spending and incurred budget deficits with his "guns and butter" policy of an expanded war in Vietnam and Great Society benefits. The Federal Reserve accommodated this spending, and that accommodation continued through President Nixon's 1972 reelection. Inflation was gradual at first; it climbed to 2.9 percent in 1966 and 3.1 percent in 1967. Then it spun out of control, reaching 5.7 percent in 1970, finally peaking at 13.5 percent in 1980. It was not until 1986 that inflation returned to the 1.9 percent level more typical of the early 1960s.

Two lessons from the 1960s and 1970s are highly pertinent today. The first is that inflation can gain substantial momentum before the general public notices it. It was not until 1974, nine years into an inflationary cycle, that inflation became a potent political issue and prominent public policy concern. This lag in momentum and perception is the essence of money illusion.

Second, once inflation perceptions shift, they are extremely difficult to reset. In the Vietnam era, it took nine years for everyday Americans to focus on inflation, and an additional eleven years to reanchor expectations. Rolling a rock down a hill is much faster than pushing it back up to the top.

More recently, since 2008 the Federal Reserve has printed over $3 trillion of new money, but without stoking much inflation in the United States. Still, the Fed has set an inflation target of at least 2.5 percent, possibly higher, and will not relent in printing money until that target is achieved. The Fed sees inflation as a way to dilute the real value of U.S. debt and avoid the specter of deflation.

Therein lies a major risk. History and behavioral psychology both provide reason to believe that once the inflation goal is achieved and expectations are altered, a feedback loop will emerge in which higher inflation leads to higher inflation expectations, to even higher inflation, and so on. The Fed will not be able to arrest this feedback loop because its dynamic is a function not of monetary policy but of human nature.

As the inflation feedback loop gains energy, a repetition of the late 1970s will be in prospect. Skyrocketing gold prices and a crashing dollar, two sides of the same coin, will happen quickly. The difference between the next episode of runaway inflation and the last is that Russia, China, and the IMF will stand ready with gold and SDRs, not dollars, to provide new reserve assets. When the dollar next falls from the high wire, there will be no net.

■ Deflation

There has been no episode of persistent deflation in the United States since the period from 1927 to 1933; as a result, Americans have practically no living memory of deflation. The United States would have experienced severe deflation from 2009 to 2013 but for massive money printing by the Federal Reserve. The U.S. economy's prevailing deflationary drift has not disappeared. It has only been papered over.

Deflation is the Federal Reserve's worst nightmare for many reasons. Real gains from deflation cannot easily be taxed. If a school administrator earns $100,000 per year, prices are constant, and she receives a 5 percent raise, her real pretax standard of living has increased $5,000, but the government taxes the increase, leaving less for the individual. But if her earnings are held constant, and prices drop 5 percent, she has the same $5,000 increase in her standard of living, but the government *cannot tax the gain* because it comes in the form of lower prices rather than higher wages.

Deflation increases the real value of government debt, making it harder to repay. If deflation is not reversed, there will be an outright default on the national debt, rather than the less traumatic outcome of default-by-inflation. Deflation slows nominal GDP growth, while nominal debt rises every year due to budget deficits. This tends to increase the debt-to-GDP ratio, placing the United States on the same path as Greece and making a sovereign debt crisis more likely.

Deflation also increases the real value of private debt, creating a wave of defaults and bankruptcies. These losses then fall on the banks, causing a banking crisis. Since the primary mandate of the Federal Reserve is to prop up the banking system, deflation must be avoided because it induces bad debts that threaten bank solvency.

Finally, deflation feeds on itself and is nearly impossible for the Fed to reverse. The Federal Reserve is confident about its ability to control inflation, although the lessons of the 1970s show that extreme measures may be required. The Fed has no illusions about the difficulty of ending deflation. When cash becomes more valuable by the day, deflation's defining feature, people and businesses hoard it and do not spend or invest. This hoarding crushes aggregate demand and causes GDP to plunge. This is why the Fed has printed over $3 trillion of new money since 2008—to bar deflation from starting in the first place. The most likely path of Federal Reserve policy in the years ahead is the continuation of massive money printing to fend off deflation. The operative assumption at the Fed is that any inflationary consequences can be dealt with in due course.

In continuing to print money to subdue deflation, the Fed may reach the political limits of printing, perhaps when its balance sheet passes $5 trillion, or when it is rendered insolvent on a mark-to-market basis. At that point, the Fed governors may choose to take their chances with deflation. In this dance-with-the-Devil scenario, the Fed would rely on fiscal policy to keep aggregate demand afloat. Or deflation may prevail despite money printing. This can occur when the Fed throws money from helicopters, but citizens leave it on the ground because picking it up entails debt. In either scenario, the United States would suddenly be back to 1930 facing outright deflation.

In such a circumstance, the only way to break deflation is for the United States to declare by executive order that gold's price is, say, $7,000 per ounce, possibly higher. The Federal Reserve could make this price stick by conducting open-market operations on behalf of the Treasury using the gold in Fort Knox. The Fed would be a gold buyer at $6,900 per ounce and a seller at $7,100 per ounce in order to maintain a $7,000-per-ounce price. The purpose would not be to enrich gold holders but to reset general price levels.

Such moves may seem unlikely, but they would be effective. Since nothing moves in isolation, this kind of dollar devaluation against gold would quickly be reflected in higher dollar prices for everything else. The world of $7,000 gold is also the world of $400-per-barrel oil and $100-per-ounce silver. Deflation's back can be broken when the dollar is devalued against gold, as occurred in 1933 when the United States revalued gold from $20.67 per ounce to $35.00 per ounce, a 41 percent dollar devaluation. If the United States faces severe deflation again, the antidote of dollar devaluation against gold will be the same, because there is no other solution when printing money fails.

■ Market Collapse

The prospect of a market collapse is a function of systemic risk independent of fundamental economic policy. The risk of market collapse is amplified by regulatory incompetence and banker greed. Complexity theory is the proper framework for analyzing this risk.

The starting place in this analysis is the recognition that capital markets exhibit all four of complex systems' defining qualities: diversity of agents, connectedness, interdependence, and adaptive behavior. Concluding that capital markets are complex systems has profound implications for regulation and risk management. The first implication is that the proper measurement of risk is the gross notional value of derivatives, not the net amount. The gross size of all bank derivatives positions now exceeds $650 trillion, more than nine times global GDP.

A second implication is that the greatest catastrophe that can occur in a complex system is an exponential, nonlinear function of systemic scale. This means that as the system doubles or triples in scale, the risk of catastrophe is increasing by factors of 10 or 100. This is also why stress tests based on historic episodes such as 9/11 or 2008 are of no value, since unprecedented systemic scale presents unprecedented systemic risk.

The solutions to this systemic risk overhang are surprisingly straightforward. The immediate tasks would be to break up large banks and ban most derivatives. Large banks are not necessary to global finance. When large financing is required, a lead bank can organize a syndicate, as was routinely done in the past for massive infrastructure projects such as the Alaska pipeline, the original fleets of supertankers, and the first Boeing 747s. The benefit of breaking up banks would not be that bank failures would be eliminated, but that bank failure would no longer be a threat. The costs of failure would become containable and would not be permitted to metastasize so as to threaten the system. The case for banning most derivatives is even more straightforward. Derivatives serve practically no purpose except to enrich bankers through opaque pricing and to deceive investors through off-the-balance-sheet accounting.

Whatever the merits of these strategies, the prospects for dissolving large banks or banning derivatives are nil. This is because regulators use obsolete models or rely on the bankers' own models, leaving them unable to perceive systemic risk. Congress will not act because the members, by and large, are in thrall to bank political contributions.

Banking and derivatives risk will continue to grow, and the next collapse will be of unprecedented scope because the system scale is unprecedented. Since Federal Reserve resources were barely able to prevent complete collapse in 2008, it should be expected that an even larger collapse will overwhelm the Fed's balance sheet. Since the Fed has printed over $3 trillion in a time of relative calm, it will not be politically feasible to respond in the future by printing another $3 trillion. The task of re-liquefying the world will fall to the IMF, because the IMF will have the only clean balance sheet left among official institutions. The IMF will rise to the occasion with a towering issuance of SDRs, and this monetary operation will effectively end the dollar's role as the leading reserve currency.

■ A Deluge of Dangers

These threats to the dollar are ubiquitous. The endogenous threats are the Fed's money printing and the specter of galloping inflation. The exogenous threats include the accumulation of gold by Russia and China (about which more in chapter 9) that presages a shift to a new reserve asset.

There are numerous ancillary threats. If inflation does not emerge, it will be because of unstoppable deflation, and the Fed's response will be a radical reflation of gold. Russia and China are hardly alone in their desire to break free from the dollar standard. Iran and India may lead a move to an Asian reserve currency, and Gulf Cooperation Council members may chose to price oil exports in a new regional currency issued by a central bank based in the Persian Gulf. Geopolitical threats to the dollar may not be confined to economic competition but may turn malicious and take the form of financial war. Finally, the global financial system may simply collapse on its own without a frontal assault due to its internal complexities and spillover effects.

For now, the dollar and the international monetary system are synonymous. If the dollar collapses, the international monetary system will collapse as well; it cannot be otherwise. Everyday citizens, savers, and pensioners will be the main victims in the chaos that follows a collapse, although such a collapse does not mean the end of trade, finance, or banking. The major financial players, whether they be nations, banks, or multilateral institutions, will muddle through, while finance ministers, central bankers, and heads of state meet nonstop to patch together new rules of the game. If social unrest emerges before financial elites restore the system, nations are prepared with militarized police, armies, drones, surveillance, and executive orders to suppress discontent.

The future international monetary system will not be based on dollars because China, Russia, oil-producing countries, and other emerging nations will collectively insist on an end to U.S. monetary hegemony and the creation of a new monetary standard. Whether the new monetary standard will be based on gold, SDRs, or a network of regional reserve currencies remains to be seen. Still, the choices are few, and close study of the leading possibilities can give investors an edge and a reasonable prospect for preserving wealth in this new world.

The system has spun out of control; the altered state of the economic world, with new players, shifting allegiances, political ineptitude, and technological change has left investors confused. In *The Death of Money* you will glimpse the dollar's final days and the resultant collapse of the international monetary system, as well as take a prospective look at a new system that will rise from the ashes of the old.

PART ONE

MONEY AND GEOPOLITICS

CHAPTER 1

PROPHESY

One of our biggest fears is that something happens today, and when we do the autopsy we find that two weeks ago we had it, [but] we didn't know because it was buried in something else that wasn't getting processed.

B. "Buzzy" Krongard
CIA executive director
September 1, 2001

The unconditional evidence supports the proposition that there was unusual trading in the option markets leading up to September 11, which is consistent with the terrorists or their associates having traded on advance knowledge of the impending attacks.

Allen M. Poteshman
University of Illinois at Urbana-Champaign
2006

Never believe anything until it has been officially denied.

Claud Cockburn
British journalist

▪ Trading in Plain Sight

"No one trades alone." An axiom of financial markets, this truism means that every trade leaves transaction records there to be seen. If one knows where to look and how to examine the history and data, much can be learned not only about quotidian sales of stock by the obvious players, large and small, but about more troubling truths and trends. The market evidence surrounding 9/11—most of which is little understood by the public—is a case in point.

The secure meeting rooms at the CIA's Langley headquarters—windowless, quiet, and cramped—are called "vaults" by those who use them. On September 26, 2003, John Mulheren and I were seated side by side in a fourth-floor vault in the headquarters complex. Mulheren was one of the most legendary stock traders in Wall Street history. I was responsible for modeling terrorist trading for the CIA, part of a broad inquiry into stock trading on advance knowledge of the 9/11 attacks.

I looked in his eyes and asked if he believed there was insider trading in American Airlines stock immediately prior to 9/11. His answer was chilling: "It was the most blatant case of insider trading I've ever seen."

Mulheren started his stock trading career in the early 1970s and, at age twenty-five, became one of the youngest managing directors ever appointed at Merrill Lynch. He was found guilty of insider trading in 1990 as part of the trading scandals of the 1980s, but the verdict was overturned on appeal. His conviction was based on testimony provided by Ivan Boesky, himself a notorious insider trader. During the case, Mulheren had been apprehended by police at his Rumson, New Jersey, estate as he set out with a loaded assault rifle in his car to kill Boesky in broad daylight.

Mulheren was expert in options trading and the mathematical connections between the prices of options and the prices of the underlying stocks on which the options were written. He was also a seasoned trader in takeover stocks and knew that deal information was often leaked in advance, an open invitation to insider trading. No one knew more about the linkage between insider trading and telltale price signals than Mulheren.

When we met at Langley, Mulheren was CEO of Bear Wagner, one of seven New York Stock Exchange specialist firms at the time. Recently, specialist firms have faded in importance, but on 9/11 they were the most important link between buyers and sellers. Their job was to make a market and stabilize prices. Specialists used options markets to lay off the risk they took in their market making. They were a crucial link between New York stock trading and Chicago options trading.

Mulheren's firm was the designated market maker in American Airlines stock at the time of the 9/11 attacks. When the planes hit the twin towers, Mulheren saw the smoke and flames from his office near the World Trade Center and understood immediately what had happened. While others speculated about a "small plane, off-course," Mulheren furiously sold S&P 500 futures. In the ninety minutes between the time of the attack and the time the futures exchange closed, Mulheren made $7 million shorting stocks. He later donated all the gains to charity.

Mulheren was an eyewitness: he watched both the unfolding of the 9/11 attack and the insider trading that preceded it. His presence at Langley in 2003 was part of a CIA project whose roots reached back to a time before the attack itself.

■ The Terror Trade

September 5, 2001, was the day Osama bin Laden learned that the attacks on New York and Washington would take place on 9/11. The countdown to terror had begun. There were four trading days left before the streets around the New York Stock Exchange would be choked with death and debris. Terrorist traders with inside information on the attack had only those few days to execute strategies to profit from the terror. Insider trading on advance knowledge of the 9/11 plot was in full swing by September 6.

Bin Laden was financially sophisticated, having been raised in one of the wealthiest families in Saudi Arabia. The other leaders of Al Qaeda, including the 9/11 hijackers, were not drawn from the ranks of the ignorant and impoverished; they were doctors and engineers. Many lived in developed countries such as Germany and the United States. Al Qaeda was financially backed by wealthy Saudis who traded stocks on a regular basis.

Al Qaeda's familiarity with the workings of the New York Stock Exchange is well known. In an interview with a Pakistani journalist just weeks after the 9/11 attacks, Bin Laden made the following comments, which show how closely he drew the connection between terror and trading:

I say the events that happened on Tuesday 11th September on New York and Washington, that is truly a great event in all measures. . . .

And if the fall of the towers . . . was an event that was huge, then consider the events that followed it . . . let us talk about the economic claims which are still continuing. . . .

The losses on the Wall Street Market reached 16%. They said that this number is a record, which has never happened since the opening of the market more than 230 years ago. . . . The gross amount that is traded in that market reaches 4 trillion dollars. So if we multiply 16% with $4 trillion to find out the loss that affected the stocks, it reaches $640 billion of losses from stocks, with Allah's grace.

American Airlines and United Airlines, the operators of the four flights that were hijacked on 9/11, are public companies whose stock is traded on the New York Stock Exchange. In 2001 American Airlines traded with the ticker symbol AMR, and United Airlines with the ticker UAL.

An investigator looking for evidence of insider trading usually starts with the options markets, closely linked to the stock market. Decades of insider trading cases have shown that options are the insider trader's tool of choice. The reason is obvious: options offer much greater leverage for the same amount of cash than regular stock trading. What makes sense for Wall Street crooks also makes sense for terrorists. When one is betting on a sure thing, leverage amplifies the expected profits, and the terrorists were betting on a sure thing—the panic that would follow their attack.

While the operational details of the 9/11 terror attacks were known in advance to only a small cadre of operatives, the coming of an attack on September 11, 2001, was known to a larger circle. This group included immediate associates of the hijackers, housemates, and financial backers, as well as family and friends. Those who learned of the coming attacks from the terrorists told others, and the information spread through a social network in much the same way a video goes viral.

Advance knowledge of an attack communicated in social networks does not help intelligence agencies unless the messages are intercepted. Interception presents challenges both in directing collection resources at the right channels and in separating signals from noise. But at least one channel was blinking red before 9/11, telling the world that disastrous events involving airlines were imminent. That channel was the pinnacle of the U.S. financial establishment—the New York Stock Exchange.

As the terror clock ticked away, market signals rolled in like a tsunami. A normal ratio of bets that a stock will fall to bets it will rise is 1 to 1. On September 6 and 7, option bets that United Airlines stock would fall outnumbered bets it would rise by 12 to 1. Exchanges were closed on September 8 and 9 for the weekend. The last trading session before the attack was September 10, and that day option bets that American Airlines stock would fall outnumbered bets it would rise by 6 to 1. On September 11, 2001, United Airlines and American Airlines flights struck the World Trade Center and Pentagon. The first trading day after the attacks, United Airlines stock fell 43 percent and American Airlines stock fell 40 percent from where they had last closed. Thousands of Americans were dead. The options traders had made millions.

One-sided trading, involving more bearish than bullish bets of the kind seen just prior to 9/11, would not be unusual if there were negative news about the stocks. But there was no news on airlines on those days. The stocks of other major airlines, such as Southwest and US Airways, did not exhibit the massively bearish trading that affected American and United.

All that appeared was a huge one-way bet on a decline in the stock prices of American and United Airlines in the last four trading days before 9/11. Seasoned traders and sophisticated computer programs recognize this pattern for what it is—insider trading in advance of adverse news. Only the terrorists themselves and their social network knew that the news would be the most deadly terrorist attack in U.S. history.

The trading records are not the only evidence of a terrorist connection to insider trading in advance of the attacks. Yet notwithstanding such evidence, the official 9/11 Commission concluded:

Exhaustive investigations by the Securities and Exchange Commission, FBI, and other agencies have uncovered no evidence that anyone with advance knowledge of the attacks profited through securities transactions.

This language used in the 9/11 Commission Report is a lawyer's dodge. Saying that agencies uncovered no evidence does not mean there is no evidence, merely that they failed to find it. The conclusion that no one profited does not mean that transactions did not take place, merely that the profits could not be ascertained. Perhaps the perpetrators failed to collect their winnings, like a bank robber who drops a satchel of stolen cash in flight. The inside terrorist traders may not have known the exchange would be closed for days after the attack, making it impossible to settle trades and collect winnings.

Despite the official denial, proof of the terrorist trading connection is found through a deeper dive into the world of forensics and the phenomenon of signal amplification. The unusual options trading in advance of 9/11 has been closely studied by academics. The literature, most of it published *after* the 9/11 Commission completed its work, is emphatically of the view that the pre-9/11 options trading was based on inside information.

The leading academic study of terrorist insider trading connected to 9/11 was done over four years, from 2002 to 2006, by Allen M. Poteshman, then at the University of Illinois at Urbana-Champaign. His conclusions were published by the University of Chicago in 2006.

These conclusions were based on strong statistical techniques. This is like using DNA to prove a crime when there was no eyewitness. In murder cases, prosecutors compare a defendant's DNA to samples found at the crime scene. A DNA match might implicate a defendant in error, but the chance is so slight, so exceedingly remote, that juries routinely convict. Certain statistical correlations are so strong that the obvious conclusion must be drawn despite a microscopic chance of error.

Academics like Poteshman take large sets of data and establish the normal behavior of stocks, called the baseline. Researchers then compare actual trading in a target period to the baseline to see if the target period represents normal or extreme activity. Explanatory variables are tested to account for extreme activity. These techniques have proved reliable in many investigatory and enforcement contexts. During the dot-com bubble, for example, they were used to uncover widespread illegal backdating of options by technology companies.

Poteshman's data for the purposes of establishing a baseline included a daily record of options trades on all stocks in the S&P Index from 1990 through September 20, 2001, shortly after the 9/11 attacks. He focused on several relevant ratios before turning to the one most likely to be used by terrorists—the simple purchase of put options on AMR and UAL. A put option on a stock is a bet that the stock's price will fall.

He arranged the data in decimal brackets from 0.0 to 1.0, with 0.0 representing extremely low activity in put options and 1.0 representing extremely high activity. He discovered that in the four trading days prior to 9/11, the maximum daily value for either hijacked airline was 0.99 and the maximum value over the entire four-day window was 0.96. In the absence of any news that would explain such an extreme skew, the inescapable conclusion is that this activity represents insider trading. Poteshman writes:

> There is evidence of unusual option market activity in the days leading up to September 11 that is consistent with investors trading on advance knowledge of the attacks.

Another leading study, conducted by the Swiss Finance Institute, reached the same conclusion. This study covered the period 1996 to 2009 and analyzed over 9.6 million options trades in thirty-one selected companies, including American Airlines. With respect to 9/11, the study concluded:

> Companies like American Airlines, United Airlines, Boeing and to a lesser extent Delta Air Lines and KLM seem to have been targets for informed trading activities in the period leading up to the attacks. The number of new put options issued during that period is statistically high and the total gains . . . realized by exercising these options amount to more than $16 million. These findings support the evidence in Poteshman (2006) who also documents unusual activities in the option market before the terrorist attacks.

The 9/11 Commission was aware of the trading records used by subsequent scholars, and it was familiar with media reports that insider trading by terrorists had taken place. Yet the 9/11 Commission denied any connection between the options trading and terrorists. Its failure to conclude that terrorist insider trading took place is due to its failure to understand *signal amplification*.

＊　　＊　　＊

Signal amplification in stock trading describes a situation where a small amount of illegal trading based on inside information leads to a much greater amount of *legal* trading based on the view that "someone knows something I don't." It is a case of legitimate traders piggybacking on the initial illegal trade without knowing of the illegality.

Again, no one can trade in isolation. For every buyer of put options, there is a seller who sees the transaction take place. Each trade is entered on price reporting systems available to professional traders. A small purchase of put options by a terrorist would not go unnoticed by those professionals. There was no news of any importance on American or United Airlines in the days before 9/11. Anyone seeing a small trade would ask herself why a trader would make a bet that the stock was going down. She would not know who was doing the trading, but would assume the trader knew what he was doing and must have a basis for a bear bet. This pro might buy a much larger amount of put options for her personal account as a piggyback bet on the stranger's informed trade.

Soon other traders begin to notice the activity and also buy put options. Each trade adds to the total and amplifies the original signal a little more. In extreme cases, the dynamic resembles the chaotic climax of the film *Wall Street,* in which initial insider trading in Blue Star Airlines by Charlie Sheen's character cascades out of control amid shouts of "Dump it all!" and "We're getting out now!"

In the event, 4,516 put options, equivalent to 451,600 shares of American Airlines, were traded on September 10, 2001, the day before the attack. The vast majority of those trades were legitimate. Yet it only takes a small amount of terrorist insider trading to start the ball rolling on a much larger volume of legitimate piggyback trading. The piggyback traders had no inside information about an attack; they were betting that other traders knew negative news on AMR that had not been made public.

They were right.

A standard rejoinder, by many in the intelligence community, to suggestions of terrorist insider trading is that terrorists would never compromise their own operational security by recklessly engaging in insider trading because of the risks of detection. This reasoning is easily rebutted. No one suggests that terrorist hijacker Mohamed Atta bought put options on AMR through an E*Trade account on his way to hijack American Airlines Flight 11 from Logan Airport, Boston. The insider trading was done not by the terrorists themselves but by parties in their social network.

As for operational security, those imperatives are easily overridden by old-fashioned greed. A case in point is home decorating maven Martha Stewart. In 2001 Stewart was one of the richest women in the world due to the success of her publishing and media ventures related to cooking and home decorating. That year she sold stock in ImClone Systems based on a tip from her broker and avoided a loss of about $45,000; that sum was a pittance relative to her fortune. In 2004, however, she was convicted of conspiracy, obstruction of justice, and making false statements in connection with the trade and was sent to prison.

When it comes to betting on a sure thing, greed trumps common sense and makes the bet irresistible. The record of insider trading is replete with such cases. A terrorist associate is not likely to show better judgment than a superrich celebrity when the opportunity arises.

Given the weight of the social network analysis, statistical methods, signal amplification, and expert opinion, why did the 9/11 Commission fail to conclude that terrorists traded in AMR and UAL in advance of the attack? The answer lies in the 9/11 Commission Report itself, in footnote 130 of chapter 5.

Footnote 130 admits that activity in AMR and UAL before 9/11 was "highly suspicious." It also says, "Some unusual trading did in fact occur, but each such trade proved to have an innocuous explanation." A closer look at these "innocuous" explanations reveals the flaws in the commission's reasoning.

For example, the report finds "a single U.S.-based institutional investor with no conceivable ties to al Qaeda purchased 95 percent of the UAL puts on September 6 as part of a trading strategy that also included *buying* 115,000 shares of American." This explanation falls down in two ways. First, the fact that a high percentage of the trades were found to be innocent is completely consistent with signal amplification. Only the small initial trade is done by terrorists. The 9/11 Commission Report presented no evidence that it had made any effort to drill down to the small initial signal. Instead, the staff were beguiled by the innocent noise.

Second, the 9/11 Commission relies on the fact that the investor it interviewed said he bought UAL puts as part of a strategy involving the purchase of AMR shares, a kind of long-short trade. This shows naïveté on the part of the commission staff. Large institutional investors have numerous positions that have nothing to do with one another but that can be selected post facto to show innocent motives to investigators. On its face, this investor's AMR position says nothing about why it so heavily shorted UAL.

The report goes on to say that "much of the seemingly suspicious trading in American on September 10 was traced to a specific U.S.-based options trading newsletter, faxed to its subscribers on Sunday, September 9, which recommended these trades." This analysis shows that the commission staff had a limited understanding of how Wall Street research works.

There are thousands of trading tip sheets in circulation. On any given day, it is possible to find at least one recommending the purchase *or* sale of most major companies listed on the New York Stock Exchange. Going back after the fact to find a newsletter that recommended buying puts on American Airlines is a trivial exercise. No doubt there were other newsletters in circulation recommending the opposite. Selecting evidence that fits a theory while ignoring other evidence is an example of confirmation bias, a leading cause of erroneous intelligence analysis.

Another problem with the newsletter rationale is the belief that the recommendation arose independently of the insider trading already going on in AMR. Why treat the newsletter as a signal when it was actually part of the noise? For example, on September 7, trading volume in AMR doubled from the previous day and reached a near three-month high with a declining stock price. This pattern is consistent with insider trading ahead of an attack on September 11. It is more likely that the September 7 put volume caused the September 9 newsletter recommendation than it is that the newsletter caused the September 10 put buying.

The more likely explanation is that the entire sequence from September 6 through 10 was a signal amplification caused by a small initial insider trade. To isolate a single event like the newsletter and give it explanatory power without reference to prior events is poor forensic technique. It is better to take a step back and look at the big picture, to separate signal and noise.

Insider traders and those piggybacking are notorious for retaining research reports to support their activities in case the SEC comes calling. SEC after-the-fact inquiries are routine whenever the SEC identifies suspicious trading related to a market-moving event. Waving a research report at SEC investigators is a standard technique to make them go away. Stock trading criminals have gone so far as to prepare their own research reports for the sole purpose of having a cover story in case their insider trading is ever questioned. Given this well-known technique for foiling investigations, it is unfortunate that the 9/11 Commission Report gave weight to a single newsletter.

Viewed through the lens of signal amplification, the 9/11 Commission's "large buyer theory" and the "newsletter theory" contained in footnote 130 are more consistent with terrorist trading than a refutation. Moreover, these theories never address the put buying in United Airlines on September 7 and the other suspicious trades.

It is important to disassociate this insider trading analysis from the so-called 9/11 Truth Movement, a collective name for groups and individuals who assert conspiracy theories related to the 9/11 attacks. Many of these theorists claim that agencies and officials of the U.S. government were involved in planning the attacks and that the twin towers collapsed from prepositioned explosives and not from the impact of the hijacked planes. This nonsense is a disservice to the memory of those killed or injured in the attack and in subsequent military responses. The hard evidence that the attacks were planned and executed by Al Qaeda is irrefutable. The 9/11 Commission Report is a monumental and excellent summary, a brilliant work of history despite the inevitable flaws that arise in such a wide-ranging effort. Furthermore, there is nothing inconsistent between the widely accepted narrative of 9/11 and terrorist insider trading. Given the magnitude of the attack and the imperatives of human nature, such trading should have been expected. The statistical, behavioral, and anecdotal evidence for insider trading are overwhelming.

Terrorist insider trading was not a U.S. government plot but a simple extension of the main terrorist plot. It was despicable yet, in the end, banal. Small-time terrorist associates could not resist betting on a sure thing, and signal amplification took care of the rest. Still, the signal was not hidden. On trading screens all over the world, evidence of the coming attacks was visible by watching options trading in American and United Airlines.

In the chilling words of CIA director George Tenet, "The system was blinking red."

■ Project Prophesy

If the 9/11 Commission was finished with the topic of terrorist insider trading, one government agency was still willing—though initially ill equipped—to dig deeper.

The Central Intelligence Agency had been mobilized before 9/11, based on the volume of reporting that indicated a spectacular attack might be in the works. A body of intelligence concerning reports of unusual trading in airline and other stocks in the days before the attack came to the CIA's attention immediately after 9/11. But it had a problem pursuing those leads because it had almost no expertise in capital markets and options trading.

This gap in intelligence capabilities at the time is not surprising. Prior to globalization, capital markets were not part of the national security arena. Markets were mostly local, controlled by national champions in each country. Some banks, such as Citibank, were international, but they conducted traditional lending businesses and were not involved in stock trading. The CIA did not have capital markets expertise because it had not been required during the Cold War; markets were not part of the battlespace.

As a result, when reports of possible terrorist insider trading rolled in after 9/11, practically no one at the agency had the experience necessary to evaluate how it might have occurred and its implications for national security. Fortunately, one senior intelligence analyst understood the implications quite well.

Randy Tauss lives quietly in the upscale Washington, D.C., suburb of McLean, Virginia, not far from CIA headquarters. He retired from the CIA in 2008 after a thirty-seven-year career, mostly in the agency's Directorate of Intelligence, the analytic branch. He is a brilliant physicist and mathematician who won numerous medals from the agency for his technical and deductive work. Although most of his work involved complex weapons systems, he won fame both inside and outside the agency for his role in solving the mystery of the 1996 midair explosion of TWA Flight 800.

Tauss had another avocation, one not required in his day job but to which he applied the same passion he showed while working with weapons and technology. He was an avid stock and options trader who used his mathematics skills to look for small anomalies in options prices that could be traded to advantage in his personal accounts. He pursued this options trading with such vigor and over such a long period of time that he was almost as well known for it among his colleagues as he was for his intelligence analyses. When the story of insider trading surfaced in the aftermath of 9/11, it was no surprise that Tauss's name came to the attention of CIA senior management.

In October 2001, just weeks after the attacks, the CIA's Office of Terrorism Analysis asked Tauss to serve as director of a project to consider whether terrorists might use advance knowledge of their actions to profit in financial markets, and whether the intelligence community could identify such efforts and possibly thwart the attack. Thus began one of the longest and most unusual analytic projects in CIA history.

The effort was dubbed "Project Prophesy." By the time the project wound down in 2004, almost two hundred finance professionals—including stock exchange executives, hedge fund managers, Nobel Prize winners, and floor traders, along with technologists and systems analysts—would be tapped to contribute their time and effort. Tauss led a massive undertaking that simultaneously modeled the mind of the terrorist and the mind of the Wall Street trader. He found that the two domains had more than a few things in common.

Project Prophesy was formally launched in April 2002, and the core team assembled by the end of May. The first task was to create a threat board of potential targets for terrorist attacks and link those targets to publicly traded stocks that might provide advance warning through unusual price activity. These stocks included a broad list of airlines, cruise lines, utilities, theme parks, and other companies with symbolically important assets.

By early 2003, the Prophesy team led by Tauss had reached out to Wall Street and other government agencies and assembled teams to participate in targeted panels to flesh out the practical details of Tauss's theory. It was widely assumed that terrorists would strike again in some spectacular way. Would there be information leakage? Would a terrorist associate engage in insider trading? Could this trading be detected so as to identify the trader and his target? Would there be time to react and stop the attack? These were the problems Prophesy set out to solve.

My involvement with Project Prophesy began at the mountaintop Kaiser estate on the island of St. Croix, a site exotic enough to make the final cut of a James Bond film. The estate is a complex of three mansions connected by private roads on Recovery Hill overlooking the town of Christiansted on the north shore of the island. The centerpiece of the complex is the White House, a sprawling, multitiered, bleach-white International Style home with a large outdoor pool trimmed with the obligatory steel-post-and-Kevlar tenting reminiscent of the Denver Airport.

I was there in the winter of 2003 for a private gathering of top financiers from the institutional, hedge fund, and private equity worlds to discuss the next big thing in alternative investing—a project to blend hedge fund and private equity strategies to optimize risk-adjusted returns.

As typically happens at such gatherings, there was downtime for drinks and getting to know the other guests. During one such break, I chatted with the head of one of the largest institutional portfolios in the world. He asked me about my career, and I recounted my early days at Citibank on assignment in Karachi.

That had been in the 1980s, not long after the shah of Iran had been deposed in the Iranian Revolution. Grand Ayatollah Khomeini became Supreme Leader and declared Iran to be an Islamic Republic guided by principles of sharia or Islamic law. This shift in Iranian governance placed pressure on Pakistan to burnish its own Islamic credentials. Pakistani president Zia-ul-Haq issued religious ordinances, including one that prohibited banks from charging interest on loans, something forbidden by sharia.

Citibank had major operations in Pakistan. The idea of running the bank there without charging interest came as a shock to management. I was assigned to become expert in sharia and assist in the conversion of Citibank's operations from Western banking to Islamic banking.

I arrived in Karachi in February 1982 and went to work. Citibank's country head, Shaukat Aziz, later prime minister of Pakistan, would occasionally pick me up at my hotel. In monsoon season, we would barrel through flooded Karachi streets choked with ubiquitous decorated buses and three-wheeled jitneys, speeding past vendors spitting bright red betel nuts they chewed for a buzz.

As I told these tales to the fund manager, I noticed his face became taut and his stare serious. He motioned me to a corner of the deck away from the other guests. He leaned forward and said sotto voce, "Look, it seems you know a lot about Islamic finance and you know your way around Pakistan." My local knowledge was a little rusty since these things had happened decades before; still, I replied, "Yeah, I worked hard at that. I know Islamic banking."

He leaned in and said, "I'm helping the CIA on a project related to terrorist finance. They don't have much expertise, and they're doing some outreach. They've asked me to source whatever talent I can. If someone from the agency contacted you, would you take the call?" I said yes.

For those too young to recall 9/11 and the aftermath, it is difficult to describe the mix of anger and patriotic fervor that gripped the nation, especially in the New York area, where many people lost friends or family members or knew someone who did. We all asked ourselves how we could help. The only advice we got from Washington was "get down to Disney World . . . take your families and enjoy life." Here was the chance for me to do more than go shopping.

A few days later the phone rang in my New York office. The caller introduced himself as part of the CIA's Office of Transnational Issues in the Directorate of Intelligence. He asked if I would be willing to join a team looking at aspects of terrorist finance, specifically insider trading ahead of major terrorist attacks. He would send me a letter outlining the scope of the project. I agreed, the letter was soon received, and by the early summer of 2003, I was on my way to CIA headquarters to meet the rest of the Project Prophesy team.

*　　*　　*

Joining a project in midstream is never easy, because the rhythm and culture of the team are already established. But I fit right in because I had been on Wall Street longer than many of the volunteers and had more international experience than all but a few. Within months I became a co–project manager under Tauss's direction.

My first contribution was to point out that the CIA's objective was already being pursued every day by hedge funds, but for a different reason. The CIA was trying to spot terrorist traders, while hedge funds were trying to spot unannounced takeovers. But the big-data techniques applied to trading patterns were the same.

Spotting suspicious trading is a three-step process. Step one is to establish a baseline for normal trading, using metrics like volatility, average daily volume, put-call ratios, short interest, and momentum. Step two is to monitor trading and spot anomalies relative to the baseline. Step three is to see if there is any public information to explain the move. If a stock spikes because Warren Buffett bought a large position, that's not an anomaly; it is to be expected. The intriguing case is when a stock spikes on no news. The logical inference is that someone knows something you don't. A hedge fund might not care about the origin of the hidden information—it can just piggyback on the trade. For the CIA, the observation became a clue. And the stakes were higher.

Like any development project, Prophesy had its geek squad of programmers and systems administrators to design protocols for security, interconnectivity, and the user interface. The team combined the joy of a Silicon Valley garage start-up with the can-do culture of the CIA in a unique effort to preempt terrorism using the same information that viewers see every day on Bloomberg TV.

The climax of Project Prophesy was a red team exercise in September 2003. Red teaming is a classic way of testing hypotheses and models by recruiting a group of experts as the "enemy," then asking them to role-play scenarios designed to expose flaws in the original assumptions.

Our red team membership was like a Pro Bowl squad, with all-star traders from the biggest banks, hedge funds, and institutional investors in the world along with some noted academics. In addition to John Mulheren, the team included Steve Levitt, a professor at the University of Chicago and an author of *Freakonomics;* Dave "Davos" Nolan, a hedge fund billionaire; and senior figures from Morgan Stanley, Deutsche Bank, and Goldman Sachs. In the somber days after 9/11, it was inspiring to see the private sector respond to requests for help. Hundreds of calls went out for expert advice, and no one ever refused. There was an awkward moment when one Wall Street CEO asked if he could travel to the CIA by private helicopter and land on the grounds at Langley, but he was politely informed this would not be possible.

The red team was given a terror scenario and asked to think like terrorists and devise a way to trade on the inside information. We wanted to anticipate which markets they would trade in, how long before the attack they would execute the trades, the size they would trade, and how they planned to get away with the money. All this real-world expertise would be lined up against the theoretical results of Project Prophesy to see if we were on the right track and whether our proposed systems could catch what our designated bad guys were actually plotting.

The assignments and plans were handled individually outside the agency like a take-home exam. The results were debriefed in a group session at CIA headquarters on a crisp day in late September 2003. The debriefing lasted all day. The investment mavens relished their chance to be bad guys and attack our models and assumptions.

The most out-of-the-box approach came from John Mulheren. He said he would not trade *before* the attack but would wait until the moment of the attack and begin his insider trading *after*. He knew markets can be slow to react and that breaking news is often misreported or sketchy. This produces a window of thirty minutes or so after the attack when the terrorist could engage in insider trading while markets struggled to comprehend events taking place around them. The beauty of trading after the attack was there would be no telltale tape. Authorities might not even investigate that part of the time line. This approach closely mirrored what Mulheren had actually done on 9/11, as he later told us.

Notwithstanding such creativity, the actions of the red team "terrorists" tended to confirm the Prophesy team's own thinking regarding how real terrorists would behave. We had modeled terrorist trading from start to finish, anticipating that the insider traders would be not the terrorists themselves but rather members of the terrorist social network. We also concluded the insider trade was likely to be executed in the options market less than seventy-two hours before the attack to minimize risk of detection.

We conceived an alarm system, too, compiling a list of the four hundred most likely target stocks. Baseline stock behavior was programmed so that anomalies were well defined. We created an automated threat board interface that broke the markets into sectors and displayed tickers with red, amber, and green lights, indicating the probability of insider trading. The system was complete, from the terrorist order entry to agents breaking down the terrorist's door with a warrant in hand.

By late 2003, we were nearing the end of the strategic study. It was a bit melancholy because our Wall Street brain trust would be breaking up. Due to the number of people involved and the degree of talent, it seemed unlikely there would be any such group assembling at the CIA for some time to come. The complete records of the red team exercise were compiled and added to our main Project Prophesy archives.

Our job wasn't quite finished, as by early 2004, Project Prophesy was ready to build a prototype watch center. When integrated with other classified sources, the system, ideally, would have the capability of interpreting, say, a scrap of pocket litter picked up from a suspected terrorist in Pakistan. The words *cruise ship* scrawled on it would be integrated with a red signal from the watch center on a public company such as Carnival Cruise Lines to bolster the case for a planned attack on a Carnival vessel. Either clue is revealing, but the combination is exponentially more telling.

We found our project's angel investor in one of the more unusual corners of the CIA's universe. A firm called In-Q-Tel had been organized in 1999 to allow the CIA to tap into cutting-edge technology incubated in start-ups in Silicon Valley. There's no faster way to be on the inside of innovation than to show up with a checkbook ready to back the next big thing. In-Q-Tel was conceived as an independent, early-stage venture capital firm—which just happened to be funded by the CIA.

■ MARKINT

With In-Q-Tel funding a scaled-down team, Project Prophesy formally ended, and our group launched into a new phase called MARKINT, for market intelligence. This was a new branch of intelligence gathering to go along with human intelligence (HUMINT), signals intelligence (SIGINT), and a short list of other -*INTs*. MARKINT was a new milestone in the long history of intelligence collections.

Over the course of 2004 and 2005, the team refined its behavioral models and created the code and network needed for a working prototype. In addition to the CIA's Randy Tauss, our partners were Lenny Raymond, a visionary technologist, and Chris Ray, a brilliant applied mathematician and causal inference theorist.

My role was to provide the market expertise, behavioral modeling, and target selection. Chris designed the algorithms and the signal engine. Lenny would weave it all together with a cool user interface. Randy ran the traps inside the agency and made sure we got funding and support. Together we had our own capital markets skunk works, after the famous black site in California where highly classified spy planes were designed and built. By early 2006, the system was running, and signals started coming in.

The system performed beyond our expectations. We routinely picked up signals that indicated insider trading. These signals were from regular market players; there was nothing yet to indicate that the insider trading was terror related. Our project had no legal enforcement powers, so we simply referred these cases to the SEC and otherwise ignored them. We called this our catch-and-release policy. We were hunting terrorists and would leave ordinary Wall Street crooks to others.

On Monday, August 7, 2006, the system flashed red on American Airlines at the open of trading. A red light was a way to spot a signal in a sea of sectors on the threat board. The metrics behind the signal showed this one was extremely powerful, something like an 8.0 earthquake on the Richter scale. A quick scan of the news showed absolutely nothing on American Airlines. There was no reason for the stock to behave the way it was—a sure sign of insider trading on news not yet public.

Chris Ray was operating the signal engine that day and sent me an e-mail that said, "There's a possible terrorist-related event today. We did get a red signal on the open in AMR (American Airlines)." Chris and I were careful to document and time-stamp the signals and analyses in real time. We both knew that if a terror event occurred, it would not be very credible to look at the tape in hindsight and find something suggestive. We wanted to see things in advance and record them to prove the value of the signal engine.

As it was, the day came and went, and the day after that, and there was no news of any terrorist threat. The signal started to look like a false positive.

On the third day after the signal, Thursday, August 10, I was writing in my library at two a.m., not an unusual hour for me to work. A small television on a bookshelf a few feet from my desk was tuned to CNN with the sound muted. I glanced over and noticed a breaking news scroll across the bottom of the screen, together with images of London bobbies taking suspects into detention and exiting buildings with boxes of documents and computers. The scroll said that a terrorist plot to blow up airplanes was being taken down by New Scotland Yard.

I quickly turned up the sound to take in the few details that were available. It was daylight in London, and the takedown of the planes operation had been proceeding for some time and was now being widely reported. It became apparent that the plot involved transatlantic airlines flying from London to the United States and targeted those with the most American citizens likely to be aboard. American Airlines was a prime target, although apparently a large number of planes had been threatened.

I knew Chris was a night owl like me, and despite the hour, I called her at home. She was awake. "Chris," I quickly said, "turn on your TV—you won't believe what's going on." She did and grasped the significance immediately. A terrorist plot to bomb American Airlines was being broken up less than seventy-two hours after we had detected the insider trading on AMR shares. Making it all the more spooky, we realized that the plot was unfolding in exactly the time frame that our behavioral modeling had estimated.

Of course, our signal had had nothing to do with foiling the plot. British intelligence agencies MI5 and MI6, with help from the CIA and the ISI, the Pakistani intelligence service, had had the plot under surveillance for months. President Bush was briefed on the plot at his ranch in Crawford, Texas, on August 5. On August 9 the plot mastermind, Rashid Rauf, was arrested in Pakistan. Rauf escaped prison in 2007 and was believed killed in a 2008 CIA drone attack, although reports of his death are disputed by some to this day.

The terrorists sent an encrypted "go" signal to commence the operation on August 6. This message was intercepted by MI6 and relayed to Eliza Manningham-Buller, the head of MI5. It was this go signal that led MI5 and New Scotland Yard to commence the arrests we watched on CNN on August 10.

Just as Chris and I did not know of plot details in advance, the plotters did not know they were about to be arrested. Instead, one of the terrorist associates in the London social network woke up on Monday, August 7, and started the trading in American Airlines that snowballed into the highly unusual pattern that had triggered the red light on our threat board. Someone had been betting on a sure thing, exactly as our behavioral modeling had predicted.

The fact that our signal engine had generated a warning, loud and clear *and* ahead of the U.K. planes plot, soon attracted attention from the highest levels of the U.S. intelligence community. On February 2, 2007, I received an e-mail from Randy Tauss saying the CIA's executive director, Mike Morell, wanted to see Chris and me to discuss the signal engine and the status of MARKINT. The meeting would take place on February 14, which gave us time to prepare the briefing.

Morell had been with the CIA since 1980 and had a storied career. He was most famous for having been at George Bush's side during 9/11 as the president hopped around the country in Air Force One while Dick Cheney, George Tenet, and others manned the command centers in Washington and Langley. Morell was also with President Obama in May 2011 monitoring the operation that killed Osama bin Laden. He twice served as acting director of Central Intelligence, including a stint after the abrupt resignation of David Petraeus in 2012, before retiring from the agency in 2013.

At the time of our meeting in 2007, Morell reported to Director Michael Hayden. Other senior intelligence officials had been invited to join our MARKINT briefing in Morell's office. This would be the highest-ranking audience the project had ever received.

Randy's e-mail also noted that someone from the CIA general counsel's office would attend. There was no doubt that our project had legal issues, including privacy concerns, and full implementation would require coordination with the FBI, since the CIA was not a domestic law enforcement agency. We had spent an enormous amount of time on these issues and knew how sensitive they were. Still, it was not obvious why Morell wanted his lawyers on hand for a preliminary briefing on a new counterterrorist system.

Morell's office was capacious by CIA standards, with bright windows, a large desk near the back wall, and a meeting table just inside the door. A ubiquitous feature of Washington offices is framed photographs of the occupant together with powerful figures. Morell had his, but these were different. Instead of the typical two-shot taken at a name-tag event, Morell had large, somber black-and-white photos of himself in the Oval Office with the president leaning over documents in intense discussion, possibly taken during the President's Daily Brief, in which the most sensitive and highly classified information in the world is imparted. If these were meant to impress the visitor, they worked.

Chris, Randy, and I took our seats at the meeting table. The other senior officials were already there, and Morell got up from his desk to join the group. The atmosphere was cordial but businesslike, even intense. Chris and Randy briefed the group on the history of Project Prophesy and the signal engine capabilities. As the only lawyer on the MARKINT team, my job was to summarize the legal authority for our efforts and the privacy safeguards in place.

A few minutes into my presentation, the agency's counsel interrupted and said, "Look, we're concerned about what you guys are doing. You're going through trading records and making referrals to the SEC. CIA is not a law enforcement agency. We're not comfortable with that."

I countered that we did not use individual trading records but relied entirely on open-source market price feeds available to everyone; I told them it was not much different than watching TV. As for the SEC referrals, I said we were just being responsible citizens and could stop completely if the agency wanted. The SEC was building similar systems of its own and would not depend on us in the future anyway. Counsel's concerns seemed like red herrings.

Then Morell leaned forward. "What we're concerned about here is perception," he said. "You guys may be doing everything right, but *The New York Times* could spin this as 'CIA trolls through Americans' 401(k)'s.' That is not a risk we should take right now."

Morell's concern was far from imaginary. *The New York Times* had already compromised national security by revealing intelligence community access to banking transactions in the SWIFT payments system in Belgium. SWIFT is the nerve center of international banking and had been a rich source of information about terrorist finance. The *Times* story had sent terrorist financiers underground to word-of-mouth networks called *hawala* and phony front companies.

The CIA was also in the midst of a news frenzy about enhanced interrogation techniques such as waterboarding. The last thing it needed was another media black eye, even if our program was effective and legal.

In fact, Morell's instincts proved prophetic. On November 14, 2013, *The Wall Street Journal* actually did run a headline that said "CIA's Financial Spying Bags Data on Americans." But coming as it did in the midst of a wave of similar revelations by defector Edward Snowden, this disclosure went almost unnoticed.

I told Morell that we would end our SEC referrals, and I offered to provide him with the technical specifications needed to assure the agency that the information we used was open source and involved no individuals. He thanked me, and with that the meeting was over. Only later did I realize that MARKINT, at least as far as the CIA was concerned, had just become a dead letter.

Near the beginning of Project Prophesy, I remarked to Randy Tauss that the team was doing extraordinary work and a counterterrorist system that could prevent spectacular attacks seemed within reach. Randy, the thirty-three-year veteran, smiled and said, "Jim, let me tell you how things work around here. We'll do a great job, and this thing will work like a charm. Then it will go nowhere and be put on a shelf. One day there will be a spectacular attack, and it will be apparent there was advance insider trading. The agency will pull our work from the shelf, dust it off, and say, 'See, we have the solution right here. We have a system that can detect this next time.' That system will get millions in funding and be built the way we wanted. But it will be too late to save lives in the next attack."

Sadly, Randy's words proved prescient. Sure enough, MARKINT was put on the shelf. But we still felt that the signal engine had a valuable role to play, even without the CIA as a home. If the civilian agencies had scant interest, we still had one friend at court—the Department of Defense. The Pentagon had the greatest resources, the fewest operational constraints, and the most forward-leaning mind-set. The ranks of senior military officers are filled with engineers, Ph.D.'s, and many more experts with graduate-level degrees in history, languages, and strategy. After all, this is the branch of government that can claim credit for the Defense Advance Research Projects Agency (DARPA), which invented the systems that led to the Internet and World Wide Web.

As it happened, our contacts with the Pentagon developed in 2007 and 2008 at exactly the time the civilian intelligence community was backing away from our efforts. But to grow this relationship, MARKINT itself had to evolve. Chris Ray and I were aware, from the early stages, that MARKINT was not just a counterterrorist tool. If it could detect terrorist footprints in capital markets, why couldn't it also be deployed to monitor the marketplace actions of dictators, strategic rivals, and other state actors? All we needed to do was calibrate the signal engine to focus on specially tailored target sets of securities.

With this broader mission in mind, Chris and I began looking for other phenomena besides insider stock trading. One that we identified was Venezuela's conversion of its dollar reserves into gold; it presaged Hugo Chávez's war on the dollar and his later demand that Venezuela's gold be repatriated from vaults in London.

We got a chance to show our system to a military audience in December 2007, when we presented the MARKINT signal engine to the U.S. Strategic Command (STRATCOM) in Omaha, Nebraska. Participants at that meeting included civilian scientists in addition to uniformed military. We demonstrated how the system could be used for early warning of attacks on the U.S. dollar and on efforts to crash U.S. markets.

Suddenly the technology was seen in a new light. We weren't alone, of course, but we were seeing the future of warfare: not wars with kinetic weapons, but wars fought on an unrestricted battlefield that included chemical and biological weapons, cyberweapons, and in our case, financial weapons.

It was becoming apparent to the Pentagon that U.S. dominance in conventional air, land, and sea battle had caused our rivals to seek new ways to confront us. Future wars would be fought in an expanded battlespace that included stocks, bonds, currencies, commodities, and derivatives. Our signal engine was the perfect early warning device.

Remember the truism *No one trades alone.* For every buyer, there is a seller. If one side of a trade is a threat to national security, it leaves a trace that the enemy did not intend. The enemy trader is like a fish swimming in the water; it leaves ripples. Even if the fish is invisible, the ripples can be seen, and the presence of the fish inferred. The forward-thinkers at that meeting in Omaha recognized that our signal engine could detect the ripples, that we had devised the perfect early warning device.

MARKINT would have a future after all. It would be not the narrow counterterrorist tool we had set out to create, but rather a broad-based system, a sort of radar for the marketplace that was designed to detect incoming financial threats. MARKINT had grown up. Our team and technology had now entered the new, larger arena of financial war.

CHAPTER 2

THE WAR GOD'S FACE

If it's . . . possible to start a war in a computer room or a stock exchange that will send an enemy country to its doom, then is there non-battlespace anywhere? . . . If [a] young lad setting out with his orders should ask today, "Where is the battlefield?" the answer would be, "Everywhere."

Colonel Qiao Liang and Colonel Wang Xiangsui
People's Liberation Army, China
1999

Now our enemies are also seeking the ability to sabotage our . . . financial institutions. . . . We cannot look back years from now and wonder why we did nothing in the face of real threats to our security and our economy.

President Barack Obama
February 12, 2013

■ Future War

One purpose of war is to degrade the enemy's will and economic capacity. Surprising as it may sound, wealth destruction through a market attack can be more effective than sinking enemy ships, when it comes to disabling an opponent. Financial war is the future of warfare, and no one works harder to see the future than senior Defense Department official Andy Marshall.

Seated at a table in a secure Pentagon conference room on a rainy fall morning in September 2012, Marshall moved forward in his chair. Around the table were three prominent investment managers, three SEC officials, and several think-tank experts. along with members of Marshall's staff. Our carefully selected group was there to discuss financial war.

"That's interesting," Marshall said. What prompted his comment, after an hour of complete silence on his part, was our discussion of China's stockpiling of gold and its possible use as a financial weapon in undermining the dollar's exchange value.

Andy Marshall is called "Mr. Marshall" even by associates as a sign of respect, and at ninety-two years of age, he has earned the deference. His official title is Director of the Office of Net Assessment in the Office of the Secretary of Defense. Unofficially he is the Pentagon's chief futurist, the man responsible for looking over the horizon and assessing threats to U.S. national security long before others even know they exist. Marshall has held this position since 1973, through eight presidential administrations.

His involvement in national security strategy goes back even further, to 1949, when he joined the RAND Corporation, the original think tank. The list of his former associates and protégés includes Herman Kahn, James Schlesinger, Don Rumsfeld, Dick Cheney, Paul Wolfowitz, and other giants of national security policy over eight decades. Only the late Paul Nitze is comparable to Marshall in terms of the depth and breadth of his influence on strategic affairs in the period since World War II.

If Marshall is less known to the general public than the figures to whom he is compared, that is quite by design. He almost never gives interviews or speeches; nor does he appear in public, and his writings are mostly classified. In a meeting, he has a sphinxlike demeanor, listening for long periods in complete silence, occasionally uttering a few words that show he has absorbed everything and is now thinking three moves ahead.

While most Americans have not heard of Andy Marshall, the Chinese military have. Marshall was a leading theorist of the late twentieth-century "revolution in military affairs" or RMA, which presaged radical changes in weaponry and strategy based on massive computing power. Precision-guided munitions, cruise missiles, and drones are all part of RMA. People's Liberation Army general Chen Zhou, the principal author of several recent Chinese strategic white papers, told *The Economist*,

"We studied RMA exhaustively. Our great hero was Andy Marshall in the Pentagon. . . . We translated every word he wrote."

Marshall is no stranger to potential confrontation with China. In fact, he is the principal architect of the main U.S. battle plan for war with China in the western Pacific. This classified plan, called "Air-Sea Battle," involves blinding China's surveillance capabilities and precision missiles, followed up with massive air power and naval attacks.

On this occasion, Marshall was not being briefed on kinetic weapons or air-sea tactics. He was hearing about sovereign wealth funds, stealth gold acquisition, and potential threats to national security caused by U.S. Federal Reserve policy.

China has over $3 trillion of investments denominated in U.S. dollars, and every 10 percent devaluation in the dollar engineered by the Fed represents a $300 billion real wealth transfer from China to the United States. It is not clear how long China will tolerate this raid on its accumulated wealth. If China were not able to defeat the United States in the air or on the sea, it could attack through capital markets.

The threats discussed with Andy Marshall that day were entirely consistent with Chinese military doctrine. Unrestricted warfare doctrine, including financial war and cyberwarfare, has roots as far back as 1995. That year Major General Wang Pufeng, former director of strategy at Beijing's Military Science Academy, published a paper called "The Challenge of Information Warfare." After paying tribute to Andy Marshall in the paper's opening lines, Wang went on to write:

In the near future, information warfare will control the form and future of war. We recognize this developmental trend of information warfare and see it as a driving force in the modernization of China's military and combat readiness. This trend will be highly critical to achieving victory in future wars.

The People's Liberation Army of China made this doctrine even more explicit in a 1999 book entitled *Unrestricted Warfare*. Unrestricted warfare tactics include numerous ways of attacking an enemy without using kinetic weapons such as missiles, bombs, or torpedoes. Such tactics include the use of weapons of mass destruction that disperse biological, chemical, or radiological elements to cause civilian casualties, and terrorize populations. Other examples of unrestricted warfare include cyberattacks that can ground aviation, open floodgates, cause blackouts, and shut down the Internet.

Recently, financial attacks have been added to the list of asymmetric threats first articulated by Wang and others. *Unrestricted Warfare* spells this out in a chapter called "The War God's Face Has Become Indistinct." It was written not long after the 1997 Asian financial crisis, which cascaded into the global financial panic of 1998. Much of the distress in Asia was caused by Western bankers suddenly pulling hot money out of banks in emerging Asian markets; the distress was compounded by bad economic advice from the Western-dominated IMF. From an Asian perspective, the entire debacle looked like a Western plot to destabilize their economies. The instability was real enough, with riots and bloodshed from Indonesia to South Korea. The ill will escalated to the point of name-calling between Malaysian prime minister Mahathir Mohamad and hedge fund maven George Soros in an infamous confrontation at the IMF annual meeting in Hong Kong in September 1997.

The Chinese were less affected than other Asian nations by the panic, but they studied the situation and began to see how banks, working in conjunction with the IMF, could undermine civil society and possibly force regime change. One of their responses to the crisis was to accumulate massive dollar reserves so they would not be vulnerable to a sudden "run on the bank" by Western lenders. The other response was to develop a doctrine of financial war. The lessons of the 1997–98 crisis were summarized by two Chinese military leaders in a passage both poetic and prophetic:

> Economic prosperity that once excited the constant admiration of the Western world changed to a depression, like the leaves of a tree that are blown away in a single night by the autumn wind. . . . What is more, such a defeat on the economic front precipitates a near collapse of the social and political order.

The Chinese are ahead of us: their doctrine of strategic financial warfare emerged in 1999 in response to the 1997 Asian financial shock. In comparison, U.S. thinking about financial warfare did not take recognizable shape until ten years later, in 2009, in response to an even bigger shock, the global financial panic of 2008. By 2012, both China and the United States had engaged in extensive efforts to develop strategic and tactical financial warfare doctrines. It was in this context that our group was summoned to brief Andy Marshall and his team on the emerging threat.

FINANCIAL WARFARE HAS BOTH offensive and defensive aspects. Offense includes malicious attacks on an enemy's financial markets designed to disrupt trading and destroy wealth. Defense involves early detection of an attack and rapid response, such as closing markets or interdicting enemy message traffic. Offense can consist of either first-strike disruption or second-strike retaliation. In game theory, offense and defense converge, since second-strike retaliation can be sufficiently destructive to deter first-strike attacks. This line of reasoning was the same doctrine Andy Marshall helped develop in nuclear-war-fighting scenarios during the Cold War in the early 1960s. The doctrine was called Mutual Assured Destruction (MAD). Now a new doctrine of Mutual Assured Financial Destruction was emerging. To Andy Marshall, financial weapons were new, but deterrence theory was not.

The distinction between offensive and defensive capabilities in financial warfare is not the only dichotomy. There is also a distinction between physical targets, such as exchange computers, and virtual targets, such as business relationships. Virtual targets involve business conduct based on trust. A seemingly honest entity can gain trust through patient, repetitive trading, then suddenly abuse that trust by flooding a trading system with malicious, manipulative orders.

Physical targets consist of a vast network of servers, switches, fiber-optic cable, and other message traffic channels, as well as the exchange premises themselves. It is not difficult for exchange engineers or enemies to see that disrupting one link in this electronic chain through sabotage or hacking can cause chaos and force a market closure, at least temporarily. More extensive attacks can shut down markets for weeks or even months, depending on the extent of the disruption.

The financial meltdown in 2008 was not an act of financial warfare, but it did demonstrate to U.S. officials the complexity and vulnerability of the global financial system. Approximately $60 trillion of wealth was destroyed from the peak in October 2007 to the trough in March 2009. If such a catastrophe could be caused by instruments as innocuous as mortgages, imagine how much more harm could be caused by malicious market manipulation orchestrated by experts who knew exactly how the system behaved.

Thanks to Marshall and others, there's a growing awareness that a well-orchestrated cyberfinancial attack could be as disruptive as any traditional military assault.

■ The Enemy Hedge Fund Scenario

A hedge fund is the perfect cover for an intelligence operation. A malicious trader does not have to destroy a system physically in order to carry out an attack. If an enemy trader sets up a legal entity such as a hedge fund, it can open accounts with major clearing brokers and commence a pattern of ordinary trading. This trading can continue for years as the entity becomes a sleeper cell in the capital markets. In time, clearing brokers come to see the entity as a prime customer generating huge commissions, and they grant it larger lines of credit.

Hedge funds are also classic intelligence-gathering operations that seek information advantage on a continual basis. The tradecraft that intelligence agencies and hedge funds use to gather information is similar. Attending high-level professional conferences is one way to build an expert network and tap into confidential information about new products and inventions. Investing in a company gives the investor access to management. Both fund traders and intelligence agents seek such access. For hedge funds, the purpose is to acquire a trading advantage, such as an early look at a new product that will affect stock prices. For intelligence services, the purpose is to keep ahead of technological developments that will affect the relative economic power of rival states.

The hedge fund sleeper could build close relationships with many brokers around the world so that its buying power was hundreds of times its capital, once all credit lines and the notional value of derivatives were taken into account. On orders from an enemy financial command, the fund network could turn malicious. Orders to sell specific stocks such as Apple, Google, or other widely held names could come flooding in and overwhelm the market makers and buyers. A price decline could start out slowly and gather momentum until it turns into a full-fledged market panic. Circuit breakers could be tripped, but the selling pressure would not abate. Business TV channels would pick up the story, and the panic would spread.

For the enemy traders, there is no tomorrow. They are not worried about paying for their trades in a few days or in the repercussions of mark-to-market losses. Their capital might even be on its way back to banks in Beijing or Moscow, unbeknown to the clearing brokers now handling the orders. Capital markets have certain safeguards against overnight credit risk, but no effective safeguards have ever been devised to insure against losses that arise during the course of a single day. Chinese or Russian covert hedge funds could exploit this weakness while abusing trust and credit built up over years.

The malicious attack need not be confined to cash markets. While the attackers are selling stocks, they could buy put options or short the stock in a dealer swap to add selling pressure. The malicious customer becomes like a virus infecting the dealer's trading desk, forcing it to add to the mayhem.

Another force multiplier is to begin the attack on a day when markets are already crashing for unrelated reasons. Attackers could wait for a day when major stock indexes are already down 2 percent, then launch the attack in an effort to push markets down 20 percent or more. This might produce a crash comparable to the great two-day crash of 1929, which marked the beginning of the Great Depression.

Financial attackers can also utilize psychological operations, psyops, to increase the attack's effectiveness. This involves issuing false news stories and starting rumors. Stories that a Fed chairman has been kidnapped or that a prominent financier has suffered a heart attack would be effective. Stories that a top-tier bank has closed its doors or that a hedge fund manager has committed suicide would suffice. These would be followed by stories that major exchanges are having "technical difficulties" and sell orders are not being processed, leaving customers with massive losses. For verisimilitude, stories would be crafted to mimic events that have actually happened in recent years. Mainstream media would echo the stories, and the panic-inducing scenarios would be widespread.

The New York Stock Exchange and the SEC claim they have safeguards designed to prevent this kind of runaway trading. But those safeguards are designed to slow down rational traders who are trying to make money and may be temporarily irrational. They involve time-outs for the markets to allow traders to comprehend the situation and begin to see bargains they might buy. They also involve margin calls designed to cover mark-to-market losses and give the brokers a cushion against customers who default.

Those mitigation techniques do not stop the financial warrior, because he is not looking for bargains or profits. The attacker can use the time-out to pile on additional sell orders in a second wave of attacks. Also, these safety techniques rely heavily on actual performance by the affected parties. When a margin call is made, it applies the brakes to a legitimate trader due to the need to provide cash. But the malicious trader would ignore the margin call and continue trading. For the malicious trader, there is no day of reckoning. The fact that the enemy might be discovered later is also no deterrent. The United States knew the Japanese bombed Pearl Harbor *after* the attack, but it didn't see the attack coming until its battleships were sunk or in flames.

A clearing broker could close out the malicious account to prevent more trading, but that moves the open positions from the hedge funds to the brokers. In such circumstances, many brokers would fail, and the cascade of failure would ripple through the financial system and render the clearinghouses insolvent. The entire hierarchy of exchanges, clearinghouses, brokers, and customers could be pushed to the brink of collapse.

Sleeper hedge funds can serve another insidious purpose, acting as intelligence-gathering operations years in advance of an attack. Intelligence analysts today need more than state secrets. Economic intelligence—including plans for natural resource projects, energy discoveries, pipeline routes, and other initiatives—is just as valuable. This information can impact commodity markets, financial stability, economic growth, and the allocation of resources by both the private and the government sectors. Such intelligence is not always known to government officials, but is known to CEOs, engineers, and developers throughout the private sector.

Once a covert hedge fund acquires a material position in a target company, it can arrange to meet that company's management. Access to management is especially easy at small to medium-size companies that receive less attention from brokerage research departments. Companies like this are often on the cutting edge of new designs in satellites, 3-D applications, and digital imaging. Access is the key. Savvy investors pick up winks and nods and interpret hints to infer the timing and nature of the latest developments. This can continue for years as the covert hedge fund patiently builds trust, churns the account, gathers information, and spots vulnerabilities. Then, like a scorpion, the fund stings, on orders from its sovereign masters.

Skeptics claim that an intelligence or military covert operation in hedge fund form would be easy to detect because of detailed anti-money-laundering and know-your-customer rules, strictly enforced by the brokers. This objection does not withstand scrutiny. The necessary techniques for operating with cover include front companies, so-called cutouts, secret agents, cover stories, and entities layered on top of each other so that the unwitting points of contact cannot see the controlling parties. A covert hedge fund structure involves layers of legal entities in tax-haven countries offering the enemy sponsor a deep cover. Professional assistance is needed from corrupt lawyers or bankers who retain innocent professionals to handle detailed work such as fund administration. Directors are recruited from the advisory companies in offshore jurisdictions that offer administration services to investors. Having innocent parties in the food chain throws counterintelligence agents off the scent.

The covert fund manager would operate in well-appointed quarters in a cosmopolitan center such as Zurich or London. The enemy managers would be highly educated professionals groomed years before by foreign intelligence agencies to perform such tasks, with business degrees from Harvard or Stanford. They would receive experience in large bank training programs at places like Goldman Sachs and HSBC, forming a cadre of sleeper finance professionals who are then given a covert assignment to manage the enemy funds.

Counterintelligence agents might happen upon such sleepers; the interception of targeted communications may reveal something of their doings. But if their operation is structured wisely by the enemy, such hedge fund plotters are almost undetectable by outsiders unless insiders betray them. Then there's the bigger issue: Is the U.S. national security community on the lookout at all?

▪ The World in Financial War

If all this sounds far-fetched, consider that the Chinese—and others—are already perpetrating even subtler forms of financial attack.

In January 2011 *The New York Times* reported that China had been a net seller of U.S. Treasury securities in 2010 after years of being a net buyer. The *Times* report found this selling strange because China was still accumulating huge dollar reserves from its trade surpluses and was still buying dollars to manipulate the value of its currency. The implication was that China must still be a large buyer of Treasuries, even though official data showed otherwise. The *Times* noted that in 2010 Britain had emerged as the world's largest purchaser of Treasury securities, and it inferred that China had "shifted purchases to accounts managed by British money managers." In effect, China was using London bankers as a front operation to continue buying U.S. Treasury notes while Beijing officially reported that it was selling.

Another technique China uses to disguise its market intelligence operations was reported on May 20, 2007, in *The New York Times* when Andrew Ross Sorkin disclosed that the China Investment Corporation (CIC), another sovereign wealth fund, had agreed to purchase $3 billion of stock in Blackstone Group, the powerful and secretive U.S.-based private equity firm.

Blackstone Group was cofounded by former Nixon administration senior official Peter G. Peterson, later chairman of both the Council on Foreign Relations and the Federal Reserve Bank of New York. The other Blackstone cofounder, Stephen A. Schwarzman, is a multibillionaire who became notorious for his sixtieth birthday party held at the New York

Park Avenue Armory on February 13, 2007, just a few months before Blackstone's sale. That party included a thirty-minute performance by Rod Stewart, for which the singer was reportedly paid $1 million. China was now buying its own front-row seat at the Blackstone party, gaining access to top management and the ability to coinvest in pending deals.

In June 2007, shortly before global capital markets began the collapse that culminated in the Panic of 2008, Schwarzman described his deal-making style: "I want war, not a series of skirmishes. . . . I always think about what will kill off the other bidder." He was referring to conventional finance; real war was the furthest thing from his mind. Yet he was already a pawn in a financial war greater in scope than his blinkered perspective allowed him to see. Self-styled global citizens like Schwarzman, who treat New York as a pit stop in their travels from Davos to Dalian, may think real war is a thing of the past, even obsolete. Similar views were advanced in the late 1920s, even as events were moving toward the greatest war in history.

Analysts praised the fact that the CIC-Blackstone deal showed that China was willing "to put its vast reserves to work outside of China." But this emphasis on the outbound money flow ignores the inbound flow of information. It is naïve not to consider that information on America's most powerful deal machine's inner workings is being channeled to the political bureaus of the Communist Party of China. The Chinese investment due diligence teams get a look at confidential deal target information, even on deals that do not ultimately get done. The $3 billion sale price may seem like a lot of money to Schwarzman, but it is only one-tenth of one percent of China's reserves, the equivalent of dropping a dime when you have a hundred-dollar bill. China's penetration of Schwarzman and Blackstone is a significant step in its advance toward East Asian hegemony and a possible confrontation with the United States. Of course, information channels are a two-way street, and firms such as Blackstone do assist the U.S. intelligence community with insights on Chinese capabilities and intentions.

The United States is not the only potential Chinese financial warfare target. In September 2012 a senior Chinese official, writing in the Communist *China Daily,* suggested mounting an attack on the Japanese bond market in retaliation for Japanese provocations involving disputed island territories in the East China Sea. On March 10, 2013, China hacked the

Reserve Bank of Australia in an effort to obtain intelligence on delicate G20 discussions.

China's actions in the bond and private equity markets are part of its long-term effort to operate in stealth, infiltrate critical nodes, and acquire valuable corporate information in the process. These financial efforts are proceeding side by side with malicious efforts in cyberspace and attacks on systems that control critical infrastructure, launched by China's notorious military espionage Unit 61398. These combined efforts will prove useful to China in future confrontations with the United States.

The United States is not supine when it comes to cyberwarfare; in fact, U.S. cybercapabilities probably exceed those of the Chinese. Journalist Matthew Aid reported in 2013 on the most sensitive U.S. cyberoperation of all, inside the National Security Agency:

> A highly secretive unit of the National Security Agency (NSA) . . . called the Office of Tailored Access Operations, or TAO, has successfully penetrated Chinese computer and telecommunications systems for almost 15 years, generating some of the best and most reliable intelligence information about what is going on inside the People's Republic of China. . . .
>
> TAO . . . requires a special security clearance to gain access to the unit's work spaces inside the NSA operations complex. The door leading to its ultramodern operations center is protected by armed guards, an imposing steel door that can only be entered by entering the correct six-digit code into a keypad, and a retinal scanner to ensure that only those individuals specially cleared for access get through the door. . . .
>
> TAO's mission is simple. It collects intelligence information on foreign targets by surreptitiously hacking into their computers and telecommunications systems, cracking passwords, compromising the computer security systems protecting the targeted computer, stealing the data stored on computer hard drives, and then copying all the messages and data traffic passing within the targeted email and text-messaging systems.

Spying operations such as TAO are far more sophisticated than the relatively simple sweeps of e-mail and telephone message traffic revealed by Edward Snowden in 2013.

Wall Street is also improving its finance-related cyberabilities. On July 18, 2013, a securities industry trade organization sponsored a financial war game, called Quantum Dawn 2, that involved more than five hundred individuals from about fifty entities and government agencies. Quantum Dawn 2 was aimed principally at preventing attacks that would disrupt normal trading. While useful, this goal falls short of preparing for a more sophisticated type of attack that would mimic, rather than disrupt, order-entry systems.

China is not the only major power fighting a financial war. Such warfare is being waged today between the United States and Iran, as the United States seeks to destabilize the Iranian regime by denying it access to critical payments networks. In February 2012 the United States banned Iran from the U.S. dollar payments systems controlled by the Federal Reserve and the U.S. Treasury. This proved inconvenient for Iran, but it was still able to transact business in international markets by converting payments to euros and settling transactions through the Belgium-based SWIFT bank message system. In March 2012 the United States pressured SWIFT to ban Iran from its payments system, too. Iran was then officially cut off from participating in hard-currency payments or receipts with the rest of the world. The United States made no secret of its goals in the financial war with Iran. On June 6, 2013, U.S. Treasury official David Cohen said that the objective of U.S. sanctions was "to cause depreciation of the rial and make it unusable in international commerce."

The results were catastrophic for the Iranian economy. Iran is a leading oil exporter and requires access to payments systems to receive dollars for the oil it ships abroad. It is also a major importer of refined petroleum products, food, and consumer electronics such as Apple computers and HP printers. Suddenly it had no way to pay for its imports, and its local currency, the rial, collapsed. Merchants sought scarce dollars on the black market at exchange rates that made the rial worth less than half its previous value, the equivalent of 100 percent inflation. A run on the Iranian banking system commenced, as depositors tried to get their rials out to purchase black-market currencies or hard assets to preserve wealth.

The government raised interest rates in an effort to stop the run on the banks. The United States had inflicted a currency collapse, hyperinflation, and a bank run and had caused a scarcity of food, gasoline, and consumer goods, through the expedient of cutting Iran out of the global payments system.

Iran fought back, even before the escalation of U.S. efforts, by dumping dollars and buying gold to prevent the United States or its allies from freezing its dollar balances. India is a major Iranian oil importer, and the two trading partners took steps to implement an oil-for-gold swap, whereby India would buy gold on global markets and swap it with Iran for oil shipments. In turn, Iran could swap the gold with Russia or China for food or manufactured goods. In the face of extreme financial sanctions, Iran was once again proving that gold is money, good at all times and in all places.

Turkey quickly became a leading source of gold for Iran. Turkish exports of gold to Iran in March 2013 equaled $381 million, which was more than double those of the previous month. However, gold is not as easy to move as digital dollars, and gold swaps have their own risks. In January 2013 a cargo plane with 1.5 tons of gold on board was impounded by Turkish authorities at the Istanbul airport because the gold was deemed contraband. Various reports said the plane originated in Ghana, a major gold producer, and was heading for Dubai, a notorious transshipment point for gold and currencies from all over the world. Reports from the *Voice of Russia* speculated that the plane was ultimately headed for Iran. Regardless of the destination, someone, possibly Iran, was missing 1.5 tons of gold.

Another source of gold bound for Iran is Afghanistan. In December 2012 *The New York Times* reported on a healthy triangular trade among Afghanistan, Dubai, and Iran using both legitimate transportation and illegal smuggling. The *Times* reported that "passengers flying from Kabul to the Persian Gulf . . . would be well advised to heed warnings about the danger of bags falling from overhead compartments. One courier . . . carried nearly 60 pounds of gold bars, each about the size of an iPhone, aboard an early morning flight."

As Iran expanded its gold trading, the United States was quick to retaliate. The U.S. Treasury announced strict enforcement of a prohibition on gold sales to Iran effective July 1, 2013. This enforcement was aimed at Turkey and the UAE, which had been the principal suppliers to Iran. The United States had already choked off Iran's access to hard currency; now it was doing the same to gold. It was a tacit recognition by the United States that gold is money, despite public disparagement of gold by U.S. Federal Reserve officials and others.

Gold was not Iran's only alternative payments strategy. The most convenient was to accept local currency payments in local banks not subject to the embargo. Iran could ship oil to India and receive Indian rupees deposited for its account in Indian banks. The use of those rupees by Iran is limited to purchases in India itself, but Indian agents can quickly adapt to import Western goods with dollars and sell them to Iranians for rupees, at high markups to compensate for the time and trouble of reexporting the Indian imports.

Iran also uses Chinese and Russian banks to act as front operations for illegal payments through sanctioned channels. It arranged large hard-currency deposits in Chinese and Russian banks before the sanctions were in place. Those banks then conducted normal hard-currency wire transfers through SWIFT for Iran, without disclosing that Iran was the beneficial owner, as required by SWIFT rules.

Intelligence reports indicate that the amount of hard currency on deposit by Iran in Chinese banks alone is $27 billion. However, Iran's ability to move these funds is circumscribed by China's need to avoid attracting the attention of the United States in making the transfers. In April 2013 Iran requested that China make a "gift" to North Korea of $4 billion as part of China's normal humanitarian aid flows to the Hermit Kingdom. Iran did not disclose to China that the gift was actually a payment for shipments of nuclear weapons technology from North Korea to Iran.

In late 2012 the United States warned Russia and China about assisting Iran in such end runs around the sanctions, but no penalties were imposed on the Russians or Chinese and none seemed likely. SWIFT also had no appetite for enforcement because it did not want to exclude Iran from its system in the first place; it did so only under U.S. pressure. The United States did not come down hard on Russia or China because she had more important agendas to pursue with both, including Syria and North Korea.

Iran also demonstrated how financial warfare and cyberwarfare could be combined in a hybrid asymmetric attack. In May 2013 Iranian hackers had reportedly gained access to the software systems used by energy companies to control oil and natural gas pipelines around the world. By manipulating this software, Iran could wreak havoc not only on physical supply chains but also on energy derivatives markets that depended on physical supply and demand for price discovery. These probes, described by U.S. officials as reconnaissance missions, are highly dangerous on their own. Neither the Iranian hackers nor the U.S. targets seemed to consider that such activities might *accidentally* trigger a market panic that even the attacker did not intend.

Iran was not alone in bearing the brunt of U.S. financial warfare capabilities. U.S. financial sanctions aimed at Syria caused the Syrian pound to lose 66 percent of its value in the twelve months from July 2012 to July 2013. Inflation in Syria spiked to an annual rate of 200 percent as a result. The Syrian government was forced to conduct business in the currencies of its three principal allies—Iranian rials, Russian rubles, and Chinese yuan—because the Syrian pound had practically ceased to function as a medium of exchange.

By late 2013, the financial damage in Iran led to an agreement between President Obama and Iranian president Hassan Rouhani, which eased U.S. financial attacks in exchange for Iranian concessions on its uranium enrichment programs. Iran had suffered from the sanctions, but it had not collapsed, and now it had met the United States at the negotiating table. In particular, sanctions on gold purchases by Iran were removed, enabling Iran to stockpile gold using the dollar proceeds from oil sales. President Obama made it clear that although sanctions were eased, they could be reimposed if Iran failed to live up to its promises to scale back its nuclear programs. Still, for the time being, Iran had fought the United States to a standstill in its financial war, despite enormous disruption to the Iranian economy.

The U.S.-Iranian financial war of 2012–13 illustrates how nations that could not stand up to the United States militarily could prove a tough match when the battlefield is financial or electronic. Just as the United States found its allies in Europe and Turkey, Iran found hers in Russia, China, and India. Iran's allies spoke openly about building new non-dollar-based banking and payments systems. Dubai had carved out a role accommodating both sides in this war not unlike Switzerland in World War II. The United States had wanted to drive Iran out of the dollar payments system, and it succeeded. But in a case of "be careful what you wish for," an alternative non-dollar-based payment system is now taking shape in Asia, and gold has proved to be an effective financial weapon on its own.

This cat-and-mouse game among China, Russia, Iran, the United States, and North Korea involving cash, gold, weapons, and sanctions illustrates how financial weapons have moved to the fore in strategic affairs.

■ The Cyberfinancial Connection

Interest in financial war is hardly confined to Andy Marshall's office in the Pentagon. In late September 2012 the Kingdom of Bahrain played host to a private, invitation-only summit of international monetary experts to discuss the geopolitics of currencies and reserves. The three-day exercise included scenarios such as the U.S. dollar's collapse and the rise of regional reserve currencies such as the Chinese yuan and Russian ruble. Participants included European legislators, think-tank scholars, prominent journalists, and capital markets experts.

On October 12, 2012, the Federation of American Scientists conducted a financial war game in Washington, D.C., involving alternative scenarios of a shooting war between Israel and Iran. Participants were given conventional military scenarios and then asked to assess the financial impact and show how financial weapons might be used as a force multiplier.

On October 25, 2012, the Boeing Corporation conducted a financial war game during an offsite conference in Bretton Woods, New Hampshire. The conference was held at the historic Mount Washington Hotel, famous as the site of the 1944 Bretton Woods conference that established the international monetary system, which prevailed from the end of the Second World War until President Nixon closed the gold window in 1971. Although Boeing is a corporation and not a sovereign state, its interest in financial warfare is hardly surprising. Boeing has employees in seventy countries and customers in 150 countries, and it is one of the world's largest exporters. Boeing's Defense, Space and Security division builds and operates the most sensitive, heavily classified platforms for U.S. national security operations. Few if any companies in the world have as large a stake as Boeing in the possibility and implications of financial warfare.

That same month, on October 30, 2012, the National Defense University completed a one-year virtual financial war game involving contributions of six leading experts from academia, think tanks, and major banks. The sponsor for the exercise was the U.S. Pacific Command, and its findings are contained in a highly sensitive 104-page final report.

In August 2013 the Swiss Army carried out one of the most elaborate financial war games of all, called Operation Duplex-Barbara. In this exercise, Swiss troops defended their country against imagined French mobs and militias swarming over their border to recover money allegedly stolen by the Swiss banks.

Even this extensive activity and analysis of financial warfare does not encompass the full extent of the threat. Cyberattacks on U.S. infrastructure, including banks and other financial institutions, are growing and can take many forms. In one troubling instance on Christmas Eve 2011, a computer file containing personal identification information on a senior U.S. government official was hacked, and the information was downloaded. The information was then used in an effort to deplete the official's personal bank account. The official was Mary Shapiro, then the chief regulator of all U.S. capital markets.

On April 23, 2013, a Twitter account maintained by the Associated Press was hacked and used to distribute a false message that the White House had been the target of a terror attack and that President Obama had been injured. This false message came just days after the Boston Marathon terror bombing and the dramatic manhunt and shootouts with the terror bombers. The Dow Jones Industrial Index immediately plunged more than 140 points, briefly wiping out $136 billion in wealth before recovering once the message was exposed as a fake. A pro-Syrian hacker group backed by Iran called the Syrian Electronic Army claimed credit for the attack. The hackers' success and the market reaction demonstrated that markets are on a hair trigger and are easily crashed and manipulated by various means. It was an instructive episode for other potential attackers.

These events point toward the most dangerous kind of financial attack, one that *combines* cyberattacks and financial warfare in the ultimate force multiplier scenario. In this situation, a cyberattack is not used to disable U.S. capital markets; instead the cyberinvaders take control of order-entry software to spoof sell orders by major financial institutions. The intended financial collapse is similar to the rogue hedge fund scenarios, except that no cash or capital is required. The computer is programmed to mimic an out-of-control broker trying to unload trillions of dollars in stocks, bonds, and derivatives.

This scenario is a larger, more targeted version of the August 1, 2012, Knight Capital fiasco, in which a software error caused a computer to go berserk and flood the New York Stock Exchange with phony orders. Knight accumulated $7 billion in unwanted stock positions in a matter of minutes and suffered $440 million in losses to unwind them. While the disaster was taking place, no one at Knight could identify the problem's source and no one thought to pull the kill switch. Finally the NYSE, in self-defense, blocked Knight from its systems.

An even greater fiasco occurred on August 22, 2013, when the NAS-DAQ Stock Market was paralyzed for three hours due to computer and communications problems that have never been publicly explained. An attack from Iran's Cyber-Defense Command has not been ruled out. In August 2012 Iran's cyberforces destroyed 30,000 computers of oil behemoth Saudi Aramco with the Shamoon digital virus, and Iranian efforts at cyberfinancial warfare are ongoing.

In these financial warfare scenarios, an attack could be so large that the NYSE would be overwhelmed and have to close down entirely. The ensuing panic would produce hundreds of billions of dollars in paper losses.

While thinkers in the national security community have expressed concerns about financial war, officials at the U.S. Treasury and Federal Reserve routinely pour cold water on the threat analysis. Their rejoinder begins with estimates of the market impact of financial war, then concludes that the Chinese or other major powers would never engage in it because it would produce massive losses on their own portfolios. This view reflects a dangerous official naïveté. The Treasury view supposes that the purpose of financial war is financial gain. It is not.

The purpose of financial war is to degrade an enemy's capabilities and subdue the enemy while seeking geopolitical advantage in targeted areas. Making a portfolio profit has nothing to do with a financial attack. If the attacker can bring an opponent to a state of near collapse and paralysis through a financial catastrophe while advancing on other fronts, then the financial war will be judged a success, even if the attacker incurs large costs. All wars have costs, and many wars are so destructive that recovery takes years or decades. This does not mean wars do not happen or that those initiating them do not find advantage despite the costs.

Consider the following calculations. If China lost 25 percent on the value of its reserves as the result of a financial war with the United States, the cost to China would be about $750 billion. A fleet of twelve state-of-the art Ford-Class aircraft carriers, comparable to the envisioned U.S. carrier force, would cost over $400 billion to build and deploy once all construction, operating, overhaul, and other life-of-the-vessel costs were taken into account. The costs of securing those aircraft carriers with destroyers, submarines, and other support vessels, as well as the land-based systems and staff needed to operate the fleet, raise the costs to a significantly higher level. In short, the economic cost of confronting the United States in financial warfare may not be higher than confronting it at sea and in the air, and the damage inflicted may be even greater. China does not have a fleet of state-of-the-art aircraft carriers, but it does have cash and computers, and it will choose its own battlespace.

China could protect its reserves against asset freezes or devaluation in the event of a financial war by converting its paper wealth to gold—an option it is now pursuing aggressively. Every gold bullion acquisition by China reduces its financial vulnerability and tilts the trade-off between portfolio losses and armament costs in favor of financial war. China's possible intentions may be inferred from its status as the world's largest gold buyer.

The U.S. Treasury and Federal Reserve view also fails to account for intertemporal effects. An attack that is costly in the short run can be quite profitable in the long run. Whatever losses China might suffer on its portfolio in a financial war could be quickly reversed during peace talks or in a negotiated settlement. Seized accounts could be unfrozen, and market losses could be turned into gains, once conditions normalized. Meanwhile China's geopolitical gains in areas like Taiwan or the East China Sea could be permanent, and it is the U.S. economy that might suffer most in such a contest and take years to recover.

Treasury and Fed officials dismiss concerns about financial war due to their misapprehension of the statistical properties of risk and their reliance on erroneous equilibrium models. These models assume efficient markets and rational behavior that have no correspondence to real markets. As applied to financial warfare, their view is that enemy attacks on particular stocks or markets will prove self-defeating because rational investors will jump in to buy bargains once the selling pressure begins. Such behavior exists only in relatively calm, unperturbed markets, but in actual panic situations, selling pressure feeds on itself, and buyers are nowhere to be found. A major panic will spread exponentially and lead to total collapse absent an act of force majeure by government.

This panic dynamic has actually commenced twice in the past sixteen years. In September 1998 global capital markets were hours away from total collapse before the completion of a $4 billion, all-cash bailout of the hedge fund Long-Term Capital Management, orchestrated by the Federal Reserve Bank of New York. In October 2008 global capital markets were days away from the sequential collapse of most major banks when Congress enacted the TARP bailout, while the Fed and Treasury intervened to guarantee money-market funds, prop up AIG, and provide trillions of dollars in market liquidity. In neither panic did the Fed's imaginary bargain hunters show up to save the day.

In short, the Treasury and Fed view of financial warfare exhibits what intelligence analysts call *mirror imaging*. They assume that since the United States would not launch a financial attack on China, China would not launch an attack on the United States. Far from preventing war, such myopia is a principal cause of war because it fails to comprehend the enemy's intentions and capabilities. Where financial warfare is concerned, markets are too important to be left to the Treasury and the Fed.

Nor is it necessary to launch a financial war in order for financial warfare capability to be an effective policy instrument. It is only necessary that the threat be credible. A scenario can arise where the U.S. president stands down from military action to defend Taiwan because China has made it clear than any such action would result in the destruction of a trillion dollars or more in U.S. paper wealth. In this scenario, Taiwan is left to its fate. Andy Marshall's Air-Sea Battle is deterred by China's weapons of wealth destruction.

Perhaps the greatest financial threat is that these scenarios might play out by accident. In the mid-1960s, at the height of Cold War hysteria about nuclear attacks and Mutual Assured Destruction, two films, *Fail-Safe* and *Dr. Strangelove,* dealt with nuclear-war-fighting scenarios between the United States and the Soviet Union. As portrayed in these films, neither side wanted war, but it was launched nonetheless due to computer glitches and actions of rogue officers.

Capital markets today are anything but fail-safe. In fact, they are increasingly failure-prone, as the Knight Capital incident and the curious May 6, 2010, flash crash demonstrate. A financial attack may be launched by accident during a routine software upgrade or drill. Capital markets almost collapsed in 1998 and 2008 without help from malicious actors, and the risk of a similar collapse in coming years, accidental or malicious, is distressingly high.

In 2011 the *National Journal* published an article called "The Day After" that described in detail the highly classified plans for continuity of U.S. government operations in the face of invasion, infrastructure collapse, or extreme natural disaster. These plans include landing a helicopter squadron on the Washington Mall, near the Capitol, to swoop up the congressional leadership for evacuation to an emergency operations center called Mount Weather in Virginia. Defense Department officials would then be moved to a hardened bunker deep inside Raven Rock Mountain on the Maryland-Pennsylvania border, not far from Camp David.

Much of Marc Ambinder's reporting involves the chain of command and what happens if certain officials, possibly including the president, are dead or missing. He points out that these contingency plans *failed* both during the attempted assassination of President Reagan in 1981 and again on 9/11. Recent years have seen improvement in secure communications, but serious ambiguity can still arise in the chain of command, and Ambinder says more failures can be expected in another national crisis.

However, a financial war would present a different kind of crisis, with little or no physical damage. No officials should be dead or missing, and the chain of command should remain intact. Absent collateral infrastructure attacks, communications would flow normally.

Yet the nation would be traumatized just as surely as if an earthquake had leveled a major city, because trillions of dollars of wealth would be lost. Banks and exchanges would close their doors and liquidity in markets would evaporate. Trust would be gone. The Federal Reserve, having used up its dry powder printing over $3 trillion of new money since 2008, would have no capacity or credibility to do more. Social unrest and riots would soon follow.

Andy Marshall and other futurists in the national security community are taking such threats seriously. They receive little or no support from the Treasury or Federal Reserve; both are captive to mirror imaging.

Ironically, solutions are not hard to devise. These solutions involve breaking big banks into units that are not too big to fail; returning to a system of regional stock exchanges, to provide redundancy; and reintroducing gold into the monetary system, since gold cannot be wiped out in a digital flash. The first-order costs of these changes are more than compensated by increased robustness and second-order benefits. None of these remedial steps is under serious consideration by Congress or the White House. For now, the United States is only dimly aware of the threat and nowhere near a solution.

PART TWO

MONEY AND MARKETS

CHAPTER 3

THE RUIN OF MARKETS

> The man of system . . . seems to imagine that he can arrange the
> different members of a great society with as much ease as the
> hand arranges the different pieces upon a chess-board. He does
> not consider that in the great chess-board of human society,
> every single piece has a principle of motion of its own.
>
> Adam Smith
> *The Theory of Moral Sentiments*
> 1759

> The "data" from which the economic calculus starts are never
> for the whole society "given" to a single mind which could work
> out the implications and can never be so given.
>
> Friedrich A. Hayek
> 1945

> Any . . . statistical regularity will tend to collapse once pressure
> is placed on it for control purposes.
>
> Goodhart's Law
> 1975

In Shakespeare's *The Merchant of Venice*, Salanio asks, "Now, what
news on the Rialto?" He's looking for information, gathering intelligence,
and attempting to identify what's happening in the marketplace. Salanio
doesn't intend to control the business unfolding around him; he knows
he cannot. He looks to understand the flow of news, to find his place in
the market.

Janet Yellen and the Federal Reserve would do well to be as humble.

The word *market* invokes images of everything from prehistoric trade goods to medieval town fairs to postmodern digital exchanges with nanosecond-speed bids and offers converging in a computational cloud. In essence, *markets are places where buyers and sellers meet* to conduct the sale of goods and services. In the world today, *place* may be an abstracted location, a digital venue; a *meeting* may amount to nothing more than a fleeting connection. But at their core, markets are unchanged since traders swapped amber for ebony on the shores of the Mediterranean during the Bronze Age.

Still, markets—whether for tangible commodities like gold or for intangibles such as stocks—have always been about deeper processes than the mere exchange of goods and services. Fundamentally, they are about *information exchange* concerning the price of goods and services. Prices are portable. Once a merchant or trader ascertains a market price, others can use that information to expand or contract output, hire or fire workers, or move to another marketplace with an informational advantage in tow.

Information can have greater value than the underlying transactions from which the information is derived; the multibillion-dollar Bloomberg fortune is based on this insight. How should a venture capitalist price a stake in an enterprise creating an entirely new product? Neither the investor nor the entrepreneur really knows. But information about past outcomes, whether occasional huge gains or frequent failures, gives guidance to the parties and allows an investment to go forward. Information about sales and investment returns is the lubricant and the fuel that allows more sales and investments to take place. An exchange of goods and services may be the result of market activity, but price discovery is the market function that allows an exchange to occur in the first place.

Anyone who has ever walked away from a carpet dealer in a Middle Eastern bazaar, only to be chased down by the dealer yelling, "Mister, mister, I have a better price, very cheap," knows the charms of price discovery. This dynamic is no different than the digitized, automated, high-frequency trading that takes place in servers adjacent to exchange trading platforms in New York and Chicago. The computer is offering the nanosecond version of "Mister, I have a better price." Price discovery is still the primary market function.

But markets are home to more than just buyers and sellers, speculators and arbitrageurs. Global markets today seem irresistible to central bankers with plans for better times. Planning is the central bankers' baleful vanity since, for them, markets are a test tube in which to try out their interventionist theories.

Central bankers control the price of money and therefore indirectly influence every market in the world. Given this immense power, the ideal central banker would be humble, cautious, and deferential to market signals. Instead, modern central bankers are both bold and arrogant in their efforts to bend markets to their will. Top-down central planning, dictating resource allocation and industrial output based on supposedly superior knowledge of needs and wants, is an impulse that has infected political players throughout history. It is both ironic and tragic that Western central banks have embraced central planning with gusto in the early twenty-first century, not long after the Soviet Union and Communist China abandoned it in the late twentieth. The Soviet Union and Communist China engaged in extreme central planning over the world's two largest countries and one-third of the earth's population for more than one hundred years combined. The result was a conspicuous and dismal failure. Today's central planners, especially the Federal Reserve, will encounter the same failure in time. The open issues are, when and at what cost to society?

The impulse toward central planning often springs from the perceived need to solve a problem with a top-down solution. For Russian Communists in 1917, it was the problem of the czar and a feudal society. For Chinese Communists in 1949, it was local corruption and foreign imperialism. For the central planners at central banks today, the problem is deflation and low nominal growth. The problems are real, but the top-down solutions are illusory, the product of hubris and false ideologies.

In the twentieth century, Russians and Chinese adhered to Marxist ideology and the arrogance of the gun. Today central bankers embrace Keynesianism and the arrogance of the Ph.D. Neither Marxist nor Keynesian ideology allows individuals the degrees of freedom necessary to discover those solutions that emerge spontaneously from the fog of complexity characteristic of an advanced economy. Instead, individuals, sensing manipulation and control from central banks, either restrain their economic activity or pursue entirely new, smaller enterprises removed from the sights of central bank market manipulation.

Market participants have been left with speculation, churning, and a game of trying to outthink the thinkers in the boardroom at the Federal Reserve. Lately, so-called markets have become a venue for trading ahead of the next Fed policy announcement, or piggybacking on its stubborn implementation. Since 2008, markets have become a venue for wealth extraction rather than wealth creation. Markets no longer perform true market functions. In markets today, the dead hands of the academic and the rentier have replaced the invisible hand of the merchant or the entrepreneur.

This critique is not new; it is as old as free markets themselves. Adam Smith, in *The Theory of Moral Sentiments*, a philosophical work from 1759, the dawn of the modern capitalist system, makes the point that no planner can direct a system of arrayed components that are also systems with unique properties beyond the planner's purview. This might be called the Matryoshka Theory, named for the Russian dolls nested one inside the other and invisible from the outside. Only when the first doll is opened is the next unique doll revealed, and so on through a succession of dolls. The difference is that *matryoshka* dolls are finite, whereas variety in a modern economy is infinite, interactive, and beyond comprehension.

Friedrich Hayek, in his classic 1945 essay "The Use of Knowledge in Society," written almost two hundred years after Adam Smith's work, makes the same argument but with a shift in emphasis. Whereas Smith focused on individuals, Hayek focused on information. This was a reflection of Hayek's perspective on the threshold of the computer age, when models based on systems of equations were beginning to dominate economic science. Of course, Hayek was a champion of individual liberty. He understood that the information he wrote about would ultimately be created at the level of individual autonomous actors within a complex economic system. His point was that no individual, committee, or computer program would ever have all the information needed to construct an economic order, even if a model of such order could be devised. Hayek wrote:

The peculiar character of the problem of a rational economic order is determined precisely by the fact that the knowledge of the circumstances of which we must make use never exists in concentrated or integrated form but solely as the dispersed bits of incomplete and frequently contradictory knowledge which all the separate individuals possess. . . . Or, to put it briefly, it is a problem of the utilization of knowledge which is not given to anyone in its totality.

Charles Goodhart first articulated Goodhart's Law in a 1975 paper published by the Reserve Bank of Australia. Goodhart's Law is frequently paraphrased along the lines, "When a financial indicator becomes the object of policy, it ceases to function as an indicator." That paraphrase captures the essence of Goodhart's Law, but the original formulation was even more incisive because it included the phrase "for control purposes." (In original form, it reads, "Any observed statistical regularity will tend to collapse once pressure is placed upon it for control purposes.") This phrase emphasized the point that Goodhart was concerned not only with market intervention or manipulation generally but also on a particular kind of top-down effort by central banks to dictate outcomes in complex systems.

Adam Smith, Friedrich Hayek, and Charles Goodhart all concluded that central planning is not merely undesirable or suboptimal; it is *impossible*. This conclusion aligns with the more recent theory of computational complexity. This theory classifies computational challenges by their degree of difficulty as measured by the data, computing steps, and processing power needed to solve a given problem set. The theory has rules for assigning such classifications, including those problems that are regarded as impossible to compute because, variously, the data are too voluminous, the processing steps are infinite, all the computational power in the world is insufficient, or all three. Smith, Hayek, and Goodhart all make the point that the variety and adaptability of human action in the economic sphere are a quintessential case of computational complexity that exceeds the capacity of man or machine to optimize. This means not that economic systems cannot approach optimality but that optimality *emerges* from economic complexity spontaneously rather than being *imposed* by central banks through policy. Today central banks, especially the U.S. Federal Reserve, are repeating the blunders of Lenin, Stalin, and Mao without the violence, although the violence may come yet through income inequality, social unrest, and a confrontation with state power.

While the Adam Smith and Friedrich Hayek formulations of the economic complexity problem are well known, Charles Goodhart added a chilling coda. What happens when data used by central bankers to set policy is itself the result of prior policy manipulation?

■ The Wealth Effect

Measures of inflation, unemployment, income, and other indicators are carefully monitored by central bankers as a basis on which to make policy decisions. Declining unemployment and rising inflation may signal a need to tighten monetary policy, just as falling asset prices may signal a need to provide more monetary ease. Policy makers respond to economic distress by pursuing policies designed to improve the data. After a while, the data themselves may come to reflect not fundamental economic reality but a cosmetically induced policy result. If these data then guide the next dose of policy, the central banker has entered a wilderness of mirrors in which false signals induce policy, which induces more false signals and more policy manipulation and so on, in a feedback loop that diverges further from reality until it crashes against a steel wall of data that cannot easily be manipulated, such as real income and output.

A case in point is the so-called wealth effect. The idea is straightforward. Two asset classes—stocks and housing—represent most of the wealth of the American people. The wealth represented by stocks is highly visible; Americans receive their 401(k) account statements monthly, and they can check particular stock prices in real time if they so choose. Housing prices are less transparent, but anecdotal evidence gathered from real estate listings and water-cooler chatter is sufficient for Americans to have a sense of their home values. Advocates of the wealth effect say that when stocks and home prices are going up, Americans feel richer and more prosperous and are willing to save less and spend more.

The wealth effect is one pillar supporting the Fed's zero-interest-rate policy and profligate money printing since 2008. The transmission channels are easy to follow. If rates are low, more Americans can afford mortgages, which increases home buying, resulting in higher prices for homes.

Similarly, with low rates, brokers offer cheap margin loans to clients, which result in more stock buying and higher stock prices.

There are also important substitution effects. All investors like to receive a healthy return on their savings and investments. If bank accounts are paying close to zero, Americans will redirect those funds to stocks and housing in search of higher returns, which feeds on itself, resulting in higher prices for stocks and housing. At a superficial level, the zero-interest-rate and easy-money policies have produced the intended outcomes. Stock prices more than doubled from 2009 to 2014, and housing prices began rebounding sharply in mid-2012. After four years of trying to manipulate asset prices, the Fed appeared to have succeeded by 2014. The wealth was being created, at least on paper, but to what effect?

The wealth effect's power has been debated for decades, but recent research has cast considerable doubt on its impact. Few economists doubt that the wealth effect exists to an extent. The issues are, how strong is it, how long does it last, and is it worth the negative impacts and distortions needed to achieve it?

The wealth effect is typically expressed as a percentage increase in consumer spending for each dollar increase in wealth. For example, a $100 billion increase in stock market and housing prices that had a 2 percent wealth effect would produce a $2 billion increase in consumer spending. The Congressional Budget Office shows that various studies put the wealth effect from housing prices in a range from 1.7 percent to 21 percent. Such a wide range of estimated effects is risible, casts doubt on similar studies, and highlights the methodological difficulties in this field.

A leading study of the wealth effect from stock prices, published by the Federal Reserve Bank of New York, contained findings that substantially undermine the Fed's own belief in the wealth effect. The study says:

> We find . . . a positive connection between aggregate wealth changes and aggregate spending . . . but the effect is found to be rather unstable and hard to pin down. The . . . response of consumption growth to an unexpected change in wealth is uncertain and the response appears very short-lived. . . . We find that . . . the wealth effect . . . was rather small in recent years. . . . When we force con-

sumption to respond with a one-period lag, a . . . shock to the growth of wealth has virtually no impact on consumption growth.

Another study shows that the wealth effect, to the extent it exists, is heavily concentrated among the rich and has no impact on the spending of everyday Americans. David K. Backus, chairman of the economics department at New York University, echoed this view:

The idea of a wealth effect doesn't stand up to economic data. The stock market boom in the late 1990s helped increase the wealth of Americans, but it didn't produce a significant change in consumption, according to David Backus. . . . Before the stock market reversed it-self, "you didn't see a big increase in consumption," says Backus. "And when it did reverse itself, you didn't see a big decrease."

Even more disturbing than doubts about the wealth effect's size and timing is the fact that economists are not even sure about the *direction* of the effect. While conventional wisdom holds that rising stock prices increase consumption, economists have suggested that it may be the other way around; that rising consumption may increase stock prices. The prominent monetary economist Lacy H. Hunt summarizes the state of research on the wealth effect as follows:

The issue here is not whether the Fed's policies cause aggregate wealth to rise or fall. The question is whether changes in wealth alter consumer spending to any significant degree. The best evidence says that wealth fluctuations have little or no effect on consumer spending. Thus, when the stock market rises in response to massive Fed liquidity, the broader economy is unaffected.

Now consider that several of the leading studies on the wealth effect were published either in 1999 or in 2007, at the height of the two most recent stock bubbles. It's hardly surprising that academic research on the wealth effect might be of particular interest during stock bubbles when the wealth effect was supposed to be at its strongest, but this research indicates that the wealth effect is actually weak and uncertain.

Taken together, all this suggests that while the Federal Reserve is printing trillions of dollars in pursuit of the wealth effect, it may actually be in service to a mere mirage.

▪ Asset Bubbles

America is today witnessing its third stock bubble, and its second housing bubble, in the past fifteen years. These bubbles do not help the real economy but merely enrich brokers and bankers. When these bubbles burst, the economy will confront a worse panic than occurred in 2008, and the bankers' cries for bailouts will not be far behind. The hubris of central bankers who do not trust markets, but seek to manipulate them, will be partly to blame.

Asset bubble creation is one of the most visible malignancies caused by Federal Reserve money printing, but there are many others. One obvious effect is the export of inflation from the United States to its trading partners through the exchange-rate mechanism. A persistent conundrum of Fed monetary policy since 2008 has been the absence of inflation in U.S. consumer prices. From 2008 through 2012, the year-over-year increase in the consumer price index averaged just 1.8 percent per year, the lowest for any five-year period since 1965. Fed critics have expected for years that inflation would rise sharply in the United States in response to money printing, albeit with a lag, but the inflation has not yet appeared; indeed persistent deflationary signs began emerging in 2013.

A principal reason for the absence of inflation in the United States is that inflation was exported abroad through the exchange-rate mechanism. Trading partners of the United States, such as China and Brazil, wanted to promote their exports by preventing their currencies from appreciating relative to the U.S. dollar. As the Fed prints dollars, these trading partners must expand their own money supplies to soak up the dollar flood coming into their economies in the form of trade surpluses or investment. These local money-printing policies cause inflation in the trading partner economies. U.S. inflation is muted because Americans import cheap goods from our trading partners.

From the start of the new millennium, the world in general and the United States in particular have had a natural deflationary bias. Initially the United States imported this deflation from China in the form of cheap goods produced by abundant labor there, aided by an undervalued currency that caused U.S. dollar prices for Chinese goods to be lower than economic fundamentals dictated. This deflationary bias became pronounced in 2001, when annual U.S. inflation dipped to 1.6 percent, perilously close to outright deflation.

It was this deflation scare that prompted then Fed chairman Alan Greenspan to sharply lower interest rates. In 2002 the average Federal Funds effective rate was 1.67 percent, then the lowest in forty-four years. In 2003 the average Federal Funds rate was even lower, 1.13 percent, and it remained low through 2004, averaging 1.35 percent for the year. The extraordinarily low interest-rate policy during this three-year period was designed to fend off deflation, and it worked. After the usual lag, the consumer price index rose 2.7 percent in 2004 and 3.4 percent in 2005. Greenspan was like the pilot of a crashing plane who pulls the aircraft out of a nosedive just before it hits the ground, stabilizes the aerodynamics, then regains altitude. By 2007, inflation was back over 4 percent, and the Fed Funds rate was over 5 percent.

Greenspan had fended off the deflation dragon, but in so doing he had created a worse conundrum. His low-rate policy led directly to an asset bubble in housing, which crashed with devastating impact in late 2007, marking the start of a new depression. Within a year, declining asset values, evaporating liquidity, and lost confidence produced the Panic of 2008, in which tens of trillions of dollars in paper wealth disappeared seemingly overnight.

The Federal Reserve chairmanship passed from Alan Greenspan to Ben Bernanke in February 2006, just as the housing calamity was starting to unfold. Bernanke inherited Greenspan's deflation problem, which had never really gone away but had been masked by the 2002–4 easy-money policies. The consumer price index reached an interim peak in July 2008, then fell sharply for the remainder of that year. Annual inflation year over year from 2008 to 2009 actually dropped for the first time since 1955; inflation was turning to deflation again.

This time the cause was not the Chinese but deleveraging. The housing market collapse in 2007 destroyed the collateral value behind $1 trillion in subprime and other low-quality mortgages, and trillions of dollars more in derivatives based on those mortgages also collapsed in value. The Panic of 2008 forced financial firms and leveraged investors to sell assets in a disorderly fire sale to pay down debt. Other assets came on the market due to insolvencies such as Bear Stearns, Lehman Brothers, and AIG. The financial panic spread to the real economy as housing starts ground to a halt and construction jobs disappeared. Unemployment spiked, which was another boost to deflation. Inflation dropped to 1.6 percent in 2010, identical to the 1.6 percent rate that had spooked Greenspan in 2001. Bernanke's response to the looming threat from deflation was even more aggressive than Greenspan's response to the same threat almost a decade earlier. Bernanke lowered the effective Fed Funds rate to close to zero in 2008, where it has remained ever since.

The world is witnessing a climactic battle between deflation and inflation. The deflation is endogenous, derived from emerging markets' productivity, demographic shifts, and balance sheet deleveraging. The inflation is exogenous, coming from central bank interest-rate policy and money printing. Price index time series are not mere data points; they are more like a seismograph that measures tectonic plates pushing against each other on a fault line. Often the fault line is quiet, almost still. At other times it is active, as pressure builds and one plate pushes under another. Inflation was relatively active in 2011 as the year-over-year increase reached 3.2 percent. Deflation got the upper hand in late 2012; a four-month stretch from September to December 2012 produced a steady decline in the consumer price index. The economy is neither in an inflationary nor a deflationary mode; it is experiencing both at the same time from different causes; price indexes reveal how these offsetting forces are playing out.

This dynamic has profound implications for policy. It means the Fed cannot stop its easing policy so long as the fundamental deflationary forces are in place. If the Fed relented in its money printing, deflation would quickly dominate the economy, with disastrous consequences for the national debt, government revenue, and the banking system. But deflation's root causes are not going away either. At least a billion more workers will enter the labor force in Asia, Africa, and Latin America in coming decades, which will keep downward pressure on costs and prices. Meanwhile a demographic debacle in developed countries will put downward pressure on aggregate demand in these advanced economies. Finally, technological breakthroughs are accelerating and promise higher productivity with cheaper goods and services. The energy revolution in natural gas, shale oil, and fracking is another deflationary force.

In short, the world wants to deflate while governments want to inflate. Neither force will relent, so the pressure between them will continue to build. It is just a matter of time before the economy experiences more than just bubbles, but an earthquake in the form of either a deeper depression or higher inflation, as one force rapidly and unexpectedly overwhelms the other.

■ Tremors

Expected earthquakes of great magnitude near large population centers are colloquially referred to as "the big one." But before those big quakes appear, they may be preceded by small tremors that wreak havoc in localities along the fault line far from the big cities. The same can be said for the Fed's market interventions. In its desperate effort to fight deflation, the Fed is causing minor meltdowns in markets far removed from the main arena of U.S. government bond interest rates. The unintended and unforeseen consequences of the Fed's easy-money policies are becoming more visible, costly, and problematic in many ways. An overview of these malignancies reveals how the Fed's quixotic pursuit of the deflation dragon is doomed to fail.

While inflation was quite low from 2008 to 2013, it was not zero, yet growth in personal income and household income was close to zero. This meant that real incomes *declined* even in a low-inflation environment. If the Fed had instead allowed deflation, real incomes would have risen even without nominal gains, because consumer goods prices would have been lower. In this way, deflation is the workingman's bonus because it allows an increase in the living standard even when wages are stagnant. Instead,

real incomes declined. Economist Lacy Hunt captured this effect suc-
cinctly when he wrote,

> Since wages remained soft, real income of the vast majority of
> American households fell. If the Fed had not taken such extraordi-
> nary steps, interest rates and inflation would be lower currently than
> they are, and we could have avoided the unknowable risks embodied
> in the Fed's swelling balance sheet. In essence, the Fed has impeded
> the healing process, delayed a return to normal economic growth,
> and worsened the income/wealth divide while creating a new
> problem—how to "exit" its failed policies.

Another unintended consequence of Fed policy involves the impact on
savers. The Federal Reserve's zero-interest-rate policy causes a $400
billion-per-year wealth transfer from everyday Americans to large banks.
This is because a normalized interest-rate environment of 2 percent would
pay $400 billion to savers who leave money in the bank. Instead, those
savers get nothing, and the benefit goes to banks that can relend the free
money on a leveraged basis and make significant profits. Part of the Fed's
design is to penalize savers and discourage them from leaving money in
the bank, and to encourage them to invest in risky assets, such as stocks
and real estate, to prop up collateral values in those markets.

But many savers are inherently conservative and with good reason. An
eighty-two-year-old retiree does not want to invest in stocks because she
could easily lose 30 percent of her retirement savings when the next bubble bursts. A twenty-two-year-old professional saving for a down payment on his first condo may avoid stocks for the same reason. Both savers
hope to get a reasonable return on their bank accounts, but the Fed uses
rate policy to ensure that they receive nothing. As a result, many citizens
are saving even *more* from retirement checks and paychecks to make up
for the lack of a market interest rate. So a Fed manipulation designed to
discourage savings actually *increases* savings, on a precautionary basis,
to make up for lost interest. This is a behavioral response not taught in
textbooks or included in models used by the Fed.

Federal Reserve policy has also damaged lending to small and medium-size enterprises (SMEs). This does not trouble the Fed, because it favors the interests of large banks. Johns Hopkins professor Steve Hanke has recently pointed out the reason for this damage to SME lending. SME loans, he argues, are funded by banks through interbank lending. In effect, Bank A lends money to Bank B in the interbank market, so that Bank B can fund a loan to a small business. But such lending is unattractive to banks today because the interbank lending rate is zero due to Fed intervention. Since banks cannot earn a market return on such interbank lending, they don't participate in that market. As a result, liquidity in the interbank lending market is low, and banks can no longer be confident that they can obtain funds when needed. Banks are therefore reluctant to expand their SME loan portfolios because of uncertain funding.

The resulting credit crunch for SMEs is one reason unemployment remains stubbornly high. Big businesses such as Apple and IBM do not need banks to fund growth; they have no problem funding activities from internal cash resources or the bond markets. But big business does not create new jobs; the job creation comes largely from small business. So when the Fed distorts the interbank lending market by keeping rates too low, it deprives small business of working capital loans and hurts their ability to fund job creation.

Other unintended consequences of Fed policy are more opaque and insidious. One such consequence is perilous behavior by banks in search of yield. With interest rates near zero, financial institutions have a difficult time making sufficient returns on equity, and they resort to leverage, the use of debt or derivatives, to increase their returns. Leverage from debt expands a bank's balance sheet and simultaneously increases its capital requirements. Therefore financial institutions prefer derivatives strategies using swaps and options to achieve the targeted returns, since derivatives are recorded off balance sheet and do not require as much capital as borrowings.

Counterparties to derivatives trades require high-quality collateral such as Treasury notes to guarantee contractual performance. Often the quality of assets available for these bank collateral pledges is poor. In these circumstances, the bank that wants to do the off-balance-sheet transaction will engage in an "asset swap" with an institutional investor, whereby the bank gives the investor low-rated securities in exchange for highly rated securities such as Treasury notes. The bank promises to reverse the transaction at a later date so the institutional investor can get its Treasury notes back. Once the bank has the Treasury notes, it can pledge them to the derivatives counterparty as "good collateral" and enter into the trade, thus earning high returns off balance sheet with scant capital required. As a result of the asset swap, a two-party trade turns into a three-party trade, with more promises involved, and a more complex web of reciprocal obligations involving banks and nonbank investors.

These machinations work as long as markets stay calm and there is no panic to repossess collateral. But in a liquidity crisis of the kind experienced in 2008, these densely constructed webs of interlocking obligations quickly freeze up as the demand for "good" collateral instantaneously exceeds the supply and parties scramble to dump all collateral at fire-sale prices to raise cash. As a result of the scramble to seize good collateral, another liquidity-driven panic soon begins, producing tremors in the market.

Asset swaps are just one of many ways financial institutions increase risk in the search for higher yields in low-interest-rate environments. A definitive study conducted by the IMF covering the period 1997–2011 showed that Federal Reserve low-interest-rate policy is consistently associated with greater risk taking by banks. The IMF study also demonstrated that the longer rates are held low, the greater the amount of risk taking by the banks. The study concludes that extended periods of exceptionally low interest rates of the kind the Fed has engineered since 2008 are a recipe for increased systemic risk. By manipulating interest rates to zero, the Fed encourages this search for yield and all the off-balance-sheet tricks and asset swaps that go with it. In the course of putting out the fire from the last panic, the Fed has supplied kindling for an even greater conflagration.

■ The Clouded Crystal Ball

The most alarming consequence of Fed manipulation is the prospect of a stock market crash playing out over a period of a few months or less. This could result from Fed policy based on forecasts that are materially wrong. In fact, the accuracy of Fed forecasts has long been abysmal.

If the Fed underestimates potential growth, then interest rates will be too low, with inflation and negative real interest rates a likely result. Such conditions hurt capital formation and, historically, have produced the worst returns for stocks. Conversely, if the Fed overestimates potential growth, then policy will be too tight, and the economy will go into recession, which hurts corporate profits and causes stocks to decline. In other words, forecasting errors in either direction produce policy errors that will result in a declining stock market. The only condition that is not eventually bad for stocks is if the Fed's forecast is highly accurate and its policy is correct—which unfortunately is the least likely scenario.

Given high expectations for equities, bank interconnectedness, and hidden leverage, any weakness in stock markets can easily cascade into a market crash. This is not certain to happen but is likely based on current conditions and past forecasting errors by the Federal Reserve.

As these illustrations show, the consequences of Federal Reserve market manipulation extend far beyond policy interest rates. Fed policy punishes savings, investment, and small business. The resulting unemployment is deflationary, although the Fed is desperately trying to promote inflation. This nascent deflation strengthens the dollar, which then weakens the dollar price of gold and other commodities, making the deflation worse.

Conversely, Fed policies intended to promote inflation in the United States, partly through exchange rates, make deflation worse in the economies of U.S. trading partners such as Japan. These trading partners fight back by cheapening their own currencies. Japan is currently the most prominent example. The Japanese yen crashed 33 percent against the U.S. dollar in an eight-month stretch from mid-September 2012 to mid-May 2013. The cheap yen was intended to increase inflation in Japan through higher import prices for energy. But it also hurt Korean exports from companies such as Samsung and Hyundai that compete with Japanese exports from Sony and Toyota. This caused Korea to cut interest rates to cheapen its currency, and so on around the world, in a blur of rate cuts, money printing, imported inflation, and knock-on effects triggered by Fed manipulation of the world's reserve currency. The result is not effective policy; the result is global confusion.

The Federal Reserve defends its market interventions as necessary to overcome market dysfunctions such as those witnessed in 2008 when liquidity evaporated and confidence in money market-funds collapsed. Of course, it is also true that the 2008 liquidity crisis was itself the product of earlier Fed policy blunders starting in 2002. While the Fed is focused on the intended effects of its policies, it seems to have little regard for the unintended ones.

■ The Asymmetric Market

In the Fed's view, the most important part of its program to mitigate fear in markets is communications policy, also called "forward guidance," through which the Fed seeks to amplify easing's impact by promising it will continue for sustained periods of time, or until certain unemployment and inflation targets are reached. The policy debate over forward guidance as an adjunct to market manipulation is a continuation of one of the most long-standing areas of intellectual inquiry in modern economics. This inquiry involves imperfect information or information asymmetry: a situation in which one party has superior information to another that induces suboptimal behavior by both parties.

This field took flight with a 1970 paper by George Akerlof, "The Market for 'Lemons,'" that chose used car sales as an example to make its point. Akerlof was awarded the Nobel Prize in Economics in 2001 in part for this work. The seller of a used car, he states, knows perfectly well whether the car runs smoothly or is of poor quality, a "lemon." The buyer does not know; hence an information asymmetry arises between buyer and seller. The unequal information then conditions behavior in adverse ways. Buyers might assume that all used cars are lemons, otherwise the sellers would hang on to them. This belief causes buyers to lower the prices they are willing to pay. Sellers of high-quality used cars might reject the extra-low prices offered by buyers and refuse to sell. In an extreme case, there might be no market at all for used cars because buyers and sellers are too far apart on price, even though there would theoretically be a market-clearing price if both sides to the transaction knew all the facts.

Used cars are just one illustration of the asymmetric information problem, which can apply to a vast array of goods and services, including financial transactions. Interestingly, gold does not suffer this problem because it has a uniform grade. Absent fraud, there are no "lemons" when it comes to gold bars.

A touchstone for economists since 1970, Akerlof's work has been applied to numerous problems. The implications of his analysis are profound. If communication can be improved, and information asymmetries reduced, markets become more efficient and perform their price discovery functions more smoothly, reducing costs to consumers.

In 1980 the challenge of analyzing information's role in efficient markets was picked up by a twenty-six-year-old economist named Ben S. Bernanke. In a paper called "Irreversibility, Uncertainty, and Cyclical Investment," Bernanke addressed the decision-making process behind an investment, asking how uncertainty regarding future policy and business conditions impedes such investment. This was a momentous question. Investment is one of the four fundamental components of GDP, along with consumption, government spending, and net exports. Of these components, investment may be the most important because it drives GDP not only when the investment is made, but in future years through a payoff of improved productivity. Investment in new enterprises can also be a catalyst for hiring, which can then boost consumption through wage payments from investment profits. Any impediments to investment will have a deleterious effect on the growth of the overall economy.

Lack of investment was a large contributor to the duration of the Great Depression. Scholars from Milton Friedman and Anna Schwartz to Ben Bernanke have identified monetary policy as a leading cause of the Depression. But far less work has been done on why the Great Depression lasted so long compared to the relatively brief depression of 1920. Charles Kindleberger correctly identified the cause of the protracted nature of the Great Depression as *regime uncertainty*. This theory holds that even when market prices have declined sufficiently to attract investors back into the economy, investors may still refrain because unsteady public policy makes it impossible to calculate returns with any degree of accuracy. Regime uncertainty refers to more than just the usual uncertainty of any business caused by changing consumer preferences, or the more-

or-less efficient execution of a business plan. It refers to the added uncertainty caused by activist government policy ostensibly designed to improve conditions that typically makes matters worse.

The publication date of Bernanke's paper, 1980, is poised in the midst of the three great periods of regime uncertainty in the past one hundred years: the 1930s, the 1970s, and the 2010s.

In the 1930s this uncertainty was caused by the erratic on-again-off-again nature of the Hoover-Roosevelt interventionist policies of price controls, price subsidies, labor laws, gold confiscation, and more, exacerbated by Supreme Court decisions that supported certain programs and voided others. Even with huge pools of unused labor and rock-bottom prices, capitalists sat on the sidelines in the 1930s until the policy uncertainty cloud was lifted by duress during the Second World War and finally by tax cuts in 1946. It was only when government got out of the way that the U.S. economy finally escaped the Great Depression.

In the 1970s the U.S. economy was experiencing another episode of extreme regime uncertainty. This episode lasted ten years, beginning with Nixon's 1971 wage and price controls and abandonment of the gold standard, and continuing through Jimmy Carter's 1980 crude oil windfall profit tax.

The same malaise afflicts the U.S. economy today due to regime uncertainty caused by budget battles, health care regulation, tax policy, and environmental regulation. The issue is not whether each policy choice is intrinsically good or bad. Most investors can roll with the punches when it comes to bad policy. The core issue is that investors *do not know* which policy will be favored and therefore cannot calculate returns with sufficient clarity to risk capital.

In his 1980 paper, Bernanke began his analysis by recapitulating the classic distinction between risk and uncertainty first made by Frank H. Knight in 1921. In Knight's parlance, *risk* applies to random outcomes that investors can model with known probabilities, while *uncertainty* applies to random outcomes with unknown probabilities. An investor is typically willing to confront risk but may be paralyzed in the face of extreme uncertainty. Bernanke's contribution was to construct the problem as one of opportunity cost. Investors may indeed fear uncertainty, but they may also have a fear of inaction, and the costs of inaction may exceed the costs of plunging into the unknown. Conversely, the costs of inaction may be reduced by the benefits of awaiting new information. In Bernanke's formulation, "It will pay to invest . . . when the cost of waiting . . . exceeds the expected gains from waiting. The expected gain from waiting is the probability that [new] information . . . will make the investor regret his decision to invest. . . . The motive for waiting is . . . concern over the possible arrival of unfavorable news."

This passage is the Rosetta stone for interpreting all of Bernanke's policies relating to monetary policy during his time as chairman of the Federal Reserve. After 2008, Bernanke's Fed would increase the cost of waiting by offering investors zero return on cash, and it would reduce the cost of moving ahead by offering forward guidance on policy. By increasing the costs of waiting and reducing the costs of moving ahead, Bernanke would tip the scales in favor of immediate investment and help the economy grow through the jobs and incomes that go with such investment. Bernanke would be the master planner who pushes capitalists back into the investment game. He showed his hand when he wrote, "It would not be difficult to recast our example of the . . . economy in an equilibrium business cycle mold. As given, the economy . . . is best thought of as being run by a central planner."

Bernanke's logic is deeply flawed because it supposes that the agency that *reduces* uncertainty does not also *add* to uncertainty by its conduct. When the Fed offers forward guidance on interest rates, how certain can investors be that it will not change its mind? When the Fed says it will raise interest rates upon the occurrence of certain conditions, how certain can investors be that those conditions will ever be satisfied? In trying to remove one type of uncertainty, the Fed merely substitutes a new uncertainty related to its ability to perform the first task. Uncertainty about future policy has been replaced with uncertainty about the reliability of forward guidance. This may be the second derivative of uncertainty, but it is uncertainty nonetheless, made worse by dependence on planners' whims rather than the market's operation.

An important paper by Robert Hall of Stanford University, delivered at the Fed's Jackson Hole gathering in August 2013, demonstrates the counterproductive nature of Bernanke's reasoning. Hall's paper makes the point that the decision to hire a new worker implicitly involves a calculation by the employer of the present value of the worker's future output. Present value calculations depend on the discount rates used to convert future returns into current dollars. But uncertainty caused by the Fed's policy flip-flops makes the discount rate difficult to ascertain and causes employers to reduce or delay hiring. In effect, the Fed's efforts to stimulate the economy are actually retarding it.

Free markets matter not because of ideology but because of efficiency; they are imperfect, yet they are better than the next best thing. Akerlof illustrates the costs of information asymmetry at one point in time, while Bernanke shows the costs of information uncertainty over time. Both are correct about these theoretical costs, but both ignore the full costs of trying to fix the problem with government intervention. Akerlof was at least humble about these limitations, while Bernanke exhibited a central planner's hubris throughout his career.

Adam Smith and Friedrich Hayek warned of the impossibility of the Fed's task and the dangers of attempting it, but Charles Goodhart points to a greater danger. Even the central planner requires market signals to implement a plan. A Soviet-style clothing commissar who orders that all wool socks be the color green might be interested to know that green is deeply unpopular and the socks will sit on the shelves. The Fed relies on price signals too, particularly those related to inflation, commodity prices, stock prices, unemployment, housing, and many other variables. What happens when you manipulate markets using price signals that are the output of manipulated markets? This is the question posed by Goodhart's Law.

The central planner must suspend belief in one's own intervention to gather information about the intervention's effects. But that information is a false signal because it is not the result of free-market activity. This is a recursive function. In plain English, the central planner has no option but to drink his own Kool-Aid. This is the great dilemma for the Federal Reserve and all central banks that seek to direct their economies out of the new depression. The more these institutions intervene in markets, the less they know about real economic conditions, and the greater the need to intervene. One form of Knightian uncertainty is replaced by another. Regime uncertainty becomes pervasive as capital waits for the return of real markets.

Unlike Shakespeare's Salanio, we can no longer trust what the markets tell us. That's because those who control them do not trust the markets themselves; Yellen and the rest have come to think their academic hand is more powerful than Adam Smith's invisible one. The result has been the slow demise of market utility that, in turn, presages the slow demise of the real economy—and of the dollar.

CHAPTER 4

CHINA'S NEW FINANCIAL WARLORDS

> Most countries fail in the reform and adjustment process pre-
> cisely because the sectors of the economy that have benefitted
> from . . . distortions are powerful enough to block any attempt
> to eliminate those distortions.
>
> **Michael Pettis**
> **Peking University**
> **December 2012**

> China's shadow banking sector has become a potential source
> of systemic financial risk. . . . To some extent, this is fundamen-
> tally a Ponzi scheme.
>
> **Xiao Gang**
> **Chairman, Bank of China**
> **October 2012**

▪ History's Burden

To contemporary Western eyes, China appears like a monolithic jugger-
naut poised to dominate East Asia and surpass the West in wealth and
output in a matter of years. In fact, China is a fragile construct that could
easily descend into chaos, as it has many times before. No one is more
aware of this than the Chinese themselves, who understand that China's
future is highly uncertain.

China's is the longest continuous civilization in world history, encom-
passing twelve major dynasties, scores of minor ones, and hundreds of
rulers and regimes. Far from being homogeneous, however, China is com-
posed of countless cultures and ethnicities, comprising a dense, complex

network of regions, cities, towns, and villages linked by trade and infrastructure, that has avoided the terminal discontinuities of other great civilizations, from the Aztec to the Zimbabwe.

A main contributor to the longevity of Chinese civilization is the in-and-out nature of governance consisting of periods of centralization, followed by periods of decentralization, then recentralization, and so on across the millennia. This history is like the action of an accordion that expands and contracts while playing a single song. The tendency to decentralize politically has given Chinese civilization the robustness needed to avoid a complete collapse at the center, characteristic of Rome and the Inca. Conversely, an ability to centralize politically has prevented thousands of local nodes from devolving into an agrarian mosaic, disparate and disconnected. China ebbs and flows but never disappears.

Recognizing the Chinese history of centralization, disintegration, and reemerging order is indispensible to understanding China today. Western financial analysts often approach China with an exaggerated confidence in market data and not enough historical perspective to understand its cultural dynamics. The Zhou Dynasty philosopher Lao Tzu expressed the Chinese sense of history in the *Tao Te Ching*—"Things grow and grow, but each goes back to its root." Appreciating that view is no less important today.

The centralized ancient dynasties include the Zhou, from around 1100 B.C.; the Qin, from 221 B.C.; and the Han, which immediately followed the Qin and lasted until A.D. 220. In the middle period of Chinese civilization came the centralized Sui Dynasty in A.D. 581 and the Tang Dynasty, which followed the Sui in A.D. 618. The past millennium has been characterized more by political centralization than disorder, under four great centralized dynasties. These began with Kublai Khan's legendary Yuan Dynasty in 1271 and continued through the Ming in 1378, the Qing in 1644, and the Communist Dynasty in 1949.

Famous episodes of decentralization and discord include the Warring States period around 350 B.C., when fourteen kingdoms competed for power in an area between the Yangtze and Huang He Rivers. Six hundred years later, in A.D. 220, another decentralized phase began with the Three Kingdoms of the Wei, Shu, and Wu, followed by rivalries between the former Qin and the rising Jin Dynasties. Instability was intermittent through the sixth century, with fighting among the Chen, Northern Zhou, Northern Qi, and Western Liang kingdoms, before another unified period began with the Sui Dynasty. A final period of disunity arose around A.D. 923, when eight kingdoms competed for power in eastern and central China.

However, discord was not limited to the long decentralized periods. Even the periods of centralization included disorderly stages that were suppressed or that marked a tumultuous transition from one dynasty to another. Possibly the most dangerous of these episodes was the Taiping Rebellion, from 1850 to 1864. The origins of this rebellion, which turned into a civil war, seem incredible today. A candidate for the administrative elite, Hong Ziuquan, repeatedly failed the imperial examination in the late 1830s, ending his chance to join the scholars who made up the elite. He later attributed his failure to a vision that told him he was the younger brother of Jesus. With help from friends and a missionary, he began a campaign to rid China of "devils." Throughout the 1840s he attracted more followers and began to exert local autonomy in opposition to the ruling Qing Dynasty.

By 1850, Hong's local religious sect had emerged as a cohesive military force and began to win notable victories against Qing armies. The Taiping Heavenly Kingdom was declared, with its capital in Nanjing. The Heavenly Kingdom, which exercised authority over more than 100 million Chinese in the south, moved to seize Shanghai in August 1860. The attack on Shanghai was repulsed by Qing armies, now led and advised by European commanders, supplemented with Western troops and arms. By 1864, the rebellion had been crushed, but the cost was great. Scholarly estimates of those killed in the rebellion range from 20 million to 40 million.

A similarly chaotic stage emerged in the so-called Warlord Period of 1916 to 1928, when China was centrally governed in name only. Power was contested by twenty-seven cliques led by warlords, who allied and broke apart in various combinations. Not until Chiang Kai-shek and the National Revolutionary Army finally defeated rival warlords in 1928 was a semblance of unity established. Even then the Chinese Communist Party, which had been ruthlessly purged by Chiang in 1927, managed to survive in southern enclaves before undertaking the Long March, a strategic retreat from attacking Nationalist forces, finally finding refuge in the Shaanxi Province of north-central China.

The most recent period of decentralized political chaos arose in the midst of the Communist Dynasty during the Cultural Revolution of 1966 to 1976. In this chaotic period, Mao Zedong mobilized youth cadres called Red Guards to identify and root out alleged bourgeois and revisionist elements in government, military, academic, and other institutional settings. Millions were killed, tortured, degraded, or forcibly relocated from cities to the countryside. Historic sites were looted and artifacts smashed in an effort to "destroy the old world and forge the new world," in the words of one slogan. Only with Mao's death in 1976, and the arrest of the radical Gang of Four, who briefly seized power after Mao's death, were the flames of cultural and economic destruction finally extinguished.

Historical memories of these turbulent episodes run deep in the minds of China's leadership. This explains the brutal suppressions of nations such as Tibet, cultures such as the Uighurs, and spiritual sects such as Falun Gong. The Communist Party does not know when the next Heavenly Kingdom might arise, but they fear its emergence. The slaughter of students and others in Tiananmen Square in 1989 sprang from this same insecurity. A protest that in the West would have been controlled with tear gas and arrests was to Communist officials a movement that could have cascaded out of control and therefore justified lethal force to suppress.

David T. C. Lie, a senior princeling, the contemporary offspring of Communist revolutionary heroes, recently said in Shanghai that the current Communist leadership's greatest fear is not the U.S. military but a volatile convergence of migrant workers and Twitter mobile apps. China has over 200 million migrant workers who live in cities without official permission to do so, and they can be forcibly returned to the countryside on Communist Party orders. China exercises tight control over the Internet, but mobile apps, transmitting through 4G wireless mobile broadband channels, are more difficult to monitor. This combination of rootless workers and uncontrolled broadband is no less dangerous in official eyes than the zeal of a failed mandarin who believed he was the brother of Jesus Christ. This potential for instability is why economic growth is paramount to China's leadership—growth is the counterweight to emerging dissent.

Prior to 1979, the Chinese economy operated on the "iron rice bowl" principle. The leadership did not promise high growth, jobs, or opportunities; instead, it promised sufficient food and life's basic necessities. Collective farms, forced labor, and central planning were enough to deliver on these promises, but not much more. Stability was the goal, and growth was an afterthought.

Beginning in 1979, Deng Xiaoping broke the iron rice bowl and replaced it with a growth-driven economy that would not guarantee food and necessities so much as provide people the opportunity to find them on their own. It was not a free market by any means, and there was no relaxation of Communist Party control. Still, it was enough to allow local managers and foreign buyers to utilize both cheap labor and imported know-how in order to create comparative advantage in a wide range of tradable manufactured goods.

The China Miracle resulted. Chinese GDP rose from $263 billion in 1979 to $404 billion in 1990, $1.2 trillion in 2000, and over $7.2 trillion in 2011, an astounding twenty-seven-fold increase in just over thirty years. Total Chinese economic output now stands at about half the size of the U.S. economy. This high Chinese growth rate has led to numerous extrapolations and estimates of a date in the not-so-distant future when the Chinese economy will surpass that of the United States in total output. At that point, say the prognosticators, China will resume its role in the first rank of global powers, a position it held in the long-ago days of the Ming Dynasty.

Extrapolation is seldom a good guide to the future, and these predictions may prove premature. Close examination of the economic growth process from a low base shows that such growth is not a miracle at all. If reasonable policies of the kind used in Singapore and Japan had substituted for the chaos of the Cultural Revolution, high growth could have happened decades sooner. Today the same analytic scrutiny raises doubts about China's ability to continue to grow at the torrid pace of recent years.

Dynamic processes such as economic growth are subject to abrupt changes, for better or worse, based on the utilization or exhaustion of factors of production. This was pointed out in a classic 1994 article by Princeton professor Paul Krugman called "The Myth of Asia's Miracle." This article was widely criticized upon publication for predicting a slow-down in Chinese growth, but it has proved prophetic.

Krugman began with the basic point that growth in any economy is the result of increases in labor force participation and productivity. If an economy has a stagnant labor force operating at a constant level of productivity, it will have constant output but no growth. The main drivers of labor force expansion are demographics and education, while the main drivers of productivity are capital and technology. Without those factor inputs, an economy cannot expand. But when those factor inputs are available in abundance, rapid growth is well within reach.

By 1980, China was poised to absorb a massive influx of domestic labor and foreign capital, with predictably positive results. Such a transition requires training that starts with basic literacy and ultimately includes the development of technical and vocational skills. The fact that China had over half a billion peasants in 1980 did not necessarily mean that those peasants could turn into factory workers overnight. The transition also requires housing and transportation infrastructure. This takes time, but by 1980 the process had begun.

As labor flowed into the cities in the 1980s and 1990s, capital was mobilized to facilitate labor productivity. This capital came from private foreign investment, multilateral institutions such as the World Bank, and China's domestic savings. Finance capital was quickly converted into plant, equipment, and infrastructure needed to leverage the expanding labor pool.

As Krugman points out, this labor-capital factor input model is a two-edged sword. When the factors are plentiful, growth can be high, but what happens when the factors are in scarce supply? Krugman answers with the obvious conclusion—as labor and capital inputs slow down, growth will do the same. While Krugman's analysis is well known to scholars and policy makers, it is less known to Wall Street cheerleaders and the media. Those extrapolating high growth far into the future are ignoring the inevitable decline in factor inputs.

For example, five factory workers assembling goods by hand will result in a certain output level. If five peasants then arrive from the countryside and join the existing factory labor force using the same hand assembly technique, then output will double since there are twice as many workers performing the same task. Now assume the factory owner acquires machines that replace hand assembly with automated assembly, then trains his workers to use the machines. If each machine doubles output versus hand assembly, and every worker gets one machine, output will double again. In this example, factory output has increased 400 percent, first by doubling the labor force, then by automating the process. As Krugman explains, this is not a "miracle." It is a straightforward process of expanding labor and productivity.

This process does have limits. Eventually, new workers will stop arriving from the countryside, and even if workers are available, there may be physical or financial constraints on the ability to utilize capital. Once every worker has a machine, additional machines do not increase output if workers can use only one at a time. Economic development is more complex than this example suggests, and many other forces affect the growth path. But the fundamental paradigm, that fewer inputs equals lower growth, is inescapable.

China is now nearing this point. This does not mean growth will cease, merely that it will decelerate to a sustainable level. China has put itself in this position because of its one-child-per-family policy adopted in 1978, enforced until recently with abortion and the murder of millions of girls. That drop in population growth beginning thirty-five years ago is affecting the adult workforce composition today. The results are summarized in a recent report produced by the IMF:

> China is on the eve of a demographic shift that will have profound consequences on its economic and social landscape. Within a few years the working age population will reach a historical peak, and will then begin a precipitous decline. The core of this working age population, those aged 20–39 years, has already begun to shrink. With this, the vast supply of low-cost workers—a core engine of China's growth model—will dissipate, with potentially far-reaching implications domestically and externally.

Importantly, when labor force participation levels off, technology is the *only* driver of growth. The United States also faces demographic headwinds due to declining birth rates, but it is still able to expand the labor force 1.5 percent per year, partly through immigration, and it retains the potential to grow even faster through its technological prowess. In contrast, China has not proved adept at inventing new technologies despite its success at stealing existing ones. The twin engines of growth—labor and technology—are both beginning to stall in China.

Still, official statistics show China growing in excess of 7 percent per year, a growth rate that advanced economies can only watch with envy. How can these sky-high growth rates be reconciled with the decline of labor and capital factor inputs that Krugman predicted almost twenty years ago? To answer this, one must consider not only the factor inputs but the composition of growth. As defined by economists, GDP consists of consumption, investment, government spending, and net exports. Growth in any or all of those components contributes to growth in the economy. How does China appear to increase these components when the factor inputs are leveling off? It does so with leverage, debt, and a dose of fraud.

To understand how, consider the composition of China's GDP compared with those of developed economies such as the United States. In the United States, consumption typically makes up 71 percent of GDP, while in China, the consumption component is 35 percent, less than half the United States'. Conversely, investment typically makes up 13 percent of U.S. GDP, while in China investment is an enormous 48 percent of the total. Net exports are about 4 percent of the economy in the United States and China, except the signs are reversed. China has a trade surplus that *adds* 4 percent to GDP, while the United States has a trade deficit that *subtracts* 4 percent from GDP. In concise terms, the U.S. economy is driven by consumption, and the Chinese economy is driven by investment.

Investment can be a healthy way to grow an economy since it has a double payoff. GDP grows when the investment is first made, then grows again from the added productivity that the original investment provides in future years. Still, this kind of investment-led expansion is not automatic. Much depends on the *quality* of the investment: whether it in fact adds to productivity or whether it is wasted—so-called *malinvestment*. Evidence from recent years is that China's infrastructure investment involves massive waste. Even worse, this investment has been financed with unpayable debt. This confluence of wasted capital and looming bad debt makes the Chinese economy a bubble about to burst.

■ The Investment Trap

The recent history of Chinese malinvestment marks a new chapter in the repeated decline of Chinese civilization. This new story revolves around the rise of a Chinese warlord caste, financial not military in kind, that acts in its own self-interest rather than in China's interest. The new financial warlords operate through bribery, corruption, and coercion. They are a cancer on the Chinese growth model and the so-called Chinese miracle.

After the 1949 Communist takeover of China, all businesses were owned and operated by the state. This model prevailed for thirty years, until Deng Xiaoping's economic reforms began in 1979. In the decades that followed, state-owned enterprises (SOEs) took one of three paths. Some were closed or merged into larger SOEs to achieve efficiencies. Certain SOEs were privatized and became listed companies, while those remaining as SOEs grew powerful as designated "national champions" in particular sectors.

Among the best known of these super-SOEs are the China State Shipbuilding Corporation, the China National Petroleum Corporation, the China Petrochemical Corporation (SINOPEC), and China Telecom. There are more than one hundred such giant government-owned corporations in China under centralized state administration. In 2010 the ten most profitable SOEs produced over $50 billion in net profits. The super-SOEs are further organized into sixteen megaprojects intended to advance technology and innovation in China. These megaprojects cover sectors such as broadband wireless, oil and gas exploration, and large aircraft manufacture.

Regardless of the path taken by state enterprise, corruption and cronyism permeated the process. Managers of SOEs that were privatized received sweetheart deals, including share allocations ahead of the public listing, and executive appointments in the privatized entity. For the enterprises that remained as SOEs, opportunities for corruption were even more direct. Board members and executive officers were political appointees, and the SOEs were protected against foreign and domestic competition. SOEs received cheap financing from government-owned banks and got orders for goods and services from government agencies as well as other SOEs. The result was a dense, complex network of government officials, Communist Party princelings, and private owner-managers, all being enriched by Chinese growth. The elites became a parasite class gorging themselves at the expense of an otherwise healthy and normal growth process.

The rise of a parasitic elite is closely linked to the prevalence of malinvestment. The need for the Chinese economy to rebalance from investment to consumption, as urged by the IMF and other official institutions, has run headlong into the self-interest of the elites who favor infrastructure because it keeps the profits flowing at their steel, aluminum, and other heavy industrial enterprises. The new financial warlords are addicted to the profits of infrastructure, even as economists lament the lack of growth in services and consumption. The fact that this problem is recognized does not mean that it will be managed well. As in all societies, including the United States, elite interests can prevail over national interests once elite political power is entrenched.

Specific examples of infrastructure projects illustrate the waste. Nanjing is one of the largest cities in China, with a population approaching seven million. It is also one of the most historically significant cities, having served as China's capital under several dynasties as well as capital of the Taipei Rebellion's Heavenly Kingdom. More recently, Nanjing was the seat of government, intermittently from 1912 to 1949, during the Chinese Republic of Dr. Sun Yat-sen and later Chiang Kai-shek.

While Nanjing has many of the same problems of pollution and uncontrolled growth of other Chinese cities, it is altogether more pleasant, with abundant parks, museums, and broad, tree-lined boulevards built under imperial influence during the late nineteenth century. Nanjing lies on the Beijing-Shanghai high-speed railway line and is easily reached from both cities. It is among the most important political, economic, and educational hubs in China today.

Immediately south of Nanjing proper lies the Jiangning district, site of one of the most ambitious infrastructure projects now under way in China. Jiangning consists of seven new cities, still under construction, connected by a highway network and an underground metro. Each city has its own cluster of skyscrapers, luxury shopping malls, five-star hotels, man-made lakes, golf courses, recreation centers, and housing and science facilities. The entire metroplex is served by the Nanjing South Railway Station to the north and a newly constructed airport to the south. A visitor cannot help but be impressed with the project's scale, the quality of the finished phases, and the rapidity with which the entire project is being completed. What struck one as odd on a recent visit is that all of these impressive facilities were empty.

Provincial officials and project managers gladly escort interested parties on a new city tour to explain the possibilities. One laboratory is pointed out as the future source of Chinese wireless broadband technology. Another skyscraper is eagerly described as a future incubator for a Chinese alternative asset management industry. An unfinished hotel is also said to be taking reservations for world-class conferences with A-list speakers from around the world.

Meanwhile the visitor stares out at miles of mud flats, with poured concrete and steel rebar footings for dozens more malls, skyscrapers, and hotels. This vision of seven new cities would be daunting enough—until one realizes that Nanjing is among dozens of cities all over China building similar metroplexes on a mind-boggling scale. The Chinese have earned a reputation around the world as master builders to rival the Pharaoh Ramesses II.

The Nanjing South Railway Station is not empty, but it also illustrates China's deficient approach to infrastructure development. In 2009 China was reeling from the same collapse in global demand that had affected the United States after the Panic of 2008. Its policy response was a ¥4 trillion stimulus program, equal to about $600 billion, directed mainly at investment in infrastructure. The United States launched an $800 billion stimulus program at the same time. However, the U.S. economy is more than twice as large as China's, so on a comparative basis, China's stimulus was the equivalent of $1.2 trillion applied to the United States. Four years after the program was launched, results are now visible in projects like the Beijing-Shanghai high-speed railroad and the Nanjing South Railway Station.

The station has 4.9 million square feet of floor space and 128 escalators; it generates over 7 megawatts of power from solar panels on the roof. Ticketing and entry to platforms are highly automated and efficient. The new trains are not only fast but also comfortable and quiet, even at their top speed of 305 kilometers per hour. Importantly, the station took two years to build, using a force of 20,000 workers. If the object of such infrastructure is to create short-term jobs rather than transportation profits, the Nanjing South station might be judged a qualified success. The long-term problem is that a high-speed train ticket from Shanghai to Nanjing costs the equivalent of thirty dollars, while a journey of similar length in the United States costs two hundred dollars. The debt incurred by China to build this monumental train station can never be paid with these deeply discounted fares.

Chinese officials rebut the excess capacity criticism by saying that they are building high-quality infrastructure for the long term. They point out that even if it takes five to ten years to fully utilize the capacity, the investment will prove to have been well founded. But it remains to be seen if such capacity will ever be used.

Apart from the infrastructure's sheer scale, China's vision of expanding the science and technology sectors of the economy faces institutional and legal impediments. The high-tech wireless broadband laboratory in Jiangning is a case in point. The research facility has massive buildings with spacious offices, conference rooms, and large labs surrounded by attractive grounds and efficient transportation. Local officials assure visitors that fifteen hundred scientists and support staff will soon arrive, but the most talented technologists require more than nice premises. These scientists will want an entrepreneurial culture, close proximity to cutting-edge university research, and access to the kind of start-up financial mentoring that comes with more than just a checkbook. Whether or not these x-factors can be supplied along with the buildings is an open question. Another problem with building for the long run is that obsolescence and depreciation may overtake the projects while they await utilization.

China's political leaders are aware that wasted infrastructure spending has permeated the Chinese economy. But like political leaders elsewhere, they are highly constrained in their response. The projects do create jobs, at least in the short run, and no politician wants to preside over a policy that causes job losses, even if it will result in healthier long-run outcomes. Too often in politics everything is short-term, and the long run is ignored.

Meanwhile the infrastructure projects are a windfall for the princelings, cronies, and cadres who run the SOEs. The projects require steel, cement, heavy equipment, glass, and copper. The building spree is beneficial to the producers of such materials and equipment, and their interests always favor more construction regardless of costs or benefits. China has no market discipline to slow down these interests or redirect investment in more beneficial ways. Instead China has an elite oligarchy that insists that its interests be served ahead of the national interest. The political elite's capacity to stand up to this economic elite is limited because the two are frequently intertwined. *Bloomberg News* has exposed the interlocking interests of the political and economic elites through cross-ownership, family ties, front companies, and straw man stockholders. Saying no to a greedy businessman is one thing, but denying a son, daughter, or friend is another. China's dysfunctional system for pursuing infrastructure at all costs is hard-wired.

China can continue its infrastructure binge because it has unused borrowing capacity with which to finance new projects and to paper over losses on the old ones. But there are limits to expansion of this kind, and the Chinese leadership is aware of them.

In the end, if you build it, they may not come, and a hard landing will follow.

■ Shadow Finance

Behind this untenable infrastructure boom is an even more precarious banking structure used to finance the overbuilding. Wall Street analysts insist that the Chinese banking system shows few signs of stress and has a sound balance sheet. China's financial reserves, in excess of $3 trillion, are enormous and provide sufficient resources to bail out the banking system if needed. The problem is that China's banks are only part of the picture. The other part consists of a shadow banking system of bad assets and hidden liabilities large enough to threaten the stability of China's banks and cause a financial panic with global repercussions. Yet the opacity of the system is such that not even Chinese banking regulators know how large and how concentrated the risks are. That will make the panic harder to stop once it arrives.

Shadow banking in China has three tributaries consisting of local government obligations, trust products, and wealth management products. City and provincial governments in China are not allowed to incur bonded debt in the same fashion as U.S. states and municipalities. However, local Chinese authorities use contingent obligations such as implied guarantees, contractual commitments, and accounts payable to leverage their financial condition. Trust products and wealth management products are two Chinese variants of Western structured finance.

The Chinese people have a high savings rate, driven by rational motives rather than any irrational or cultural traits. The rational motives include the absence of a social safety net, adequate health care, disability insurance, and retirement income. Historically the Chinese counted on large families and respect for elders to support them in their later years, but the one-child policy has eroded that social pillar, and now aging Chinese couples find that they are on their own. A high savings rate is a sensible response.

But like savers in the West, the Chinese are starved for yield. The low interest rates offered by the banks, a type of financial repression also practiced in the United States, make Chinese savers susceptible to higher-yielding investments. Foreign markets are mostly off-limits because of capital controls, and China's own stock markets have proved highly volatile, performing poorly in recent years. China's bond markets remain immature. Instead, Chinese savers have been attracted by two asset classes—real estate and structured products.

The bubble in Chinese property markets, especially apartments and condos, is well known, but not every Chinese saver is positioned to participate in that market. For them, the banking system has devised trust structures and "wealth management products" (WMPs). A WMP is a pool or fund in which investors buy small units. The pool then takes the aggregate proceeds and invests in higher-yielding assets. Not surprisingly, the assets often consist of mortgages, properties, and corporate debt. In the WMP, China has an unregulated version of the worst of Western finance. WMPs resemble the collateralized debt obligations, collateralized loan obligations, and mortgage-backed securities, so-called CDOs, CLOs, and MBSs, that nearly destroyed Western capital markets in 2008. They are being sold in China without even the minimal scrutiny required by America's own incompetent rating agencies and the SEC.

The WMPs are sponsored by banks, but the related assets and liabilities do not appear on the bank balance sheets. This allows the banks to claim they are healthy when in fact they are building an inverted pyramid of high-risk debt. Investors are attracted by the higher yields offered in WMPs. They assume that because the WMPs are sponsored and promoted by the banks, the principal must be protected by the banks in the same manner as deposit insurance. But both the high yield and the principal protection are illusory.

The investors' funds going into the WMPs are being used to finance the same wasted infrastructure and property bubbles that the banks formerly financed before recent credit-tightening measures were put in place. The cash flows from these projects are often too scant to meet the obligations to the WMP investors. The maturities of the WMPs are often short-term while the projects they invest in are long-term. The resulting asset-liability maturity mismatch would create a potential panic scenario if investors refused to roll over their WMPs when they mature. This is the same dynamic that caused the failures of Bear Stearns and Lehman Brothers in the United States in 2008.

Bank sponsors of WMPs address the problems of nonperforming assets and maturity mismatches by issuing new WMPs. The new WMP proceeds are then used to buy the bad assets of the old WMPs at inflated values so the old WMPs can be redeemed at maturity. This is a Ponzi scheme on a colossal scale. Estimates are that there were twenty thousand WMP programs in existence in 2013 versus seven hundred in 2007. One report on WMP sales in the first half of 2012 estimates that almost $2 trillion of new money was raised.

The undoing of any Ponzi scheme is inevitable, and the Chinese property and infrastructure bubbles fueled by shadow banking are no exception. A collapse could begin with the failure of a particular rollover scheme or with exposure of corruption associated with a particular project. The exact trigger for the debacle is unimportant because it is certain to happen, and once it commences, the catastrophe will be unstoppable without government controls or bailouts. Not long after a crackup begins, investors typically line up to redeem their certificates. Bank sponsors will pay the first ones in line, but as the line grows longer in classic fashion, the banks will suspend redemptions and leave the majority with worthless paper. Investors will then claim that the banks guaranteed the principal, which the banks will deny. Runs will begin on the banks themselves, and regulators will be forced to close certain banks. Social unrest will emerge, and the Communist Party's worst nightmare, a replay of the spontaneous Taiping Rebellion or Tiananmen Square demonstrations, will then loom.

China's $3 trillion in reserves are enough to recapitalize the banks and provide for recovery of losses in this scenario. China has additional borrowing power at the sovereign level to deal with a crisis if needed, while China's credit at the IMF is another source of support. In the end, China has the resources to suppress the dissent and clean up the financial mess if the property Ponzi plays out as described.

But the blow to confidence will be incalculable. Ironically, savings will increase, not decrease, in the wake of a financial collapse, because individuals will need to save even more to make up their losses. Stocks will plunge as investors sell liquid assets to offset the impact of now-illiquid WMPs. Consumption will collapse at exactly the moment the world is waiting for Chinese consumers to ride to the rescue of anemic world growth. Deflation will beset China, making the Chinese even more reluctant to allow their currency to strengthen against trading partners, especially the United States. The damage to confidence and growth will not be confined to China but will ripple worldwide.

■ Autumn of the Financial Warlords

The Chinese elites understand these vulnerabilities and see the chaos coming. This anticipation of financial collapse in China is driving one of the greatest episodes of capital flight in world history. Chinese elites and oligarchs, and even everyday citizens, are getting out while the getting is still good.

Chinese law prohibits citizens from taking more than $50,000 per year out of the country. However, the techniques for getting cash out of China, through either legal or illegal means, are limited only by the imagination and creativity of those behind the capital flight. Certain techniques are as direct as stuffing cash in a suitcase before boarding an overseas flight. *The Wall Street Journal* reported the following episode from 2012:

> In June, a Chinese man touched down at Vancouver airport with around $177,500 in cash—mostly in U.S. and Canadian hundred-dollar bills, stuffed in his wallet, pockets and hidden under the lining of his suit case. . . . The Canadian Border Service officer who found the cash, said the man told him he was bringing the money in to buy a house or a car. He left the airport with his cash, minus a fine for concealing and not declaring the money.

In another vignette, a Chinese brewery billionaire flew from Shanghai to Sydney, drove an hour into the countryside to see a vineyard, bid $30 million for the property on the spot, and promptly returned to Shanghai as quickly as he had arrived. It is not known if the oligarch preferred wine to beer, but he preferred Australia to China when it came to choosing a safe haven for his wealth.

Other capital flight techniques are more complicated but no less effective. A favorite method is to establish a relationship with a corrupt casino operator in Macao, where a high-rolling Chinese gambler can open a line of credit backed by his bank account. The gambler then proceeds deliberately to lose an enormous amount of money in a glamorous game such as baccarat played in an ostentatious VIP room. The gambling debt is promptly paid by debiting the gambler's bank account in China. This transfer is not counted against the annual ceiling on capital exports because it is viewed as payment of a legitimate debt. The "unlucky" gambler later recovers the cash from the corrupt casino operator, minus a commission for the money-laundering service rendered.

Even larger amounts are moved offshore through the mis-invoicing of exports and imports. For example, a Chinese furniture manufacturer can create a shell distribution company in a tax haven jurisdiction such as Panama. Assuming the normal export price of each piece of furniture is $200, the Chinese manufacturer can underinvoice the Panamanian company and charge only $100 for each piece. The Panamanian company can then resell into normal distribution channels for the usual price of $200 per piece. The $100 "profit" per piece resulting from the underinvoicing is then left to accumulate in Panama. With millions of furniture items shipped, the accumulated phony profit in Panama can reach into the hundreds of millions of dollars. This is money that would have ended up in China but for the invoicing scheme.

Capital flight by elites is only part of a much larger story of income inequality between elites and citizens in China. In urban areas, the household income of the top 1 percent is twenty-four times the average of all urban households. Nationwide, the disparity between the top 1 percent and the average household is thirty times. These wide gaps are based on official figures. When hidden income and capital flight are taken into account, the disparities are even greater. *The Wall Street Journal* reported:

> Tackling inequality requires confronting the elites that benefit from the status quo and reining in the corruption that allows officials to pad their pockets. Wang Xialou, deputy director of China's National Economic Research Foundation, and Wing Thye Woo, a University of California at Davis economist, say that when counting what they call "hidden" income—unreported income that may include the results of graft—the income of the richest 10% of Chinese households was 65 times that of the poorest 10%.

Minxin Pei, a China expert at Claremont McKenna College, states that corruption, cronyism, and income inequality in China today are so stark that social conditions closely resemble those in France just before the French Revolution. The overall financial, social, and political instability is so great as to constitute a threat to the continued rule of China's Communist Party.

Chinese authorities routinely downplay these threats from malinvestment in infrastructure, asset bubbles, overleverage, corruption, and income inequality. While they acknowledge that these are all significant problems, officials insist that corrective actions are being taken and that the issues are manageable in relation to the overall size and dynamic growth of the Chinese economy. These threats are viewed as growing pains in the birth of a new China as opposed to an existential crisis in the making.

Given the history of crashes and panics in both developed and emerging markets over the past thirty years, Chinese leaders may be overly sanguine about their ability to avoid a financial disaster. The sheer scale and interconnectedness of SOEs, banks, government, and citizen savers has created a complex system in the critical state, waiting for a spark to start a conflagration. Even if the leadership is correct in saying that these specific problems are manageable in relation to the whole, they must still confront the fact that the entire economy is unhealthy in ways that even the Communist Party cannot easily finesse. The larger issue for China's leadership is the impossibility of rebalancing the economy from investment to consumption without a sharp decline in growth. This slowdown, in effect the feared hard landing, is an event for which neither the Communists nor the world at large is prepared.

Understanding the challenge of rebalancing requires taking another look at China's infrastructure addiction. Evidence for overinvestment by China is not limited to anecdotes about colossal train stations and empty cities. The IMF conducted a rigorous analytic study of capital investment by China compared to a large sample of thirty-six developing economies, including fourteen in Asia. It concluded that investment in China is far too high and has come at the expense of household income and consumption, stating, "Investment in China may currently be around 10 percent of GDP higher than suggested by fundamentals."

There is also no mystery about who is to blame for the dysfunction of overinvestment. The IMF study points directly at the state-controlled banks and SOEs, the corrupt system of crony lending and malinvestment that is visible all over China: "State-owned enterprises (SOEs) tend to be consistently implicated . . . because their implied cost of capital is artificially low. . . . China's banking system continues to be biased toward them in terms of capital allocation." State-controlled banks are funneling cheap money to state-owned enterprises that are wasting the money on overcapacity and the construction of ghost cities.

Even more disturbing is the fact that this infrastructure investment is not only wasteful, it is unsustainable. Each dollar of investment in China produces less in economic output than the dollar before, a case of diminishing marginal returns. If China wants to maintain its GDP growth rates in the years ahead, investment will eventually be well in excess of 60 percent of GDP. This trend is not a mere trade-off between consumption and investment. Households deferring consumption to support investment so that they may consume more later is a classic development model. But China's current investment program is a dysfunctional version of the healthy investment model. The malinvestment in China is a deadweight loss to the economy, so there will be no consumption payoff down the road. China is destroying wealth with this model.

Households bear the cost of this malinvestment, since savers receive a below-market interest rate on their bank deposits so that SOEs can pay a below-market interest rate on their loans. The result is a wealth transfer from households to big business, estimated by the IMF to be 4 percent of GDP, equal to $300 billion per year. This is one reason for the extreme income inequality in China. So the Chinese economy is caught in a feedback loop. Elites insist on further investment, which produces low payoffs, while household income lags due to wealth transfers to those same elites. If GDP were reduced by the amount of malinvestment, the Chinese growth miracle would already be in a state of collapse.

Nevertheless, collapse is coming. Michael Pettis of Peking University has done an interesting piece of arithmetic based on the IMF's infrastructure research. In the first instance, Pettis disputes the IMF estimate of 10 percent of GDP as the amount of Chinese overinvestment. He points out that the peer group of countries used by the IMF to gauge the correct level of investment may have overinvested themselves, so actual malinvestment by China is greater than 10 percent of GDP. Still, accepting the IMF conclusion that China needs to reduce investment by 10 percent of GDP, he writes:

Let us . . . give China five years to bring investment down to 40% of GDP from its current level of 50%. Chinese investment must grow at a much lower rate than GDP for this to happen. How much lower? . . . Investment has to grow by roughly 4.5 percentage points or more below the GDP growth rate for this condition to be met.

If Chinese GDP grows at 7%, in other words, Chinese investment must grow at 2.3%. If China grows at 5%, investment must grow at 0.4%. And if China grows at 3% . . . investment growth must actually contract by 1.5%. . . .

The conclusion should be obvious. . . . Any meaningful rebalancing in China's extraordinary rate of overinvestment is only consistent with a very sharp reduction in the growth rate of investment, and perhaps even a contraction in investment growth.

The suggestion that China needs to rebalance its economy away from investment toward consumption is hardly news; both U.S. and Chinese policy makers have discussed this for years. The implication is that rebalancing means a slowdown in Chinese growth from the 7 percent annual rate it has experienced in recent years. But it may already be too late to accomplish the adjustment smoothly; China's "rebalancing moment" may have come and gone.

Rebalancing requires a combination of higher household income and a lower savings rate. The resulting disposable income can then go into spending on goods and services. The contributors to higher income include higher interest rates to reward savers and higher wages for workers. But the flip side of higher interest rates and higher wages is lower corporate profits, which negatively impacts the Chinese oligarchs. These oligarchs apply political pressure to keep wages and interest rates low. In the past decade, the share of Chinese GDP attributable to wages has fallen from over 50 percent to 40 percent. This compares to a relatively constant rate in the United States of 55 percent. The consumption situation is even worse than the averages imply, because Chinese wages are skewed to high earners with a lower propensity to spend.

Another force, more powerful than financial warlords, is standing in the way of consumer spending. This drag on growth is demographic. Both younger workers and older retirees have a higher propensity to spend. It is workers in their middle years who maintain the highest savings rate in order to afford additional consumption later in life. The Chinese workforce is now dominated by that midcareer demographic. In effect, China is stuck with a high savings rate until 2030 or later for demographic reasons, independent of policy and the greed of the oligarchs.

Based on these demographics, the ideal moment for China to shift to a consumption-led growth model was the period 2002 to 2005. This was precisely the time when the productive stage of the investment-led model began to run out of steam, and a younger demographic favored higher spending. A combination of higher interest rates to reward savers, a higher exchange rate to encourage imports, and higher wages for factory workers to increase spending might have jump-started consumption and shifted resources away from wasted investment. Instead, oligarchs prevailed to press interest rates, exchange rates, and wages below their optimal levels. A natural demographic boost to consumption was thereby suppressed and squandered.

Even if China were to reverse policy today, which is highly doubtful, it faces an uphill climb because the population, on average, is now at an age that favors savings. No policy can change these demographics in the short run, so China's weak consumption crisis is now locked in place.

Taking into account the components of GDP, China is seen to be nearing collapse on many fronts. Consumption suffers from low wages and high savings due to demographics. Exports suffer from a stronger Chinese yuan and from external efforts to weaken the dollar and the Japanese yen. Investment suffers from malinvestment and diminishing marginal returns. To the extent that the economy is temporarily propped up by high investment, this is a mirage built on shifting sands of bad debt. The value of much investment in China is as empty as the buildings it produces. Even the beneficiaries of this dysfunction—the financial warlords—are like rats abandoning a sinking ship through the medium of capital flight.

China could respond to these dilemmas by raising interest rates and wages to boost household income, but these policies, while helping the people, would bankrupt many SOEs, and the financial warlords would steadfastly oppose them. The only other efficacious solution would be large-scale privatization, designed to unleash entrepreneurial energy and creativity. But this solution would be opposed not only by the warlords but by the Communist Party itself. Opposition to privatization is where the self-interest of the warlords and the Communists' survival instincts converge.

Four percent growth may be the best that China can hope for going forward, and if the financial warlords have their way, the results will be much worse. Continued subsidies for malinvestment and wage suppression will exacerbate the twin crises of bad debt and income inequality, possibly igniting a financial panic leading to social unrest, even revolution. China's reserves may not be enough to douse the flames of financial panic, since most of those reserves are in dollars and the Fed is determined to devalue the dollar through inflation. China's reserves are being hollowed out by the Fed even as its economy is being hollowed out by the warlords. It is unclear if the Chinese growth miracle will end with a bang or with a whimper, but it will end nonetheless.

China is not the first civilization to ignore its own history. Centralization engenders complexity, and a densely connected web of reciprocal adaptations are the essence of complex systems. A small failure in any part quickly propagates through the whole, and there are no firebreaks or high peaks to stop the conflagration. While the Communist Party views centralization as a source of strength, it is the most pernicious form of weakness, because it blinds one to the coming collapse.

China has fallen prey to the new financial warlords, who loot savings with one hand and send the loot abroad with the other. The China growth story is not over, but it is heading for a fall. Worse yet, the ramifications will not be confined to China but will ripple around the world. This will come at a time when growth in the United States, Japan, and Europe is already anemic or in decline. As in the 1930s, the depression will go global, and there will be nowhere to hide.

CHAPTER 5

THE NEW GERMAN REICH

But there is another message I want to tell you. . . . The ECB is ready to do whatever it takes to preserve the euro. And believe me, it will be enough.

Mario Draghi
President of the European Central Bank
July 2012

If there is no crisis, Europe doesn't move.

Wolfgang Schäuble
German minister of finance
December 2012

▪ The First Reich

Those blithely predicting the breakup of Europe and the euro would do well to understand that we are witnessing the apotheosis of a project first begun twelve hundred years ago. A long view of history repeating itself reveals why the euro is the strongest currency in the world. Today the euro waits in the wings, one more threat to the hegemony of the dollar.

Europe has been united before: not all of it in the geographic sense, but enough to constitute a distinct European polity in contrast to a mere city, kingdom, or country in the area called Europe. That unity arose in Charlemagne's Frankish Empire, the *Frankenreich,* near the turn of the ninth century. The similarities of Charlemagne's empire to twenty-first-century Europe are striking and instructive to those, especially in the United States, who struggle to understand European dynamics today.

While many focus on the divisions, nationalities, and distinct cultures within Europe, a small group of leaders, supported by their citizens, continue the work of European unification begun in the ashes of the Second World War. "United in diversity" is the European Union's official motto, and the word *united* is the theme most often overlooked by the critics and skeptics of a political project now in its eighth decade. Markets are powerful, but politics are more so, and this truth is slowly becoming more apparent on trading floors in London, New York, and Tokyo. Europe and its currency, the euro, despite their flaws and crises, are set to endure.

Charlemagne, a late eighth- and early ninth-century Christian successor to the Roman emperors, was the first emperor in the West following the fall of the Western Roman Empire in A.D. 476. The Roman Empire was not a true European empire but a Mediterranean one, although it extended from the Roman heartland to provinces in present-day Spain, France, and even England. Charlemagne was the first emperor to include parts of present-day Germany, the Netherlands, and the Czech Republic with the former Roman provinces and Italy, to form a unified entity along geographic lines that resemble modern western Europe. Charlemagne is called, by popes and laymen alike, *pater Europae,* the Father of Europe.

Charlemagne was more than a king and conqueror, although he was both. He prized literacy and scholarship as well as the arts, and he created a court at Aachen comprised of the finest minds of the early Middle Ages such as Saint Alcuin of York, considered "the most learned man anywhere" by Charlemagne's contemporary and biographer, Einhard. The achievements of Charlemagne and his court in education, art, and architecture gave rise to what historians call the Carolingian Renaissance, a burst of light to end an extended dark age. Importantly, Charlemagne understood the significance of uniformity throughout his empire for ease of administration, communication, and commerce. He sponsored a Carolingian minuscule script that supplanted numerous forms of writing that had evolved in different parts of Europe, and he instituted administrative and military reforms designed to bind the diverse cultures he had conquered into a cohesive realm.

Charlemagne did not pursue his penchant for uniformity past the point necessary for stability. He advocated diversity if it aided his larger goals pertaining to education and religion. He promoted the use of vernacular

Romance and German languages by priests, a practice later abandoned by the Catholic Church (and belatedly revived in 1965 by the Second Vatican Council). He accepted vassalage from conquered foes in lieu of destroying their cultures and institutions. In these respects, he embraced a policy the European Union today calls *subsidiarity:* the idea that uniform regulation should be applied only in areas where it is necessary to achieve efficiencies for the greater good; otherwise local custom and practice should prevail.

Charlemagne's monetary reforms should seem quite familiar to the European Central Bank. The European monetary standard prior to Charlemagne was a gold *sou,* derived from *solidus,* a Byzantine Roman coin introduced by Emperor Constantine I in A.D. 312. Gold had been supplied to the Roman Empire since ancient times from sources near the Upper Nile and Anatolia. However, Islam's rise in the seventh century, and losses in Italy to the Byzantine Empire, cut off trade routes between East and West. This resulted in a gold shortage and tight monetary conditions in Charlemagne's western empire. He engaged in an early form of quantitative easing by switching to a silver standard, since silver was far more plentiful than gold in the West. He also created a single currency, the *livre carolinienne,* equal to a pound of silver, as a measure of weight and money, and the coin of the realm was the *denire,* equal to one-twentieth of a *sou.* With the increased money supply and standardized coinage, along with other reforms, trade and commerce thrived in the Frankish Empire.

Charlemagne's empire lasted only seventy-four years beyond his death in A.D. 814. The empire was initially divided into three parts, each granted to one of Charlemagne's sons, but a combination of early deaths, illegitimate heirs, fraternal wars, and failed diplomacy led to the empire's long decline and final dissolution in 887. Still, the political foundations for modern France and Germany had been laid. The *Frankenreich*'s legacy lived on until it took a new form with the creation of the Holy Roman Empire and the coronation of Otto I as emperor in 962. That empire, the First Reich, lasted over eight centuries, until it was dissolved by Napoleon in 1806. By reviving Roman political unity and advancing arts and sciences, Charlemagne and his realm were the most important bridge between ancient Rome and modern Europe.

Notwithstanding the institutions of the Holy Roman Empire, the millennium after Charlemagne can be seen largely as a chronicle of looting, war, and conquest set against a background of intermittent ethnic and religious slaughter. The centuries from 900 to 1100 were punctuated by raids and invasions led by Vikings and their Norman descendants. The period 1100 to 1300 was dominated by the Crusades abroad and knightly combat at home. The fourteenth century saw the Black Death, which killed from one-third to one-half the population of Europe. The epoch starting with the Counter-Reformation in 1545 was especially bloody. Doctrinal conflicts between Protestants and Catholics turned violent in the French Wars of Religion from 1562 to 1598, then culminated in the Thirty Years' War from 1618 to 1648, a Europe-wide, early modern example of total war, in which civilian populations and nonmilitary targets were destroyed along with armies.

The sheer suffering and inhumanity of these latter centuries is captured in this description of the siege of Sancerre in 1572. Sancerre's starving population successively ate their donkeys, mules, horses, cats, and dogs. Then the *sancerrois* consumed leather, hides, and parchment documents. Lauro Martines, citing the contemporary writer, Jean de Léry, describes what came next:

> The final step was cannibalism. . . . Léry . . . then says the people of Sancerre "saw this prodigious . . . crime committed within their walls. For on July 21st, it was discovered and confirmed that a grape-grower named Simon Potard, Eugene his wife and an old woman who lived with them . . . had eaten the head, brains, liver, and innards of their daughter aged about three."

These bloodbaths were followed by the wars of Louis XIV, waged continually from 1667 to 1714, in which the Sun King pursued an explicit policy of conquest aimed at reuniting France with territory once ruled by Charlemagne.

The European major litany of carnage continued with the Seven Years' War (1754–63), the Napoleonic Wars (1803–15), the Franco-Prussian War (1870–71), the First World War, the Second World War, and the Holocaust. By 1946, Europe was spiritually and materially exhausted and looked back with disgust and horror at the bitter fruits of nationalism, chauvinism, religious division, and anti-Semitism.

France was involved in every one of these wars, and Franco-German conflict was at the heart of the three most recent, in 1870, 1914, and 1939, all occurring within a seventy-year span, a single lifetime. After the Second World War, while the U.K. wrestled with the demise of its own empire and a U.S.-Soviet condominium descended in the form of the Iron Curtain and the Cold War, Continental statesmen, economists, and intellectuals confronted the central question of how to avoid yet another war between France and Germany.

■ The New Europe

A first step toward a unified, federal Europe took place in 1948 with the Hague Congress, which included public intellectuals, professionals, and politicians from both left and right in a broad-based discussion of the potential for political and economic union in Europe. Winston Churchill, Konrad Adenauer, and François Mitterrand, among many others, took part. This was followed in 1949 by the founding of the College of Europe, an elite postgraduate university dedicated to the promotion of solidarity among western European nations and the training of experts to implement that mission. Behind both the Hague Congress and the College of Europe were the statesmen Paul-Henri Spaak, Robert Schuman, Jean Monnet, and Alcide De Gasperi.

The great insight of these leaders was that economic integration would lead to political integration, thereby making war obsolete, if not impossible.

The first concrete step toward economic integration was the European Coal and Steel Community (ECSC), launched in 1952. Its six original members were France, West Germany, Italy, Belgium, Luxembourg, and the Netherlands. The ECSC was a common market for coal and steel, two of the largest industries in Europe at the time. In 1957 it was joined by the European Atomic Energy Community (Euratom), dedicated to developing the nuclear energy industry in Europe, and also by the European Economic Community (EEC), created by the Treaty of Rome and devoted to creating a common market in Europe for goods and services beyond coal and steel.

In 1967 the Merger Treaty unified the ECSC, Euratom, and the EEC under the name of the European Communities (EC). The 1992 Maastricht Treaty recognized the European Communities as one of the "three pillars" of a new European Union (EU), along with Police and Judicial Cooperation, and a Common Foreign and Security Policy (CFSP), formed as the representative of the new EU to the rest of the world. Finally, in 2009, the Lisbon Treaty merged the three pillars into the sole legal entity of the European Union and named a European Council president to direct general objectives and policies.

Alongside this economic and political integration was an equally ambitious effort at monetary integration. At the heart of monetary union is the European Central Bank (ECB), envisioned in the 1992 Maastricht Treaty and legally formed in 1998 pursuant to the Treaty of Amsterdam. The ECB issues the euro, which is a single currency for the eighteen nations that are Eurozone members. The ECB conducts monetary policy with a single mandate to maintain price stability in the Eurozone. It also trades in foreign exchange markets as needed to affect the euro's value relative to other currencies. The ECB manages the foreign exchange reserves of the eighteen national central banks in the Eurozone and operates a payments platform among those banks called TARGET2.

At present, Europe's most tangible and visible symbol is the euro. It is literally held, exchanged, earned, or saved by hundreds of millions of Europeans daily, and it is the basis for trillions of euros in transactions conducted by many millions more around the world. In late 2014 the ECB will occupy its new headquarters building, almost six hundred feet high, located in a landscaped enclave in eastern Frankfurt. The building is a monument to the permanence and prominence of the ECB and the euro.

Many market analysts, Americans in particular, approach Europe and the euro through the lens of efficient-markets theory and standard financial models—but with a grossly deficient sense of history. The structural problems in Europe are real enough, and analysts are right to point them out. Glib solutions from the likes of Nobelists Paul Krugman and Joseph Stiglitz—that nations like Spain and Greece should exit the Eurozone, revert to their former local currencies, and devalue to improve export competitiveness—ignore how these nations got to the euro in the first place. Italians and Greeks know all too well that the continual local currency devaluations they had suffered in the past were a form of state-sanctioned theft from savers and small businesses for the benefit of banks and informed elites. Theft by devaluation is the technocratic equivalent of theft by looting and war that Europeans set out to eradicate with the entire European project. Europeans see that there are far better options to achieve competitiveness than devaluation. The strength of this vision is confirmed by the fact that pro-euro forces have ultimately prevailed in every democratic election or referendum, and pro-euro opinion dominates poll and survey results.

Charlemagne's enlightened policies of uniformity, in combination with the continuity of local custom, exist today in the EU's subsidiarity principle. The contemporary EU motto, "United in diversity," could as well have been Charlemagne's.

■ From Bretton Woods to Beijing

The euro project is a part of the more broadly based international monetary system, which itself is subject to considerable stress and periodic reformation. Since the Second World War, the system has passed through distinct phases known as Bretton Woods, the Washington Consensus, and the Beijing Consensus. All three of these phrases are shorthand for shared norms of behavior in international finance, what are called *the rules of the game.*

The Washington Consensus arose after the collapse of the Bretton Woods system in the late 1970s. The international monetary system was saved between 1980 and 1983 as Paul Volcker raised interest rates, and Ronald Reagan lowered taxes, and together they created the sound-dollar or King Dollar policy. The combination of higher interest rates, lower taxes, and less regulation made the United States a magnet for savings from around the world and thereby rescued the dollar. By 1985, the dollar was so strong that an international conference was held at the Plaza

Hotel in New York in order to reduce its value. This was followed by another international monetary conference in 1987, at the Louvre in Paris, that informally stabilized exchange rates. The Plaza and Louvre Accords cemented the new dollar standard, but the international monetary system was still ad hoc and in search of a coherent set of principles.

In 1989 the missing intellectual glue for the new dollar standard was provided by economist John Williamson. In his landmark paper, "What Washington Means by Policy Reform," Williamson prescribed the "Washington Consensus" for good behavior by other countries, in the new world of the dollar standard. He made his meaning explicit in the opening paragraphs:

> No statement about how to deal with the debt crisis . . . would be complete without a call for the debtors to fulfill their part of the proposed bargain by "setting their houses in order," "undertaking policy reforms," or "submitting to strong conditionality." The question posed in this paper is what such phrases mean, and especially what they are generally interpreted as meaning in Washington. . . .
>
> The Washington of this paper is both the political Washington of Congress and . . . the administration and the technocratic Washington of the international financial institutions, the economic agencies of the US government, the Federal Reserve Board, and the think tanks.

It is hard to imagine a more blunt statement of global dollar hegemony emanating from Washington, D.C. The omission of any reference to nations other than the United States, or any institution other than those controlled by the United States, speaks to the state of international finance in 1989 and the years that followed.

Williamson went on to describe what Washington meant by debtors "setting their houses in order." He set forth ten policies that made up the Washington Consensus. These policies included commonsense initiatives such as fiscal discipline, elimination of wasteful subsidies, lower tax rates, positive real interest rates, openness to foreign investment, deregulation, and protection for property rights. The fact that these policies favored free-market capitalism and promoted the expansion of U.S. banks and corporations in global markets did not go unnoticed.

By the early 2000s, the Washington Consensus was in tatters due to the rise of emerging market economies that viewed dollar hegemony as favoring the United States at their expense. This view was highlighted by the IMF response to the Asian financial crisis of 1997–98, in which IMF austerity plans resulted in riots and bloodshed in the cities of Jakarta and Seoul.

Washington's failure over time to adhere to its own fiscal prescriptions, combined with the acceleration of Asian economic growth after 1999, gave rise to the Beijing Consensus as a policy alternative to the Washington Consensus. The Beijing Consensus comes in conflicting versions and lacks the intellectual consistency that Williamson gave to the Washington Consensus. Author Joshua Cooper Ramo is credited with putting the phrase *Beijing Consensus* into wide use with his seminal 2004 article on the subject. Ramo's analysis, while original and provocative, candidly admits that the definition of Beijing Consensus is amorphous: "the Beijing Consensus . . . is flexible enough that it is barely classifiable as a doctrine."

Despite the numerous economic elements thrown into the stew of the Beijing Consensus, Ramo's most important analytic contribution was the recognition that the new economic paradigm was not solely about economics but rather was fundamentally geopolitical. The ubiquitous John Williamson expanded on Ramo in 2012 by defining the five pillars of the Beijing Consensus as incremental reform, innovation, export-led growth, state capitalism, and authoritarianism.

As viewed from China, the Beijing Consensus is a curious blend of seventeenth-century Anglo-Dutch mercantilism and Alexander Hamilton's eighteenth-century American School development policies. As interpreted by the Chinese Communist Party, it consists of protection for domestic industry, export-driven growth, and massive reserve accumulation.

No sooner had policy intellectuals defined the Beijing Consensus than it began to break down due to internal contradictions and deviations from the original mercantilist model. China used protectionism to support infant industries as Hamilton recommended, but it failed to follow Hamilton's support for domestic competition. Hamilton used protectionism to give new industries time to establish themselves, but he relied on competition to make them grow stronger so they could eventually hold their own in international trade. In contrast, Chinese elites coddled China's "national champions" to the point that most are not globally competitive without state subsidies. By 2012, the deficiencies and limits of the Beijing Consensus were plain to see, although the policies were still widely practiced.

■ The Berlin Consensus

By 2012, a new Berlin Consensus emerged from the ashes of the 2008 global financial crisis and the European sovereign debt crises of 2010–11. The Berlin Consensus has no pretensions to be a global one-size-fits-all economic growth model; rather it is highly specific to Europe and the evolving institutions of the EU and Eurozone. In particular, it represents the imposition of the successful German model on Europe's periphery through the intermediation of Brussels and the ECB. German chancellor Angela Merkel has summarized her efforts under the motto of "More Europe," but it would be more accurate to say that the project is about more Germany. The Berlin Consensus cannot be fully implemented without structural adjustments in order to make the periphery receptive and complementary to the German model.

The Berlin Consensus, as conceived in Germany and applied to the Eurozone, consists of seven pillars:

- Promotion of exports through innovation and technology
- Low corporate tax rates
- Low inflation
- Investment in productive infrastructure
- Cooperative labor-management relations
- Globally competitive unit labor costs and labor mobility
- Positive business climate

Each one of the seven pillars implies policies designed to promote specific goals and produce sustained growth. These policies, in turn, presuppose certain monetary arrangements. At the heart of the Berlin Consensus is a recognition that savings and trade, rather than borrowing and consumption, are the best path to growth.

Taking the elements of the Berlin Consensus singly, one begins with the emphasis on *innovation and technology* as the key to a robust export sector. German companies such as SAP, Siemens, Volkswagen, Daimler, and many others exemplify this ethic. The World Intellectual Property Organization (WIPO) reports that six of the top ten applicants for international trademark protection in 2012 were EU members. Of 182,112 applications filed under the WIPO Patent Cooperation Treaty in 2011, 27.5 percent were filed by EU members, 26.8 percent by the United States, and 9.0 percent by China. The EU's attainments in university education, basic research, and intellectual property are now on a par with those of the United States and well ahead of China's.

Intellectual property drives economic growth only to the extent that business can utilize it to create value-added products. A key factor in the ability of business to drive productivity through innovation is a *low corporate tax rate*. Statutory tax rates are an imperfect guide because they may be higher than the tax rate actually paid due to deductions, credits, and depreciation allowances; still, the statutory rate is a good starting place for analysis. Here Europe once again stands out favorably. The average European corporate tax rate is 20.67 percent, compared to 40 percent for the United States and 25 percent for China, once local income taxes are added to national taxes. Corporations in the EU are predominantly taxed on a national basis, meaning tax is paid to a host country only based on profits made in that country, which contrasts favorably with the U.S. system of global taxation, in which a U.S. corporation pays tax on foreign as well as domestic profits.

Both the EU and the United States have managed to maintain *low inflation* in recent years, but Europe has done so with significantly less money printing and yield-curve manipulation, which means its potential for future inflation based on changes in the turnover or velocity of money is reduced. In contrast, China has had a persistent problem with inflation due to Chinese efforts to absorb Federal Reserve money printing to maintain a peg between the yuan and the dollar. Of the three largest economic zones, the EU has the best track record on inflation both in terms of recent experience and prospects going forward.

The EU's approach to *infrastructure investment* has resulted in higher quality and more productive investment than that of either the United States or China. Because large infrastructure projects in Europe typically involve cross-border collaboration, they tend to be more economically rational and less subject to political pressures. A prominent example is the Gotthard Base Tunnel, scheduled to open in 2017, which will run thirty-four miles end to end beneath the Swiss Alps, which tower ten thousand feet above it. The tunnel will be the longest in the world and has rightly been compared to the Panama Canal and the Suez Canal as a world-historic achievement in the advancement of transportation infrastructure for the benefit of trade and commerce. Although the Gotthard Base Tunnel lies entirely in Switzerland, it is a critical link in a Europe-wide high-speed rail transportation network.

For passengers, the tunnel will cut an hour off the current three-hour-and-forty-minute travel time from Milan to Zurich. For rail freight traffic, the tunnel will increase annual capacity through the Gotthard Pass by 250 percent, from the current 20 million tons to a projected 50 million tons. The Gotthard Base Tunnel will be linked to scores of high-speed rail corridors coordinated by the EU's Trans-European high-speed rail network, called TEN-R. These and many similar European infrastructure projects compare favorably in terms of long-term payoffs with Chinese ghost cities and the U.S. practice of wasted investments such as solar cell maker Solyndra and electric car maker Fisker, which both filed for bankruptcy.

The German labor-management coordination model for large enterprises, called *Mitbestimmung,* or codetermination, has been in place since the end of the Second World War. It was expanded significantly in 1976 with the requirement that worker delegates hold board seats of any corporation with more than five hundred employees. Codetermination does not replace unions but complements them by allowing worker input in corporate decision making in a regular and continuous way, in addition to the sporadic and often disruptive processes of collective bargaining and occasional strikes. The model is unique to Germany and may not be copied specifically by other EU members. What is significant about co-determination for Europe is not the exact model but the example it sets with regard to improving productivity and competitiveness for business. The German model compares favorably with that of China, where workers have few rights, and the United States, where labor-management relations are adversarial rather than cooperative.

Of the Berlin Consensus pillars, the one most difficult to engender in the EU as a whole, especially in the periphery, is the efficient labor pillar including *lower unit labor costs*. Here the policy is to force internal adjustment through lower nominal wages in euros, rather than external adjustment either by devaluing the euro or by abandoning it in favor of local currencies in countries such as Greece or Spain. Keynesians have argued that wages are "sticky" and do not respond to normal supply and demand forces. Paul Krugman puts the conventional Keynesian view as follows:

So if there were really a large excess supply of labor, shouldn't we be seeing wages plummeting?

And the answer is no—wages (and many prices) don't behave like that. It's an interesting question why . . . but it's simply a fact that actual cuts in nominal wages happen only rarely and under great pressure. . . .

So there is no reason to believe that cutting wages would be helpful.

As with much of Keynesianism, this analysis applies at best to the special case of heavily unionized labor in closed markets rather than nonunion labor in more open markets. With regard to Europe, Krugman misses the most important point. The emphasis on sticky wages and pay cuts assumes the workers involved already have or had jobs. In Spain, Italy, Greece, Portugal, France, and elsewhere, millions of well-educated youth have never had a job. This labor pool does not have any anchored expectations about how much one should be making. Any job with decent working conditions, training, and possibilities for advancement will prove attractive, even at wages that an older generation might have rejected.

The second part of the efficient labor pillar of the Berlin Consensus is *labor mobility*. As long ago as 1961, Robert Mundell highlighted its importance to a single-currency area in his landmark article "A Theory of Optimum Currency Areas":

> In a currency area comprising many regions and a single currency, the pace of inflation is set by the willingness of central authorities to allow unemployment in deficit regions. . . . Unemployment could be avoided . . . if central banks agreed that the burden of international adjustment should fall on surplus countries, which would then inflate until unemployment in deficit countries is eliminated. . . . A currency area . . . cannot prevent both unemployment and inflation among its members.

Although this article was written almost forty years before the euro's launch, the implications for the Eurozone are pertinent. When the terms of trade turn adverse to the periphery and in Germany's favor, either the periphery will have unemployment or Germany will have inflation, or there will be a combination of the two. Since Germany indirectly controls the ECB and has so far been unwilling to tolerate inflation, rising unemployment in the periphery is inevitable.

Mundell, however, also pointed out that the solution to this dilemma is capital and labor factor mobility across national boundaries. If capital could shift from Germany to Spain to take advantage of abundant labor, or if labor could shift from Spain to Germany to take advantage of abundant capital in the form of plant and equipment, then the unemployment problem could be solved without inflation. EU directives and use of the euro have gone far toward increasing the mobility of capital. However, Europe has lagged behind the rest of the developed world in mobility-of-labor terms, partly due to linguistic and cultural differences among the national populations. This problem is widely recognized, and because steps are being taken to improve labor mobility within the EU, prospects for growth are greater than many observers believe.

This brings the analysis to the final element of the Berlin Consensus—a *positive business climate*. What economists call regime uncertainty is a principal differentiator between long, anemic depressions and short, sharp ones. Monetary policy and fiscal policy uncertainty can negatively impact an economy, as was seen in the United States during the Great Depression of 1929 to 1940, and as is being seen again in the depression that began in 2007. But policy cannot improve an economy if businesses are unwilling to invest capital and create the new jobs associated with such investment. Once the panic phase of a financially induced depression is over, the greatest impediment to capital investment is uncertainty about policy regimes related to matters such as taxes, health care, regulation, and other costs of doing business. Both the United States and the EU suffer from regime uncertainty. The Berlin Consensus is designed to remove as much uncertainty as possible by providing for price stability, sound money, fiscal responsibility, and uniformity across Europe on important regulatory matters.

In turn, a positive business climate becomes a magnet for capital not just from local entrepreneurs and executives but also from abroad. This points to an emerging driver of EU growth harnessed to the Berlin Consensus—Chinese capital. As the Beijing Consensus collapses and Chinese capital seeks a new home, Chinese investors looks increasingly to Europe. Chinese leaders realize they have overinvested in U.S.-dollar-denominated assets; they also know they cannot divest those assets quickly. But at the margin they can invest new reserves in diverse ways, including euro-denominated assets. China was in no hurry to prop up a flailing Eurozone in 2011, but now that the EU has stabilized, they find the euro an attractive alternative to dollar-denominated assets. *The Washington Post* reported on this phenomenon in 2013:

> As Chinese companies and entrepreneurs have moved to invest more overseas, they have been drawn increasingly to Europe, where a two-year surge in foreign direct investment from China has eclipsed the amount flowing to the United States. Over the past two years, Chinese companies invested more than $20 billion in the European Union, compared with $11 billion in the United States.

The Wall Street Journal reported in July 2013 that the Chinese State Administration for Foreign Exchange (SAFE), which manages China's reserves, "was an early investor in bonds issued by the European Financial Stability Fund . . . and has invested regularly since then in the bailout fund." A sound euro is an important attraction for Chinese capital because a stable currency mitigates exchange-rate risk to investors. Indeed, capital inflows from China provided support for the euro—an example of a positive feedback loop between a sound currency and capital flows.

Increasing capital inflows to the Eurozone were not limited to those coming from China. The U.S. money-market industry has also been investing heavily in the Eurozone. After panicked outflows in 2011, the ten largest money-market funds in the United States almost doubled their investments in the Eurozone between the summer of 2012 and early 2013.

The Berlin Consensus is taking root in Europe, based on the seven pillars and directed as much from the EU in Brussels as from Berlin, to mitigate resentment of Germany's economic dominance. The consensus is powered by a virtuous troika of German technology, periphery youth labor, and Chinese capital. It receives its staying power from a farsighted blend of low inflation, sound money, and positive real interest rates. The new Berlin Consensus has the potential to replicate the *Wirtschaftswunder*, Germany's "economic miracle" reconstruction after the Second World War, on a continental scale.

German chancellor Angela Merkel was born during German reconstruction in the 1950s, grew up in Communist East Germany, and had firsthand experience with German reunification in the 1990s. Few political leaders anywhere have her experience in facing such daunting development challenges. She is now turning those skills to the greatest development challenge of all: growing the European periphery and preserving the euro at the same time.

■ The Euro Skeptics

Europe may have the will to preserve both its unity and the euro, but does it have the means? Events since the 2008 financial crisis have raised considerable doubt in many quarters about Europe's capacity to deal with successive crises, notwithstanding the overriding political objectives of the Berlin Consensus. A close examination reveals that these doubts are misplaced, and that the euro project is considerably more durable than the critics suppose.

Foreign exchange and debt markets have existed in a state of continual turmoil since the global sovereign debt crisis erupted with the announcement of default by Dubai World on November 27, 2009. Any visitor to Dubai in the months leading up to the default could see the real estate bubble forming, in the shape of a skyline with miles of empty office buildings and luxury condos for sale. Investors assumed that Dubai, with oil wealth provided by rich neighbors in Abu Dhabi, would muddle through, but it did not. Its collapse became contagious, spreading to Europe and Greece in particular.

By early 2010, serious fraud had been uncovered in Greece's national accounting, enabled by off-the-books swaps provided by Goldman Sachs and other Wall Street banks. It became apparent that Greece could not pay its debts without both massive structural reforms and outside assistance. The sovereign debt crisis had gone global and would soon push Ireland and Portugal to the brink of default, raising serious doubts about the public finances of the much larger economies of Spain and Italy.

Fears about sovereign finances spread quickly to the banks in those countries most affected, and a feedback loop emerged. Since the banks owned sovereign bonds, any distress in the bonds would impair bank capital. If the banks needed bailouts, the sovereign regulators would have to provide the funds. But this meant issuing more bonds, further impairing sovereign credit, which hurt bank balance sheets more, spawning a death spiral of simultaneously imploding sovereign and bank credit. Only new capital from outside sources, whose own credit was not impaired, could break the cycle.

After three years of on-again, off-again crises and contagion, the solution was finally found in the troika of the IMF, the ECB, and the EU, backstopped by Germany. The IMF obtained its funds by borrowing from nations with healthy reserve balances, such as China and Canada. The EU raised funds by pooling member resources, largely from Germany. Finally, the ECB created funds by printing money as needed. The troika members operated under the central bankers' new mantra, "Whatever it takes." By late 2012, the European sovereign debt and bank crisis was largely contained, although rebuilding bank balance sheets and making the required structural adjustments will take years to complete.

Despite this turmoil, the euro held up quite well, to the surprise of many analysts and investors, especially those in the United States. In July 2008 the euro reached a peak of $1.60 and remained in a trading range between $1.20 and $1.60 during the sovereign debt crisis. Throughout the turmoil, the euro *always* traded at a higher dollar price than where it began in 1999.

The euro has also increased its share of global reserves significantly since its issue date. The IMF maintains a data time series showing the composition of official foreign exchange reserves broken down by currency. Data for the first quarter of 1999 show that the euro comprised 18.1 percent of global allocated foreign exchange reserves. By the end of 2012, after three years of crisis, the euro's share had *risen* to 23.9 percent of global reserves.

Such objective data is at odds with the histrionics produced by the Euro skeptics, and that helps explain why, by early 2013, the prophets of Euro-doom were mostly mute on the subject of a Eurozone breakup. The skeptics had committed a succession of analytic failures, easily seen even at the hysteria's height in early 2012. The first analytic failure involved the zero-sum nature of cross exchange rates.

Beginning in 2010, the United States initiated a cheap-dollar policy, intended to import inflation from abroad in the form of higher import prices on energy, electronics, textiles, and other manufactured goods. The cheap-dollar policy was made explicit in numerous pronouncements, including President Obama's 2010 State of the Union address, where he announced the National Export Initiative, and former Federal Reserve chairman Ben Bernanke's Tokyo speech on October 14, 2012, in which he threatened trading partners with higher inflation if they did not allow their currencies to strengthen against the dollar. Since the United States wanted a cheap dollar, it wanted a strong euro in dollar terms. In effect, the United States was using powerful policy tools to strengthen the euro. Why this obvious point was lost on many U.S. analysts is a mystery, but a permanently weak euro was always contrary to U.S. policy.

The second analytic failure had to do with the tendency to conflate the simultaneous crises in debt, banking, and currencies. Analysts looked at defaulting sovereign bonds in Greece and at weak banks in Spain, then breezily concluded that the euro must weaken also. This is superficial: economically, there is nothing inconsistent about weak bonds, weak banks, and a strong currency.

Lehman Brothers is a case in point. In 2008 Lehman defaulted on billions of dollars in bond obligations. This default meant the end of the bonds but not the end of the dollar, since the currency in which bonds are issued has a different dynamic than the bonds themselves. A currency's strength has more to do with central bank policy and global capital flows than with the fate of specific bonds in that currency. Analysts who treated European banks and bonds and the single currency as subject to the same distress made a fundamental error. The euro could do quite well despite the fate of Greek bonds and Irish banks.

The third analytic blind spot was a failure to recognize that capital flows dominate trade flows in setting exchange rates. Too much emphasis was placed on Europe's perceived lack of export competitiveness, especially in the Eurozone periphery of Ireland, Portugal, Spain, Italy, Greece, and Cyprus. Export competitiveness is important when it comes to growth, but it is not the decisive factor in determining exchange rates. Capital flows to the euro from the Federal Reserve in the form of central bank swaps with the ECB, and from China in the form of reserve allocations and direct foreign investment, placed a solid floor under the euro. If the two largest economies in the world, the United States and China, did not want the euro to go down, then it would not go down.

The fourth blind spot had to do with the need to lower unit labor costs as part of the structural adjustment required to make peripheral Eurozone economies globally competitive. Euro skeptics suffer from the legacy of misguided Keynesian economics and the sticky-wage myth, technically called downward nominal wage rigidity. Keynesians rely on a theory of sticky wages to justify inflation, or theft from savers. The idea is that wages will rise during periods of inflation but will not decline easily during periods of deflation; they will tend to stick at the old nominal wage levels.

As a result, wages fail to adjust downward, employers fire workers, unemployment rises, and aggregate demand is weakened. A liquidity trap then develops, and deflation becomes worse as the cycle feeds on itself, resulting in impossibly high debt, bankruptcies, and depression. Inflation is considered advisable policy because it allows employers to give workers a nominal raise, even if there is no raise in real terms due to higher prices. Workers receive raises in nominal terms, while wages adjust downward in real terms. This is a form of money illusion or deception of workers by central banks, but it works in theory to lower real unit labor costs. As applied to Europe, the Keynesian view is that the quickest way to achieve the needed inflation is for member nations to quit the euro, revert to a former local currency, and then devalue these currencies. This was the theoretical basis for the many predictions that the euro must fail and that members would quit to help their economies grow.

In twenty-first-century economies, all aspects of this theory are flawed, starting with the premise. Sticky wages are a special case, arising in limited conditions where labor is a predominant factor input to productivity, labor substitutes do not exist, unionization is strong, globalized outsourcing is unavailable, and unemployment is reasonably low. Today all those factors are reversed.

Capital is the predominant factor input, robotics and outsourcing are readily available, and the union movement is weak in the private sector. Consequently, workers will accept lower nominal wages if that enables them to retain their jobs. This form of lowering unit labor costs is known as *internal adjustment* via lower wages versus *external adjustment* through a cheaper currency and inflation. External adjustment may have worked in the 1930s in the U.K., when Keynes first advanced his ideas on sticky wages. However, under twenty-first-century globalized conditions, internal adjustment is a far superior remedy because it treats the problem directly and avoids the exogenous costs of breaking up the Eurozone. As a case in point, on July 2, 2013, Greece's Hellenic Statistical Authority (ELSTAT) reported that private-sector salaries in Greece had dropped an average of 22.3 percent since the first quarter of 2012, a clear refutation of the obsolete sticky-wage theories of Keynes and Krugman.

The sentiment that sticking with the euro is desirable, despite contracting economies and falling wages, is widely shared among everyday citizens in the Eurozone periphery despite the pretensions of academic theory. In 2013 Marcus Walker and Alessandra Galloni did extensive reporting on this topic for *The Wall Street Journal* and revealed the following:

Across Europe's southern rim, people recoil at the idea of returning to national currencies, fearing such a step would revive inflation, remove checks on corruption and derail national ambitions to be part of Europe's inner circle. Such fears outweigh the bleak growth outlook that has prompted many U.S. and U.K. economists to predict a split of the currency.

Only 20% of Italians say leaving the euro would help the economy. . . . Strong majorities in Spain, Portugal, Greece and Ireland also reject an exit from the euro, recent polls show. . . .

"Europeans who now use the euro have no desire to abandon it and return to their former currency," according to a survey by the Pew Research Center. In Spain and Portugal, 70% or more of people want to stick with the euro, recent polls found.

The fifth and final analytic blind spot of the Euro skeptics was a failure to understand that the euro is—and always has been—a political project rather than an economic one and that the political will to preserve it was never in doubt. A true understanding of the euro is summarized by leading French intellectual Guy Sorman:

Europe was not built for economic reasons, but to bring peace between European countries. It is a political ambition. It is the only political project for our generation. We'll pay the price to save this project.

In sum, the euro is strong and getting stronger.

■ The Euro's Future

This *tour d'horizon* of the Euro skeptics' analytic blind spots not only rebuts their criticism of the euro but reveals the euro's underlying strengths and future direction. These strengths are part of a larger, emergent worldview of how to prosper in a highly competitive, globalized economy.

The most encouraging reports involve Greece, the economy that was most reviled. Over $175 million of new money entered the Greek stock market between June 2012 and February 2013, and according to *The Wall Street Journal,* "everything from Greek real estate to energy stocks are finding buyers." In April 2013 the troika approved the disbursement of further bailout assistance to Greece based on its progress in cutting government spending and moving toward a balanced budget. On May 14, 2013, the Fitch service upgraded Greece's credit rating, and in a review of the Greek economy, *The New York Times* reported, "The drive to improve competitiveness, mainly through much lower wage costs, is finally bearing fruit, too. This is most visible in tourism, which accounts for 17 percent of gross domestic product. Revenues are expected to jump 9 percent to 10 percent this year." Greece is also benefiting from the privatization of government-owned assets. The fifteen-hundred-acre former Athens airport site is expected to attract €6 billion of investment to establish a mixed-use development that should create more than twenty thousand well-paying jobs.

Another recent story from Greece involves events tantamount to a controlled experiment, something economists seek but seldom find. Prior to 2010, port facilities in the major Greek port of Piraeus had been owned by the government. That year the government sold half the port for €500 million to Cosco, a Chinese shipping concern, while retaining the other half. A comparison of operations in the Chinese- and Greek-controlled halves of the facility in 2012 showed a striking contrast:

> On Cosco's portion of the port, cargo traffic has more than doubled over the last year, to 1.05 million containers. And while profit margins are still razor thin . . . that is mainly because the Chinese company is putting a lot of its money back into the port. . . . The Greek-run side of the port . . . endured a series of debilitating worker strikes in the three years before Cosco came to town. . . . On the Greek side of the port, union rules required that nine people work a gantry crane; Cosco uses a crew of four.

This comparison perfectly illustrates the fact that there is nothing intrinsically noncompetitive about Greek workers or Greek infrastructure.

Greece needs only more flexible work rules, lower unit labor costs, and new capital. Chinese capital is a conspicuous part of the solution, and Chinese investors such as Cosco are willing to commit capital when a productive business climate can be assured.

Developments in Spain are equally encouraging. Spanish unit labor costs have already dropped over 7 percent relative to Germany, and economists expect further decreases. In February 2012 Spain's prime minister, Mariano Rajoy, implemented laws that increased labor flexibility by allowing employers to terminate workers in a downturn, reduce severance pay, and renegotiate contracts entered into during the property boom prior to 2008. The result was a drastic increase in Spain's competitiveness in manufacturing, especially the automotive industry.

The positive effect was immediate. Renault announced plans to increase production in the northern Spanish city of Palencia. Ford Motor Company and Peugeot also announced increased production at their plants in Spain. In October 2012 Volkswagen announced an €800 million investment in its plant near Barcelona. All these investment and expansion plans will have positive ripple effects because the large manufacturers are tied to a network of parts suppliers and subcontractors throughout Spain.

The expanded employment and output as the result of lower wages in Spain is a refutation of the sticky-wage theories of Keynes and Krugman, and it is happening on a widespread scale from Greece to Ireland. Although this is a difficult and painful adjustment, the shift is sustainable, and it leaves Europe well positioned to be a globally competitive manufacturing base and magnet for capital inflows.

The Economist, along with many others, has cited adverse demographics as a major hurdle in the way of more robust European growth. Europe does have a rapidly aging society (as do Russia, Japan, China, and other major economies). Over a twenty-year horizon, the demographics of working-age populations are rigid in a closed society, which can be a large determinant of economic outcomes, but this view ignores forms of flexibility even in a closed society.

A working-age population is not the same as a workforce. When unemployment is high, as it is in much of Europe, new entrants can come into the workforce at a much higher rate than population growth, assuming jobs are available. The pools of well-educated unemployed are so large in Europe today that demography places no short-term constraints on productive labor factor inputs. As noted, improved labor mobility can also facilitate growth in the productive workforce by enabling unemployed workers in the Eurozone's depressed regions to move to more productive regions to supply the labor needed. Immigration from eastern Europe and Turkey can supply ample labor to western Europe, much as the Chinese interior has supplied labor to Chinese coastal factories for decades. In short, demographics are not a constraint on European growth as long as there is underutilized labor, labor mobility, and immigration.

Internal economic adjustment alone may not be enough to secure the future of the euro and the EU more broadly. Expansion of the institutions of the EU will also be required, as captured in Merkel's phrase "More Europe." The EU is like an aircraft with a single wing; it can choose to remain grounded, or it can build the other wing. Efforts to deal with the immediate crises in 2010 and 2011, including monetary ease and multilateral bailout packages, have been sufficient to avoid a collapse, but they are not sufficient to correct the fundamental contradictions in the design of the euro and the ECB. A single currency has been shown to be dysfunctional without uniformity of fiscal policy and bank regulation, along with improved mobility of labor and capital among currency union members.

The good news is that these deficiencies are well understood by political and financial leaders in Europe and are being remedied at a rapid pace. On January 1, 2013, the EU Fiscal Stability Treaty entered into force for the sixteen EU member nations that had ratified it as of that date, including all the periphery nations. The treaty contains binding procedures requiring signatories to have budget deficits of less than 3 percent of GDP when their debt-to-GDP ratio is under 60 percent. In cases where the debt-to-GDP ratio exceeds 60 percent, the deficit must be less than 0.5 percent of GDP. The treaty also contains the so-called debt brake that requires signatories with a debt-to-GDP ratio in excess of 60 percent to reduce the ratio by 5 percent of the excess each year until the ratio is less than 60 percent. Treaty provisions are implemented and enforced at the member level for the time being, but the treaty stipulates that the members will incorporate the treaty rules in the overall EU legal framework before January 1, 2018.

An EU-wide bank deposit insurance program to mitigate banking panics is currently under consideration, as are proposals to replace separate sovereign bonds issued by Eurozone members with true Eurobonds backed by the credit of the Eurozone as whole. Action on these fronts may follow, but first further progress must be made on fiscal restraint and other market reforms.

The threads of banking union and consolidated bailout funds have begun to intertwine. In June 2013 a Euro Working Group of senior finance ministry officials from the Eurozone announced a €60 billion bailout fund to provide direct support to banks in distress.

Beyond these fiscal and banking reforms, the EU's future is further brightened by the accession of new members either to the EU, the Eurozone, or both. In July 2013 Latvia received approval from the European Commission and the ECB to adopt the euro as its currency. Croatia officially became an EU member on July 1, 2013, and its central bank governor, Boris Vujčić, announced that Croatia wanted to move as quickly as possible to full adoption of the euro as its currency. Candidate countries whose membership in the EU is under way but not yet completed are Montenegro, Serbia, Macedonia, and Turkey. Potential candidates who do not yet meet the requirements for EU membership but are working toward conformity are Albania, Bosnia and Herzegovina, and Kosovo. In the future, it is not too much to expect that Scotland and Ukraine may apply for membership.

The EU is already the largest economic power in the world, with combined GDP greater than that of the United States and more than double that of China and Japan. Over the next ten years, the EU is destined to evolve into the world's economic superpower, stretching from Asia Minor to Greenland and from the Arctic Ocean to the Sahara Desert.

Germany sits at the heart of this vast economic and demographic domain. While Germany cannot control the entire region politically, it will be the greatest economic power within the region. Through its indirect control of the ECB and the euro, it will dominate commerce, finance, and trade. Eurobonds will provide a deep, liquid pool of investable assets larger than the U.S. Treasury bond market. If needed, the euro can be supported by its members' combined gold holdings, which exceed 10,000 tonnes, about 25 percent more than the U.S. Treasury's official gold holdings. This combination of large, liquid bond markets, a sound currency, and huge gold reserves may enable the euro to displace the dollar as the world's leading reserve currency by 2025. This prospect will hearten Russia and China, which have been seeking escape from U.S. dollar hegemony since 2009. Germany is also the key to this monetary evolution because of its insistence on sound money, and because of the example it has set of how to be an export giant without a weak currency.

Germany's new Reich, intermediated through the EU, the euro, and the ECB, will be the greatest expression of German social, political, and economic influence since Charlemagne's reign. Even though it will come at the expense of the dollar, the changes will be positive in most ways, because of Germany's productivity and its adherence to democratic values. Europe's diverse historical and cultural landscape will be preserved within an improved economic framework. With German leadership and foresight, the EU motto, "United in diversity," will be realized in its truest form.

CHAPTER 6

BELLS, BRICS, AND BEYOND

> We aim at progressively developing BRICS into a full-fledged mechanism of . . . coordination on a wide range of key issues. . . . As the global economy is being reshaped, we are committed to exploring new models.
>
> Declaration of the BRICS
> March 2013

> Citizens of the Baltic countries can be grateful that their leaders never listened to Krugman.
>
> Anders Åslund
> September 2012

■ Supranational

The European Union, the United States, China, and Japan constitute a global Gang of Four that comprises 65 percent of the world's economy. The remaining 157 nations tracked by the IMF make up the other 35 percent of global output. Among these 157 nations is a Gang of Ten consisting of Brazil, Russia, India, Canada, Australia, Mexico, Korea, Indonesia, Turkey, and Saudi Arabia, which each produce between 1 percent and 3 percent of global output. Each of the smallest 147 nations produces less than 1 percent of global output, and most produce far less. The wealth concentration *among* nations is as starkly skewed as it is *within* nations. Among the 80 percent of nations with the lowest output, any one could disappear tomorrow and the impact on global growth would scarcely be noticed.

This is important to recall when Wall Street analysts promote theses on investing in emerging markets, frontier markets, and more exotic lo-

cales. The fact is there are few significant capital markets, their capacity
to absorb inflows is limited, and they have a tendency to overheat when
they try to absorb more than a modest amount of capital. Yet as China
heads for a hard landing, as the United States is stuck in low gear, as
Japan endures its third decade in depression, and as Europe muddles
through a structural adjustment, it is difficult to deny the Gang of Ten's
investment appeal, and the appeal of those not far behind, such as Poland,
Taiwan, South Africa, Colombia, and Thailand.

Consider the BRICS. For convenience, as well as for marketing purposes, analysts bundle smaller nations into groups tagged with acronyms
made of members' names. BRICS is the granddaddy of such groups, consisting of Brazil, Russia, India, China, and a late entry to the club, South
Africa. Each BRICS member has its own attractions and problems; what
the BRICS do not have is much in common. The Russian economy is best
understood as a natural-resource-extraction racket run by oligarchs and
politicians who skim enormous amounts off the top and reinvest just
enough to keep the game going. China has produced real growth but has
also produced waste, pollution, and corruption to the point that China
has an unsustainable model hostile to any foreign investor from whom it
cannot steal technology. India has growth and great promise but has not
come close to realizing its potential because its world-class red-tape *raj*
stifles innovation. Among the BRICS, Brazil and South Africa come closest to being "real" economies in the sense that growth is sustainable,
corruption is not completely rampant, and entrepreneurship has room to
breathe.

Yet there is no denying the success of the BRICS moniker. The original
term *BRIC* was created by Jim O'Neill and his colleagues at Goldman
Sachs in 2001 to highlight the group's share of global GDP and higher
growth rates compared to established large economy groups such as the
G7. But O'Neill's analysis was not primarily economic; it was political.
Beyond the basic facts about size and growth, O'Neill called for rethinking the G7's international governance model to reduce Europe's role and
increase the role of emerging economies in a new G5 + BRICs = G9 formula.

In his proposed G9, O'Neill glossed over differences in social development, including bedrock principles such as civil rights and the rule of law,

with the comment "The other members would need to recognise that not all member countries need to be the 'same.'" He recognized that the BRICs were not at all homogeneous as economic models: "The four countries under consideration are very different economically, socially and politically."

How O'Neill's original work morphed from a political manifesto to an investment theme is best explained by Wall Street's penchant for salespeople engaging their customers with a good story. But it is difficult to fault O'Neill for this; he had a political agenda, and it worked. By 2008, the G7 was practically a museum piece, and the G20, including the BRICS and others, was the de facto board of directors of the international monetary system. O'Neill correctly foresaw that in the post–Cold War, globalized world, the economic had become the political. Economic output trumped civil society and other traditional metrics of inclusion in global leadership groups. The BRICS concept was never an investment thesis so much as a political injunction, and the world took heed.

The BRICS success bred a host of acronymic imitators. Among the recent entrants in this naming derby are the BELLs, consisting of Bulgaria, Estonia, Latvia, and Lithuania; and the GIIPS of the EU periphery, consisting of Greece, Ireland, Italy, Portugal, and Spain. As a group, the GIIPS are best understood as a Eurozone subset that share the euro and are undergoing arduous internal economic adjustments. Within the GIIPS, one should distinguish between Spain and Italy on the one hand, which are true economic giants making up almost 5 percent of the global economy, and Portugal, Ireland, and Greece on the other, whose combined output is less than 1 percent of global total. On the whole, the BELLs and GIIPS have more economic factors in common than do the BRICS, and their proponents have explicit economic themes in mind versus the overtly political perspectives of O'Neill and Goldman Sachs.

■ BELLs

The BELLs are small, almost inconsequential, as their economies add up to just 0.2 percent of global GDP combined. But their geopolitical significance is enormous, since they form the EU's eastern frontier and are the frontline states buffering Europe and the traditional eastern powers, Russia and Turkey. Unlike the BRICS, the BELLs do have much in common. In addition to being EU members, they had all fixed the value of their local currencies to the euro. Pegging to the euro has led the BELLs into the same internal adjustment and devaluation as the Eurozone periphery, since they cannot use currency devaluation as a quick fix for dealing with economic adjustment issues.

Economists lament that they cannot conduct scientific experiments on national economies because many variables cannot be controlled and processes cannot be replicated. But certain cases have enough controlled variables to produce telling results when divergent polices are pursued under similar conditions. Two such quasi-experiments involving the BELLs have played out recently. The first contrasts the BELLs and the GIIPS; the second contrasts each BELLs member to the others.

Experiments are typically conducted by controlling certain variables among all participants and measuring differences in the factors that are not controlled. The first control variable in this real-world experiment is that neither the BELLs nor the GIIPS devalued their currencies. The BELLs have maintained a local currency peg to the euro and have not devalued. Indeed, Estonia actually joined the euro on January 1, 2011, at the height of anti-euro hysteria, and Latvia joined on January 1, 2014.

The second control variable is the depth of the economic collapse in both the BELLs and the GIIPS beginning in 2008 and continuing into 2009. Each BELL suffered approximately a 20 percent decline in output in those two years, and unemployment reached 20 percent. The decline in output in the GIIPS in the same period was only slightly less. The third control variable is that both the BELLs and the GIIPS suffered an evaporation of direct foreign investment and lost access to capital markets, a shortfall that had to be made up with various forms of official assistance. In short, the BELLs and the GIIPS both experienced collapsing output, rising unemployment, and a sudden stop in foreign investment in 2008 and 2009. At the same time, the governments never seriously considered devaluation, despite wails from the pundits.

From these comparable initial conditions, divergent policies were pursued. The GIIPS initially continued so-called economic stimulus and made only slight cuts in public spending. Greece actually increased the number of government employees between 2010 and 2011. The principal way of addressing fiscal issues in the GIIPS was through tax increases. The internal adjustment process of lowering unit labor costs began in the GIIPS only in 2010, and serious fiscal and labor market reform was begun in 2013; much work remains.

In contrast, the BELLs took immediate, drastic measures to put their fiscal houses in order, and strong growth resumed as early as 2010 and is now the highest in the EU. The turnaround was dramatic. Latvia's economy contracted 24 percent in 2008–9, but then grew over 10 percent in 2011–12. Estonia contracted 20 percent in 2008–9 but grew at a robust 7.9 percent rate in 2011. Lithuania's economy did not suffer as much as the other BELLs in the crisis and actually grew 2.8 percent in 2008. Lithuania's growth did decline in 2009, but it bounced back quickly and rose 5.9 percent in 2011. This pattern of collapse followed by robust growth in the Baltic BELLs is the classic V pattern that is much discussed but seldom seen in recent years because governments such as the United States use money printing to truncate the V, leaving protracted, anemic growth in its wake.

How does one account for this sharp turnaround in the Baltic states' growth compared to the EU periphery? Anders Åslund, a scholar at the Peterson Institute for International Economics in Washington, D.C., and an expert on the eastern European and Russian economies, has written extensively on this topic. He attributes economic success in the Baltics and failure in southern Europe from 2009 to 2012 to specific factors. When confronted with severe economic contraction, he suggests, an affected nation must embrace the crisis and turn it to political advantage. Political leaders who explain clearly the economic choices to their citizens will gain support for tough policies, while leaders such as those in the United States and southern Europe who deny the problem's depth will find that the sense of urgency recedes and that citizens are less willing over time to make the needed sacrifices. Åslund also urges that countries facing economic crises should embrace new leaders with new ideas. Vested interests associated with old leadership will be most likely to cling to failed policies, while new leaders are able to pursue the cuts in government spending needed to restore fiscal health.

Åslund also recommends that the emergency economic responses be clearly communicated, front-loaded, and weighted more to spending cuts than tax increases. Citizens will support policies they understand but will be ambivalent about the need for spending cuts if politicians sugarcoat the situation and prolong the process. He also says that "credible culprits are useful." In Latvia's case, three oligarchs dominated the economy in 2006, and 51 percent of the seats in parliament were held by parties they controlled. Reform politicians campaigned against their corruption, and by 2011 the oligarchs' representation had shrunk to 13 percent. The United States also had corrupt bankers as ready-made culprits but chose to bail them out rather than hold them accountable for the precrisis excesses.

Finally and most important, Åslund emphasizes that the restructuring process must be equitable and take the form of a social compact. All societal sectors, government and nongovernment, union and nonunion, must sacrifice to restore vigor to the economy. With regard to Latvia, he writes, "The government prohibited double incomes for senior civil servants . . . and cut salaries of top officials more than of junior public employees, with 35 percent salary cuts for ministers." Again, the process in the Baltics contrasts sharply with that of countries such as the United States, where government spending has increased since the crisis. In the United States, public union and government employee salaries and benefits have mostly been protected, while the brunt of adjustment has fallen on the nonunion private sector. Åslund concludes by noting that these recommendations were mostly followed in the Baltics and disregarded in the southern periphery, with the result that the Baltics are now growing robustly while Europe's southern periphery is stuck in recession with uncertain prospects.

The BELLs' success in quickly restoring growth and competitiveness contrasts sharply with the GIIPS, which have stretched the process out over six years and still have a considerable way to go to achieve fiscal sustainability. Reports from the Baltic region are overwhelmingly positive on the economies there. Reporting on Estonia in 2012, CNBC's Paul Ames writes, "Shoppers throng Nordic design shops and cool new restaurants in Tallinn, the medieval capital, and cutting-edge tech firms complain they can't find people to fill their job vacancies." The BELLs have also made good use of their human capital and a relatively well-educated workforce. Estonia in particular has become a high-tech hub centered on its most successful company, Skype, which has more than four hundred employees in a worker-friendly campus near Tallinn.

The New York Times published a story on Latvia in 2013 that accurately captured the trajectory of steep collapse and strong recovery that used to be typical of business cycles but is now mostly avoided by Western governments at the expense of long-term growth:

> When a credit-fueled economic boom turned to bust in this tiny Baltic nation in 2008, Didzis Krumins, who ran a small architectural company, fired his staff . . . and then shut down the business. He watched in dismay as Latvia's misery deepened under a harsh austerity drive that scythed wages, jobs and state financing for schools and hospitals.
>
> But instead of taking to the streets to protest the cuts, Mr. Krumins . . . bought a tractor and began hauling wood to heating plants that needed fuel. Then, as Latvia's economy began to pull out of its nose-dive, he returned to architecture and today employs 15 people—five more than he had before.

Even the IMF, which has generally counseled against the sharp government spending cutbacks used in Baltic states, acknowledged the Baltics' success in a 2013 speech by its managing director, Christine Lagarde, in Riga:

> While challenges remain today, you have pulled through. You have returned to strong growth and reduced unemployment. . . . You have lowered budget deficits and kept government debt ratios to some of the lowest in the European Union. You have become more competitive in world markets through wage and price cuts. You have restored confidence and brought down interest rates through good macroeconomic policies. We are here today to celebrate your achievements.

The peg to the euro and, in the Estonian and Latvian cases, actual conversion to the euro, have proved instrumental in the recovery and growth stories in the BELLs. Anchoring a local currency to the euro, and ultimately adopting it, removes exchange-rate uncertainty for trading partners, investors, and lenders. The benefits of offering economic certainty were illustrated in a recent *Bloomberg* report:

> Today, Estonia's economy is the fastest-growing in the currency bloc, consumers and businesses are paying lower interest rates, and business ties with Finland—a euro member state and Estonia's main trading partner—are tighter than ever. . . .
>
> "The most important thing was that we ended all the speculation about a possible devaluation" of the kroon, says Priit Perens, the chief executive officer of Swedbank AS, Estonia's biggest lender and a part of Stockholm-based Swedbank. . . . Fears that all the Baltic countries would eventually devalue had hampered investor confidence for a long time. Devaluation would have been ruinous, since Estonia's banks had started lending in euros before the country switched to the common currency. Paying off euro-denominated loans in devalued kroon would have imposed a crushing burden on businesses and consumers.

Lithuania and Bulgaria constitute an experiment within an experiment since they have not pursued fiscal consolidation as strenuously as Latvia and Estonia and, as a result, have not recovered as robustly. But overall, the BELLs have implemented fiscal consolidation and other reforms far more rigorously than have the GIIPS, and they are achieving sustainable debt and deficit levels, trade surpluses, and improved credit ratings as a reward.

If not a perfectly controlled experiment, the contrast between the BELLs' and the GIIPS' policy choices is a powerful case study. The findings show that economic prudence works and Keynesian-style stimulus fails. The results are not surprising, given Keynesianism's dismal track record over the decades and the lack of empirical support for its claims. But the BELLs example is likely to resonate for decades among objective observers, who look for empirical economic proof as opposed to classroom hypotheticals.

The cases of the BELLs and the GIIPS illustrate both the benefits of fiscal consolidation (as practiced by the former) and the costs of delay and denial (as practiced by the latter). The overriding lesson is that currency devaluation is not a precondition to recovery but rather a hindrance. A strong, stable currency is a magnet for investment and a catalyst for expanded trade. The essential ingredients for rapid growth following a crisis are accountability, transparency, fiscal consolidation, and an equitable distribution of sacrifices. The BELLs' experience from 2008 to 2014 offers powerful lessons for Europe's southern periphery as it continues to adjust in the years ahead.

■ BRICS

While the BELLs were breaking new ground in demonstrating fiscal consolidation's benefits, the more powerful BRICS have unsettled conventional wisdom and cast doubt on the U.S. dollar's future as the world's leading reserve currency.

When the BRICS leaders convened a finance ministers' summit in September 2006 in New York City, they showed every sign of evolving in line with O'Neill's original prescription, not so much as a coherent economic bloc but as a political force. The meetings evolved into a formal leaders' summit in Yekaterinburg, Russia, in June 2009, and the summits have continued at the ministerial and leaders' level. In 2010 the original BRIC group of Brazil, Russia, India, and China invited South Africa to join its ranks, and the acronym was changed to BRICS. In April 2011 South Africa attended its first BRICS leaders' summit as a full member in Sanya, China.

O'Neill has consistently downplayed the idea that South Africa should be among the BRICS, because the size of its economy and population coupled with its unemployment problem do not put it in the first rank of developing economies. This is true economically, but ironically South Africa's addition vindicates O'Neill's original thesis that the BRIC project was more political than economic. The other BRICS were located in eastern Europe, Asia, and Latin America. The African continent was a conspicuous gap in the alignment of the East and the South against the

West. South Africa, as the largest economy in Africa, filled that gap with its advanced infrastructure and highly educated workers, despite its relatively small size.

The BRICS' combined economic heft is undeniable. The members represent over 40 percent of global population, 20 percent of global economic output, and 40 percent of total foreign exchange reserves. The BRICS have emerged as a counterweight to the original G7 of highly developed economies and a powerful caucus within the more inclusive G20. However, the BRICS have not taken any measures to integrate their economies into a free-trading area or EU-style currency union except on a limited bilateral basis. The BRICS' principal impact has been to weigh in on global governance and the future of the international monetary system with one voice.

The BRICS leaders have begun to stake out radical new positions on five key issues: IMF voting, UN voting, multilateral assistance, development assistance, and global reserve composition. Their manifesto calls for nothing less than a rethinking or overturning of the post–Second World War arrangements made at Bretton Woods and San Francisco that led to the original forms of the IMF, World Bank, and the United Nations. The BRICS insist that unless those institutions are reformed to be more inclusive of BRICS' priorities, the BRICS will take concrete steps to create their own institutions to perform their functions on a regional basis. The evolution of such institutions would inevitably entail a diminution in the role of the institutions they were meant to replace. It is unclear whether these proposals are a stalking horse to promote real reform in the existing forums or whether there are concrete plans to proceed in the direction announced. Perhaps both intentions are true. In any case, the BRICS are unwilling to accept the international monetary and governance status quo.

Specifically, the BRICS have called for expansion of the UN Security Council permanent members to include Brazil and India. Russia and China are already permanent members. This would create a seven-member permanent membership with the BRICS holding four seats—a slight majority. There would be no elimination of the U.S. veto in this scenario, but the addition of a Brazilian or Indian veto would significantly increase BRICS leverage in the behind-the-scenes negotiations that precede formal Security Council votes. Inclusion of Brazil and India would increase the occasions on which BRICS hold the rotating Security Council presidency. The Security Council presidency gives the presiding nation the ability to set the agenda and affect Security Council processes.

The BRICS, especially China, have also pushed for voting reform at the IMF. If population, reserves, and economic output are the relevant criteria, then current voting power in the IMF is skewed in western Europe's favor and against the BRICS. The IMF leadership recognizes this, and managing director Christine Lagarde has been outspoken in favor of the needed voting reforms (called "voice" in IMF jargon), especially with regard to China. The difficulty lies in getting countries such as Belgium and the Netherlands to reduce their voice in favor of China. This process has dragged on for years. The BRICS have played their cards astutely by conditioning BRICS' pledges for badly needed IMF lending facilities to progress on voting reform. The BRICS' trump card in this game is to launch an alternative multilateral reserve lending institution if the IMF does not increase their voting power.

A blueprint for BRICS alternatives to the IMF and World Bank was a principal result of their March 2013 summit in Durban, South Africa. At that summit's conclusion, the BRICS issued a communiqué, which stated in part:

> We directed our Finance Ministers to examine the feasibility and viability of setting up a New Development Bank for mobilising resources for infrastructure and . . . we are satisfied that the establishment of a New Development Bank is feasible and viable. We have agreed to establish the New Development Bank. . . .
>
> We tasked our Finance Ministers and Central Bank Governors to explore the construction of a financial safety net through the creation of a Contingent Reserve Arrangement (CRA) amongst BRICS countries. . . . We are of the view that the establishment of the CRA with an initial size of US$100 billion is feasible. . . .
>
> We call for the reform of the International Financial Institutions to make them more representative and to reflect the growing weight of BRICS. . . . We remain concerned with the slow pace of the reform of the IMF.

The BRICS summit also specifically addressed the U.S. dollar's role as the world's leading reserve currency, and its possible replacement by SDRs:

We support the reform and improvement of the international monetary system, with a broad-based international reserve currency system providing stability and certainty. We welcome the discussion about the role of the SDR in the existing international monetary system including the composition of the SDR's basket of currencies.

Finally, and so as to leave no doubt about the BRICS' status as a political rather than an economic project, the Durban summit devoted substantial time to topics such as the crisis in Syria, a Palestinian state, Israeli settlements, Iranian nuclear weapons development, the war in Afghanistan, instability in the Congo, and other purely geopolitical issues.

The BRICS reaffirmed their commitment to their new multilateral lending facility at their summit in St. Petersburg on September 5, 2013, held in conjunction with the G20 Leaders Summit. At that summit, the BRICS agreed that their contributions to the new fund would come 41 percent from China, 18 percent each from Russia, Brazil, and India, and 5 percent from South Africa.

In a surprising coda to the revelations of U.S. spying on allies emerging from defector Edward Snowden, Brazil announced plans in September 2013 to build a twenty-thousand-mile undersea fiber optic cable network from Fortaleza, Brazil, to Vladivostok, Russia, with links in Cape Town, South Africa, Chennai, India, and Shantou, China, to be completed by 2015. This system is tantamount to a BRICS Internet intended to be free from U.S. surveillance. The United States has long had excellent capability in tapping into undersea cables, so the actual security of the new system may be problematic. Nevertheless, the proprietary nature of this system could easily be adapted to include a BRICS interbank payments system, which would facilitate the use of any BRICS-sponsored alternatives to dollar payments.

In addition to the regular meetings of BRICS leaders, a large number of ancillary and shadow institutions have sprung up around the BRICS, including the BRICS Think Tanks Council, the BRICS Business Council, and a BRICS virtual secretariat, among others. The BRICS are also coordinating foreign policy through the BRICS foreign affairs ministers' meetings in conjunction with the annual UN General Assembly meeting in New York. These initiatives have spawned a new international facilitator class: the "BRICS Sherpa" and their "Sous-Sherpas." These BRICS institutions form a formidable caucus in the midst of other multilateral forums conducted by the IMF, UN, and G20.

Today the BRICS must be regarded as a powerful economic and political force, notwithstanding a recent slowdown in growth rates in certain members, especially China. The global BRICS footprint in terms of territory, population, output, natural resources, and financial reserves is impossible to ignore. The world should anticipate a gradual convergence between the BRICS' vision for the future and the West's legacy institutions, now that the BRICS have found policies and processes that unite them.

This convergence has many facets, which can be condensed into a single theme: the diminution in the dollar's international role and a decline in the ability of the United States and its closest allies to affect outcomes in major forums and in geopolitical disputes. The BRICS may have had humble origins in O'Neill's brief research paper, but the group has taken on a life of its own.

■ The Shanghai Cooperation Organization

Wall Street analysts are not alone in identifying commonalities in emerging market economies, as other regional groups have come to the fore in recent years. These linkages, based upon regional proximity or community of interest, are beginning to challenge the postwar arrangements of the leading Western economies. They include the Shanghai Cooperation Organization (SCO) and the Gulf Cooperation Council (GCC). Once again, these groupings share an inclination to reduce the U.S. dollar's role as the leading reserve currency. Their agendas go beyond the free-trade areas and common markets found throughout the world and include strategic, military, natural resource, and international monetary initiatives. Depending on how well these groups pursue their agendas and overcome internal rivalries, they stand to play a significant role in any reformation or evolution of the international monetary system from its current configuration.

The Shanghai Cooperation Organization was formed in June 2001 as the continuation of a predecessor organization, the Shanghai Five. The SCO members are the original Shanghai Five members—Russia, China, Kazakhstan, Kyrgyzstan, and Tajikistan—plus new member Uzbekistan. However, the SCO includes India, Iran, and Pakistan among its observer states and regularly invites the former Soviet republics and members of the Association of South-East Asian Nations (ASEAN) to their meetings.

The SCO had its origins in security issues indigenous to its member states, including suppression of secessionist tendencies in the Caucasus, Tibet, and Taiwan. The members also had a shared interest in defeating Al Qaeda and other terrorist groups in Chechnya and western China. But the SCO quickly evolved into an Asian counterweight to NATO. Russia gained China's support in its confrontation with NATO in eastern Europe, and China gained the support of the Russians in its confrontation with the United States in East Asia. In this context, the SCO's rejection of a U.S. application for observer status in 2005 was unsurprising.

In addition to conducting joint military exercises and cooperating in dozens of large-scale infrastructure projects related to energy, telecommunications, and water, the SCO has also launched initiatives in banking and multilateral finance, which are pertinent to the international monetary system's future. The Prime Ministers Council of the SCO signed an agreement at its Moscow summit on October 26, 2005, creating the SCO Interbank Consortium, designed to facilitate economic cooperation among its central banks, joint infrastructure financing, and formation of specialized development lenders to its members.

At the SCO Prime Ministers Summit in Astana, Kazakhstan, in October, 2008, Chinese premier Wen Jiabao and Russian prime minister Vladimir Putin endorsed Iran's application to become a full member of the SCO. At that summit, Iranian vice president Parviz Davoudi remarked that "the Shanghai Cooperation Organisation is a good venue for designing a new banking system which is independent from international banking systems." The SCO summit in June 2009 was conducted side by side with the BRICS summit in Yekaterinburg, Russia. Chinese president Hu

Jintao and Russian president Dmitry Medvedev used the occasion of the SCO and BRICS summits to sign a joint Sino-Russian declaration calling for reform of the global financial system and international financial institutions and greater developing economy representation in the IMF.

Newly elected Iranian president Hassan Rouhani had a kind of international coming-out party at the SCO summit in Kyrgyzstan's capital, Bishkek, on September 13, 2013. At the summit, Iran received strong support from Russia, China, and the rest of the SCO for noninterference in Iran's uranium-enrichment efforts.

As geopolitics are increasingly played out in the realm of international economics rather than purely military-diplomatic spheres, the SCO's evolution from a security alliance to a potential monetary zone should be expected. This has already happened covertly through Russian and Chinese banks' role in facilitating Iranian hard-currency transactions, despite sanctions on Iranian money transfers imposed by the United States and the EU.

The convergence of the BRICS' and SCO's agendas on international monetary matters should be most worrying for traditional Western elites. The drivers are Russia and China, the two most powerful members of both organizations. The BRICS and the SCO may have separate agendas in military and strategic affairs, but they are like-minded on the subjects of IMF voting rights, and they share an emerging antipathy to the dollar's dominant role.

■ The Gulf

Another strategic and geographically contiguous alliance, the Gulf Cooperation Council (GCC), genuinely has the potential to form a single-currency area that would diminish the U.S. dollar's role.

The GCC was founded on May 25, 1981, when Bahrain, Kuwait, Oman, Qatar, Saudi Arabia, and the United Arab Emirates signed a pact in Riyadh, Saudi Arabia. There have been no additions to this original group, although Morocco and Jordan are currently under consideration for membership.

The GCC does not have links to Iraq or Iran, despite the fact that both of those nations border the Persian Gulf along with all the GCC members. The reasons are obvious. Iraq ruined its GCC relations with the invasion of member Kuwait in 1990. Iran is not a candidate for membership because it is ethnically and religiously distinct from the Arab states with which it shares the Persian Gulf and because it is Saudi Arabia's bitter enemy. But the possible additions of Jordan and Morocco make sense. The existing GCC members are all Arab monarchies. Jordan is an Arab monarchy, and Morocco is an Arabic-speaking monarchy and Arab League member. While the GCC pursues relatively liberal economic and trade policies, it is still a de facto club for the remaining kings of Arabia.

The GCC has pursued a path not unlike the EU in that it successfully launched a common market in 2008 and is now moving toward a single currency. The GCC's significance for the international monetary system lies more in its single-currency initiative than in other facets of strategic and economic cooperation, which are of mostly regional rather than international importance. As was the case with the euro, implementation of a single currency in the GCC will take a decade or more to complete. Key issues that need to be resolved include convergence criteria for members' fiscal and monetary policies and the powers of the new central bank. Most vexing in the short run are the inevitable politics that swirl around issues such as the physical location of the central bank's headquarters and the membership and governance of its board.

The GCC members are already in a quasi-currency union because their individual currencies are pegged to the U.S. dollar and therefore to one another using fixed exchange rates. However, each GCC member retains an independent central bank. This arrangement resembles the European Rate Mechanism (ERM), which lasted from 1979 to 1999 and was a predecessor to the euro, although the GCC has had more success than the ERM, which witnessed numerous breaks with designated exchange-rate parities by its members.

The conversion from the current GCC arrangement to a single currency would appear to be a straightforward process. But recent stresses in the Eurozone have given pause to the GCC members and impeded the monetary integration process. The most prominent impediment is running a single monetary policy with divergent fiscal policies. This problem was one of the principal contributors to the European sovereign debt crisis. Countries such as Greece and Spain engaged in nonsustainable fiscal policies financed with debt issued in a strong currency, the euro, to investors who inferred incorrectly that Euro-denominated sovereign debt had the implicit support of all the Eurozone members. The core problem for any proposed currency union (such as the GCC) is how to enforce fiscal discipline among members when there is a single central bank and a single monetary policy. The need is to prevent a recurrence of Greek-style free-riding on the stronger members' fiscal discipline.

The GCC has already witnessed this free-riding problem in the 2009 Dubai World collapse. Dubai is part of the United Arab Emirates along with six other principalities, most prominently Abu Dhabi. The emirates share a single currency, the dirham, issued by a central bank located in Abu Dhabi.

Dubai World, an investment holding company, was created in 2006 by Dubai's ruler, Sheikh Mohammed bin Rashid Al Maktoum. Although Dubai World insisted its debts were not government guaranteed, its debt appeared to investors as tantamount to a UAE member's sovereign debt. Between 2006 and 2009, Dubai World borrowed approximately $60 billion to finance infrastructure projects, including office buildings, apartments, and transportation systems, many of which remain empty or underused to this day.

On November 27, 2009, Dubai World unexpectedly announced it was requesting a "standstill" among creditors and called for debt-maturity extensions across the board. This default, rather than any specific event in Europe, was the catalyst for the sovereign debt crisis that quickly engulfed Europe and lasted from 2010 to 2012. Eventually Abu Dhabi and the UAE central bank intervened to bail out Dubai World in much the same manner as the EU and the European Central Bank intervened to bail out Greece, Portugal, Ireland, and Spain. These lessons from the UAE and Europe are not lost on Saudi Arabia, Qatar, and the other wealthy GCC members. An enforceable GCC fiscal pact with limits on deficit spending is likely to be required before the single-currency project moves forward.

The other major issue looming over the GCC single currency is the question of an initial par value relative to the U.S. dollar. Too low a value would be inflationary, while too high a value would prove deflationary. This is the same dilemma that confronted the U.K. when it returned to the gold standard in 1925 after suspending it in 1914 to fight the First World War. The U.K. blundered then by setting sterling's value against gold too high, which caused extreme deflation and contributed to the Great Depression.

When a country or group of countries peg to the U.S. dollar, those countries effectively outsource their monetary policy to the Federal Reserve. If the Fed is engaged in monetary ease and the pegging country is running a trade surplus or experiencing capital inflows, the pegging country has to print its own money to purchase the incoming dollars in order to maintain the peg. In effect, the Fed's easy-money policy is exported through the exchange-rate mechanism, which forces the pegging country to engage in its own easy-money policy. If the pegging country economy is stronger than the U.S. economy, this easy-money policy will produce inflation, as has occurred in China and the GCC since 2008. The simplest solution is to abandon the peg and allow the local currency to appreciate against the dollar. Such reductions in the dollar's value are the Fed's goal under its cheap-dollar policy.

An alternative solution is to maintain a single currency with a value fixed to a currency *other* than the dollar. Monetary experts have suggested several candidates for an alternative peg. One obvious candidate is the IMF's special drawing right, the SDR. The SDR itself is valued relative to a currency basket that includes the dollar but with significant weight given to the euro, sterling, and the yen. Importantly, the IMF retains the ability to change the SDR basket composition periodically, adding new currencies to better reflect trade patterns, changes in comparative advantage, and the relative economic performance of the countries whose currencies are included in the basket. An SDR peg would align the future GCC currency more closely with the economies of its trading partners and decrease the Fed's impact on GCC monetary policy.

GCC member economies are highly dependent on oil exports for revenue and growth. Volatility in the dollar price of oil translates into volatility in economic performance when the GCC currency is pegged to the dollar. A logical extension, then, of the SDR basket approach would be to include the dollar price of oil in the basket. By doing so, the exchange value of the GCC currency would move in tandem with the dollar price of oil. If the Fed pursued a cheap-dollar policy and the dollar price of oil increased due to the resulting inflation, the GCC currency would appreciate automatically, mitigating inflation in the GCC. This way the GCC currency can be both pegged and free of the Fed's cheap-dollar policy.

A more intriguing solution to the peg issue—and one with large implications for the future of the international monetary system—is more radical: *to price oil and natural gas exports in the GCC currency itself,* thereby allowing the GCC currency to float relative to other currencies. This could truly mark the beginning of the dollar's demise as the benchmark currency for oil prices, and it would create immediate global demand for the GCC currency.

This trend toward the abandonment of the dollar as the benchmark for pricing oil was dramatically accelerated in late 2013 as a result of White House efforts to legitimize Iran as the regional hegemon of the Middle East. Implicitly since 1945 and explicitly since 1974, the United States has guaranteed Saudi Arabia's security in exchange for Saudi support for the dollar as the sole medium of exchange for energy exports and for Saudi promises to purchase weapons and infrastructure from the United States. This nearly seventy-year-long relationship was thrown into grave doubt in late 2013 by President Obama's modus vivendi with Iran and implicit tolerance of Iranian nuclear ambitions.

The U.S.-Iranian rapprochement occurred after Saudi-U.S. relations had already been badly strained by President Obama's abandonment of Saudi ally Hosni Mubarak in Egypt in 2011 during the Arab Spring uprisings, and by the president's failure to support Saudi rebel allies in the Syrian Civil War. The Saudis then spent billions of dollars to help restore military rule in Egypt and to crush the Egyptian Muslim Brotherhood favored by President Obama. More recently the Saudis publicly displayed their displeasure with the United States and moved decisively to secure weapons from Russia, nuclear technology from Pakistan, and security assistance from Israel. The resulting Saudi-Russian-Egyptian alliance removes another prop from under the dollar and creates a community of interest between Saudi Arabia and Russia, which had already announced its preference for an international monetary system free from dollar hegemony.

For a GCC currency to become a true global reserve currency as opposed to a trade currency, further deepening of GCC financial markets and infrastructure would be needed. However, Saudi Arabia's reevaluation of its security relations with the United States combined with the euro's expansion and the efforts of the BRICS and the SCO to acquire gold and escape dollar dominance could presage a quite rapid diminution in the dollar's international reserve-currency role.

■ The Island Twins

Two nations stand apart from this survey of monetary multilateralism and rising discontent with the international monetary system: the U.K. and Japan. The U.K. is a member of NATO and the EU, while Japan is an important and long-standing treaty ally of the United States.

Neither nation has joined in a monetary union or spoken out vociferously against U.S. dominance in international monetary institutions. Both Japan and the U.K. maintain their own currencies and their own central banks; they host the respective financial centers of Tokyo and London. The Japanese yen and the U.K. pound sterling are both officially recognized as reserve currencies by the IMF, and both Japan and the U.K. have the large, robust bond markets needed to support that designation.

Still, Japan and the U.K. are weak in gold reserves, with only about 25 percent of the gold needed to equal the United States or Russia in a gold-to-GDP ratio; Japan and the U.K. have an even lower gold-to-GDP ratio than China, which is itself short of gold. The United States, the Eurozone, and Russia all have sufficient gold to sustain confidence in their currencies in the event of a crisis. In contrast, Japan and the U.K. represent the purest cases of reliance on fiat money. Both countries are out on a limb, with printing presses, insufficient gold, no monetary allies, and no Plan B.

Japan and the U.K. are part of a global monetary experiment orchestrated by the U.S. Federal Reserve and articulated by former Fed chairman Ben Bernanke in two speeches, one given in Tokyo on October 14, 2012, and one given in London on March 25, 2013. In his 2012 Tokyo speech, Bernanke stated that the United States would continue its loose monetary policy through quantitative easing for the foreseeable future. Trading partners therefore had two choices. They could peg their currencies to the dollar, which would cause inflation—exactly what the GCC was experiencing. Or, according to Bernanke, those trading partners could allow their currencies to appreciate—the desired outcome under his cheap-dollar policy—in which case their exports would suffer. For trading partners that complained that this was a Hobson's choice between inflation and reduced exports, Bernanke explained that if the Fed did *not* ease, the result would be even worse for them: a collapsing U.S. economy that would hurt world demand as well as world trade and sink developed and emerging markets into a global depression.

Despite Bernanke's rationale, his cheap-dollar policy had the potential to ignite beggar-thy-neighbor rounds of currency devaluations—a currency war that could lead to a trade war, as happened in the 1930s. Bernanke addressed this concern in his 2013 London speech. One problem with the 1930s devaluations, he said, was that they were *sequential* rather than contemporaneous. Each country that devalued in the 1930s might have gained growth and export market share, but it came at the expense of the countries that had not devalued. The desired growth from devaluation was suboptimal because it came with high costs. Bernanke's solution was for *simultaneous* rather than sequential ease by the United States, Japan, the U.K., and the ECB. In theory, this would produce stimulus in the major economies without imposing temporary costs on trading partners:

> Today most advanced industrial economies remain . . . in the grip of slow recoveries from the Great Recession. With inflation generally contained, central banks in these countries are providing accommodative monetary policies to support growth. Do these policies constitute competitive devaluations? To the contrary, because monetary policy is accommodative in the great majority of advanced industrial economies, one would not expect large and persistent changes in . . . exchange rates among these countries. The benefits of monetary accommodation in the advanced economies are not created in any significant way by changes in exchange rates;

they come instead from the support for domestic aggregate demand in each country or region. Moreover, because stronger growth in each economy confers beneficial spillovers to trading partners, these policies are not "beggar-thy-neighbor" but rather are positive-sum, "enrich-thy-neighbor" actions.

Bernanke's "enrich-thy-neighbor" rhetoric ignored the neighbors in emerging markets such as China, Korea, Brazil, Thailand, and elsewhere whose currencies would have to appreciate (and their exports suffer) in order for Bernanke's "stimulus" to work in the developed economies. In other words, Japanese exports might benefit, but this could come at the expense of Korea's exports, and so on. It might not be a currency war of all against all, but it was still one that pitted the United States, the U.K., and Japan against the remaining G20 members.

Japan and the U.K. had another reason to support the money printing and resultant devaluation being urged by the Fed. Money printing was being done not only to promote exports but to increase import prices. These more expensive imports would cause inflation to offset deflation, which was a danger to the United States and the U.K. and had long existed in Japan. In Japan's case, inflation would come primarily through higher prices for energy imports, and in the cases of the United States and the U.K., it would come from higher prices for clothing, electronics, and certain raw materials and foodstuffs.

The United States and the U.K. both have debt-to-GDP ratios of approximately 100 percent and rising, while Japan's debt-to-GDP ratio is over 220 percent. These levels are historically high. The trend in these ratios is more important to investors than the absolute levels, and the trend is worsening. All three nations are moving toward a sovereign debt crisis if their policies cannot be adjusted to put these debt-to-GDP ratios on a declining path.

Debt-to-GDP ratios are calculated in nominal rather than real terms. Nominal debt needs to be repaid with nominal growth in income. Nominal growth equals real growth plus inflation. Since real growth is anemic, the central banks *must* cause inflation to have any hope of increasing nominal growth and reducing these debt-to-GDP ratios. When policy interest-rate cuts are no longer possible because the rates are effectively zero, quantitative easing, designed in part to import inflation through currency devaluation, is the central bankers' preferred technique.

The Bank of England (BOE) has engaged in four rounds of quantitative easing (QE), beginning in March 2009. Subsequent rounds were launched in October 2011, February 2012, and July 2012. Increased asset purchases have ceased for the time being, but the BOE's near-zero-interest-rate policy has continued. The BOE is refreshingly candid about the fact that it is targeting nominal rather than real growth, although it hopes that real growth might be a by-product. Its official explanation on the bond purchases to carry out QE states, "The purpose of the purchases was and is to inject money directly into the economy in order to boost nominal demand. Despite this different means of implementing monetary policy, the objective remains unchanged—to meet the inflation target of 2 percent on the CPI measure of consumer prices."

The situation in Japan differs. Japan has been in what may be described as a long depression since December 1989, when the 1980s stock and property bubbles collapsed. Japan relied primarily on fiscal stimulus through the 1990s to keep its economy afloat, but a more pernicious phase of the depression began in the late 1990s. Japan's nominal GDP peaked in 1997, declining almost 12 percent by 2011. The Japanese consumer price index peaked in 1998 and has declined steadily since, with relatively few quarters of positive CPI readings. It is a truism, if not intuitive, that an economy with declining *nominal* GDP can still have *real* growth when inflation turns to deflation. But this type of real growth does nothing to help the government with debt, deficits, and tax collections since those functions are based on nominal growth.

The Bank of Japan's (BOJ) relationship to QE, inflation, and nominal GDP targeting is more opaque than the Bank of England's. The BOJ's efforts at monetary ease prior to 2001 were desultory and controversial even within the BOJ. A modest QE program was begun in March 2001 but was too small to have much effect. A detailed IMF survey of the impact of QE in Japan from 2001 to 2011 concluded, "The impact on economic activity . . . was found to be limited."

Suddenly on December 16, 2012, Japanese politics and monetary policy were transformed with Shinzo Abe's election as prime minister, in a landslide victory for his Liberal Democratic Party. The election gave

Abe's party a supermajority in the Japanese Diet that could override ve-
toes by the Senate. Abe campaigned explicitly on a platform of money
printing, including threats to amend the laws governing the Bank of Japan if it failed to print. "It's very rare for monetary policy to be the focus
of an election," Abe said. "We campaigned on the need to beat deflation,
and our argument has won strong support. I hope the Bank of Japan
accepts the results and takes an appropriate decision."

Even Abe's election did not fully convince markets that the BOJ would
actually take extraordinary measures, given the bank's indifferent approach to monetary ease for the prior twenty years. On March 20, 2013,
Abe's handpicked candidate, Haruhiko Kuroda, became governor of the
BOJ. Within days, Kuroda persuaded the BOJ's policy board to implement the largest quantitative easing program the world had ever seen. The
BOJ pledged to purchase $1.4 trillion of Japanese government bonds over
the two-year period of 2013 and 2014 using printed money. Japan simultaneously announced a plan to lengthen the maturity structure of the
bonds it purchased, comparable to the Fed's "Operation Twist." Relative
to the size of the U.S. economy, Japan's money-printing program was
more than twice as large as the Fed's QE3 program, announced in 2012.
As was the case with the Bank of England, the Bank of Japan was explicit
about its goal to increase inflation in order to increase nominal, if not
real, GDP: "The Bank will achieve the . . . target of 2 percent in terms of
the year-on-year rate of change in the consumer price index . . . at the
earliest possible time."

By 2014, it was as if the Federal Reserve, the BOJ, and the BOE were
in a monetary poker game and had gone all in on their bet. All three
central banks had used money printing and near-zero rates to create inflation in order to increase nominal GDP. Whether nominal GDP turned
into real GDP was beside the point. In fact, real growth since 2009 was
on a path characteristic of depression in all three countries. Inflation and
nominal GDP were the explicit and primary goals of their respective
monetary policies.

The U.S. dollar, the U.K. pound sterling, and the Japanese yen together
comprise 70 percent of global allocated reserves and 65 percent of the
SDR basket. If the Federal Reserve is the keystone of the international
monetary system, the Bank of Japan and the Bank of England are adja-

cent arch stones. But all three central banks, now engaged in a monetary experiment on an unprecedented scale, face highly uncertain outcomes. Their announced goal is not real growth but inflation and nominal growth in order to pay their debts.

Creditors and reserve holders in the BRICS, the SCO, the GCC, and other emerging markets are watching this money-printing pageant with undisguised frustration and increasing determination to end an international monetary system that allows such economic free-riding at the cost of inflation, lost exports, and diminished wealth in their own countries. It remains to be seen whether the international monetary system collapses of its own weight or is overthrown by emerging-market losers in response to this crime of the century being perpetrated by the U.S., U.K., and Japanese central banks.

PART THREE

MONEY AND WEALTH

CHAPTER 7

DEBT, DEFICITS, AND THE DOLLAR

> Forward guidance . . . should promise that monetary policy will not remove the punch bowl but allow the party to continue until very late in the evening to ensure that everyone has a good time.
>
> Charles I. Plosser
> President of the Federal Reserve Bank of Philadelphia
> February 12, 2013

> Adopting a nominal income . . . target is viewed as innovative only by those unfamiliar with the debate on the design of monetary policy of the past few decades. No one has yet designed a way to make it workable. . . . Rather, a . . . target would be perceived as a thinly disguised way of aiming for higher inflation.
>
> Charles Goodhart
> March 18, 2013

▦ The Meaning of Money

What is a dollar? This question has no easy answer. Most people respond that a dollar is money, something they make, spend, or save. That raises another question: What is money? Experts recite the three-part definition of money as a medium of exchange, a store of value, and a unit of account. The *unit of account* part of the definition is useful but almost trivial. Bottle caps can be a unit of account; so can knots on a string. A unit of account is merely a way of adding or subtracting perceived value. *Medium of exchange* also refers indirectly to value, since each party to an exchange must perceive value in the unit being exchanged for goods or services. Two of the three parts of the definition implicitly reference value. The entire standard definition can thus be collapsed into the one remaining part, the *store of value*.

If, then, money is value, what is *value*? At this point, the analysis becomes philosophical and moral. Values can be held by individuals yet shared within a culture or community. Values can be subjective (as is the case with ethics) or absolute (as is the case with religion). Values can come into conflict when competing or contiguous groups have widely varied values.

Despite this breadth in the meaning of *value,* two facets stand out. The first is the idea of a metric: that there is a way of measuring the presence, absence, or degree of value. The second is the idea of trust: that when one ascribes values to an individual or group, one trusts that the individual or group will act consistently with those values. Trust embodies consistent behavior in the form of reciprocal or altruistic acts.

At heart, a dollar is money, money is value, and value is trust consistently honored. When one buys a bottle of Coca-Cola anywhere in the world, one trusts that the original formula is being used, and that the contents are not adulterated; in this respect, Coca-Cola does not disappoint. This is trust consistently honored, meaning that a bottle of Coke has value.

When a customer buys a bottle of Coke, he hands the seller a dollar. This is not mere barter, but rather a value exchange. What is the source of the dollar's value? How does it hold up as an example of trust consistently honored?

To answer that question, one needs to dig deeper. The dollar itself, whether in paper or digital form, is a representational object. What does the dollar represent? To whom is the trust directed? When trust is required, Ronald Reagan's dictum applies: *Trust, but verify.* The Federal Reserve System, owned by private banks, is the issuer of the dollar. The Fed asks for our trust, but how can one verify if the trust is being honored?

In a rule-of-law society, a customary way of verifying trust is the written contract. A first-year law student in contracts class immediately learns to "get it in writing." The beliefs and expectations of the parties to a contract are written down and read by both parties. Assuming both parties agree, the contract is signed, and from then forward, the contract embodies the trust. At times, disputes arise about the meaning of words in the contract or the performance of its terms. Countries have courts to resolve those disputes. This system of contracts, courts, and decisions guided by a constitution is what is meant by a rule-of-law society.

How does the Federal Reserve fit into this system? On one level, the Fed follows the written contract model. One can begin by reading the fine print on a dollar bill. That is where one finds the written money contract. The parties to this contract are specified as "The Federal Reserve" and "The United States of America" on behalf of the people.

One-dollar contracts are entered into by each of the Fed's twelve regional reserve banks. Some of these written contracts are entered by the Dallas Fed, some by the Philadelphia Fed, and so on. Larger denominations such as twenty-dollar contracts are entered into by the "System." These contracts are all signed by an agent, the U.S. secretary of the Treasury, on behalf of the people.

The most important clause in the written dollar contract appears on the front at the top of each bill. It is the phrase "Federal Reserve Note." A note is an obligation, a form of debt. Indeed, this is how the Fed reports money issued on its balance sheet. Balance sheets show assets on the left-hand side, liabilities on the right-hand side, and capital, which is assets minus liabilities, at the bottom. Notes issued by the Fed are reported on the right-hand side of the balance sheet, as a liability, exactly where one would place debt.

Fed notes are an unusual form of debt because they bear no interest and have no maturity. Another way to describe a dollar, using the contract theory, is that it is a perpetual, non-interest-bearing note issued by the Fed. Any borrower will attest that perpetual, non-interest-bearing debt is the best kind of debt because one never pays it back, and it costs nothing in the meantime. Still, it is a debt.

So the dollar is money, money is value, value is trust, trust is a contract, and the contract is debt. By application of the transitive law of arithmetic, the dollar is debt owed by the Fed to the people in contractual form. This view may be called the contract theory of money, or *contractism*. As applied to the dollar, one way to understand the theory is to substitute the word *debt* every time one sees the word *money*. Then the world looks like a different place; it is a world in debt.

This approach to money through the lens of contract is one of many monetary theories. The most influential of these is the quantity theory of money, or *monetarism,* advocated in the twentieth century by Irving Fisher and Milton Friedman. Monetarism is one of the Fed's chosen guides to money creation, although the original formulation advocated by Friedman is no longer in vogue.

Another approach is the state theory of money, which posits that unbacked paper money has value since the state may demand such money as tax payments. The state may use coercion unto death to collect taxes; therefore citizens work for and value money because it can satisfy the state. This relationship of money and state means paper money has extrinsic value in excess of its intrinsic value due to the medium of state power. This type of money is known as chartal money, and *chartalism* is another name for the state theory of money. In the 1920s John Maynard Keynes adopted chartalism in his calls for the abolition of gold standards. More recent acolytes of the theory of money as an arm of state power are Paul McCulley, former executive at bond giant PIMCO, and Stephanie Kelton, economist at the University of Missouri, who marches under the banner of modern monetary theory.

A new entrant in the money theory sweepstakes is the quantity theory of credit. This theory, advanced by Richard Duncan, is a variant of the quantity theory of money. Duncan proposes that credit creation has become so prolific and pervasive that the idea of money is now subsumed in the idea of credit, and that credit creation is the proper focus of monetary study and policy. Duncan brings impressive statistical and forensic analyses of government data to the study of credit expansion. His work could properly be called *creditism,* although it is really a twenty-first-century version of a nineteenth-century view of money called the British Banking School.

Monetarism, chartalism, and creditism all have one idea in common: a belief in *fiat* money. The word *fiat* has a Latin origin that means "let it be done." As applied to money, *fiat* refers to the case where the state orders that a particular form of money serve as currency and be treated as legal tender. All three theories agree that money does not have to have intrinsic value as long as it possesses extrinsic value supplied by the state. When fiat money opponents say money "is not backed by anything," these theorists answer, "So what?" In their view, money has value because the state dictates it be so, and nothing else is required to give money its value.

A theory is useful only to the extent it accords with real-world phenomena and helps observers to understand and anticipate events in that world. Theories of money that rely on state power are a thin reed on which to lean because the application of state power is changeable. In that sense, these competing theories of money may be said to be contingent.

Returning to where we started, the contract theory of money focuses on money's intrinsic value. The money may be paper, but the paper has writing, and the writing is a legal contract. A citizen may deem the contract valuable for her own reasons independent of state dictates. The citizen may value contract performance rather than fiat. This theory is useful for understanding not only the dollar but also whether the dollar contract is being honored, both now and in the future.

Although the dollar as debt bears no interest and has no maturity, the dollar still involves duties of performance on the parts of both the Fed and the Treasury, the two named parties on the contract. This performance is made manifest in the economy. If the economy is doing well, the dollar is useful, and contract performance is satisfactory or valuable. If the economy is dysfunctional, performance may be thought poor to the point of default under the contract.

A gold standard is a way to enforce the money contract. Advocates for gold insist that all paper money has no intrinsic value, which can be supplied only by tangible precious metal in the form of gold, or perhaps silver. This view misapprehends the role of gold in a gold standard, but for the few who insist that coins or bullion be the sole medium of exchange—a highly impractical state of affairs. All gold standards involve a relationship between physical gold and paper representations of gold, whether these representations are called notes, shares, or receipts. Once this relationship is accepted, one is quickly back to the world of contract.

On this view, gold is the collateral or bond posted to ensure satisfactory performance of the money contract. If the state prints too much money, the citizen is then free to declare the money contract in default and redeem her paper money for gold at the market exchange rate. In effect, the citizen takes her collateral.

Gold advocates suggest that the exchange rate between paper money and gold should be fixed and maintained. There is merit to this idea, but a fixed exchange rate is not essential to gold's role in a contract money system. It is necessary only that the citizen be free to buy or sell gold at any time. Any citizen can go on a personal gold standard by buying gold with paper dollars, while anyone who does not buy gold is expressing comfort with the paper-money contract for the time being.

The money price of gold is therefore a measure of contractual performance by the Fed and Treasury. If performance is satisfactory, gold's price should be stable, as citizens rest easy with the paper-money deal. If performance is poor, the gold price will spike, as citizens terminate the money-debt contract and claim their collateral through gold purchases on the open market. Like any debtor, the Fed prefers that the citizen-creditors be unaware of their right to claim collateral. The Fed is betting that citizens will not claim the gold collateral en masse. This bet depends on a high degree of complacency among citizens about the nature of the money contract, the nature of gold, and their right to take collateral for nonperformance.

This is one reason the Fed and fiat money economists use phrases like "barbarous relic" and "tradition" to describe gold and insist that gold has no role in a modern monetary system. The Fed's view is absurd, akin to saying land and buildings have no role in a mortgage. Money is a paper debt with gold as its collateral. The collateral can be claimed by the straightforward purchase of gold.

The Fed prefers that investors not make this connection, but one investor who did was Warren Buffett. In his case, he moved not into gold but into hard assets, and his story is revealing.

In November 2009, not long after the depths of the market selloff resulting from the Panic of 2008, Buffett announced his acquisition of 100 percent of the Burlington Northern Santa Fe Railway. Buffett described this purchase as a "bet on the country."

Maybe. A railroad is the ultimate hard asset. Railroads consist of a basket of hard assets, such as rights of way, adjacent mining rights, tracks, switches, signals, yards, and rolling stock. Railroads make money by transporting other hard assets, such as wheat, steel, ore, and cattle. Railroads are hard assets that move hard assets.

By acquiring 100 percent of the stock, Buffett effectively turned the railroad from an exchange-traded public equity into private equity. This means that if stock exchanges were closed in a financial panic, there would be no impact on Buffett's holdings because he is not seeking liquidity. While others might be shocked by the sudden illiquidity of their holdings, Buffett would just sit tight.

Buffett's acquisition is best understood as getting out of paper money and into hard assets, while immunizing those assets from a stock exchange closure. It may be a "bet on the country"—but it is also a hedge against inflation and financial panic. The small investor who cannot acquire an entire railroad can make the same bet by buying gold. Buffett has been known to disparage gold, but he is the king of hard asset investing, and when it comes to the megarich, it is better to focus on their actions than on their words. Paper money is a contract collateralized by gold, the latter a hard asset nonpareil.

■ Debt, Deficits, and Sustainability

The Federal Reserve is not the only government-linked debtor in the U.S. money system; in fact, it is far from the largest. The U.S. Treasury has issued over $17 trillion of debt in the form of bills, notes, and bonds, compared to about $4 trillion of debt-as-money notes issued by the Fed.

Unlike Federal Reserve notes, Treasury notes are not thought of as money, although the most liquid instruments are often called "cash equivalents" on corporate balance sheets. Another difference between Federal Reserve notes and Treasury notes is that Treasury notes have maturity dates and pay interest. Fed notes can be issued in indefinite quantities and remain outstanding indefinitely, but Treasury notes are more subject to the discipline of bond markets, where investors trade over $500 billion in Treasury securities every day.

Market discipline includes continual evaluation by investors as to whether the Treasury's debt burden is *sustainable*. This evaluation asks whether the Treasury can pay its outstanding debts as agreed. If the answer is yes, the market will gladly accept more Treasury debt at reasonable interest rates. If the answer is no, the market will dump Treasury debt, and interest rates will skyrocket. In cases of extreme uncertainty due to lack of funds or lack of willingness to pay, government debt can become nearly worthless, as happened in the United States after the Revolutionary War and in other countries many times before and since.

Analysis of government debt is most challenging when the answer is neither yes nor no but maybe. It is at these tipping points (which complexity theorists call phase transitions) that the bond market stands poised between confidence and panic, and debt default seems like a real possibility. European sovereign bond markets approached this point in late 2011 and remained poised on the brink until September 2012, when the European Central Bank head, Mario Draghi, offered his famous "whatever it takes" pronouncement. He meant that the ECB would substitute its money debt for sovereign debt in the quantities needed to reassure the sovereign debt holders. This reassurance worked, and European sovereign debt markets pulled back from the brink.

In recent years, purchases of government securities with money printed by the Federal Reserve account for a high percentage of net new debt issued by the Treasury. The Fed insists that its purchases are a policy tool to ease monetary conditions and are not intended to monetize the national debt. The Treasury, at the same time, insists that it is the world's best debtor and has no difficulty satisfying the funding requirements for the U.S. government. Still, the casual observer could be forgiven for believing that the Fed is monetizing the debt by debasing money— historically a step on the road to collapse for economic and political systems, from ancient Rome to present-day Argentina. The Fed's great confidence game is to swap its non-interest-bearing notes for the Treasury's interest-bearing notes, then rebate the interest earned back to the Treasury. The challenge for bond markets, and investors generally, is to decide how much Treasury note issuance is sustainable and how much substitution of Fed notes for Treasury notes is acceptable before the phase transition emerges and a collapse begins.

The dynamics of government debt and deficits are more complicated than the conventional argument admits. Too often the debate over debt and deficits degenerates into binary choices: Is debt good or bad for an economy? Is the U.S. deficit too high, or is it affordable? Tea Party conservatives take the view that deficit spending is intrinsically bad, that a balanced budget is desirable in and of itself, and that the United States is well down the path to becoming Greece. Krugman-style liberals take the view that debt is necessary to fund certain desirable programs, and that the United States has been here before in terms of its debt-to-GDP ratio. After World War II, the U.S. debt-to-GDP ratio was 100 percent—about where it is today. The United States gradually reduced it during the 1950s and 1960s, and liberals say America can do it again with slightly more taxation.

There are valid points in both positions, but there are also strong rebuttals to both. The policy problem is that a debate framed in this way creates false dichotomies that facilitate not resolution but rhetoric. Debt is inherently neither positive nor negative. Debt's utility is determined by what the borrower does with the money. Debt levels are not automatically too high or too low; what matters to creditors is their trend toward sustainability.

Debt can be ruinous if it is used to finance deficits, and with no plan for paying the debt other than through additional debt. Debt can be productive if it funds projects that produce more than they cost and that pay for themselves over time. Debt-to-GDP ratios can be relatively low, but still troubling, if they are getting higher. Debt-to-GDP ratios can be relatively high and not be a cause for concern if they are getting lower.

▓ The Debt Debate

Framing the debt and deficit debates in these terms raises further questions. What are the proper guidelines for determining whether debt is being used for a desirable purpose and whether debt-to-GDP trends are moving in the right direction? Fortunately, both questions can be answered in a rigorous, nonideological way, without retreating to the rhetoric of conservatives or liberals.

Debt used to finance government spending is acceptable when three conditions are met: the benefits of the spending must be greater than the costs, the government spending must be directed at projects the private sector cannot do on its own, and the overall debt level must be sustainable. These tests must be applied independently, and all must be satisfied. Even if government spending can be shown to produce net benefits, it cannot be justified if private activity can do the job better. When government spending produces net costs, it destroys the stock of wealth in society and can never be justified except in an existential crisis such as war.

Difficulties arise when costs and benefits are not well defined and when ideology substitutes for analysis in the decision-making process. Two cases illustrate these problems—the Internet and the 2009 Obama stimulus.

Government-spending advocates point out that the government financed the early development of the Internet. In fact, the government sponsored ARPANET, a robust message traffic system among large-scale university computers designed to facilitate research collaboration during the Cold War. However, ARPANET's development into today's Internet was advanced by the private sector through the creation of the World Wide Web, the Web browser, and many other innovations. This history shows that certain government spending can be highly beneficial when it jump-starts private-sector innovation. ARPANET had fairly modest ambitions by today's standards, and it was a success. The government did not freeze ARPANET for all time; instead, it made the protocols available to private developers and got out of the way. The Internet is an example of government leaving the job to the private sector.

An example of destructive government spending is the 2009 Obama stimulus plan. The expected benefits were based on erroneous assumptions about so-called Keynesian multipliers. In fact, the Obama stimulus was directed largely at supplementing state and local payrolls for union jobs in government and school administration, many of which are redundant, nonproductive, and wealth-destroying. Much of the rest went to inefficient, nonscalable technologies such as solar panels, wind turbines, and electric cars. Not only did this spending not produce the mythical multiplier, it did not even produce nominal growth equal to nominal spending. The Obama stimulus is an example of government spending that does not pass the cost-benefit test.

An example of a government initiative that meets all tests for acceptable spending is the interstate highway system. In 1956 President Eisenhower championed and Congress authorized the interstate highway system, which cost about $450 billion in today's dollars. The benefits of that system vastly exceeded $450 billion and continue to accrue to this day. It is difficult to argue that the private sector could have produced anything like this matrix of highways; at best, we would have a hodge-podge of toll roads with many areas left unserved. Only government could have completed the project on a nationwide scale, and debt-to-GDP ratios were stable at the time. Thus the interstate highway system passes the three-pronged test of efficient government spending that justifies debt.

Today long-term interest rates are near all-time lows, and the United States could easily borrow $150 billion for seven years at 2.5 percent interest. With that money, the government could, for example, construct a new natural gas pipeline adjacent to the interstate highway system and place natural gas fueling stations at existing facilities. This interstate pipeline could be connected to large natural gas trunk pipelines at key nodes, and the government could then require a ten-year conversion of all interstate trucking from diesel to natural gas.

With this pipeline and fueling station network in place, private companies like Chevron, ExxonMobil, and Ford would then take over the innovation and expansion of natural-gas-powered transportation, a public-to-private handoff as happened after ARPANET. The shift to natural-gas-powered trucks would facilitate the growth of natural-gas-powered automobiles. The demand for natural gas would then boost exploration and production along with related technologies in which the United States excels.

As with the interstate highway system, the results of an interstate natural-gas-fueling system would be transformative. The boost to the economy would come immediately—not from mythical multipliers but from straightforward productive spending. Hundreds of thousands of jobs would be created in the actual pipeline construction, and more jobs would come from the conversion of vehicles from gasoline to natural gas. Dependence on foreign oil would end, and the U.S. trade deficit would evaporate, boosting growth. The environmental benefits are obvious since natural gas burns cleaner than diesel or gasoline.

Will this happen? It is doubtful. Republicans are more focused on debt reduction than on growth, and Democrats are ideologically opposed to all carbon-based energy, including natural gas. The political stars seem aligned against this kind of out-of-the-box solution. However, it remains the case that government debt to finance spending can be acceptable if it passes the three-pronged test of positive returns, no displacement of private-sector efforts, and sustainable debt levels. The third prong is the most problematic today.

■ Sustainable Debt

Another essential question must be asked: Are debt levels sustainable? That, in turn, leads to other questions: How can policy makers know if they are pushing the debt-to-GDP trend in the desired direction? What role does the Fed play in making deficits sustainable and debt affordable?

The relation of Federal Reserve monetary policy to national debt and deficits is fraught with grave risks for the debt-as-money contract. At a primitive level, the Fed actually can monetize any amount of debt the Treasury issues, up to the point of a collapse of confidence in the dollar. The policy issue is one of rules or limitations imposed on the Fed's money-printing ability. What are the guidelines for discretionary monetary policy?

Historically, a gold standard was one way to limit discretion and reveal when monetary policy was off track. Under the classic gold standard, gold outflows to trading partners showed that monetary policy was too easy and tightening was required. The tightening would have a recessionary effect, lower unit labor costs, improve export competitiveness, and once again start the inward flow of physical gold. This process was as self-regulating as an automatic thermostat. The classic gold standard had its problems, but it was better than the next-best system.

In more recent decades, the Taylor Rule—named after its creator, the economist John B. Taylor—was a practical guide for Fed monetary policy. It had the virtue of recursive functions so that data from recent events would feed back into the next policy decision, to produce what network scientists call a path-dependent outcome. The Taylor Rule was one tool in the broader sweep of the sound-dollar standard created by Paul Volcker and Ronald Reagan in the early 1980s. The sound-dollar policy was carried forward through the late 1980s and 1990s in Republican and Democratic administrations by Treasury secretaries as diverse as James Baker and Robert Rubin. If the dollar was not quite as good as gold, at least it maintained its purchasing power as measured by price indexes, and at least it served as an anchor for other countries looking for a monetary reference point.

Today every reference point is gone. There is no gold standard, no dollar standard, and no Taylor Rule. All that remains is what financial writer James Grant calls the "Ph.D. Standard": the conduct of policy by neo-Keynesian, neo-monetarist academics with Ph.D.'s granted by a small number of elite schools.

Rules used by academic policy makers to define sustainable deficits are argued among elite economists and revealed in speeches, papers, and public comments of various kinds. In an environment of deficit spending, one of the most important tools is the primary deficit sustainability (PDS) framework. This analytic framework, which can be expressed as an equation or identity, measures whether national debt and deficits are sustainable, or conversely when the trend in deficits could cause a loss of confidence and rapidly increasing borrowing costs. PDS is a way to tell if America is becoming Greece.

This framework has been used for decades, but its use was crystallized in the current context by economist John Makin, one of the most astute analysts of monetary policy. In 2012 Makin wrestled with the relationship of U.S. debt and deficits to gross domestic product (GDP), using the PDS framework as a guide.

The key factors in PDS are borrowing costs (B), real output (R), inflation (I), taxes (T), and spending (S); together, the BRITS. Real output plus inflation (R + I) is the total value of goods and services produced in the U.S. economy, also called nominal gross domestic product (NGDP). Taxes minus spending (T − S) is called the *primary deficit*. The primary deficit is the excess of what a country spends over what it collects in taxes. In calculating the primary deficit, spending does *not* include interest on the national debt. This is not because interest expense does not matter; it matters a lot. In fact, the whole purpose of the PDS framework is to illuminate the extent to which the United States can afford the interest and ultimately the debt. Interest is excluded from the primary deficit calculation in order to see if the other factors combine in such a way that the interest is affordable. Interest on the debt *is* taken into account in the formula as B, or borrowing costs.

In plain English, U.S. deficits are sustainable if economic output minus interest expense is *greater* than the primary deficit. This means the U.S. economy is paying interest and producing a little "extra" to pay down debt. But if economic output minus interest expense is *less* than the primary deficit, then over time the deficits will overwhelm the economy, and the United States will be headed for a debt crisis, even financial collapse.

To a point, what matters is not the debt and deficit *level* but the *trend* as a percentage of GDP. If the levels are trending down, the situation is manageable, and debt markets will provide time to remain on that path. Sustainability does not mean that deficits must go away; in fact, deficits can grow larger. What matters is that total debt as a percentage of GDP becomes *smaller,* because nominal GDP grows *faster* than deficits plus interest.

Think of nominal GDP as one's personal income and the primary deficit as what gets charged on a credit card. Borrowing costs are interest on the credit card. If personal income increases fast enough to pay the interest on the credit card, with money left over to pay down the balance, this is a manageable situation. However, if one's income is not going up, and *new* debt is piled on after paying the *old* interest, then bankruptcy is just a matter of time.

The PDS framework is an economist's formal expression of the credit card example. If national income can pay the interest on the debt, with enough left over to reduce total debt as a percentage of GDP, then the situation should remain stable. This does not mean that deficits are beneficial, merely that they are affordable. But if there is not enough national income left over after the interest to reduce the debt as a percentage of GDP, and if this condition persists, then the United States will eventually go broke.

Expressed in the form of an equation, sustainability looks like this:

If $(R + I) - B > |T - S|$,

then U.S. deficits are *sustainable.* Conversely,

If $(R + I) - B < |T - S|$,

then U.S. deficits are *not sustainable.*

The PDS/BRITS framework and the credit card example encapsulate the recent drama, posturing, and rhetoric of the great economic debates in the United States. When Democrats and Republicans fight over taxes, spending, deficits, debt ceilings, and the elusive grand bargain, these politicians are really arguing over the relative sizes of the BRITS.

PDS by itself does not explain which actions to take or what ideal policy should be. What it does is allow one to understand the consequences of specific choices. PDS is a device for conducting thought experiments on different policy combinations, and it acts as the bridge connecting fiscal and monetary solutions. The BRITS are a Rosetta stone for understanding how all of these policy choices interact.

For example, one way to improve debt sustainability is to increase taxes. If taxes are larger, the primary deficit is smaller, so a given amount of GDP will bring the United States closer to the sustainability condition. Alternatively, if taxes are held steady but spending is cut, then the primary deficit also shrinks, producing a move toward sustainability. A blend of spending cuts and tax increases produces the same beneficial results. Another way to move toward sustainability is to increase real growth. An increase in real growth means more funds are available, after interest expense, to reduce debt as a percentage of GDP.

There are also ways for the Federal Reserve to affect the PDS factors. The Fed can use financial repression to keep a lid on borrowing costs. Lower borrowing costs have the same impact as higher real growth in terms of increasing the amount of GDP remaining after interest expense. Importantly, the Fed can cause inflation, which increases *nominal* growth, even in the absence of *real* growth. Nominal growth minus borrowing costs is the left side of the PDS equation. Inflation increases the funds that are left over after interest expense, which also helps to reduce the debt as a percentage of GDP.

These potential policy choices in the PDS framework each involve a change in one BRITS component and assume the other components are unchanged, but the real world is more complex. Changes in one BRITS component can cause changes in another, which can then amplify or negate the desired effect of the original change. Democrats and Republicans disagree not only about higher taxes and less spending but also about the impact of these policy choices on the other BRITS. Democrats believe that taxes can be increased without hurting growth, while Republicans believe the opposite. Democrats believe that inflation can be helpful in a depression, while Republicans believe that inflation will lead to higher borrowing costs that will worsen the situation.

The result of these disagreements is political stalemate and policy dysfunction. The political stalemate has played out in a long series of debates and quick fixes, beginning with the August 2011 debt ceiling debacle, continuing through the January 2013 fiscal cliff drama, and then the spending sequester and debt ceiling showdowns in late 2013 and early 2014.

The PDS can be used to quantify trends, but it cannot forecast the exact level at which a trend becomes unsustainable; that is the job of bond markets. The bond markets are driven by investors who risk money every day betting on the future path of interest rates, inflation, and deficits. These markets may be tolerant of political stalemate for long periods of time and give policy makers the benefit of a doubt. But at the end of the day, the bond markets can render a harsh judgment. If the United States is on an unsustainable path as revealed by PDS, and that downward path is accelerating with no end in sight, then the markets may suddenly and unexpectedly cause interest rates to spike. The interest-rate spike makes PDS less sustainable, which makes interest rates higher still. A feedback loop is created between progressively worsening PDS results and progressively higher rates. Eventually the system can collapse into outright default or hyperinflation.

▨ Fed Policy and the Money Contract

Today the Federal Reserve confronts a daunting mixture of unforgiving math, anxious markets, and dysfunctional politics. The U.S. economy is like a sick patient, with politicians as the concerned relatives at the patient's bedside arguing over what to do next. The PDS framework is the thermometer that reveals whether the patient's condition is deteriorating, and bond markets are the undertaker, waiting to carry the patient to her grave. Into this melodramatic mise-en-scène walks Dr. Fed. The doctor may not have the medicine needed to provide a cure, but newly printed money is like morphine for the economy. It can ease the pain, as long as it does not kill the patient.

As the proprietor of the debt-as-money contract with the American people and creditors around the world, the Fed must not be seen to dishonor the trust placed in it by holders of Fed notes. From the perspective of the international monetary system, the only scenario worse than a collapse of confidence in Treasury bonds is a collapse of confidence in the dollar itself. Debt, deficits, and the dollar are three strands in a knot that secures the world financial system. By issuing unlimited dollars to prop up Treasury debt, the Fed risks unraveling the knot and undoing the dollar confidence game. The difference between success and failure for the Fed is a fine line.

In strict terms, government finance can be thought of as two large circles in a classic Venn diagram. One circle is the world of monetary policy controlled by the Federal Reserve. The other circle is fiscal policy, consisting of taxes and spending, controlled by Congress and the White House. As in a Venn diagram, the two circles have an area of intersection. That area is inflation. If the Fed can create enough inflation, the real value of debt will melt away, and spending can continue without tax increases. The trick is to increase inflation without increasing borrowing costs, since higher borrowing costs increase debt. The PDS framework shows how this can be done.

To understand this, it is useful to consider conditions revealed by PDS using model inputs. An ideal situation for the Fed consists of 4 percent real growth, 1 percent inflation, 2 percent borrowing costs (measured as a percentage of GDP), and a 2 percent primary deficit (also measured as a percentage of GDP). Plugging these numbers into the PDS framework results in:

$$(4 + 1) - 2 > 2, \text{ or}$$

$$3 > 2$$

In other words, real growth plus inflation, minus interest expense, is greater than the primary deficit, which means that debt as a percentage of GDP is *declining*. This is the condition of debt sustainability with high real growth and low inflation.

Unfortunately the example above is not what the Fed is confronting in markets today. Borrowing costs are low, at 1.5 percent of GDP, which helps the equation relative to the first example; but some other terms are *worse* for sustainability. Real growth is closer to 2.5 percent, and the primary deficit is about 4 percent (inflation is the same at about 1 percent). Plugging these actual numbers into the PDS framework results in:

$$(2.5 + 1) - 1.5 < 4, \text{ or}$$

$$2 < 4$$

In this example, real growth plus inflation minus interest expense is *less* than the primary deficit, which means that debt as a percentage of GDP is *increasing*. This is the unsustainable condition. Again, what matters in this model is not the *level* but the *trend,* as played out in the dynamics of the BRITS and their interactions. Contrary to the oft-cited Carmen Reinhart and Kenneth Rogoff thesis, the absolute level of debt to GDP is not what triggers a crisis; it is the trend toward unsustainability.

One beauty of PDS is that the math is simple. Starting with the identity as 2 < 4 means that to achieve sustainability, either the 2 must go up, the 4 must go down, or both. Real growth in the United States today is stuck at 2.5 percent, partly due to policy uncertainty. The U.S. primary deficit may decrease to 3 percent because of the 2013 tax increases and spending sequester, but otherwise the tax and spending stalemate seems set to continue. The math is basic but rigid: if real growth is 2.5 percent, the primary deficit is 3 percent, and borrowing costs won't go lower, then the *only* path to sustainability is for the Fed to *raise inflation above borrowing costs*. Of course, inflation tends to increase borrowing costs, a good example of feedback loops within the BRITS.

For example, the Fed could cap borrowing costs at 2 percent and raise inflation to 3 percent. With all of these new inputs, the PDS framework results in:

$(2.5 + 3) - 2 > 3$, or

$3.5 > 3$

This result satisfies the condition for sustainability, and bond markets should not panic but show patience and give the United States more time to increase real growth, reduce the primary deficit, or both.

Through PDS and BRITS, it becomes possible to unravel the acrimony, political dysfunction, and televised shouting matches. The policy solution is unavoidable. In the absence of higher real growth, *either politicians must reduce deficits, or the Fed must produce inflation.* There is no other way to avoid a debt crisis.

Political success in reducing deficits so far has been modest and insufficient, and increases in real growth continue to disappoint expectations. Therefore, the burden of avoiding a debt crisis falls on the Fed in the form of higher inflation through monetary policy. Inflation is a prominent solution in the PDS framework despite the unfairness this imposes on small savers.

Savers may have few alternatives, but bond buyers have many. The issue is whether bond buyers will tolerate the capital erosion that comes from inflation. This condition in which inflation is higher than the nominal interest rate produces *negative real rates.* For example, a nominal 2 percent interest rate with 3 percent inflation produces a real interest rate of *negative* 1 percent. In normal markets, bond buyers would demand higher interest rates to offset inflation, but these are not normal markets. The bond market may want higher nominal rates, but the Fed won't permit it. The Fed enforces negative real rates through financial repression.

The theory of financial repression was explained incisively by Carmen Reinhart and M. Belen Sbrancia in their 2011 paper "The Liquidation of Government Debt." The key to financial repression is the use of law and policy to prevent interest rates from exceeding the rate of inflation. This strategy can be carried out in many different ways. In the 1950s and 1960s it was done through bank regulation that made it illegal for banks to pay more than a stated amount on savings deposits. Meanwhile the Fed engineered a mild form of inflation, slightly higher than the bank deposit rate, which eroded those savings. It was executed with such subtlety that savers barely noticed. Besides, savers had few alternatives, as this was a time before money-market accounts and 401(k)s. The 1929 stock market crash was still a living memory for many, and most investors considered equities too speculative. Money in the bank was a primary form of wealth preservation. As long as the Fed did not steal the money too quickly or too overtly, the system remained stable.

This condition of modest negative real rates for a sustained period of time also worked its wonders on the debt-to-GDP ratio. During this golden age of financial repression, national debt declined from over 100 percent of GDP in 1945 to less than 30 percent by the early 1970s.

By the late 1960s, the game of financial repression was over, and inflation became too prevalent to ignore. The theft of wealth from traditional savers had become painful. Merrill Lynch responded in the 1970s with the creation of higher-yielding money-market funds, and others quickly followed. Mutual fund families like Fidelity made stock ownership easy. Investors broke free of financial repression, left the banks behind, and headed for the new frontier of risky assets.

The problem confronting the Fed today is how to use financial repression to cap interest rates without the benefit of 1950s-style regulated bank deposit rates and captive savers. The Fed's goal is the same as in the 1950s—higher inflation and a cap on rates, but tactics have evolved. Inflation comes from money printing, and rate caps come from bond buying. Conveniently for the Fed, money printing and bond buying are two sides of the same coin, because the Fed buys bonds with printed money.

The name for this type of operation is quantitative easing (QE). The first of several QE programs commenced in 2008, and over $2 trillion of new money was printed by the end of 2012. By early 2014, printing was proceeding at the rate of over $1 trillion of new money per year.

Money that sits in banks as excess reserves does not produce inflation. Price inflation emerges only if consumers or businesses borrow and spend the printed money. From the Fed's perspective, the manipulation of consumer behavior to encourage borrowing and spending is a critical policy component. The Fed has chosen to manipulate consumers with both carrots and sticks. The stick is an inflation shock, intended to scare consumers into spending before prices go up. The carrot is the negative real interest rate, designed to encourage borrowing money to buy risky assets such as stocks and housing. The Fed will ensure negative real rates by using its own bond buying power, and that of the commercial banks if necessary, to suppress nominal interest rates.

In order to make the carrots and sticks effective, at least 3 percent inflation is needed. At that level, real interest rates will be negative, and consumers should be sufficiently worried to start spending. These powerful inducements to lend and spend are designed to grow nominal GDP at a rate closer to historical trends. Over time the Fed hopes this growth becomes self-sustaining, so it can then reverse policy and let nominal GDP turn into real GDP through an accelerating real growth process. The Fed is using policies of zero interest rates and quantitative easing to reach its goals of higher inflation and negative real rates.

Banks can make significant profits by borrowing at the zero short-term rates offered by the Fed and lending for longer terms at higher rates. But this type of lending can produce losses if short-term rates rise quickly while the banks are stuck with the long-term assets, such as mortgages and corporate debt. The Fed's solution to this problem is *forward guidance*. In effect, the Fed tells the banks not to worry about short-term rates rising until well into the future.

In March 2009 the Fed issued an announcement that short-term rates would remain at zero for "an extended period." In August 2011 the "extended period" phrase was dropped and a specific date of "mid-2013" was announced as the earliest on which rates would increase. By January 2012 this date had been pushed back to "late 2014." Finally, in September 2012 the Fed announced that the earliest that rates would increase was "mid-2015."

Even this assurance was not enough for all banks and investors. There was concern that the Fed might bring the rate hike date forward just as easily as it had pushed it back. The criteria on which the Fed might change its mind were unclear, and so the impact of forward guidance was muted. A debate raged within the Fed about whether forward guidance should be converted from an ever-changing series of dates to a set of hard numeric goals that were more easily observed.

This debate was captured in historic and analytic detail in a paper presented by Michael Woodford of Columbia University at the Fed's Jackson Hole Symposium at the end of August 2012. While Woodford's argument is nuanced, it boils down to one word—*commitment*. His point was that forward guidance is far more effective in changing behavior today if that guidance is clear and framed in such a way that the central bank will not repudiate the guidance in the future:

> A . . . reason why forward guidance may be needed . . . is in order to facilitate *commitment* on the part of the central bank. . . . In practice, the most logical way to make such commitment achievable and credible is by publicly stating the commitment, in a way that is sufficiently unambiguous to make it embarrassing for policymakers to simply ignore the existence of the commitment when making decisions at a later time.

The impact of Woodford's tour de force on Fed thinking was immediate. On December 12, 2012, just three months after the Jackson Hole Symposium, the Fed scrapped its practice of using target dates for forward guidance and substituted strict numeric goals. In customary Fedspeak, the new goals were described as follows:

> In particular, the committee decided to keep the target range for the federal funds rate at 0 to 1/4 percent and currently anticipates that this exceptionally low range for the federal funds rate will be appropriate at least as long as the unemployment rate remains above 6-1/2 percent, inflation between one and two years ahead is projected to be no more than a half percentage point above the Committee's 2 percent longer-run goal, and longer-term inflation expectations continue to be well anchored.

The Fed is now publicly wedded to a set of numeric goals and committed to zero rates until those goals are achieved and perhaps even longer.

Three aspects of the Fed's commitment stand out. The first is that the numeric targets of 6.5 percent unemployment and 2.5 percent inflation are thresholds, not triggers. The Fed did not say that it would raise rates *when* those levels were hit; it said it would not raise rates *before* those levels were hit. This leaves ample room to continue easy money even if unemployment falls to 6 percent or inflation rises to 3 percent. Second, the Fed said *both* targets would have to be satisfied before it raised rates, not just one or the other. This means that if unemployment is 7 percent, the Fed can continue its easy-money policy even if inflation rises to 3 percent or higher. Finally, the Fed's inflation target is based on *projected* inflation, not actual inflation. This means that if actual inflation is 4 percent, it can continue with easy money so long as its subjective inflation projection is 2.5 percent or less.

This new policy is a brilliant finesse by the Fed. Superficially it pays lip service to Woodford's recommendation for commitment to unambiguous goals; but in reality the goals are slippery and ill defined. No one knows if the Fed will slam on the brakes at 3 percent inflation, if unemployment is still 7 percent. No one knows how much time will elapse between the end of money printing and a rate increase. Yet the Fed's new policy is consistent with its hidden 3 percent inflation goal under the carrots-and-sticks approach. The Fed can justify higher inflation if its employment goal is unmet. It can justify higher inflation if projected inflation is lower. It can justify higher inflation in all events because the numeric targets are thresholds and not triggers. The new policy puts no real constraints on higher inflation.

The PDS and BRITS framework and the Fed's new policies converge around the specter of inflation, which lurks behind the academic theories and public pronouncements. Low borrowing costs and higher inflation are the only ways the Fed can improve deficit sustainability. Financial repression lowers borrowing costs, and quantitative easing can create higher inflation if the markets believe it will continue. The Fed's December 2012 policy is a muddled version of Woodford's recommendations. The Fed is pretending to have numeric goals while preserving the degrees of freedom it needs to reach any inflation target it finds necessary, but that involves a certain sleight of hand.

The Fed's form of theft from savers has a name: it's called *money illusion* by economists. The idea is that money printing on its own cannot create real growth but can create the illusion of growth by increasing nominal prices and nominal GDP. Eventually the illusion will be shattered, as it was in the late 1970s, but it can persist for a decade or more before inflation emerges with a lag and steals the perceived gains.

While the Fed's goals of higher inflation and rising nominal GDP are clear, there is good reason to believe the Fed will fail to achieve these goals and may even produce disastrous consequences for the United States by trying. The Fed's own staff have expressed reservations about whether forward guidance works at all in the time horizons the Fed is using. Prominent economist Charles Goodhart has said that nominal GDP targeting is "a thinly disguised way of aiming for higher inflation" and that "no one has yet designed a way to make it workable."

Perhaps the most compelling critique of the flaws in nominal GDP targeting and the inflation embedded within it comes from inside the Fed board of governors itself. In February 2013 Fed governor Jeremy Stein offered a highly detailed critique of the Fed's easy-money policy and obliquely pointed to its greatest flaw: that increased turnover is not the only channel money creation can find, and that other channels include asset bubbles and financial engineering.

Stein's thesis is that a low-interest-rate environment will induce a search for higher yields, which can take many forms. The most obvious form is a bidding up of the price of risky assets such as stocks and housing. This can be observed directly. Less obvious are asset-liability mismatches, where financial institutions borrow short and lend long on a leveraged basis to capture a spread. Even more opaque are collateral swaps, where a financial institution such as Citibank pledges junk bonds to a counterparty in exchange for Treasury securities on an overnight basis, then uses those Treasury securities as collateral on a higher-yielding off-balance-sheet derivative. Such transactions set the stage for a run on Citibank or others if the short-term asset providers suddenly want their securities back and Citibank must dump other assets at fire-sale prices to pay up. The invisible web of counterparty risk increases systemic risk—and moves the system closer to a replay of the Panic of 2008 on a larger scale.

The scenarios sketched by Stein would rapidly undo the Fed's efforts if such events came to pass. A market panic stemming from excessive leverage and risk taking occurring so soon after the Panic of 2008 would destroy the Fed's efforts to lure consumers back into the lending and spending game of the early 2000s.

Stein's paper has been taken to say that Fed must end QE sooner rather than later to avoid the buildup of hidden risk in financial institutions. But there is another interpretation. Stein himself warns that if banks do not take the hint and curtail risky financial engineering, the Fed might force them to do so with increased regulation. The Federal Reserve has life-and-death powers over banks in areas such as loss reserves, dividend policies, stress tests, acquisitions, capital adequacy, and more. Bank managers would be foolhardy to defy the Fed in the areas Stein highlights. Stein's paper suggests a partial return to an older kind of financial repression through regulation.

The Fed's manipulations have left it in the position of a tightrope walker with no net, one who must exert all his energy in a concentrated effort just to keep moving forward, even as the slightest slip or unexpected gust could cause a catastrophic end to the enterprise. The Fed must promote inflation (while not acknowledging it) and must inflate asset prices (without causing bubbles to burst). It must exude confidence while having no idea whether its policies will work or when they might end.

In short, the Fed is caught between its roles as proprietor of the debt-as-money contract and as the singular savior of sovereign debt. It is unlikely to succeed in only one of these roles; it shall succeed, or fail, at both.

CHAPTER 8

CENTRAL BANK OF THE WORLD

> The optimum currency area is the world.
>
> Robert A. Mundell
> Recipient, Nobel Prize in Economics

> I haven't read the Governor's proposal. . . . But as I under-
> stand . . . it's a proposal designed to increase the use of the
> IMF's special drawing rights, . . . ah . . . and . . . ah . . . we're ac-
> tually quite open to that.
>
> Timothy Geithner
> U.S. Treasury secretary
> in reply to a reporter's question about a Chinese government proposal
> March 25, 2009

> The IMF has refined, repurposed, and restocked its toolkit.
>
> Christine Lagarde
> IMF managing director
> September 19, 2013

■ One World

To meet Dr. Min Zhu is to see the future of global finance. He stands out in a crowd, his six-foot-four-inch frame reminding financiers of the late twentieth century's most powerful bankers, Paul Volcker and Walter Wriston, who dominated a room not just with intellect but with physical presence. Min Zhu belongs not to the twentieth century but to the twenty-first, and it is difficult to name anyone who better personifies the conflicting forces—east versus west, gold versus paper, state versus markets—coursing through the world today.

Min Zhu is the IMF's deputy managing director, among the most senior positions in the IMF, reporting directly to the managing director, Christine Lagarde. The IMF is one of the key institutions established at the 1944 Bretton Woods Conference, which created the framework for the international monetary system in the aftermath of the Great Depression as the Second World War drew to a close. Since its founding, the IMF has been the great enigma of global finance.

The IMF is quite public about its operations and objectives. At the same time, it is little understood even by experts, in part because of the unique role it performs and the highly technical jargon it uses in doing so. Specialized university training at institutions like the School of Advanced International Studies in Washington, D.C., is a typical admission ticket to a position at the IMF. This combination of openness and opaqueness is disarming; the IMF is transparently nontransparent.

The IMF's mission has repeatedly morphed over the decades since Bretton Woods. In the 1950s and 1960s, it was the caretaker of the fixed-exchange-rate gold standard and a swing lender to countries experiencing balance-of-payments difficulties. In the 1970s, it was a forum for the transition from the gold standard to floating exchange rates, engaging in massive sales of gold at U.S. insistence to help suppress the price. In the 1980s and 1990s, the IMF was like a doctor who made house calls, dispensing bad medicine in the form of incompetent advice to emerging economies. This role ended abruptly with blood in the streets of Jakarta and Seoul and scores killed as a result of the IMF's mishandling of the 1997–98 global financial crisis. The early 2000s were a period of drift, during which the IMF's mandate was unclear and experts suggested that the institution had outlived its usefulness. The IMF reemerged in 2008 as the de facto secretariat and operating arm of the G20, coordinating policy responses to the financial panic that year. Today the IMF has capitalized on its newfound role as global lender of last resort: it has become the central bank of the world.

Min Zhu holds the highest-ranking position ever held by a Chinese citizen at the IMF, the World Bank, or the Bank for International Settlements, the international monetary system's three multilateral pillars. His career personifies China's financial rise *in nuce*. He graduated in 1982 from Fudan University in Shanghai, among the most prestigious schools in China. He obtained a Ph.D. in economics in the United States, before moving through various jobs at the World Bank and the international division of the Bank of China. In 2009 he became China's central bank deputy governor. In May 2010 he was handpicked by Dominique Strauss-Kahn, then IMF chief, to be his special adviser. Finally in 2011 Strauss-Kahn's successor, Christine Lagarde, selected him to be the IMF's deputy managing director.

Zhu has a relaxed demeanor and good sense of humor, but when pressed hard on a policy he feels strongly about, he can suddenly turn strident, as if he were lecturing students rather than engaging in debate. His slightly accented English is excellent, but his soft-spoken style is difficult to hear at times. His background is unique: he has operated at the highest levels at a central bank under Chinese Communist Party control and at the highest levels of the IMF, an institution ostensibly committed to free markets and open capital accounts.

Zhu travels continually on official IMF business, for university lectures, and to attend prestigious international conferences such as the Davos World Economic Forum. Private bankers and government officials eagerly seek his advice at the IMF's Washington, D.C., headquarters and on the sidelines of G20 summits, while Communist Party Central Politburo members do the same on his periodic trips to Beijing. From East to West, from communism to capitalism, Min Zhu straddles the contending forces in world finance today, with a foot in both camps.

No one, including central bank governors and Madame Lagarde herself, is more aware than Zhu of the international monetary system's hidden truths, which makes his global economic and financial views especially significant. He is an adamant globalist, reflecting his position between the worlds of state capitalism and free markets. He does not think of the world in traditional categories of north-south or east-west but rather as country clusters based on economic factors, supply-chain linkages, and historical bonds. These clusters intersect and overlap. For example, Austria belongs to a European manufacturing cluster that includes Germany and Italy, but it is also part of a central European clutch of former Austro-Hungarian Empire nations, including Hungary and Slovenia. As that group's leader, Austria is a "gatekeeper" that gives the Austro-Hungarian group access to the European manufacturing cluster through a nexus of subcontracting, supply chains, and bank lending. These linkages might, for example, facilitate sales by a Slovenian auto parts manufacturer to Fiat in Italy. The Slovenian-Italian link runs through gatekeeper Austria.

This paradigm of clusters, overlaps, and gatekeepers results in unexpected alignments. Zhu places South America in a China–western hemisphere supply-chain cluster, a point also made by Riordan Roett, a leading scholar of Latin American economics. Zhu's view is that U.S. economic hegemony stops at the Panama Canal, while most of South America is now properly regarded as a Chinese sphere of influence.

Zhu's cluster paradigm is of more than academic interest because it is beginning to have a direct impact on IMF policy as it relates to surveillance of its 188 member countries. The paradigm provides a basis for the study of national policy "spillover" effects as labeled by the IMF. The IMF treats spillovers in the same way that bank risk managers talk about contagion—the rapid uncontrolled transmission of collapse from one market to another through a dense web of counterparty obligations and collateral pledges, in a blind stampede for liquidity in a financial panic. Spillovers happen within clusters when national economies are tightly linked, and between clusters when gatekeepers are in distress. Min Zhu is helping the IMF to develop a working risk-management model based on complexity, one that is far more advanced than those used by individual central banks or private financial institutions.

⬛ Updating Keynes

Zhu is showing traditional Keynesians how their model of policy action, in conjunction with an individual or corporate response, is obsolete. This two-part action-response model must be modified to place financial intermediation between the policy maker and the economic agent. This distinction is illustrated as follows:

Classic Keynesian Model
Fiscal/Monetary Policy > Individual/Corporate Response

New IMF Model
Fiscal/Monetary Policy > Financial Intermediary > Individual/
Corporate Response

While financial institutions in earlier decades had been predictable and passive players in policy transmission to individual economic actors, today's financial intermediaries are more active and materially mute or amplify policy makers' wishes. Private banks may use securitization, derivatives, and other forms of leverage to greatly increase the impact of policy easing, and they can tighten lending standards or migrate to safe assets like U.S. Treasury notes to diminish the impact. Banks are also the main transmission channels for spillover effects. Zhu makes the point that Keynesian analysis fails in part because it has not fully incorporated the role of banks into its functions.

Clustering, spillover, and financial transmission are the three theoretical legs supporting the platform from which the IMF surveys the international monetary system. New concepts of this kind can percolate in university economics departments for decades before they have practical effect. Despite a preponderance of Ph.D.'s in its ranks, the IMF is not a university. It is a powerful institution with the ability either to preserve or condemn regimes through its policy decisions on lending and the conditionality attached. Zhu's paradigm offers a glimpse of the IMF's plans: clustering implies that economic linkages are more important than sovereignty. Spillover effects mean top-down control is needed to contain risk. Financial transmission suggests that banks are the key nodes in the exercise of control. In a nutshell, the IMF seeks to control finance, to contain risk, and to condition economic development on a global basis.

This one-world mission requires assistance from the most talented and politically powerful players available. The IMF executive suite is an exquisitely balanced microcosm of the global economy. In addition to Min Zhu and managing director Christine Lagarde, the IMF top management includes David Lipton from the United States, Naoyuki Shinohara from Japan, and Nemat Shafik from Egypt. Group diversity is more than an exercise in multinationalism. Lagarde represents the European interest, Min Zhu the Chinese, Lipton the American, Shinohara the Japanese, and

Shafik the developing economies. The top five managers at the IMF, seated around a conference table, effectively speak for the world.

David Lipton's is the single most powerful voice, more powerful than Christine Lagarde's, because the United States has a veto over all important actions by the IMF. This doesn't mean Lipton doesn't play for the team; on many issues the United States and the IMF see eye to eye—including the dollar's eventual replacement as the global reserve currency. Lipton's veto power means that changes will take place at a tempo dictated by any quid pro quo that the United States demands.

Lipton is one of numerous Robert Rubin protégés, who include Timothy Geithner, Jack Lew, Michael Froman, Larry Summers, and Gary Gensler. These men have for years controlled U.S. economic strategy in the international arena. Robert Rubin was Treasury secretary from 1995 to 1999, after having worked several years in the Clinton White House as National Economic Council director. Before joining the U.S. government, Rubin was Goldman Sachs co-chairman; he worked at Citigroup in the chairman's office from 1999 to 2009, and he briefly served as Citigroup chairman at the start of the financial markets collapse in 2007. Lipton, Froman, Geithner, Summers, and Gensler all worked for Rubin at the U.S. Treasury in the late 1990s, Lew at the White House. Lipton, Lew, and Froman later followed Rubin to Citigroup, while Summers later worked as a Citigroup consultant.

After being vetted and groomed in midlevel positions in the 1990s, this bland bureaucratic team was carefully placed and promoted within the White House, Treasury, IMF, and elsewhere in the 2000s, to ensure Rubin's web of influence and role as the de facto godfather of global finance. Geithner is the former Treasury secretary and former president of the Federal Reserve Bank of New York. Lew currently holds the Treasury secretary position. Froman was a powerful behind-the-scenes figure in the White House National Economic Council and National Security Council from 2009 through 2013 and then the U.S. trade representative. Larry Summers is a former Treasury secretary and chaired President Obama's National Economic Council. During his White House years, Froman was the U.S. "sherpa" at G20 meetings, sometimes seen whispering in the president's ear just as a key policy dispute was about to be ironed out with Chinese president Hu Jintao or another world leader.

From 2009 through 2013, Gensler was chairman of the Commodity Futures Trading Commission, the agency that regulates Treasury bond and gold futures trading.

The members of the Rubin clique are extraordinary in the incompetence they displayed during their years in public and private service, and in the financial devastation they left in their wake. Rubin and his subordinate and successor, Larry Summers, promoted the two most financially destructive legislative changes in the past century: Glass-Steagall repeal in 1999, which allowed banks to operate like hedge funds; and derivatives regulation repeal in 2000, which opened the door to massive hidden leverage by banks. Geithner, while at the New York Fed from 2003 to 2008, was oblivious to the unsafe and unsound banking practices under his direct supervision, which led to the subprime mortgage collapse in 2007 and the Panic of 2008. Froman, Lipton, and Lew were all at Citigroup along with Rubin and contributed to catastrophic failures in risk management that led to the once-proud bank's collapse and its takeover by the U.S. government in 2008, with over fifty thousand jobs lost at Citigroup alone. Gensler was instrumental in the 2002 passage of Sarbanes-Oxley legislation, which has done much to stifle capital formation and job creation in the years since. He was also on watch at the Commodity Futures Trading Commission in 2012 during the catastrophic collapse of MF Global, a bond and gold broker. Recently Gensler has shown better sense, calling for tougher derivatives regulation.

The lost wealth and personal hardship resulting from the Rubin clique's policies are incalculable, yet their economic influence continues unabated. Today Rubin still minds the global store from his seat as cochairman of the nonprofit Council on Foreign Relations. David Lipton, the Rubin protégé par excellence, with the lowest public profile of the group, is now powerfully placed in the IMF executive suite, at a critical juncture in the international financial system's evolution.

The Rubin web of influence is not a conspiracy. True conspiracies rarely involve more than a few individuals because they continually run the risk of betrayal, disclosure, or blunders. A large group like the Rubin clique actually welcomes conspiracy claims because they are easy to rebut, allowing the insiders to get back to work in the quiet, quasi-anonymous way they prefer. The Rubin web is more a fuzzy network of like-minded individuals with a shared belief in the superiority of elite thought and with faith in their coterie's capacity to act in the world's best interests. They exercise global control not in the blunt, violent manner of Hitler, Stalin, or Mao but in the penumbra of institutions like the IMF, behind a veneer of bland names and benign mission statements. In fact, the IMF's ability to topple a regime by withholding finance in a crisis is no less real than the power of Stalin's KGB or Mao's Red Guards.

The executive team at the IMF holds the view, more gimlet-eyed than any central bank's, that the international monetary system is severely impaired. Because of massive money printing since 2008, a new collapse could emerge at any time, playing out not just with failures of financial institutions or sovereigns but with a loss of confidence in the U.S. dollar itself. Institutional memory reaches back to the dollar crash of October 1978, reversed only with Fed chairman Paul Volcker's strong-dollar policies beginning in August 1979 and IMF issuance of its world money, the special drawing right or SDR, in stages from 1979 to 1981. The dollar gained strength in the decades that followed, but the IMF learned how fragile confidence in the dollar could be when U.S. policy was negligently managed.

Min Zhu sees these risks as well, even though he was a college student during the last dollar collapse. He knows that if the dollar collapses again, China has by far the most to lose, given its role as the world's largest external holder of U.S.-dollar-denominated debt. Zhu believes the world is in a true depression, the worst since the 1930s. He is characteristically blunt about the reasons for it; he says the problems in developed economies are not cyclical—they are structural.

Economists publicly disagree about whether the current economic malaise is cyclical or structural. A cyclical downturn is viewed as temporary, a phase that can be remedied with stimulus spending of the classic Keynesian kind. A structural downturn, by contrast, is embedded and lasts indefinitely unless adjustments in key factors—such as labor costs, labor mobility, taxes, regulatory burdens, and other public policies—are made. In the United States, the Federal Reserve and Congress have acted as if the U.S. output gap, the difference between potential and actual growth, is temporary and cyclical. This reasoning suits most policy makers and politicians because it avoids the need to make hard decisions about public policy.

Zhu cuts through this myopia. "Central bankers like to say the problem is mostly cyclical and partly structural," he recently said. "I say to them it's mostly structural and partly cyclical. But actually, it's structural." The implication is that a structural problem requires structural, not monetary, solutions.

The IMF is currently confronted with a full plate of contradictions. IMF economists such as José Viñals have warned repeatedly about excessive risk taking by banks, but the IMF has no regulatory authority over banks in its member countries. Anemic global growth gives rise to calls for stimulus-style policies, but stimulus will not work in the face of structural impediments to growth. Any stimulus effort requires more government spending, but spending involves more debt at a time when sovereign debt crises are acute. Christine Lagarde calls for short-term stimulus combined with long-term fiscal consolidation. But markets do not trust politicians' long-term commitments. There is scant appetite for benefit cuts, even by countries on the brink of collapse like Greece. Proposed solutions are all either politically infeasible or economically dubious.

Min Zhu's new paradigm points the way out of this bind. His clustering and gatekeeper analysis suggests that policies should be global, not national, and his spillover analysis suggests that more direct global bank regulation is needed to contain crises. The specter of the sovereign debt crisis suggests the urgency for new liquidity sources, bigger than those that central banks can provide, the next time a liquidity crisis strikes. The logic leads quickly from one world, to one bank, to one currency for the planet. The combination of Christine Lagarde's charismatic leadership, Min Zhu's new paradigm, and David Lipton's opaque power have positioned the IMF for its greatest role yet.

■ One Bank

The Federal Reserve's status as a central bank has long been obvious, but in its origins, from 1909 to 1913, following the Panic of 1907, supporters went to great lengths to disguise the fact that the proposed institution was a central bank. The most conspicuous part of this exercise is the name itself, the Federal Reserve. It is not called the Bank of the United States of America, as the Bank of England and the Bank of Japan proclaim themselves. Nor does the name contain the key phrase "central bank" in the style of the European Central Bank.

The obfuscation was much by design. The American people had rejected central banks twice before. The original central bank, the Bank of the United States chartered by Congress in 1791, was closed in 1811 after its twenty-year charter expired. A Second Bank of the United States, also a central bank, existed from 1817 to 1836, but its charter was also allowed to expire in the midst of acrimonious debate between supporters and opponents. From 1836 to 1913, a period of great prosperity and invention, the United States had no central bank. Well aware of this history and the American people's deep suspicion of central banks, the Federal Reserve's architects, principally Senator Nelson Aldrich of Rhode Island, were careful to disguise their intentions by adopting an anodyne name.

Likewise, the IMF is best understood as a de facto central bank of the world, despite the fact that the phrase "central bank" does not appear in its name. The test of central bank status is not the name but the purpose. A central bank has three primary roles: it employs leverage, it makes loans, and it creates money. Its ability to perform these functions allows it to act as a lender of last resort in a crisis. Since 2008, the IMF has been doing all three in a rapidly expanding way.

A key difference between a central bank and ordinary banks is that a central bank performs these three functions for other banks, rather than for public customers such as individuals and corporations. Buried in the IMF's Articles of Agreement, its 123-page governing document, is a provision that states, "Each member shall deal with the Fund only through its . . . central bank . . . or other similar fiscal agency, and the Fund shall deal only with or through the same agencies." According to its charter, then, the IMF is to function as the world's central bank, a fact carefully disguised by nomenclature and by the pose of IMF officials as mere international bureaucrats dispensing dispassionate technical assistance to nations in need.

The IMF's central-bank-style lending role is the easiest to discern of its functions. It has been the IMF's mission from its beginnings in the late 1940s and is one still trumpeted today. This function grew at a time when most major currencies had fixed exchange rates to the dollar and when countries had closed capital accounts. When trade deficits or capital flight arose, causing balance-of-payments problems, countries could not resort to a devaluation quick fix unless they could show the IMF that the problems were structural and persistent. In those cases, the IMF might approve devaluation. More typically, the IMF acted as a swing lender, providing liquidity to the deficit country for a time, typically three to five years, in order for that country to make policy changes necessary to improve its export competitiveness. The IMF functioned for national economies the way a credit card works for an individual who temporarily needs to borrow for expenses but plans to repay from a future paycheck.

Structural changes required by the IMF in exchange for the loan might include labor market reforms, fiscal discipline to reduce inflation, or lower unit labor costs, all aimed at making the country more competitive in world markets. Once the adjustments took hold, the deficits would then turn to surpluses, and the IMF loans would be repaid. However, that theory seldom worked smoothly in practice, and as trade deficits, budget deficits, and inflation persisted in certain member nations, devaluations were permitted. While devaluation can improve competitiveness, it can also impose large losses on investors in local markets, who relied on attractive exchange rates to the dollar to make their initial investments. On the other hand, if it so chooses, the IMF can make loans to help countries avoid devaluation and thereby protect investors such as JPMorgan Chase, Goldman Sachs, and their favored clients.

Today the IMF website touts loans to countries such as Yemen, Kosovo, and Jamaica as examples of its positive role in economic development. But such loans are window dressing, and the amounts are trivial compared to the IMF's primary lending operation, which is to prop up the euro. As of May 2013, 45 percent of all IMF loans and commitments were extended to just four countries—Ireland, Portugal, Greece, and Cyprus—as part of the euro bailout. Another 46 percent of loans and commitments were extended to just two other countries: Mexico, whose stability is essential to the United States, and Poland, whose stability is essential to both NATO and the EU. Less than 10 percent of all IMF lending was to the neediest economies in Asia, Africa, or South America. Casual visitors to the IMF's website should not be deceived by images of smiling dark-skinned women wearing native dress. The IMF functions as a rich nations' club, lending to support those nations' economic interests.

If the IMF's central-bank-lending function is transparent, its deposit-taking function is more opaque. The IMF does not function like a retail commercial bank with teller windows, where individuals can walk up and make a deposit to a checking or savings account. Instead, it runs a highly sophisticated asset-liability management program, in which lending facilities are financed through a combination of "quotas" and "borrowing arrangements." The quotas are similar to bank capital, and the borrowing arrangements are similar to the bonds and deposits that a normal bank uses to fund its lending. The IMF's financial activities are mostly conducted off balance sheet as contingent lending and borrowing facilities. In this way, the IMF resembles a modern commercial bank such as JPMorgan Chase whose off-balance-sheet contingent liabilities dwarf those shown on the balance sheet.

To see the IMF's true financial position, one must look beyond the balance sheet to the footnotes and other sources. IMF financial reports are stated in its own currency, the SDR, which is easily converted into dollars. The IMF computes and publishes the SDR-to-dollar exchange rate daily. In May 2013 the IMF had almost $600 billion of unused borrowing capacity, which, when combined with existing resources, gave the IMF $750 billion in lending capacity. If this borrowing and lending capacity were fully utilized, the IMF's leverage ratio would only be about 3 to 1, if quotas were considered to be equity. This is extremely conservative compared to most major banks, whose leverage ratios are closer to 20 to 1 and are higher still when hidden off-balance-sheet items are considered.

The interesting aspect of IMF leverage is not that it is high today but that it exists at all. The IMF operated for decades with almost no leverage; advances were made from members' quotas. The idea was that members would contribute their quotas to a pool, and individual members could draw from the pool for temporary relief as needed. As long as total borrowings did not exceed the total quota pool, the system was stable and did not need leverage. This is no longer the case. As corporations and individuals deleveraged after the Panic of 2008, sovereign governments, central banks, and the IMF have employed leverage to keep the global monetary system afloat. In effect, public debt has replaced private debt.

The overall debt burden has not been reduced—it has increased, as the global debt problem has been moved upstairs. The IMF is the penthouse, where the problem can be passed no higher. So far the IMF has been able to facilitate the official leveraging process as an offset to private deleveraging. Public leverage has mostly occurred at the level of national central banks such as the Federal Reserve and the Bank of Japan. But as those central banks reach practical and political limits on their leverage, the IMF will emerge as the *last* lender of last resort. In the next global liquidity crisis, the IMF will have the only clean balance sheet in the world because national central bank balance sheets are overleveraged with long-duration assets.

The biggest single boost to the IMF's borrowing and leverage capacity came on April 2, 2009, very near the depths of the stock market crashes that began in 2008, a time of pervasive fear in financial markets. The occasion was the G20 Leaders' Summit in London, hosted by the U.K. prime minister Gordon Brown and attended by U.S. president Obama, French president Sarkozy, German chancellor Merkel, China's Hu Jintao, and other world leaders. The summit pledged to expand the IMF's lending capacity to $750 billion. For every dollar the IMF lends, it must first obtain a dollar from its members; so expanded lending capacity implied expanded borrowing and greater leverage. It took the IMF over a year to obtain most of the needed commitments, although for a panoply of political reasons, the full amount has not yet been subscribed.

The largest IMF commitments came from the European Union and Japan, each committing $100 billion, and China, which committed another $50 billion. Other large commitments of $10 billion each came from the other BRIC nations, Russia, India, and Brazil, and from the developed nations of Canada, Switzerland, and Korea.

The most contentious commitment to the IMF's new borrowing facility involved the United States. On April 16, 2009, just days after the G20 summit, President Obama sent letters to the congressional leadership requesting its support for a $100 billion commitment to the new IMF borrowings. The president, guided by Rubin protégé Mike Froman, had made a verbal pledge of the $100 billion at the summit, but he needed legislation to deliver on the actual funding. The letters to Congress stated that the new funding was a package deal intended to increase IMF votes for China and to force gold sales by the IMF. President Obama's letters also called for "a special one-time allocation of Special Drawing Rights, reserve assets created by the IMF . . . that will increase global liquidity." The president's letters were refreshingly candid on the IMF's ability to print world money.

China wanted additional votes at the IMF, and it wanted more gold dumped on the market to avoid a run-up in the price at a time when it was acquiring gold covertly. The United States wanted the IMF to print more world money. The IMF wanted hard currency from the United States and China to conduct bailouts. The deal, which had something for everyone, had been carefully structured by Mike Froman and other sherpas at the summit and signed on by Geithner, Obama, and the G20 leaders.

Looking a bit deeper, the Obama letter to Congress contained another twist. The new commitments to the IMF came not as quotas but as loans, consistent with the IMF's growing role as a leveraged bank. The president sought to reassure Congress that the loan to the IMF was not an expenditure and therefore would have no impact on the U.S. budget deficit. The president's letter said, "That is because when the United States transfers dollars to the IMF . . . the United States receives in exchange . . . a liquid, interest-bearing claim on the IMF, which is backed by the IMF's strong financial position, including . . . gold." This statement is entirely true. The IMF does have a strong financial position, and it has the third-largest gold hoard in the world after the United States and Germany. It was curious that just as Federal Reserve officials were publicly disparaging gold's role in the monetary system, the president felt the need to mention gold to the Congress as a confidence booster. Despite disparagement of gold by academics and central bankers, gold has never fully lost its place as the bedrock of global finance.

Drilling still further down, we find a curious feature of the IMF loan proposal. If the United States gave the IMF $100 billion in cash, it would receive an interest-bearing note from the IMF in exchange. However, the note would be denominated not in dollars but in SDRs. Since the SDR is a nondollar world currency, its value fluctuates against the U.S. dollar.

The SDR exchange value is calculated partly by reference to the dollar, but also by reference to a currency basket that includes the Japanese yen, the euro, and the U.K. pound sterling. This means that when the IMF note matures, the United States will receive back *not* the original $100 billion but a different amount depending on the fluctuation of the dollar against the SDR. If the dollar were to grow stronger against the other currencies in the SDR basket, the United States would receive *less* than the original $100 billion loan in repayment, because the nondollar basket components would be worth less. But if the dollar were to grow weaker against the other currencies in the SDR basket, the United States would receive *more* than the original $100 billion loan in repayment, because the nondollar basket components would be worth more. In making the loan, the U.S. Treasury was betting *against* the dollar since only a *decline* in the dollar would enable the United States to get its money back. This $100 billion bet against the dollar was not mentioned in the president's letter and went largely unrecognized by Congress at the time. As it happens, it proved a political time bomb that came back to haunt the United States and the IMF ahead of the 2012 presidential election.

The president's letters also misled Congress about the loan commitment's purpose. They state in several places that the loan proceeds would be used by the IMF for assistance "primarily to developing and emerging market countries." In fact, the IMF's new borrowing capacity was used primarily to bail out the Eurozone members Ireland, Portugal, Greece, and Cyprus. Little of the cash was used for emerging markets lending. The misleading language was intended to dodge criticism from Congress that U.S. taxpayer money would be used to bail out Greek bureaucrats who retired at age fifty with lifetime pensions, while Americans were working past seventy to make ends meet.

These deceptions and the Treasury's bet against the dollar went unnoticed in the frenzy of auto company bailouts and stimulus packages. Under the leadership of House Democrat Barney Frank and Senate Republican Richard Lugar, the U.S. commitment to the IMF borrowings was buried in a war spending bill and was passed by Congress on June 16, 2009. The IMF issued a press release with remarks by then managing director Dominique Strauss-Kahn touting the legislation and describing it as a "significant step forward."

While the legislation provided for the $100 billion U.S. commitment, the IMF did not actually borrow the funds right away. The commitment was like a credit line on a MasterCard that the cardholder has not yet used. The IMF could swipe the MasterCard at any time and get the $100 billion from the United States simply by issuing a borrowing notice.

In November 2010 the Obama plan to finance IMF bailouts had the rug pulled out from under it by the midterm elections and the Republican takeover of the House of Representatives. Republican success was fueled by Tea Party resentment at earlier bailouts for Wall Street banks Goldman Sachs and JPMorgan Chase. Barney Frank lost his House Financial Services Committee chairmanship, and the new Republican leadership began examining the implications of the U.S. commitment to the IMF.

By early 2011, the European sovereign debt crisis had reached a critical state, and it was impossible to disguise the fact that U.S. funds, if drawn by the IMF, would be used to bail out retired Greek and Portuguese bureaucrats. Conservative publications featured headlines like "Why Is the U.S. Bankrolling IMF's Bailouts in Europe?" On November 28, 2011, Barney Frank announced his retirement. Also in 2011 Senator Jim DeMint (R-S.C.) introduced legislation to rescind the U.S. commitment to the IMF. The DeMint bill was defeated in the Senate on a 55–45 vote. That defeat needed votes from Republicans, which were provided by Richard Lugar (R-Ind.) and a few others. On May 8, 2012, the Tea Party struck back by supporting Richard Mourdock, who went on to defeat Lugar in a primary election, forcing Lugar's retirement after thirty-six years as a senator. One by one the IMF's friends in the U.S. Congress were stepping aside or being forced out. With regard to the Frank and Lugar departures from Congress, the IMF's Lagarde gave a Gallic shrug and said, "We will miss them."

By late 2013, the sparring match between the White House and Congress over funding for the IMF had grown more intense. After the London G20 Summit, the IMF had taken further steps to increase its borrowing power beyond the original commitments, shifting some of the U.S. lending commitment away from debt toward a quota increase—in effect, it moved part of the U.S. money from temporary lending to permanent capital. These 2010 changes, which also followed through on the London Summit commitments to increase the voting power of China, required congressional approval beyond that contained in the 2009 Barney Frank legislation. Hundreds of eminent international economists, and prominent former officials such as Treasury secretary Hank Paulson, who had engineered the Goldman Sachs bailout in 2008, publicly called on Congress to approve the legislation. However, President Obama did not include the new requests in his 2012 or 2013 budgets, in order to avoid making a campaign issue out of U.S. taxpayer support for European bailouts.

At this point Christine Lagarde's impatience with the process began to boil over. During the World Economic Forum in Davos on January 28, 2012, she hoisted her Louis Vuitton handbag in the air and said, "I am here with my little bag, to actually collect a bit of money." In an interview with *The Washington Post* published on June 29, 2013, she was more pointed and said, "We have been able to significantly increase our resources . . . notwithstanding the fact that the U.S. did not contribute or support that move. . . . I think everybody would like to complete the process. Let's face it. It has been around a long time."

Fortunately for the IMF, the controversial U.S. funds commitment was not needed in the short run. By late 2012, the European sovereign debt crisis had stabilized, as growth continued in the United States and China, albeit at a slower rate than hoped for by the IMF. But after the history of debt crises in Dubai, Greece, Cyprus, and elsewhere from 2009 to 2013, it appeared to be just a matter of time before the situation somewhere destabilized and the U.S. commitment would be needed to finance another rescue package.

The IMF's role as a leveraged lender, in effect a bank, is now institutionalized. The IMF has evolved from a quota-based swing lender to a leveraged lender of last resort like the Federal Reserve. Its borrowing and lending capabilities are well understood by economic experts, if not by the public at large. But even experts are largely unfamiliar with or confused by the IMF's greatest power—the ability to create money. Indeed, the name of the IMF's world money, the special drawing right, seems designed more to confuse than to enlighten. The IMF's printing press is standing by, ready for use when needed in the next global liquidity crisis. It will be a key tool in engineering the dollar's demise.

■ One Currency

John Maynard Keynes once mused that not one man in a million was able to understand the process by which inflation destroys wealth. It is as likely that not one woman or man in ten million understands special drawing rights, or SDRs. Still, the SDR is poised to be an inflationary precursor par excellence. The SDR's mix of opacity and unaccountability permits global monetary elites to solve sovereign debt problems using an inflationary medium, which in turn allows individual governments to deny political responsibility.

The SDR's stealth qualities begin with its name. Like *Federal Reserve* and *International Monetary Fund,* the name was chosen to hide its true purpose. Just as the Federal Reserve and IMF are central banks with disguised names, so the SDR is world money in disguise.

Some monetary scholars, notably Barry Eichengreen of the University of California at Berkeley, object to the use of the term *money* as applied to SDRs, viewing the units as a mere accounting device used to shift reserves among members. But the IMF's own financial reports refute this view. Its annual report contains the following disclosures:

> The SDR may be allocated by the IMF, as a supplement to existing reserve assets. . . . Its *value* as a reserve asset derives from the commitments of participants to hold and accept SDRs. . . . The SDR is also used by a number of international and regional organizations as a *unit of account.* . . . Participants and prescribed holders can *use and receive SDRs in transactions* . . . among themselves.

As money is classically defined as having three essential qualities—store of value, unit of account, and medium of exchange—this disclosure clinches the case for the SDR as money. The IMF itself says the SDR has value, is a unit of account, and can be used as a medium of exchange in transactions among designated holders. The three-part money definition is satisfied in full.

The amount of SDRs in circulation is minuscule compared to national and regional currencies such as the dollar and euro. The SDR's use is limited to IMF members and certain other official institutions and is controlled by the IMF Special Drawing Rights Department. Further, SDRs will perhaps never be issued in banknote form and may never be used on an everyday basis by citizens around the world. But even such limited usage does not alter the fact that the SDR is world money controlled by elites. In fact, it enhances that role by making the SDR invisible to citizens.

The SDR can be issued in abundance to IMF members and can also be used in the future for a select list of the most important transactions in the world, including balance-of-payments settlements, oil pricing, and the financial accounts of the world's largest corporations such as Exxon-Mobil, Toyota, and Royal Dutch Shell. Any inflation caused by massive SDR issuance would not immediately be apparent to citizens. The inflation would show up eventually in dollars, yen, and euros at the gas pump or the grocery, but national central banks could deny responsibility with ease and point a finger at the IMF. Since the IMF is not accountable to any electoral process and is a self-perpetuating supranational organization, the buck would stop nowhere.

The SDR's history is as colorful as its expected future. It was not part of the original Bretton Woods monetary architecture agreed to in 1944. It was an emergency response to a dollar crisis that began in 1969 and continued in stages through 1981.

During the Bretton Woods system's early decades, from 1945 to 1965, international monetary experts worried about a so-called dollar shortage. At that time the dollar was the dominant global reserve currency, essential to international trade. Europe's and Japan's industrial bases had been devastated during the Second World War. Both Europe and Japan had human capital, but neither possessed the dollars or gold needed to pay for the machinery and raw materials that could revive their manufacturing. The dollar shortage was partly alleviated by Marshall Plan aid and Korean War spending, but the greatest boost came from the U.S. consumer's newfound appetite for high-quality, inexpensive imported goods. American baby boomers, as teenagers in the 1960s, may recall driving to the beach in a Volkswagen Beetle with a Toshiba transistor radio in hand. By 1965, competitive export nations such as Germany and Japan were rapidly acquiring the two principal reserve assets at the time, dollars and gold. The United States understood that it needed to run substantial trade deficits to supply dollars to the rest of the world and facilitate world trade.

The international monetary system soon fell victim to its own success. The dollar shortage was replaced with a dollar glut, and trading partners became uneasy with persistent U.S. trade deficits and potential inflation. This situation was an illustration of Triffin's dilemma, named after Belgian economist Robert Triffin, who first described it in the early 1960s. Triffin pointed out that when one nation issues the global reserve currency, it must run persistent trade deficits to supply that currency to its trading partners; but if the deficits persist too long, confidence in the currency will eventually be lost.

Paradoxically, both a dollar shortage *and* a dollar glut give rise to consideration of alternative reserve assets. In the case of a dollar shortage, a new asset is sought to provide liquidity. In the case of a dollar glut, a new asset is sought to provide substitutes for investing reserves and to restore confidence. Either way, the IMF has long been involved in the contemplation of alternatives to the dollar.

By the late 1960s, confidence in the dollar was collapsing due to a combination of U.S. trade deficits, budget deficits, and inflation brought on by President Lyndon Johnson's "guns and butter" policies. U.S trading partners, notably France and Switzerland, began dumping dollars for gold. A full-scale run on Fort Knox commenced, and the U.S. gold hoard was dwindling at an alarming rate, leading to President Nixon's decision to end the dollar's gold convertibility, on August 15, 1971.

As caretaker of the international monetary system, the IMF confronted collapsing confidence in the dollar and a perceived gold shortage. The U.K. pound sterling had already devalued in 1967 and was suffering its own crisis of confidence. German marks were considered attractive, but German capital markets were far too small to provide global reserve assets in sufficient quantities. The dollar was weak, gold was scarce, and no alternative assets were available. The IMF feared that global liquidity could evaporate, triggering a collapse of world trade and a depression, as had happened in the 1930s. In this strained environment, the IMF decided in 1969 to create a new global reserve asset, the SDR, from thin air.

From the start, the SDR was world fiat money. Kenneth W. Dam, a leading monetary scholar and former senior U.S. government official who served in the Treasury, the White House, and Department of Defense, explains in his definitive history of the IMF:

> The SDR differed from nearly all prior proposals in one crucial respect. Previously it had been thought essential that any new international reserves created through the Fund, and particularly any new reserve asset, be "backed" by some other asset. . . . The SDR, in contrast, was created out of (so to speak) whole cloth. It was simply allocated to participants in proportion to quotas, leading some to refer to the SDR as "manna from heaven." Thereafter it existed and was transferred without any backing at all. . . . A ready analogy is to "fiat" money created by national governments but not convertible into underlying assets such as gold.

Initially the SDR was valued as equivalent to 0.888671 grams of fine gold, but this IMF gold standard was abandoned in 1973 not long after the United States itself abandoned the gold standard with respect to the dollar. Since 1973, the SDR's value has been computed with reference to a reserve-currency basket. This does not mean that the SDR is *backed* by hard currencies, as Dam points out, merely that its *value* in transactions and accounting is calculated in that manner. Today the basket consists of dollars, euros, yen, and pounds sterling in specified weights.

SDRs have been issued to IMF members on four occasions since their creation. The first issue was for 9.3 billion SDRs, handed out in stages from 1970 to 1972. The second issue was for 12.1 billion SDRs, also done in stages from 1979 to 1981. There was no SDR issuance for almost thirty years, from 1981 to 2009. This was the King Dollar era engineered by Paul Volcker and Ronald Reagan, which continued through the Republican and Democratic administrations of George Bush, Bill Clinton, and George W. Bush. Then in 2009, in the wake of the financial crisis and in the depths of a new depression, the IMF issued 161.2 billion SDRs on August 28 and 21.5 billion SDRs on September 9. The cumulative SDR issuance since their creation is 204.1 billion, worth over $300 billion at the current dollar-SDR exchange rate.

The history makes it clear that there is a close correspondence between periods of SDR issuance and periods of collapsing confidence in the dollar. The best index of dollar strength or weakness is the Price-adjusted Broad Dollar Index, calculated and published by the Federal Reserve. The Fed's dollar index series begins in January 1973 and is based on a par value expressed as 100.00 on the index. The first SDRs issued in 1970 to 1972 predate this index but were linked to the dollar's 20 percent collapse against gold at the time.

The second SDR issuance, from 1979 to 1981, immediately followed a dollar breakdown from a Fed index level of 94.2780 in March 1977 to 84.1326 in October 1978—an 11 percent decline in nineteen months. After the issuance, the dollar recovered its standing, and the index hit 103.2159 in March 1982. This was the beginning of the King Dollar period.

The third and fourth SDR issuances began in August 2009, not long after the dollar crashed to an index level of 84.1730 in April 2008, near its level in the crisis of 1978. The lags of approximately a year between index lows and SDR issuance are a reflection of the time it takes the IMF to obtain board approval to proceed with new issuance.

Unlike the issuance in the 1980s King Dollar period, the massive 2009 issuance did not result in the dollar regaining its strength. In fact, the dollar index reached an all-time low of 80.5178 in July 2011, just before gold hit an all-time high of $1,895.00 on September 5. The difference in 2011 compared to 1982 was that the Fed and Treasury were pursuing a weak-dollar policy, in contrast to Paul Volcker's strong-dollar policy. Nevertheless, the 2009 SDR issuance served its purpose, reliquefying global financial markets after the Panic of 2008. Markets regained their footing by late 2012 with the stabilization of the European sovereign debt crisis after Mario Draghi's "whatever it takes" pledge on the ECB's behalf. By 2012, global liquidity was restored, and SDRs were once again placed on the shelf, awaiting the next global liquidity crisis.

Although the SDR is a useful tool for emergency liquidity creation, thus far the dollar retains its status as the world's leading reserve currency. Performing a reserve-currency role requires more than just being money; it requires a pool of investable assets, primarily a deep, liquid bond market. Any currency can be used in international trade if the trading partners are willing to accept it as a medium of exchange. But a problem arises after one trading partner has acquired large trade currency balances. That party needs to invest the balances in liquid assets that pay market returns and preserve value. When the balances are large—for example, China's $3 trillion in reserves—the investable asset pool must be correspondingly large. Today U.S.-dollar-denominated government bond markets are the only markets in the world large and diversified enough to absorb the investment flows coming from surplus nations such as China, Korea, and Taiwan. The SDR market is microscopic in comparison.

Still, the IMF makes no secret of its ambitions to transform the SDR into a reserve currency that could replace the dollar. This was revealed in an IMF study released in January 2011, consisting of a multiyear, multistep plan to position the SDR as the leading global reserve asset. The study recommends increasing the SDR supply to make them liquid and more attractive to potential private-sector market participants such as Goldman Sachs and Citigroup. Importantly, the study recognizes the need for natural sellers of SDR-denominated bonds such as Volkswagen and IBM. Sovereign wealth funds are recommended as the most likely SDR bond buyers for currency diversification reasons. The IMF study recommends that the SDR bond market replicate the infrastructure of the U.S. Treasury market, with hedging, financing, settlement, and clearance mechanisms substantially similar to those used to support trading in Treasury securities today.

Beyond the SDR bond market creation, the IMF blueprint goes on to suggest that the IMF could change the SDR basket composition to reduce the weight given to the U.S. dollar and increase the weights of other currencies such as the Chinese yuan. This is a stealth mechanism to enhance the yuan's role as a reserve currency long before China itself has created a yuan bond market or opened its capital account. If the SDR market becomes liquid, and the yuan is included in the SDR, bank dealers will discover ways to arbitrage one currency against the other and thereby increase the yuan's use and attractiveness. With regard to a future SDR bond market, the IMF study candidly concludes, "If there were political willingness to do so, these securities could constitute an embryo of global currency." This conclusion is highly significant because it is the first time the IMF has publicly moved beyond the idea of the SDR as a liquidity supplement and presented it as a leading form of world money.

Indeed, the IMF's distribution of SDRs is not limited to IMF members.

Article XVII of the IMF's governing Articles of Agreement permits SDR issuance to "non-members . . . and other official entities," including the United Nations and the Bank for International Settlements (BIS), in Basel, Switzerland. The BIS is notorious for facilitating Nazi gold swaps while being run by an American, Thomas McKittrick, during the Second World War, and is commonly known as the central bank for central banks. The IMF can issue SDRs to the BIS today to finance its ongoing gold market manipulations. Under Article XVII authority, the IMF could also issue SDRs to the United Nations, which could put them to use for population control or climate change regimes.

An expanded role for SDRs awaits further developments that may take years to evolve. While the SDR is not ready to replace the dollar as the leading reserve currency, it is moving slowly in that direction. Still, the SDR's rapid-response role as a liquidity source in a financial panic is well practiced. The 2009 SDR issuance can be viewed as "test drive" prior to a much larger issuance in a future liquidity crisis.

SDRs granted to an IMF member are not always immediately useful, because that member may need to pay debts in dollars or euros. However, SDRs can be swapped for dollars with other members who do not mind receiving them. The IMF has an internal SDR Department that facilitates these swaps. For example, if Austria has obligations in Swiss francs and receives an SDR allocation, Austria can arrange to swap SDRs for dollars with China. Austria then sells the dollars for Swiss francs and uses the francs to meet its obligations. China will gladly take SDRs for dollars as a way to diversify its reserves out of dollars. In actual swaps, China had acquired the equivalent of $1.24 billion in SDRs above its formal allocations by April 30, 2012. IMF deputy managing director Min Zhu cryptically summarized the SDR's liquidity role when he stated, "They are fake money, but they are a kind of fake money that can be real money."

The IMF is transparent when it comes to the purpose of SDR issuance. The entire Bretton Woods architecture, which gave rise to the IMF, was a reaction to the 1930s Depression and deflation. The IMF Articles of Agreement address this issue explicitly:

> In all its decisions with respect to the allocation . . . of special drawing rights the Fund shall seek to meet the long-term global

need, as and when it arises, to supplement existing reserve assets in
such manner as will . . . avoid . . . deflation.

Deflation is every central bank's nemesis because it is difficult to reverse, impossible to tax, and makes sovereign debt unpayable by increasing the real value of debt. By explicitly acknowledging its mission to
prevent deflation, the IMF's actions are consistent with the aims of other
central banks.

With its diverse leadership, leveraged balance sheet, and the SDR, the
IMF is poised to realize its one-world, one-bank, one-currency vision and
exercise its intended role as Central Bank of the World. The next global
liquidity crisis will shake the stability of the international monetary system to its core; it may also be the catalyst for the realization of the IMF's
vision. The SDR is the preferred pretender to the dollar's throne.

CHAPTER 9

GOLD REDUX

Gold and silver are the only substances, which have been, and continue to be, the universal currency of civilized nations. It is not necessary to enumerate the well-known properties which rendered them best fitted for a general medium of exchange. They were used . . . from the earliest times. . . . And when we see that nations, differing in language, religion, habits, and on almost every subject susceptible of doubt, have, during a period of near four thousand years, agreed in one respect; and that gold and silver have, uninterruptedly to this day, continued to be the universal currency of the commercial and civilized world, it may safely be inferred, that they have also been found superior to any other substance in that permanency of value.

Albert Gallatin
Longest-serving Treasury secretary (1801–1814)
1831

If a gold standard is going to be effective, you've got to fix the price of gold and you've got to really stick to it. . . . To get on a gold standard technically now, an old-fashioned gold standard, and you had to replace all the dollars out there in foreign hands with gold, God, the price . . . of gold would have to be enormous.

Paul Volcker
Former chairman of the board of governors of the Federal Reserve
System
October 15, 2012

Money is gold, and nothing else.

J. P. Morgan, 1912

■ Gold Realities, Gold Myths

Thoughtful discussion of gold is as rare as the metal itself. The topic seems too infused with emotion to admit of much rational discourse. On the one hand, opponents of a role for gold in the international monetary system are as likely to resort to ad hominem attacks as to economic analysis in their efforts to ridicule and marginalize the topic. A 2013 column by a well-known economist used the words *paranoid, fear-based, far-right fringe,* and *fanatics* to describe gold investors, while flitting through a shopworn list of supposed objections that do not hold up to serious scrutiny.

On the other hand, many so-called gold bugs are no more nuanced, with their charges that the vaults in Fort Knox are empty, the gold having been long ago shipped to bullion banks like JPMorgan Chase and replaced with tungsten-filled look-alikes. This fraud is alleged to be part of a massive, multidecade price suppression scheme to deprive gold investors of the profits of their prescience and to deny gold its proper place in the monetary cosmos.

Legitimate concerns about gold's use in conjunction with discretionary monetary policy do exist, of course, and there's evidence of government intervention in gold markets. Both argue for an examination of the issue that sorts fact from fantasy. Understanding gold's real role in the monetary system requires reliance on history, not histrionics; analysis should be based on demonstrable data and reasonable inference rather than accusation and speculation. When a refined view is taken on the subject of gold, the truth turns out to be more interesting than either the gold haters or the gold bugs might lead one to believe.

Lord Nathan Rothschild, bullion broker to the Bank of England and head of the legendary London bank N. M. Rothschild & Sons, is said to have remarked, "I only know of two men who really understand the value of gold—an obscure clerk in the basement vault of the Banque de Paris and one of the directors of the Bank of England. Unfortunately, they disagree." This comment captures the paucity of well-founded views and the opacity that infuses discussion of gold.

At the most basic level, gold is an element, atomic number 79, found in ore, sometimes nuggets, in scarce quantities, in or on the earth's crust. The fact that gold is an element is important because that means pure gold is of uniform grade and quality at all times and in all places. Many commodities such as oil, corn, or wheat come in various grades with greater or lesser impurities, which are reflected in the price. Leaving aside alloys and unrefined products, pure gold is the same everywhere.

Because of its purity, uniformity, scarcity, and malleability, gold is money nonpareil. Gold has been money for at least four thousand years, perhaps much longer. Genesis describes the Patriarch Abraham as "very rich in livestock, gold and silver." King Croesus minted the first gold coins in Lydia, modern-day Turkey, in the sixth century B.C. The 1792 U.S. Coinage Act, passed just three years after the U.S. Constitution went into effect, authorized the newly established Mint to produce pure gold coins called eagles, half eagles, and quarter eagles. Gold's long history does not mean that it must be used as money today. It does mean that anyone who rejects gold as money must feel possessed of greater wisdom than the Bible, antiquity, and the Founding Fathers combined.

To understand gold, it is useful to know what gold is *not*.

Gold is not a derivative. A gold exchange-traded fund listed on the New York Stock Exchange is not gold. A gold futures contract traded on the CME Group's COMEX is not gold. A forward contract offered by a London Bullion Market Association bank is not gold. These financial instruments, and many others, are contracts that offer price exposure to gold and are part of a system that has physical gold associated with it, but they are contracts, not gold.

Contracts based on gold have many risks that are not intrinsic to gold itself, starting with the possibility that counterparties may default on their obligations. Exchanges where the gold contracts are listed may be closed as a result of panics, wars, acts of terror, storms, and other acts of God. Hurricane Sandy in 2012 and the 9/11 attack on the World Trade Center are two recent cases in which the New York Stock Exchange closed. Exchange rules may also be abruptly changed, as happened on the COMEX in 1980 during the Hunt brothers' attempted silver market corner. Banks may claim force majeure to terminate contacts and settle in cash rather than bullion. In addition, governments may use executive orders to abrogate outstanding contracts. Power outages and Internet backbone collapses may result in an inability to close out or settle exchange-traded contracts. Changes in exchange-margin requirements may prompt forced liquidations that cascade into panic selling. None of these occurrences affects the physical gold bullion holder.

Outright physical gold ownership, without pledges or liens, stored outside the banking system, is the only form of gold that is true money, since every other form is a mere conditional claim on gold.

Gold is not a commodity. The reason is that it is not consumed or converted to anything else; it is just gold. It is traded on commodity exchanges and is thought of as a commodity by many market participants, but it is distinct. Economists as diverse as Adam Smith and Karl Marx defined commodities generally as undifferentiated goods produced to satisfy various needs or wants. Oil, wheat, corn, aluminum, copper, and countless other true commodities satisfy this definition. Commodities are consumed as food or energy, or else they serve as inputs to other goods that are demanded for consumption. In contrast, gold has almost no industrial uses and is not food or energy in any form. It is true that gold is desired by almost all of mankind, but it is desired as money in its store-of-value role, not for any other purpose. Even jewelry is not a consumption item, although it is accounted as such, because gold jewelry is ornamental wealth, a form of money that can be worn.

Gold is not an investment. An investment involves converting money into an instrument that entails both risk and return. True money, such as gold, has no return because it has no risk. The easiest way to understand this idea is to remove a dollar bill from a wallet or purse and look at it. The dollar bill has no return. In order to get a return, one must convert the money to an investment and take a risk. An investor who takes her dollar bills to the bank and deposits them can earn a return, but it is not a return on money; it is a return on a bank deposit. Bank deposit risks may be quite low, but they are not zero. There is maturity risk if the deposit is for a fixed term. There is credit risk if the bank fails. Bank deposit insurance may mitigate bank failure risk, but there is a chance the insurance fund will become insolvent. Those who believe that bank deposit risk is a thing of the past should consider the case of Cyprus in March 2013, when certain bank deposits were forcibly converted into bank stock after an earlier scheme to confiscate the deposits by taxation was rejected. This conversion of deposits to equity in order to bail out insolvent banks was looked upon favorably in Europe and the United States as a template for future bank crisis management.

There are innumerable ways to earn a return by taking risk. Stocks, bonds, real estate, hedge funds, and many other types of pooled vehicles are all investments that include both risk and return. An entire branch of economic science, particularly options pricing theory, was based on the flawed assumption that a short-term Treasury bill is a "risk-free" investment. In fact, recent U.S. credit downgrades below the AAA level, a rising U.S. debt-to-GDP ratio, and continuing congressional dysfunction about debt-ceiling legislation have all shown the "risk-free" label to be a myth.

Gold involves none of the risks inherent in these investments. It has no maturity risk since there is no future date when gold will mature into gold; it is gold in the first place. Gold has no counterparty risk because it is an asset to the holder, but it is not anyone else's liability. No one "issues" gold the way a note is issued; it is just gold. Once gold is in your possession, it has no risks related to clearance or settlement. Banks may fail, exchanges may close, and the peace may be lost, but these events have no impact on the intrinsic value of gold. This is why gold is the true risk-free asset.

Confusion about the role of gold arises because it usually treated as an investment and is reported as such in financial media. Not a day goes by without a financial reporter informing her audience that gold is "up" or "down" on the day, and in terms of gold's dollar price per ounce, this is literally true. But is gold fluctuating, or is it the dollar? On a day that gold is reported to be "up" 3.3 percent, from $1,500 per ounce to $1,550 per ounce, it would be just as accurate to treat gold as a constant and report that the dollar is "down" from 1/1,500th of an ounce of gold to 1/1,550th of an ounce. In other words, one dollar buys you less gold, so the dollar is down. This highlights the role of the *numeraire,* or the unit of account, which is part of the standard definition of money. If gold is the *numeraire,* then it is more accurate to think of dollars or other currencies as the fluctuating assets, not gold.

This *numeraire* question can also be illustrated by the following example involving currencies. Assume that on a given trading day, gold's dollar price moves from $1,500 per ounce to $1,495 per ounce, a 0.3 percent *decline,* and on the same day the yen exchange rate to one dollar moves from 100 yen to 101 yen. Converting dollars to yen, it is seen that gold's price in yen moved from ¥150,000 ($1,500 × 100) to ¥150,995 ($1,495 × 101), a 0.6 percent *increase.* On the *same* trading day, gold was *down* 0.3 percent in dollars but *up* 0.6 percent in yen. Did gold go up or down? If one views the dollar as the only form of money in the world, then gold declined, but if one views gold as the *numeraire,* or monetary standard, then it is more accurate to say that gold was constant, that the dollar rose against gold and the yen fell against gold. This unified statement resolves the contradiction of whether gold went up or down. It did neither; instead, the currencies fluctuated. This also illustrates the fact that gold's value is intrinsic and not a mere function of global currency values. It is the currencies that are volatile and that lack intrinsic value.

If gold is not a derivative, a commodity, or an investment, then *what is it?* Legendary banker J. P. Morgan said it best: "Money is gold, and nothing else."

While money was gold for J. P. Morgan—and everybody else—for four thousand years, money suddenly ceased to be gold in 1974, at least according to the IMF. President Nixon ended U.S. dollar convertibility into gold by foreign central banks in 1971, but it was not until 1974 that an IMF special reform committee, at the insistence of the United States, officially recommended gold's demonetization and the SDR's elevation in the workings of the international monetary system. From 1975 to 1980, the United States worked strenuously to diminish gold's monetary role, conducting massive gold auctions from official U.S. stocks. As late as 1979, the United States dumped 412 tonnes of gold on the market in an effort to suppress the price and deemphasize gold's importance. These efforts ultimately failed. Gold's market price briefly spiked to $800 per ounce in January 1980. There have been no significant official U.S. gold sales since then.

The demotion of gold as a monetary asset by the United States and the IMF in the late 1970s means that the economics curricula of leading universities have not seriously studied gold for almost two generations. Gold might be taught in certain history classes, and there are many gold experts who are self-taught, but any economist born since 1952 almost certainly has no formal training in the monetary uses of gold. The result has been an accretion of myths about gold in place of serious analysis.

The first myth is that gold cannot form the basis of a modern monetary system because there's *not enough gold* to support the requirements of world trade and finance. This myth is transparently false, but it is cited so often that its falsity merits rebuttal.

The total gold supply in the world today, exclusive of reserves in the ground, is approximately 163,000 tonnes. The portion of that gold held by official institutions, such as central banks, national treasuries, and the IMF, is 31,868.8 tonnes. Using a $1,500-per-ounce price, the official gold in the world has a $1.7 trillion market value. This value is far smaller than the total money supply of the major trading and financial powers in the world. For example, U.S. money supply alone, using the M1 measure provided by the U.S. Federal Reserve, was $2.5 trillion at the end of June 2013. The broader Fed M2 money supply was $10.6 trillion at the same period. Combining this with money supplies of the ECB, the Bank of Japan, and the People's Bank of China pushes global money supply for the big four economic zones to $20 trillion for M1 and $48 trillion for M2. If global money supply were limited to $1.7 trillion of gold instead of $48 trillion of M2 paper money, the result would be disastrously deflationary and lead to a severe depression.

The problem in this scenario is not the amount of gold but the *price*. There is ample gold at the right price. If gold were $17,500 per ounce, the official gold supply would roughly equal the M1 money supply of the Eurozone, Japan, China, and the United States combined. The point is not to predict the price of gold or to anticipate a gold standard but merely to illustrate that the *quantity* of gold is never an impediment to a gold standard as long as the *price* is appropriate to the targeted money supply.

The second myth is that gold cannot be used in a monetary system because *gold caused the Great Depression* of the 1930s and contributed to its length and severity. This myth is half true, but in that half-truth lies much confusion. The Great Depression, conventionally dated from 1929 to 1940, was preceded by the adoption of the "gold exchange standard," which emerged in stages from 1922 to 1925 and functioned with great difficulty until 1939. The gold exchange standard was agreed in principle at the Genoa Conference in 1922, but the precise steps toward implementation were left to the participating countries to work out in the years that followed.

As the name implies, the gold exchange standard was not a pure gold standard of the type that had existed from 1870 to 1914. It was a hybrid in which both *gold* and foreign *exchange*—principally U.S. dollars, U.K. pounds sterling, and French francs—could serve as reserves and be used for settlement of any balance of payments. After the First World War, citizens in most major economies no longer carried gold coins, as had been common prior to 1914.

In theory, a country's foreign exchange reserves were redeemable into gold when a holder presented them to the issuing country. Citizens were also free to own gold. But international redemptions were meant to be infrequent, and physical gold possession by citizens was limited to large bars, which are generally unsuitable for day-to-day transactions. The idea was to create a gold standard but have as little gold in circulation as possible. The gold that was available was to remain principally in vaults at the Federal Reserve Bank of New York, the Bank of England, and the Banque de France, while citizens grew accustomed to using paper notes instead of gold coins, and central bankers learned to accept their trading partners' notes instead of demanding bullion. The gold exchange standard was, at best, a pale imitation of a true gold standard and, at worst, a massive fraud.

Most important, nations had to choose a conversion rate between their currencies and gold, then stick to that rate as the new system evolved. In view of the vast paper money supply increases that had occurred during the First World War, from 1914 to 1918, most participating nations chose a value for their currencies that was far below the prewar rates. In effect, they devalued their currencies against gold and returned to a gold standard at the new, lower exchange rate. France, Belgium, Italy, and other members of what later became known as the Gold Bloc pursued this policy. The United States had entered the war later than the European powers, and its economy was less affected by the war. The United States also received large gold inflows during the war, and as a result, it had no difficulty maintaining gold's prewar $20.67-per-ounce exchange rate. After the Gold Bloc devaluations, and with the United States not in distress, the future success of the gold exchange standard now hinged on the determination of a conversion rate for U.K. pounds sterling.

The U.K., under the guidance of chancellor of the exchequer Winston Churchill, chose to return sterling to gold at the prewar rate equivalent to £4.86 per ounce. He did this both because he felt duty bound to honor Bank of England notes at their original value, but also for pragmatic reasons having to do with maintaining London's position as the reliable sound money center of world finance. Given the large amount of money printed by the Bank of England to finance the war, this exchange rate greatly overvalued the pound and forced a drastic decrease in the money supply in order to return to the old parity. An exchange rate equivalent to £7.50 per ounce would have been a more realistic peg and would have put the U.K. in a competitive trading position. Instead, the overvaluation of pounds sterling hurt U.K. trade and forced deflationary wage cuts on U.K. labor in order to adjust the terms of trade; the process was similar to the structural adjustments Greece and Spain are experiencing today. As a result, the U.K. economy was in a depression by 1926, years before the conventional starting date of 1929 associated with the Great Depression and the U.S. stock market crash.

With an overvalued pound and disadvantageous terms of trade, the U.K.'s gold began flowing to the United States and France. The proper U.S. response should have been to ease monetary policy, controlled by the Federal Reserve, and allow higher inflation in the United States, which would have moved the terms of trade in the U.K.'s favor and given the U.K. economy a boost. Instead, the Fed ran a tight money policy, which contributed to the 1929 market crash and helped to precipitate the Great Depression. By 1931, pressure on the overvalued pound became so severe that the U.K. abandoned the 1925 parity and devalued sterling. This left the dollar as the most overvalued major currency in the world, a situation rectified in 1933, when the United States also devalued from $20.67 per ounce to $35.00 per ounce, cheapening the dollar to offset the effect of the sterling devaluation two years earlier.

The sequence of events from 1922 to 1933 shows that the Great Depression was caused not by gold but rather by *central bank discretionary policies*. The gold exchange standard was fatally flawed because it did not take gold's free-market price into account. The Bank of England overvalued sterling in 1925. The Federal Reserve ran an unduly tight money policy in 1927. These problems have to do not with gold per se but with the *price* of gold as manipulated and distorted by central banks. The gold exchange standard did contribute to the Great Depression because it was not a true gold standard. It was a poorly designed hybrid, manipulated and mismanaged by discretionary monetary policy conducted by central banks, particularly in the U.K. and the United States. The Great Depression is not an argument against gold; it is a cautionary tale of central bank incompetence and the dangers of ignoring markets.

The third myth is that *gold caused market panics* and that modern economies are more stable when gold is avoided and central banks use monetary tools to smooth out periodic panics. This myth is one of economist Paul Krugman's favorites, and he recites it ad nauseam in his anti-gold, pro-inflationary writings.

In fact, panics do happen on a gold standard, and panics *also* happen in the absence of a gold standard. Krugman likes to recite a list of panics that arose during the classical gold standard and the gold exchange standard; it includes market panics or crashes in 1873, 1884, 1890, 1893, 1907, and the Great Depression. Fair enough. But panics also occurred in the absence of a gold standard. Examples include the 1987 stock market crash, when the Dow Jones Industrial Index fell over 22 percent in a single day, the 1994 Mexican peso collapse, the 1997–98 Asia-Russia-Long-Term Capital market panic, the 2000 tech stock collapse, the 2007 housing market collapse, and the Lehman-AIG financial panic of 2008.

Panics are neither prevented nor caused by gold. Panics are caused by credit overexpansion and overconfidence, followed by a sudden loss of confidence and a mad scramble for liquidity. Panics are characterized by rapid declines in asset values, margin calls by creditors, dumping of assets to obtain cash, and a positive feedback loop in which more asset sales cause further valuation declines, which are followed by more and more margin calls and asset sales. This process eventually exhausts itself through bankruptcy, a rescue by solvent parties, government intervention, or a convergence of all three. Panics are a product of human nature, and the pendulum swings between fear and greed and back to fear. Panics will not disappear. The point is that panics have little or nothing to do with gold.

In practice, gold standards worked well in the past and remain entirely feasible today. Still, daunting design questions arise in the creation of any gold standard. Designing a gold standard is challenging in the same way that designing a digital processor can be challenging; there is good design and bad design. There are technical issues that deserve serious consideration, and spurious issues that do not. There is enough gold in the world—it is just a matter of price. Gold did not cause the Great Depression, but central bank policy blunders did. Panics are not the result of gold; they are the result of human nature and easy credit. Puncturing these myths is the way forward to an authentic debate of gold's pros and cons.

■ The Scramble for Gold

While academics and pundits debate gold's virtues as a monetary standard, central banks are past the debate stage. For central banks, the debate is over—gold is money. Today central banks are acquiring gold as a reserve asset at a pace not seen since the early 1970s, and this scramble for gold has profound implications for the future role of every currency, especially the U.S. dollar.

The facts speak for themselves and require little elaboration. Central banks and other official institutions such as the IMF were net sellers of gold every year from 2002 through 2009, although sales dropped sharply during that time from over 500 tonnes in 2002 to less than 50 tonnes in 2009. Beginning in 2010, central banks became net buyers, with purchases rising sharply from less than 100 tonnes in 2010 to over 500 tonnes in 2012. In the ten-year span from 2002 to 2012, the shift from net sales to net purchases was over 1,000 tonnes per year, an amount greater than one-third of annual global mining output. Increasingly, gold is moving directly from mines to central bank vaults.

Table 1 shows increases in gold reserves for selected countries from the first quarter of 2004 to the first quarter of 2013, measured in tonnes:

Table 1. Gold Reserves in Selected Countries

Country	Q1 2004	Q1 2013	% Change
Argentina	28.61 mt	61.74 mt	+ 216%
Belarus	12.44 mt	49.29 mt	+ 396%
China	599.98 mt	1,054.09 mt	+ 176%
India	357.75 mt	557.75 mt	+ 156%
Kazakhstan	54.70 mt	122.89 mt	+ 225%
Korea	14.05 mt	104.44 mt	+ 743%
Laos	3.64 mt	8.88 mt	+ 244%
Mexico	6.80 mt	124.24 mt	+ 2,043%
Russia	389.79 mt	981.62 mt	+ 252%
Thailand	80.87 mt	152.41 mt	+ 188%
Turkey	116.10 mt	408.86 mt	+ 352%
Ukraine	19.60 mt	36.08 mt	+ 184%
Total	1,684.33 mt	3,662.29 mt	+ 217%

All these large central bank acquirers are in Asia, Latin America, and eastern Europe. Over this same period, from 2004 to 2013, Western central banks were net sellers of gold, although such sales stopped abruptly in 2009. Since then emerging economies have had to acquire gold from mine production, scrap gold recycling, or open-market sales, including sales of over 400 tonnes by the IMF in late 2009 and early 2010. Taking into account all national central banks, exclusive of the IMF, official gold reserves increased 1,481 tonnes from the fourth quarter of 2009 through the first quarter of 2013—a 5.4 percent increase. Central banks have become significant gold buyers, and the movement of gold is from west to east.

These statistics all need to be qualified by the curious case of China. China reported a gold reserve position of 395 tonnes for over twenty years from 1980 through the end of 2001. Then the reported position suddenly leaped to 500 tonnes, where it remained for a year; then it leaped again to 600 tonnes at the end of 2002, where it remained for over six years. Finally, the reported position was increased to 1,054 tonnes in April 2009, where it has remained for almost five years through early 2014.

Officially, China has reported a series of sudden spikes in its gold holdings of 105 tonnes in 2001, 100 tonnes in 2002, and 454 tonnes in 2009. Increases of this size are extremely difficult to conduct in a single transaction except by prearrangement between two central banks or the IMF. No such prearranged central bank or IMF sales to China have been reported, and no reported central bank or IMF holdings show the necessary sudden drops at the appropriate times that would correspond to such increases by China. The conclusion is inescapable that China is actually accumulating gold in smaller quantities over long periods of time, and reporting the changes in a lump sum on an irregular basis.

This covert, piecemeal gold-acquisition program makes perfect sense. Physical gold is marketable in the sense that it can be readily purchased or sold, but it is also thinly traded, and the price is volatile. Large buyers in any thinly traded market try to disguise their intentions to avoid market impact, in which bank dealers move the price adversely to the buyer in anticipation of large, inelastic buy orders.

China minimizes the market impact of its buying program through the use of secret agents and direct purchases from mines. The agents are principally located in the HSBC headquarters building on Queen's Road Central in Hong Kong and in the Shanghai branch of ANZ Bank, although the network of buying agents is worldwide. These agents place purchase orders for commercial-size gold lots of several tonnes each with brokers and London-based bullion banks. The buyer's true identity is not disclosed. The gold is paid for by one of China's sovereign wealth funds, the State Administration for Foreign Exchange, which is managed by former PIMCO bond trader Zhu Changhong. Once purchased, the gold is shipped by air transport to secure vaults in Shanghai. The agents are highly disciplined and patient in their buying activity and typically "buy the dips" in market price, as indicated on the New York–based COMEX exchange. In a masterpiece of market savvy, China bought 600 tonnes of gold directly from Australia's Perth Mint and other sellers near the interim low price of $1,200 per ounce reached in the April to July 2013 price dip. Partly as a result of these large-scale covert operations, in addition to more customary commercial purchases, China is estimated to have imported approximately 1,000 tonnes of gold per year in 2012 and 2013.

China's direct gold ore purchases are principally from gold mines located in China, but they have expanded rapidly to include newly acquired mines in southern Africa and western Australia. As recently as 2001, China produced less than 200 tonnes per year from its own mines. Output increased steadily from 2001 to 2005 and then surged in 2006, so that by 2007 China surpassed South Africa as the world's largest gold producer, a position it has maintained since. By 2013, China was producing over 400 tonnes per year—about 14 percent of worldwide mine production. Gold ore produced in Chinese-controlled mines, whether inside China or elsewhere, is sent to refineries in China, Australia, South Africa, and Switzerland, where it is refined to pure gold, cast into one-kilo gold bars, and shipped to vaults in Shanghai. Through these channels, Chinese gold bypasses the London market, minimizing the market impact and keeping the exact size of China's gold hoard a state secret.

The combination of internal gold mining output and imports from abroad means that China has increased its domestic gold holdings, both public and private, by approximately 4,500 tonnes since the last official update of its central bank gold reserves in 2009. It is impossible for observers outside the Chinese government to gauge exactly how much of that increase is waiting to be added to official reserves at the next announcement, and how much was devoted to Chinese domestic demand from consumers for jewelry, bars, and coins. It is well known that Chinese citizens are avid gold consumers, both for reasons of wealth preservation and as a convenient medium for flight capital. Gold is sold in various forms in thousands of bank branches and boutiques throughout China.

In the absence of better data, a first approximation is that half the increase in China's gold since 2009 went to domestic consumption and half, or 2,250 tonnes, has secretly been added to official reserves. If this approximation is correct, then China's official gold reserves as of early 2014 are not the reported 1,054 tonnes but instead are closer to 3,300 tonnes. At the current pace of mine output and imports, and assuming half the available gold goes to official reserves, China will add another

700 tonnes to its reserves-in-waiting throughout 2014, which would put total Chinese gold reserves at 4,000 tonnes by early 2015. China waited over six years, from late 2002 to early 2009, before publicly announcing its last increase in official reserves. If China repeats that tempo, the next update to the gold reserve figures can be expected in 2015.

Even these estimates based on known mining output and known imports must be qualified by the fact that certain gold imports to China are completely unreported. A senior manager of G4S, one of the world's leading secure logistics firms, recently revealed to a gold industry executive that he had personally transported gold into China by land through central Asian mountain passes at the head of a column of People's Liberation Army tanks and armored transport vehicles. This gold was in the form of the 400-ounce "good delivery" bars favored by central banks rather than the smaller one-kilo bars imported through regular channels and favored by retail investors. What is clear from such disclosures is that any estimates of China's official gold reserves are more likely to be too low than too high.

An announcement by China in 2015 that it holds 4,000 tonnes of gold in its official reserves will discredit the view of Western pundits and economists that gold is not a monetary asset. With 4,000 tonnes, China will surpass France, Italy, Germany, and the IMF in the ranks of the world's largest gold holders, and it will be second only to the United States. This would be in keeping with China's status as the world's second-largest economy.

China's covert gold acquisition is in sharp contrast to Russia's far more transparent efforts to increase its own gold reserves. In the nine years from early 2004 to late 2013, Russian gold reserves increased over 250 percent, from approximately 390 tonnes to over 1,000 tonnes. Unlike China's, this increase was achieved almost entirely through domestic mine production and did not rely on imports. Russia is the world's fourth-largest gold producer, with output of approximately 200 tonnes per year. The Russian reserve increase was also done in steady increments of about 5 tonnes per month, announced regularly on the website of the Central Bank of Russia. Since the central bank does not rely on imports or the London bullion market to increase its gold holdings, Russia can afford to be more transparent than China because it is less vulnerable to price manipulation and front-running by the London bullion banks. Russia's acquisition program is ongoing, and its official gold holdings should surpass 1,100 tonnes in 2014. Reserves of 1,100 tonnes are over one-eighth the size of U.S. gold reserves, but the Russian economy is also about one-eighth the size of the U.S. economy. Measured in proportion to the size of their respective economies, Russian gold reserves have pulled ahead of those of the United States.

Many analysts have been baffled by the paradox of strong demand for physical gold around the world and the simultaneous weakness in the price of gold futures traded on the COMEX exchange since the August 2011 peak in gold prices. Physical buying is coming not only from central banks but also from individuals, as reflected in the demand for one-kilo bars versus the 400-ounce "good delivery" bars favored by central banks. Swiss refineries have been working overtime to convert large bars to smaller ones to meet this demand. This seeming paradox is easily explained. If the price of any good, whether gold or bread, is held below its intrinsic value by intervention in any form, the behavioral response is always to strip the shelves bare.

The scramble for gold, epitomized in the central bank gold-acquisition programs of China and Russia, also manifests itself in the urgency with which central banks are attempting to repatriate gold from foreign depositories to vaults on their home soil.

Apart from the U.S. hoard, almost half the official gold in the world is *not* stored in the home country of the holder but in vaults at the Federal Reserve Bank of New York and at the Bank of England in London. The Federal Reserve vaults hold approximately 6,400 tonnes of gold, and the Bank of England vaults approximately 4,500 tonnes. Almost none of the gold in the New York Federal Reserve vaults belongs to the United States, and less than 300 tonnes of the gold in the Bank of England belongs to the U.K. U.S. gold is mostly kept in two U.S. Army facilities at Fort Knox, Kentucky, and West Point, New York, with a small amount held at the U.S. Mint in Denver, Colorado. The Federal Reserve and the Bank of England together have about 10,600 tonnes of official gold belonging to Germany, Japan, the Netherlands, the IMF, and other large holders, as well as many smaller holders around the world. Third-party gold held at the Fed and the Bank of England constitutes 33 percent of the official gold in the world.

This concentration of official gold in New York and London is mostly a legacy of the various gold standards that existed on and off from 1870 to 1971. When gold was used to settle balance of payments between countries, it was easier to keep the gold in financial centers such as New York and London, then reassign legal title as needed, rather than ship the gold around the world. Today balance of payments are settled mostly in dollars or euros, not gold, so the money center rationale for gold no longer applies.

Centralized gold holdings are also a legacy of the Cold War (1946–91), when it was considered safer for Germany to keep its gold in New York than to risk confiscation by the Soviet armored divisions that surrounded Berlin. Now the risks to Germany of gold confiscation by the United States in the event of a financial meltdown are considerably higher than the risks of confiscation by Russian invasion. Countries such as Germany no longer have a compelling reason to keep their gold in New York or London, and there are significant risks in doing so. If the United States or the U.K. suddenly deemed it necessary to confiscate foreign gold to defend its paper currency in a crisis, that gold would be conveyed from the original owners to the possession of the United States or the U.K.

As a result of these changed circumstances and emerging risks, gold-owning nations have begun a movement to repatriate their gold. The first prominent repatriation was initiated by Venezuela, which ordered the Bank of England to return 99 tonnes from London to Caracas in August 2011. The first gold shipments took place in November 2011, and upon their arrival, President Hugo Chávez paraded the gold-filled armored cars through Caracas streets, to the cheers of everyday Venezuelans.

A larger and more significant gold-repatriation program was launched by Germany in 2013. Germany holds 3,391 tonnes of official gold and is currently the world's second-largest holder after the United States. At the end of 2012, German gold was located as follows: 1,051 tonnes in Frankfurt; 1,526 tonnes in New York; 441 tonnes in London; and 374 tonnes in Paris. On January 16, 2013, the Deutsche Bundesbank, the central bank of Germany, announced an eight-year plan to repatriate all the gold in Paris and 300 tonnes of the gold in New York back to Frankfurt. The gold in London would be left in place, and at the end of the repatriation plan in December 2020, German gold would be 50 percent in Frankfurt, 37 percent in New York, and 13 percent in London.

Commentators quickly fell upon the fact that the 300-tonne transfer from New York to Frankfurt would take eight years to complete as prima facie evidence that the New York Fed did not have the German gold in its vaults or was otherwise financially embarrassed by the request. But the Deutsche Bundesbank *does not want* the gold returned quickly. It prefers to have it in New York, where it can more efficiently be used for market manipulation. The Deutsche Bundesbank did not want to request the transfer at all but was pressured to do so by political supporters of Angela Merkel, who was facing reelection in September 2013. The physical security of Germany's gold had become a political issue in the Bundestag, the German parliament. The Deutsche Bundesbank's announced plan was merely a way to defuse the political issue while still leaving most of Germany's gold in New York. Even after full implementation of the plan in 2020, Germany will still have 1,226 tonnes in New York, an amount greater than the total reserves of all but three other countries in the world. It is more convenient for the Deutsche Bundesbank to have its gold in New York, where it can be utilized in gold swaps and gold leases, as part of central bank efforts to manipulate gold markets. Still, a significant amount of gold is on its way to Frankfurt—part of a global movement to repatriate national gold.

The same populist political pressures that forced the German central bank to repatriate part of its gold have also swelled up in Switzerland. While the central banks of China, Russia, and other nations were avidly purchasing gold, Switzerland was one of the largest sellers. At the beginning of 2000, Switzerland's gold reserves were over 2,590 tonnes. That amount dropped steadily, as the gold price was rising sharply, and by late 2008, Switzerland held only 1,040 tonnes, down 60 percent from the amount eight years earlier. Swiss gold reserves have remained at this level since, while gold's price rose significantly from its 2008 level.

There was sharp reaction in the Swiss parliament to these massive sales despite rising prices. On September 20, 2011, four Swiss parliament members, led by Luzi Stamm of the Swiss People's Party, introduced an initiative that requires all Swiss gold to be stored in Switzerland and that strips the Swiss National Bank of its ability to sell Switzerland's gold. The initiative also requires the Swiss National Bank to hold at least 20 percent of its total assets in gold. The last provision might actually require Switzerland to acquire even more bullion, since gold was only 8.9 percent of total Swiss reserves as of July 2013. On March 20, 2013, the initiative sponsors announced they had obtained the one hundred thousand signatures required to place the initiative on a ballot to be voted on by Swiss citizens—a key feature of Swiss democracy. The exact date of the Swiss gold referendum is not known but is expected by 2015.

In 2003 Kaspar Villiger, then the Swiss minister of finance, when asked in parliament about the location of Swiss gold, infamously replied, "I don't know . . . don't have to know, and don't want to know." Such arrogance, typical of global financial elites, is increasingly unacceptable to citizens, who see their gold reserves being dissipated by bureaucrats operating behind closed doors in central banks and enclaves like the IMF and BIS. The actions of Swiss officials cost their citizens over $35 billion in lost wealth, compared to the value of their reserves had Switzerland kept its gold.

The Venezuelans, Germans, and Swiss may be the most prominent exemplars of the gold-repatriation movement, but they are not alone in raising the issue. In 2013 the sovereign wealth fund of Azerbaijan, a major energy exporter, ordered its gold reserves moved from JPMorgan Chase in London to the Central Bank of Azerbaijan in Baku. The gold-repatriation issue was also raised publicly in 2013 in Mexico. In the Netherlands, members of the center-right Christian Democratic Appeal Party and the leftist Socialist Party have petitioned De Nederlandsche Bank, the Dutch central bank, to repatriate its 612 tonnes of gold. Only 11 percent of the Dutch gold, or 67 tonnes, is actually in the Netherlands. The remainder is divided with about 312 tonnes in New York, 122 tonnes in Canada, and 110 tonnes in London. When asked in 2012 about the possibility of Dutch gold stored in New York being confiscated by the United States, Klaas Knot, then president of De Nederlandsche Bank, replied, "We are regularly confronted with the extra-territorial functioning of laws from the United States and usually these are not cheerfully received in Europe." A small movement in Poland under the name "Give Our Gold Back," launched in August 2013, focused on the repatriation of Poland's 100 tonnes of gold held by the Bank of England. Of course, many countries, such as Russia, China, and Iran, already store their gold at home and are free of confiscation risk.

The issues of gold acquisition and gold repatriation by central banks are closely related. They are two facets of the larger picture of gold resuming its former role as the crux of the international monetary system. Major gold holders do not want to acknowledge it because they prefer the paper money system as it is. Smaller gold holders do not want to acknowledge it because they want to obtain gold at attractive prices and avoid the price spike that will result when the scramble for gold becomes disorderly. There is a convergence of interests, between those who disparage gold and those who embrace it, to keep the issue of gold as money off the table for the time being. This will not last, because the world is witnessing the inexorable remonetization of gold.

■ Gold Redux

There are few more tendentious comments on gold than the a priori statement that a gold standard cannot work today. In fact, a well-designed gold standard could work smoothly if the political will existed to enact it and to adhere to its noninflationary disciplines. A gold standard is the ideal monetary system for those who create wealth through ingenuity, entrepreneurship, and hard work. Gold standards are disfavored by those who do not create wealth but instead seek to extract wealth from others through inflation, inside information, and market manipulation. The debate over gold versus fiat money is really a debate between entrepreneurs and rentiers.

A new gold standard has many possible designs and would be effective, depending on the design chosen and the conditions under which it was launched. The classical gold standard, from 1870 to 1914, was hugely successful and was associated with a period of price stability, high real growth, and great invention. In contrast, the gold exchange standard, from 1922 to 1939, was a failure and a contributing factor in the Great Depression. The dollar gold standard, from 1944 to 1971, was a middling success for two decades before it came undone due to a lack of commitment by its principal sponsor, the United States. These three episodes from the past 150 years make the point that gold standards come in many forms and that their success or failure is determined not by gold per se but by the system design and the willingness of participants to abide by the rules of the game.

Consideration of a new gold standard begins with the understanding that the old gold standard was never completely left behind. When the Bretton Woods system broke down in August 1971, with President Nixon's abandonment of gold convertibility by foreign central banks, the gold standard was not immediately deserted. Instead, in December 1971 the dollar was devalued 7.89 percent so that gold's official price increased from $35 per ounce to $38 per ounce. The dollar was devalued again on February 12, 1973, by an additional 10 percent so that gold's new official price was $42.22 per ounce; this is still gold's official price today for certain central banks, for the U.S. Treasury, and for IMF accounting purposes, although it bears no relationship to the much higher market price. During this period, 1971–73, the international monetary system moved haltingly toward a floating-exchange-rate regime, which still prevails today.

In 1972 the IMF convened the Committee of Twenty, C-20, consisting of the twenty member countries represented on its executive board, to consider the reform of the international monetary system. The C-20 issued a report in June 1974, the "Outline of Reform," that provided guidelines for the new floating-rate system and recommended that the SDR be converted from a gold-backed reserve asset to one referencing a basket of paper currencies. The C-20 recommendations were hotly debated inside the IMF during 1975 but were not adopted at the time. At a meeting in Jamaica in January 1976, the IMF did initiate substantial reforms along the lines of the C-20 report, which were incorporated in the Second Amendment to the IMF Articles of Agreement. They became effective on April 1, 1978.

The international monetary debate, from the C-20 project in 1972 to the Second Amendment in 1978, was dominated by the disposition of IMF gold. The United States wanted to abandon any role for gold in international finance. The U.S. Treasury dumped 300 tonnes of gold on the market during the Carter administration to depress the price and demonstrate U.S. lack of interest. Meanwhile, France and South Africa were insisting on a continued role for gold as an international reserve asset. The Jamaica compromise was a muddle, in which 710 tonnes of IMF gold was returned to members, another 710 tonnes was sold on the market, and the remainder of approximately 2,800 tonnes was retained by the IMF. The IMF changed its unit of account to the SDR, and the pricing of SDRs was changed from gold to a basket of paper currencies. The United States was satisfied that gold's role had been demoted; France was satisfied that gold remained a reserve asset; and the IMF continued to own a substantial amount of gold. The essence of this U.S.-Franco compromise remains to this day.

With the coming of the Reagan administration in 1981, the United States went through a profound shift in its attitude toward gold. It sold less than 1 percent of its remaining gold from 1981 to 2006, and it has sold no gold at all since 2006. The retention of gold by the United States and the IMF since 1981, as well as the continuation of large gold hoards by Germany, Italy, France, Switzerland, and others, have left the world with a shadow gold standard.

Gold's continued role as a global monetary asset was brought home in a stunningly candid address given by Mario Draghi, head of the European Central Bank, at the Kennedy School of Government on October 9, 2013. In reply to a question from a reporter, Tekoa Da Silva, about central bank attitudes toward gold, Draghi remarked:

> You are . . . asking this to someone who has been Governor of the Bank of Italy. Bank of Italy is [the] fourth largest owner of gold reserves in the world. . . .
>
> I never thought it wise to sell [gold] because for central banks this is a reserve of safety. It's viewed by the country as such. In the case of non-dollar countries, it gives you a fairly good protection against fluctuations of the dollar, so there are several reasons, risk diversification and so on. So, that's why central banks, which had started a program for selling gold a few years ago, substantially . . . stopped. By and large they are not selling it any longer. Also the experience of some central banks that liquidated the whole stock of gold about ten years ago was not considered to be terribly successful.

France's insistence at Jamaica in 1976 that gold continue as a reserve asset has returned to the IMF's monetary banquet like Banquo's ghost.

Just as Banquo was promised in *Macbeth* that he would beget a line of kings, so gold may persevere as the once and future money.

▪ A New Gold Standard

How would a twenty-first-century gold standard be structured? It would certainly have to be global, involving at least the United States, the Eurozone, Japan, China, the U.K., and other leading economies. The United States is capable of launching a gold-backed dollar on its own, given its massive gold reserves, but if it were to do so, other currencies in the world would be unattractive to investors relative to a new gold-backed dollar. The result would be deflationary, with a diminution of transactions in those other currencies and reduced liquidity. Only a global gold standard could avoid the deflation that would accompany an effort by the United States to go it alone.

The first step would be a global monetary conference, similar to Bretton Woods, where participants would agree to establish a new global monetary unit. Since the SDR already exists, it is a perfectly suitable candidate for the new global money. But this new SDR would be gold backed and freely convertible into gold or the local currency of any participant in the system. It would not be the paper SDR that exists today.

The system would also have to be two-tiered. The top tier would be the SDR, which would be defined as equal to a specified weight in gold. The second tier would consist of the individual currencies of the participating nations, such as the dollar, euro, yen, or pound sterling. Each local currency unit would be defined as a specified quantity of SDRs. Since local currency is defined in SDRs, and SDRs are defined in gold, by extension every local currency would be worth a specified weight in gold. Finally, since every local currency is in a fixed relationship to SDRs and gold, each currency would also be in a fixed relationship to one another. As an example, if SDR1.00 = €1.00, and SDR1.00 = $1.50, then €1.00 = $1.50, and so on.

In order to participate in the new gold SDR system, a member nation would have to have an open capital account, meaning that its currency would have to be freely convertible into SDRs, gold, or currencies of the other participating members. This should not be a burden for the United States, Japan, the Eurozone, or others who already maintain open capital accounts, but it could be an impediment for China, which does not. However, China may find the attractions of a nondollar, gold-backed currency such as the new SDR sufficiently enticing that it would open its capital account in order to join and allow the new system to succeed.

Participants would be encouraged to adopt the new gold SDR as a unit of account as broadly as possible. Global markets in oil and other natural resources would now be priced in SDRs rather than dollars. The financial records of the largest global corporations, such as IBM and Exxon, would be maintained in SDRs, and various economic metrics, such as global output and balance-of-payments accounts, would be computed and reported in SDRs. Finally, an SDR bond market would develop, with issuance by sovereign nations, global corporations, and regional development banks, and with purchases by sovereign wealth funds and large pension funds. It might be intermediated by the largest global banks, such as Goldman Sachs, under IMF supervision.

One of the more daunting technical issues in this potential global gold SDR system is the determination of the proper fixed rates at which currencies can convert to one another. For example, should €1.00 be equivalent to $1.30, $1.40, $1.50, or another amount? This is essentially the same issue that the founders of the euro faced after the Maastricht Treaty was signed in 1992, which committed the parties to create a single currency from diverse currencies such as the Italian lira, the German mark, and the French franc. In the euro's case, years of technical study and economic theory developed by specialized institutions were applied to the task. Technical consideration is warranted today, too, but the best approach would be to use market signals to solve the problem. The parties in the new system could announce that the fixed rate would be determined in four years based on the weighted average of bank foreign currency transactions during the last twelve months prior to the fixing date. The four-year period would give markets sufficient time to adjust and consider the implications of the new system, and the twelve-month averaging period would smooth out short-term anomalies or market manipulation.

The most challenging issue involves the SDR's value measured in a weight of gold, and the fractional gold reserve required to make the system viable. The problem can be reduced to a single issue: the implied, nondeflationary price of gold in a global gold-backed monetary system. Once that issue was resolved with respect to one *numeraire,* conversion to other units of account using fixed exchange rates would be trivial.

Initially, the new system would operate without an expansion of the global money supply. Any nation that wanted SDRs could buy them from banks or dealers, earn them in trade, or acquire them from the IMF in exchange for its own currency. Local currency delivered to the IMF in exchange for SDRs would be sterilized so the global money supply did not expand. Discretionary monetary policy would be reserved to national central banks such as the Fed and ECB, subject to the need to maintain fixed rates to gold, SDRs, and other currencies. The IMF would resort to discretionary monetary policy through the unsterilized creation of new SDRs only in extraordinary circumstances and with approval of a supermajority of IMF members participating in the new system.

Given these constraints on the creation of new SDRs, the system would launch with the SDR as an anchor and unit of account but a relatively small amount of SDRs in existence. The combined base money supplies of the participants would constitute the global money supply, as it does today, and that money supply would be the reference point for determining the appropriate price for gold.

Another key issue would be determining the amount of gold backing needed to support the global money supply. Austrian School economists insist on 100 percent backing, but this is not strictly required. In practice, the system requires only enough gold to supply anyone with a preference for physical gold over gold-backed paper money, and adequate assurance that the fixed gold price will not be changed once established. These two goals are related; the stronger the assurance of consistency, the less gold is required to maintain confidence. Historically, gold standards have operated successfully with between 20 percent and 40 percent backing relative to money supply. Given the abandonment of gold in 1914, 1931, and 1971, a high figure will be required to engender confidence by justifiably cynical citizens. For illustrative purposes, take 50 percent of money supply as the target backing; the United States, the Eurozone, China, and

Japan as the participating economies; global official gold holdings as the gold supply; and M1 as the money supply. Dividing the money supply by the gold supply gives an implied, nondeflationary price for gold, under a gold-backed SDR standard, of approximately $9,000 per ounce.

The inputs in this calculation are debatable, but $9,000 per ounce is a good first approximation of the nondeflationary price of gold in a global gold-backed SDR standard. Of course, nothing moves in isolation. The world of $9,000-per-ounce gold is also the world of $600-per-barrel oil, $120-per-ounce silver, and million-dollar starter homes in mid-America. This new gold standard would not cause inflation, but it would be a candid recognition of the inflation that has already occurred in paper money since 1971. This one-time price jump would be society's reckoning with the distortions caused by the abuse of fiat currencies in the past forty years. Participating nations would need legislation to nominally adjust fixed-income payments to the neediest in forms such as pensions, annuities, social welfare, and savings accounts up to the insured level. Nominal values of debt would be left unchanged, instantaneously solving the global-sovereign-debt-and-deleveraging conundrum. Banks and rentiers would be ruined—a healthy step toward future growth. Theft by inflation would be a thing of the past, for as long as the system was maintained. Wealth extraction would be replaced with wealth creation, and the triumph of ingenuity could commence.

Discretionary monetary policy conducted by national central banks would be preserved in this new system. Indeed, the percentage of physical gold backing the currency issues could even be increased or decreased from time to time if needed. However, central banks participating in the system would be required to *maintain the fixed gold price* in their currency by acting as buyers and sellers in physical gold. Any central bank perceived as too easy for too long would find citizens lined up at its doors and would be quickly stripped of its gold. IMF gold-swap lines backed by other central banks would be made available to deal with temporary adjustment requirements—an echo of the old Bretton Woods system. These gold market operations would be conducted transparently to instill confidence in the process.

Importantly, the IMF would have emergency powers to increase the SDR supply with the approval of a supermajority of its members to deal with a global liquidity crisis, but SDRs and national currencies would remain freely convertible to gold at all times. If citizens had confidence in the emergency actions, the system would remain stable. If citizens perceived that money creation was occurring to rescue elites and rentiers, a run on gold would commence. These market signals would act as a brake on abuse by the IMF and the central banks. In effect, a democratic voice, mediated by market mechanisms, would be injected into global monetary affairs for the first time since the First World War.

Austrian School supporters of a traditional gold standard are unlikely to endorse this new gold standard because it has fractional, even variable gold backing. The conspiracy-minded are also unlikely to support it because it is global and has the look and feel of a new world order. Even the milder critics will point out that this system depends completely on promises by governments, and such promises have consistently been broken in the past. Yet it has the virtue of practicality; it could actually get done. It forthrightly addresses the problems of deflation that would occur if the United States took a go-it-alone approach, and it mitigates the hyperinflationary shock that would result if fractional backing were not used. The new gold standard comes close to Mundell's prescription that the optimal currency zone is the world, and it revives a version of Keynes's vision at Bretton Woods before the United States insisted on dollar hegemony.

Most profoundly, a new gold standard would address the three most important economic problems in the world today: the dollar's decline, the debt overhang, and the scramble for gold. The U.S. Treasury and Federal Reserve have decided that a weak-dollar policy is the remedy for the lack of world growth. Their plan is to generate inflation, increase nominal aggregate demand, and rely on the United States to pull the global economy out of the ditch like a John Deere tractor hitched to a harvester up to its axles in mud. The problem is that the U.S. solution is designed for cyclical problems, not for the structural problems that the world currently faces. The solution to structural problems involves new structures, starting with the international monetary system.

There is no paper currency that will come close to replacing the dollar as the leading reserve currency in less than ten years. Even now the dollar is being discarded and gold remonetized at an increasing tempo—both perfectly sensible reactions to U.S. weak-dollar policies. The United States and the IMF should lead the world to the gold-backed SDR, which would satisfy Chinese and Russian interests while leaving the United States and Europe with the leading reserve positions. The world cannot wait ten years for the paper SDR, the yuan, and the euro to converge into Barry Eichengreen's "Kumbaya" world of multiple reserve currencies. The consequences of misguided monetary leadership will be on display in far fewer than ten years.

CHAPTER 10

CROSSROADS

I'm the fellow who takes away the punch bowl just when the party is getting good.

William McChesney Martin Jr.
Chairman of the Federal Reserve Board, 1951–70

The trouble is that this is no ordinary recession, and a lot of people have not had any punch yet.

Kenneth Rogoff
June 6, 2013

Developed countries have no reason to default. They can always print money.

George Soros
April 9, 2013

▪ The Inflation-Deflation Paradox

Federal Reserve policy is at a crossroads facing unpleasant paths in all directions. Monetary policy around the world has reached the point where the contradictions embedded in years of market manipulation have left no choices that do not involve either contraction or catastrophic risk. Further monetary easing may precipitate a loss of confidence in money; policy tightening will restart the collapse in asset values that began in 2007. Only structural change in the U.S. economy, something outside the Fed's purview, can break this stalemate.

This much was clear by 2013, as weary economists and policy makers waited for the robust recovery they had eagerly anticipated since the stock market rally started in 2009. Annual GDP growth in the United States touched 4 percent in the fourth quarter of 2009, prompting talk of "green shoots" amid signs that the economy was bouncing back from the worst recession since the Great Depression. Even when growth fell to a 2.2 percent annual rate by the second quarter of 2010, the optimistic spin continued, with happy talk by Treasury secretary Timothy Geithner of a "recovery summer" in 2010. Reality slowly sank in. Annual growth was an anemic 1.8 percent in 2011 and was only slightly better at 2.2 percent in 2012. Then, despite predictions from the Fed and private analysts that 2013 would be a turnaround year, growth fell again to 1.1 percent in the first quarter of 2013, although it revived to 4.1 percent in the third quarter.

The economy was in a phase not seen in eighty years. It was neither a recession as technically defined, nor a robust recovery as widely expected. It was a depression, exactly as Keynes had defined it, "a chronic condition of sub-normal activity for a considerable period without any marked tendency either towards recovery or towards complete collapse." There was no cyclical recovery because the problems in the economy were not cyclical; they were structural. This depression should be expected to continue indefinitely in the absence of structural changes.

Fed forecasters and most private analysts use models based on credit and business cycles from the seventy-odd years since the end of the Second World War. Those baselines do not include any depressions. One must reach back eighty years, to the 1933–36 period, a recovery within a depression, to find a comparable phase. The Great Depression ended in 1940 with structural changes: the economy was put on a war footing. In early 2014 no war was imminent, and no structural changes were being contemplated. Instead, depressionary low growth and high unemployment have become normal in the U.S. economy.

The American Enterprise Institute's John Makin, who has an uncanny record of accurately predicting economic cycles, pointed out that based on historical patterns, the United States might actually be headed for a recession in 2014—the second recession within a depression since 2007, an eerie replay of the Great Depression. Makin pointed out that despite below-trend growth since 2009, the expansion has lasted over four years and is approaching the average longevity for modern economic expansions in the United States. Based on duration if not strength, U.S. real growth should be expected to turn negative in the near future.

Even if the United States does not enter a technical recession in 2014, the depression will continue, the strongest evidence coming from depression-level employment data. Despite cheerleading in late 2013 about the creation of two hundred thousand new jobs per month and a declining unemployment rate, the reality behind the headline data is grim. As analyst Dan Alpert points out, almost 60 percent of jobs created in the first half of 2013 were in the lowest-wage sectors of the U.S. economy. These sectors normally account for one-third of total jobs, meaning that new job creation was disproportionately low wage by a factor of almost two to one. Low-wage jobs are positions such as the order taker at McDonald's, the bartender at Applebee's, and the checkout clerk at Walmart. All work has dignity, but not all work has pay that can ignite a self-sustaining economic recovery.

About 50 percent of the jobs created during the first half of 2013 were part-time, defined as jobs with thirty-five hours of work per week or less. Some part-time jobs offer as little as one hour per week. If the unemployment rate were calculated by counting those working part-time who want full-time work, and those who want a job but have given up looking, the unemployment rate in mid-2013 would be 14.3 percent instead of the officially reported 7.1 percent. The 14.3 percent figure is comparable to levels reached during the Great Depression, a level consistent with an economic depression.

New hiring since 2009 has been roughly equal to the number of new entrants into the workforce in that time period, which means that it did nothing to reduce the total number of those who became unemployed during the acute phase of the panic and downturn in 2008 and 2009. Alpert also shows that even the supposed "good news" of a declining unemployment rate is misleading because the declining rate reflects those workers dropping out of the workforce entirely rather than new job creation in an expanding labor pool. The percentage of Americans counted in the labor force had dropped from a high of 66.1 percent before the new depression to 63.5 percent by mid-2013. Even with the reduced labor force, real wage gains adjusted for inflation were not being realized, and in fact real wages have been falling for the past fifteen years.

Added to this dismal employment picture is the striking increase in dependency on government programs. By late 2013, the United States had over 50 million citizens on food stamps; over 26 million citizens unemployed, underemployed, or discouraged from looking for work; and over 11 million citizens on permanent disability, many of those because their unemployment benefits had run out. These numbers are a national disgrace. Combined with feeble growth, borderline recession conditions, and over five years of zero interest rates, these figures made talk of an economic recovery seem misplaced.

Though overall conditions suggest a new depression, one element was missing from the portrait—namely, deflation, defined as a generalized drop in consumer prices and asset values. During the darkest stage of the Great Depression, from 1930 to 1933, cumulative deflation in the United States was 26 percent, part of a broader, worldwide deflationary collapse. The United States experienced slight deflation in 2009 compared to 2008, but nothing at all comparable to the Great Depression; in fact, mild inflation has persisted in the new depression, and the official consumer price index shows a 10.6 percent increase from the beginning of 2008 to mid-2013. The contrast between the extreme deflation of the Great Depression and the mild inflation of the new depression is the most obvious difference between the two episodes and is also the source of the greatest challenge now facing the Federal Reserve. It raises the vexing question of when and how to reduce and eventually reverse money printing.

A depression's natural state is deflation. Businesses faced with declining revenue and individuals faced with unemployment will rapidly sell assets to reduce debt, a process known as deleveraging. As asset sales continue and as spending declines, prices decline further, which is deflation's immediate cause. Those price declines then add further economic stress, leading to additional asset sales, more unemployment, and so on in a feedback loop. In deflation, the real value of cash increases, so individuals and businesses hoard cash instead of spending it or investing in new land, plant, and equipment.

This entire process of asset sales, hoarding, and price declines is called a liquidity trap, famously described by Irving Fisher in his 1933 work *The Debt-Deflation Theory of Great Depressions* and by John Maynard Keynes in his most influential work, *The General Theory of Employ-*

ment, Interest and Money. In a liquidity trap, the response to money printing is generally weak, and from a Keynesian perspective, fiscal policy is the preferred medicine.

While the response to money printing may be weak, it is not nil. Working against potential deflation has been a massive money-printing operation by the Federal Reserve. In the six years from 2008 to 2014, the Federal Reserve has increased base money from about $800 billion to over $4 trillion, a more than 400 percent increase. While the turnover or velocity of money has been in sharp decline, the quantity of money has skyrocketed, helping to offset the slower pace of spending. The combination of massive money printing and zero interest rates has also propped up asset prices, leading to a stock market rally and a strong recovery in housing prices since 2009. But asset values are being inflated from other sources too.

■ Tuition Tally

Another reason deflation has not prevailed over inflation, despite faint economic growth, is that the U.S. Treasury has promoted a new cash injection into the economy, larger than subprime housing finance in the 2002–7 period. This injection is in the form of student loans.

Student loans are the new subprime mortgages: another government-subsidized bubble about to burst. Students have a high propensity to spend, whether on tuition itself or on books, apartments, furniture, and beer. If you give students money, they will spend it; there is little danger that they will buy gold or otherwise hoard the money as savings. Tuition payments financed by student loans are a mere conduit since the payments are passed along as union faculty salaries or university overhead. Loan proceeds remaining after tuition are spent directly by the students.

Annual borrowing in all undergraduate and graduate student loan programs surged to over $100 billion per year in 2012, up from about $65 billion per year at the start of the 2007 depression. By August 2013, total student loans backed by the U.S. government exceeded $1 trillion, an amount that has doubled since 2009. A provision contained in the 2010 Obamacare legislation provided the U.S. Treasury with a near monopoly on student loan origination and sidelined most private lenders who formerly participated in this market. This meant that the Treasury could relax lending standards to continue the flow of easy money.

The student loan market is politically untouchable because higher education historically produces citizens with added skills who repay the loans and earn higher incomes over time. No member of Congress wants to support legislation that would crimp Johnnie or Susie's ability to afford college. But the program has morphed into direct government pump priming, in the same manner that historically productive home lending programs morphed into a housing bubble between 1994 and 2007. In the mortgage market, Fannie Mae and Freddie Mac used government subsidies to push home ownership beyond levels that buyers could afford, giving rise to subprime mortgages without documentation or down payments. The mortgage market crashed in 2007, marking the start of the depression.

Student loans now pose a similar dynamic. Most of the loans are sound and will be repaid as agreed. But many borrowers will default because the students did not acquire needed skills and cannot find jobs in a listless economy. Those defaults will make federal budget deficits worse, a development not fully reflected in official budget projections. In effect, student loans are being pumped out by the U.S. Treasury and directed to borrowers with a high propensity to spend and limited ability to repay.

These monies have helped prop up the U.S. economy, but the flow of tuition dollars isn't sustainable. It is economically no different than the Chinese building ghost cities with borrowed money that cannot be repaid. Chinese ghost cities and U.S. diplomas are real, but productivity increases and the ability to repay the borrowings are not.

While student loans may provide a short-term lift to discretionary spending, the long-term effects of excessive debt combined with the absence of jobs are another encumbrance on the economy. A record 21 million young adults between ages eighteen and thirty-one are living with their parents. Many of these stay-at-homes are recent graduates who cannot pay rent or afford down payments on homes because of student loans. For now, student loan cash flows and spending have helped to defer the deflation threat, but the student loan bubble will burst in the years ahead, making the debt and deficit crises worse.

■ The Inflation Conundrum

Former Fed chairman Bernanke once said that the Federal Reserve could combat deflation by throwing money from helicopters. His metaphor assumed that people would gladly pick up the money and spend it. In the real world, however, picking up the money means going into debt in the form of business loans, mortgages, or credit cards. Businesses and individuals are unwilling to go into debt because of policy uncertainty and the threat of even more deflation.

Going back to 2009, Bernanke's critics have claimed that quantitative easing would lead to unacceptably high inflation, even imminent hyperinflation. These critics focused exclusively on money printing, failing to perceive that inflation is only partially a function of money supply. The other key factor is behavior in the form of lending and spending. Underlying weakness in the economy, and extreme uncertainty about policies on taxes, health care, environmental regulation, and other business cost determinants, resulted in stagnation both in consumer spending and in business investment, two main drivers of economic growth.

A standoff in the battle between deflation and inflation does not mean that price stability prevails. The opposing forces may have neutralized each other for the time being, but neither has gone away. Collapsing growth in China and a reemergence of the sovereign debt crisis in Europe could give deflation the upper hand. Conversely, a war in the Middle East followed by a commodity price shock, surging oil prices, and panicked gold buying could cause dollar dumping and an inflationary groundswell that the Fed would be unable to contain. Either extreme is possible.

This dilemma is reflected in a difference of opinion at the Federal Open Market Committee (FOMC), the Fed's policy-making arm, between those who favor reduced money printing and those who favor a continuation or even expansion of the money supply through Fed asset purchases. The group that favors reduced money printing, so-called tapering, led by

Fed governor Jeremy Stein, contends that continued money printing is having only limited positive effects and may create asset bubbles and systemic risk. Since money is practically free because of zero-rate policy, and since leverage magnifies returns to investors, the inducement to borrow money and take a chance on rising asset prices is hard to resist. Leverage is available to stock traders in the form of margin loans and to home buyers in the form of cheap mortgages. Since rising stock and home prices are based on cheap money rather than economic fundamentals, both markets are forming new bubbles, which will eventually burst and damage confidence again.

Under certain scenarios, the outcome could be worse than a bursting bubble and might include systemic risk and outright panic. The stock market is poised for a crash worse than 2000 or 2008. Business television anchors and sell-side analysts are only too happy to announce each new "high" in the stock market indexes. In fact, these highs are mostly nominal—they are not entirely real. When the reported index levels are adjusted for inflation, a different picture emerges. The 2008 peak was actually below the 2000 peak in real terms. The nominal peak in 1973 was followed in 1974 by one of the worst stock market crashes in U.S. history. Past is not necessarily prelude; still, the combination of extreme leverage, economic weakness, and a looming recession all put the stock market at risk of a historic crash. Any such crash would result in a blow to confidence that no amount of Fed money printing could assuage. It would trigger an extreme version of Fisher's debt-deflation cycle. In this scenario, deflation would finally gain the upper hand over inflation, and the economic dynamics of the early 1930s would return with a vengeance.

Another factor that could contribute to a worst-case result is the hidden leverage on bank balance sheets in the form of derivatives and asset swaps. The concern here relates not to a stock market crash but to a counterparty failure that triggers a liquidity crisis in financial markets and precipitates a panic.

The pro-tapering group around Fed governor Stein understands that reduced money printing may hurt growth, but they fear that a stock market crash or a financial panic could hurt growth much more by destroying confidence. In their view, reduced money printing now is a way to let a little air out of the bubbles without deflating them entirely.

In opposition to this view are FOMC members like Fed chairwoman Janet Yellen, who see no immediate inflation risk due to excess capacity in labor markets and manufacturing, and who favor continued large asset purchases and money printing as the only hope for continued growth, especially in light of the recent tightening in fiscal policy. For Yellen, the money printing should continue until persistent inflation above 2.5 percent actually emerges *and* until unemployment is 6.5 percent or less. Yellen favors continued money printing even if inflation rises to 3 percent or more so long as unemployment is above 6.5 percent. She regards the risks of financial panic as remote and is confident that inflation can be controlled in due course with available tools if inflation does rise too far.

Yellen's confidence in the remoteness of inflation and in the Fed's ability to control inflation, if it does emerge, is based on her application of conventional general equilibrium models that do not include the most advanced theoretical work on complexity theory, interconnectedness, and the sudden emergence of systemic risk. On the other hand, her understanding that inflation was not imminent due to slack in labor and industrial capacity made her economic forecasts consistently more accurate than those of her colleagues and the Fed staff from 2011 to 2013. These forecasting successes added to her credibility inside the Federal Reserve and were important in her selection as the new Fed chairwoman. As a result, her views on the need for continued money printing carry great weight with the Fed staff and the FOMC.

It is not surprising that the FOMC members are deeply divided between the contrasting views espoused by Stein and Yellen. Stein is no doubt correct that systemic risk is building up unseen in the banking system through off-balance-sheet transactions and that new bubbles are emerging. Yellen is undoubtedly right that the economy is fundamentally weak and needs all the policy support it can get to avoid outright recession and deflation. The fact that both sides in the debate are correct means both sides are also incorrect to the extent that they fail to incorporate their opponents' valid points in their own views. The resulting policy incoherence is the inevitable outcome of the Fed's market manipulation. Valid price signals are suppressed or distorted, which induces banks to take risky positions that serve no business purpose except to eke out profits in a zero-rate environment. At the same time, asset values are inflated, which means that capital is not devoted to its most productive uses but instead chases evanescent mark-to-market gains in stocks and housing. Both continued money printing *and* the reduction of money printing pose risks, albeit different kinds.

The result is a standoff between natural deflation and policy-induced inflation. The economy is like a high-altitude climber proceeding slowly, methodically on a ridgeline at twenty-eight thousand feet without oxygen. On one side of the ridge is a vertical face that goes straight down for a mile. On the other side is a steep glacier that offers no way to secure a grip. A fall to either side means certain death. Yet moving ahead gets more difficult with every step and makes a fall more likely. Turning back is an option, but that means finally facing the pain that the economy avoided in 2009, when the money-printing journey began.

The great American novelist F. Scott Fitzgerald wrote in 1936 that "the test of a first-rate intelligence is the ability to hold two opposed ideas in the mind at the same time, and still retain the ability to function." By 2014, the Federal Reserve board members were being put to Fitzgerald's test. Inflation and deflation are opposed ideas, as are tapering and nontapering. No doubt, the Fed board members start with first-rate intelligence; they are now confronted with opposing ideas. The question is whether, as Fitzgerald phrased it, they can "still retain the ability to function."

■ Confidence

Former Federal Reserve chairman Paul Volcker joined the Fed as a staff economist in 1952 and has witnessed or led every significant monetary and financial development since. As the Treasury undersecretary, he was at President Nixon's side when the dollar's convertibility into gold was ended in 1971. Appointed Fed chairman by President Carter in 1979, he raised interest rates to 19 percent in 1981 to break the back of the borderline hyperinflation that gripped America from 1977 onward. In 2009 President Obama selected him to head the Economic Recovery Advisory Board, to formulate responses to the worst economic slump since the

Great Depression. From this platform, he advanced the Volcker Rule, an attempt to restore sound banking practices that were abandoned with the repeal of Glass-Steagall in 1999. The Volcker Rule finally got past the big bank lobbyists in 2013. Volcker correctly perceived the riskiest facet of the banking system and deserves much credit for working to fix it. No banker or policy maker knows more about money, and how it works, than Volcker.

When pressed about the dollar's role in the international monetary system today, Volcker acknowledges the challenges facing the U.S. economy, and the dollar in particular, with a kind of been-there-done-that attitude. He points out that circumstances are not as dire as they were in 1971, when there was a run on Fort Knox, or in 1978, when, because international creditors had begun to reject the U.S. dollar as a store of value, the U.S. Treasury issued the infamous Carter Bonds, denominated in Swiss francs.

When pressed harder, Volcker is candid about China's rise and acknowledges talk of the dollar being knocked off its pedestal as the world's leading reserve currency. But he just as quickly points out that despite the talk, no currency comes close to the dollar in terms of the deep, liquid pools of investable assets needed for true reserve-currency status. Volcker is no fan of the gold standard and believes a return to gold is neither feasible nor desirable.

Finally, when presented with issues such as bonded debt, massive entitlements, continuing deficits, and legislative dysfunction that suggests the dollar dénouement has already begun, Volcker narrows his gaze, hardens his demeanor, and utters one word: "Confidence."

He believes that, if people have confidence in it, the dollar can weather any storm. If people lose confidence in the dollar, no army of Ph.D.s can save it. On this point, Volcker is certainly right, yet no one can say whether confidence in the dollar has passed the point of no return due to Fed blunders, debt-ceiling debacles, and the precautions of the Russians and Chinese.

Unfortunately, there are growing signs that confidence in the dollar is evaporating. In October 2013 the Fed's Price-adjusted Broad Dollar Index, the best gauge of the dollar's standing in foreign exchange markets, stood at 84.05, an improvement on the all-time low of 80.52 of July 2011 but approximately equal to prior lows in October 1978, July 1995, and April 2008. Demand for physical gold bullion, a measure of lost confidence in the dollar, began rising sharply in mid-to-late 2013, another sign of a weaker dollar. The foreign currency composition of global reserves shows a continuing decline in the dollar's use as a reserve currency from about 70 percent in 2000 to about 60 percent today. No one of these readings indicates an immediate crisis, but all three show declining confidence.

Other indications are anecdotal and difficult to quantify but are no less telling. Among them are the rise of alternative currencies and of virtual or digital currencies such as bitcoin. Digital currencies exist within private peer-to-peer computer networks and are not issued by or supported by any government or central bank. The bitcoin phenomenon began in 2008 with the pseudonymous publication of a paper (by Satoshi Nakamoto) describing the protocols for the creation of a new electronic digital currency. In January 2009 the first bitcoins were created by Nakamoto's software. He continued making technical contributions to the bitcoin project until 2010, at which point he withdrew from active participation. However, by that time a large community of developers, libertarians, and entrepreneurs had taken up the project. By late 2013, over 11.5 million bitcoins were in circulation, with the number growing steadily. The value of each bitcoin fluctuates based on supply and demand, but it had exceeded $700 per bitcoin in November 2013. Bitcoin's long-term viability as a virtual currency remains to be seen, but its rapid and widespread adoption can already be taken as a sign that communities around the world are seeking alternatives to the dollar and traditional fiat currencies.

Beyond the world of alternative currencies lies the world of transactions without currencies at all: the electronic barter market. Barter is one of the most misunderstood of economic concepts. A large economic literature is devoted to the inefficiencies of barter, which requires the simultaneous coincidence of wants between the two bartering parties. If one party wanted to trade wheat for nails, and the counterparty wanted wheat but had only rope to trade, the first party might accept the rope and go in search of someone with nails who wanted rope. In this telling, money was an efficient medium of exchange that solved the simultaneity problem because one could sell her wheat for money and then use the money to buy nails without having to barter the rope. But as author David Graeber points out, the history of barter is mostly a myth.

Economists since Adam Smith have assumed that barter was the historical predecessor of money, but there is no empirical, archaeological, or other evidence for the existence of a widespread premoney barter economy. In fact, it appears that premoney economies were based largely on credit—the promise to return value in the future in exchange for value delivered today. The ancient credit system allowed intertemporal exchanges, as it does today, and solved the problem of the simultaneous coincidence of wants. Historical barter is one more example of economists developing theories with scant attachment to reality.

Mythical history notwithstanding, barter *is* a rapidly growing form of economic exchange today, because networked computers solve the simultaneity problem. One recent example involved the China Railway Corporation, General Electric, and Tyson Foods. China Railway had a customer, a poultry processor, that filed for bankruptcy, resulting in the railroad taking possession of frozen turkeys pledged as collateral. General Electric was selling gas turbine-electric locomotives to the railroad, and China Railway inquired if it could pay for the locomotives with the frozen turkeys. GE, which has an eighteen-person e-barter trading desk, quickly ascertained that Tyson Foods China would take delivery of the turkeys for cash. China Railway delivered the turkeys to Tyson Foods, which paid cash to GE, and then GE delivered the locomotives to China Railway. The transaction between GE and China Railway was effectively the barter of turkeys for turbines, with no money changing hands. Cashless barter may not have been part of the past, but it will increasingly be part of the future.

The bitcoin and barter examples both illustrate that the dollar grows less essential every day. This is also seen in the rise of regional trade currency blocs, such as Northeast Asia and the China–South America connection. Three-way trade among China, Japan, and Korea, and the bilateral trade between China and its respective trading partners in South America, are among the largest and fastest-growing trading relationships in the world. None of the currencies involved—yuan, yen, won, real, or peso—are close to becoming reserve currencies. But all serve perfectly well as trade currencies for transactions that would previously have been invoiced in dollars. Trade currencies are used as a temporary way to keep score in the balance of trade, while reserve currencies come with deep pools of investable assets used to store wealth. Even if these local currencies are used for trade and not as reserves, each transaction represents a diminution in the role of the dollar.

To paraphrase Hemingway, confidence in the dollar is lost slowly at first, then quickly. Virtual currencies, new trade currencies, and the absence of currency (in the case of barter) are all symptoms of the slow, gradual loss of confidence in the dollar. They are the symptoms but not the cause. The causes of declining confidence in the dollar are the dual specter of inflation *and* deflation, the perception on the part of many that the dollar is no longer a store of value but a lottery ticket, potentially worth far more, or far less, than face value for reasons beyond the holder's control. Panic gold buying, and the emergency issuance of SDRs to restore liquidity when it comes, will signal the stage of a rapid loss of confidence.

Volcker was right in his assertion that confidence is indispensable to the stability of any fiat currency system. Unfortunately, the academics who are now responsible for monetary policy focus exclusively on equilibrium models and take confidence too much for granted.

■ Failure of Imagination

Following the 9/11 attacks in New York and Washington, D.C., the U.S. intelligence community was reproached for its failure to detect and prevent the hijacking plots. These criticisms reached a crescendo when it was revealed that the CIA and the FBI had specific intelligence linking terrorists and flying lessons but failed to share the information or connect the dots.

The *New York Times* columnist Tom Friedman offered the best description of what went wrong: "Sept. 11 was not a failure of intelligence or coordination. It was a failure of imagination." Friedman's point was that even if all the facts had been known and shared by the various intelligence agencies, they still would have missed the plot because it was too unusual and too evil to fit analysts' preconceived notions of terrorist capabilities.

A similar challenge confronts U.S. economic policy makers today. Data on economic performance, unemployment, and the buildup of derivatives inside megabanks are readily available. Conventional economic models abound, and the analysts applying those models are among the best and brightest in their field. There is no lack of information and no shortage of intelligence; the missing piece is imagination. Fed and Wall Street analysts, tied to the use of models based on past business cycles, seem incapable of imagining the dangers actually confronting the U.S. economy. The 9/11 attacks demonstrated that the failure to imagine the worst often results in a failure to prevent it.

The worst economic danger confronting the United States is deceptively simple. It looks like this:

$$(-1) - (-3) = 2$$

In this equation, the first term represents nominal growth, the second term represents inflation or deflation, and the right side of the equation equals real growth. A more familiar presentation of this equation is:

$$5 - 2 = 3$$

In this familiar form, the equation says that we begin with 5 percent nominal growth, then subtract 2 percent inflation, in order to reach 3 percent real growth. Nominal growth is the gross value of goods and services produced in the economy, and inflation is a change in the price level that does not represent real growth. To arrive at real growth, one subtracts inflation from the nominal value. This same inflation adjustment can be applied to asset values, interest rates, and many other data points. One must subtract inflation from the stated or nominal value in order to get the real value.

When inflation turns to deflation, the price adjustment becomes a negative value rather than a positive one, because prices decline in a deflationary environment. The expression $(-1) - (-3) = 2$ describes nominal growth of negative 1 percent, minus a price change of negative 3 percent, producing positive 2 percent real growth. In effect, the impact of declining prices more than offsets declining nominal growth and therefore produces real growth. This condition has almost never been seen in the United States since the late nineteenth century. But it is neither rare elsewhere nor impossible in the United States; in fact, it has been Japan's condition for parts of the past twenty-five years.

The first thing to notice about this equation is that there is *real growth* of 2 percent, which is weak by historic standards but roughly equal to U.S. growth since 2009. As an alternative scenario, using the formula above, assume annual deflation of 4 percent, as actually occurred from 1931 to 1933. Now the expression is (-1) − (-4) = 3. In this case, *real* growth would be 3 percent, much closer to trend and arguably not at depressionary levels. However, a condition of *high deflation, zero interest rates, and continuing high unemployment closely resembles a depression.* This is an example of the through-the-looking-glass quality of economic analysis in a world of deflation.

Despite possible real growth, the U.S. Treasury and the Federal Reserve fear deflation more than any other economic outcome. Deflation means a persistent decline in price levels for goods and services. Lower prices allow for a higher living standard even when wages are constant, because consumer goods cost less. This would seem to be a desirable outcome, based on advances in technology and productivity that result in certain products dropping in price over time, such as computers and mobile phones. Why is the Federal Reserve so fearful of deflation that it resorts to extraordinary policy measures designed to cause inflation? There are four reasons for this fear.

The first is deflation's impact on government debt repayment. Debt's real value may fluctuate based on inflation or deflation, but the nominal value of a debt is fixed by contract. If one borrows $1 million, then one must repay $1 million plus interest, regardless of whether the real value of $1 million is greater or less due to deflation or inflation. U.S. debt is at a point where no feasible combination of real growth and taxes will finance repayment of the amount owed. But if the Fed can cause inflation— slowly at first to create money illusion, and then more rapidly—the debt will be manageable because it will be repaid in less valuable nominal dollars. In deflation, the opposite occurs, and the real value of the debt increases, making repayment more difficult.

The second problem with deflation is its impact on the debt-to-GDP ratio. This ratio is the debt amount divided by the GDP amount, both expressed in nominal terms. Debt is continually increasing in nominal terms because of continuing budget deficits that require new financing, and interest payments that are financed with new debt. However, as shown in the previous example, real growth can be positive even if nominal GDP is shrinking, provided deflation exceeds nominal growth. In the debt-to-GDP ratio, when the debt numerator expands and the GDP denominator shrinks, the ratio increases. Even without calculating entitlements, the U.S. debt-to-GDP ratio is already at its highest level since the Second World War; including entitlements makes the situation far worse. Over time, the impact of deflation could drive the U.S. debt-to-GDP ratio above the level of Greece, closer to that of Japan. Indeed, this deflationary dynamic is one reason the Japanese debt-to-GDP ratio currently exceeds 220 percent, by far the highest of any developed economy. One impact of such sky-high debt-to-GDP ratios on foreign creditors is ultimately a loss of confidence, higher interest rates, worse deficits because of the higher interest rates, and finally an outright default on the debt.

The third deflation concern has to do with the health of the banking system and systemic risk. Deflation increases money's real value and therefore increases the real value of lenders' claims on debtors. This would seem to favor lenders over debtors, and initially it does. But as deflation progresses, the real weight of the debt becomes too great, and debtor defaults surge. This puts the losses back on the bank lenders and causes bank insolvencies. Thus the government prefers inflation, since it props up the banking system by keeping banks and debtors solvent.

The fourth and final problem with deflation is its impact on tax collection. This problem is illustrated by comparing a worker making $100,000 per year in two different scenarios. In the first scenario, prices are constant and the worker receives a $5,000 raise. In the second scenario, prices drop 5 percent and the worker receives no raise. On a pretax basis, the worker has the same 5 percent increase in her standard of living in both scenarios. In the first scenario, the improvement comes from a higher wage, and in the second it comes from lower prices, but the economic result is the same. Yet on an after-tax basis, these scenarios produce entirely different outcomes. The government taxes the raise, say, at a 40 percent rate, but the government *cannot tax* the declining prices.

In the first scenario, the worker keeps only 60 percent of the raise after taxes. But in the second scenario, she keeps 100 percent of the benefit of lower prices. If one assumes inflation in the first example, the worker may be even worse off because the part of the raise remaining after taxes is diminished by inflation, and the government is better off because it collects more taxes, and the real value of government debt declines. Since inflation favors the government and deflation favors the worker, governments always favor inflation.

In summary, the Federal Reserve prefers inflation because it erases government debt, reduces the debt-to-GDP ratio, props up the banks, and can be taxed. Deflation may help consumers and workers, but it hurts the Treasury and the banks and is firmly opposed by the Fed. This explains Alan Greenspan's extraordinary low-interest-rate policies in 2002 and Ben Bernanke's zero-rate policy beginning in 2008. From the Fed's perspective, aiding the economy and reducing unemployment are incidental by-products of the drive to inflate. The consequence of these deflationary dynamics is that the government must have inflation, *and the Fed must cause it.*

The dynamics amount to a historic collision between the natural forces of deflation and government's need for inflation. So long as price index data show that deflation is a threat, the Fed will continue with its zero-rate policy, money printing, and efforts to cheapen the dollar in foreign exchange markets in order to import inflation through higher import prices. When the data show a trend toward inflation, the Fed will allow the trend to continue in the hope that nominal growth will become self-sustaining. This will cause inflation to take on a life of its own through behavioral feedback loops not included in Fed models.

Japan is a large canary in a coal mine in this regard. The Asian nation has undergone persistent core deflation since 1999 but also saw positive real growth from 2003 to 2007 and negative nominal growth in 2001 and 2002. Japan has not experienced the precise combination of negative nominal growth, deflation, and positive real growth on a persistent basis, but it has flirted with all those elements throughout the past fifteen years. To break out of this coil, Japan's new prime minister, Shinzo Abe, elected in December 2012, declared his policy of the "three arrows": money printing to cause inflation, deficit spending, and structural reforms. A corollary to this policy was to weaken the exchange value of the yen to import inflation, mostly through higher prices for energy imports.

The initial response to "Abenomics" was highly favorable. In the five months following Abe's election, the yen, measured against dollars, dropped 17 percent, from 85 to 1 to 102 to 1, while the Japanese Nikkei stock index rose 50 percent. The combination of a cheaper yen, the wealth effect from rising stock prices, and the promise of more money printing and deficit spending seemed like a page from a central banker's playbook on how to break out of a deflationary spiral.

Despite the burst of market enthusiasm for Abenomics, a cautionary note was raised in a speech on May 31, 2013, in Seoul, South Korea, by one of the most senior figures in Japanese finance, Eisuke Sakakibara, a former deputy finance minister, nicknamed "Mr. Yen." Sakakibara emphasized the importance of real growth even in the absence of nominal growth and pointed out that the Japanese people are wealthy and have prospered personally despite decades of low nominal growth. He made the often-overlooked point that because of Japan's declining population, real GDP *per capita* will grow faster than real *aggregate* GDP. Far from a disaster story, a Japan that has deflation, depopulation, and declining nominal GDP can nevertheless produce robust real per capita GDP growth for its citizens. Combined with the accumulated wealth of the Japanese people, this condition can result in well-to-do society even in the face of nominal growth that would cause most central bankers to flood the economy with money.

Sakakibara is not unaware of the impact of deflation on the real value of debt. The Japanese debt-to-GDP ratio is mitigated by zero interest rates, which prevent the debt from compounding rapidly. Most Japanese government debt is owned by the Japanese themselves, so a foreign financing crisis of the kind that struck Thailand in 1997 and Argentina in 2000 is unlikely. Sakakibara's most telling point is that Japan's growth problems are structural, not cyclical, and therefore cyclical remedies such as money printing will not work; he sees no chance of Japanese inflation hitting the 2 percent target rate.

Sakakibara's insights, that monetary remedies will not solve structural problems, and that real growth is more important than nominal growth, are being ignored by central banks in both the United States and Japan.

The Federal Reserve and the Bank of Japan will pursue the money-printing pseudoremedy as far as possible until investors finally lose confidence in their currencies, their bonds, or both. Japan, the canary, will likely suffer this crisis first.

The Federal Reserve's supporters ask defensively, *What else could the Fed have done?* If the Fed had not resorted to extraordinary money creation in 2008 and the years since, it does seem likely that asset prices would have plunged further, unemployment would have been significantly higher, and GDP growth significantly worse. A sharp contraction with rising bankruptcies and crashing industrial output, akin to the depression of 1920, might have resulted. In short, the Fed defenders argue, there really was no choice except to create money on an unprecedented scale.

In this view, the problems of executing an exit strategy from monetary expansion are more manageable than the problems of economic depression. Defenders assert that the Fed took the right path in 2008 and persevered with great skill. This is the mainstream view that has resulted in the contemporary lore of Bernanke-as-hero, a halo that has now been transferred to Janet Yellen.

The history of depressions in the United States from 1837 onward supports another perspective on the Fed's actions. Under this view, the Fed should have provided only enough liquidity to mitigate the worst phase of the financial panic in late 2008. Thereafter the Fed should have capped the amount of excess reserves and normalized interest rates in a range of 1 to 2 percent. Most of the large banks—including Citibank, Morgan Stanley, and Goldman Sachs—should have been temporarily nationalized, their stockholders wiped out, and their bondholders subject to principal reductions as needed to restore capital. Nonperforming assets could have been stripped from these banks in receivership, then placed in a long-term government trust, to be liquidated for the taxpayers' benefit as circumstances permitted. Management of the banks should have been fired, while enforcement actions and criminal prosecutions were pursued against them as the facts warranted. Finally asset prices, particularly housing and stocks, should have been allowed to fall to much lower levels than were seen in 2009.

In this scenario, bankruptcies and unemployment in 2009–10 would have been much higher and asset values much lower than what actually occurred. The year 2009 would have resembled 1920 in the severity of its depression, with skyrocketing unemployment, collapsing industrial production, and widespread business failure. But an inflection point would have been reached. The government-owned banks could have been taken public with clean balance sheets and would have exhibited a new willingness to lend. Private equity funds would have found productive assets at bargain prices and begun investing. Abundant labor, with lower unit labor costs, could have been mobilized to expand productivity, and a robust recovery, rather than a lifeless one, would have commenced. The depression would have been over by 2010, and real growth would have been 4 to 5 percent in 2011 and 2012.

The benefit of a severe depression in 2009 is not severity for its own sake. No one wishes to play out a morality tale involving greedy bankers getting their just deserts. The point of a severe depression in 2009 is that it would have prompted the structural adjustments that are needed in the U.S. economy. It would also have diverted assets from parasitic pursuits in banking toward productive uses in technology and manufacturing. It would have moved unit labor costs to a new, lower level that would have been globally competitive when higher U.S. productivity was taken into account. Normalized interest rates would have rewarded savers and helped strengthen the dollar, making the United States a magnet for capital flows from around the world. The economy would have been driven by investment and exports rather than relying on the lending-and-spending consumption paradigm. Growth composition would have more nearly resembled the 1950s, when consumption was about 60 percent of GDP, instead of recent decades, when consumption was closer to 70 percent. These types of healthy, long-term structural adjustments would have been forced on the U.S. economy by a one-time liquidation of the excesses of debt and leverage and the grotesque overexpansion of finance.

It is not correct to say the Federal Reserve had no choice in its handling of the economy at the start of the Depression. It is correct to say, in Tom Friedman's phrase, that there was a failure of imagination to see that the economy's problems were structural, not cyclical. The Fed applied obsolete general equilibrium models and took a blinkered view of the structural challenge. Policy makers at the Fed and the Treasury avoided a sharp depression in 2009 but created a milder depression that continues today and will continue indefinitely. Federal Reserve and U.S. Treasury officials and staff said repeatedly in 2009 that they wanted to avoid Japan's mistakes in the 1990s. Instead, they have repeated every one of Japan's mistakes in their failure to pursue needed structural changes in labor markets, eliminate zombie banks, cut taxes, and reduce regulation on the nonfinancial sector. The United States is Japan on a larger scale, with the same high taxes, low interest rates that penalize savers, labor market rigidities, and too-big-to-fail banks.

Abenomics and Federal Reserve money printing share a frenzied focus on avoiding deflation, but the underlying deflation in both Japan and the United States is not anomalous. It is a valid price signal that the system had too much debt and too much wasted investment prior to the crash. Japan was overinvested in infrastructure, just as the United States was overinvested in housing. In both cases, the misallocated capital reached the point where it had to be written off in order to free up bank balance sheets to make new, more productive loans. But that isn't what happened.

Instead, as a result of political corruption and cronyism, regulators in both countries preserved the ailing balance sheets in amber along with banker job security. The deflationary price signals were muted with money printing, the same way pain in athletes is masked with steroids. But the deflation did not go away, and it will never go away until the structural adjustments are made.

The United States may find false courage in Japan's apparent success, using its model as ammunition for evaluating its own QE policies. But the signs in Japan are misleading, consisting of more money illusion and new asset bubbles. Japan reached the crossroads first; it opted for Abenomics. The Fed needs to look more critically at Japan's putative escape from depression. If it follows the Japanese path, both nations will be headed for an acute debt crisis. The only difference may be that Japan gets there first.

CHAPTER 11

MAELSTROM

Nobody really understands gold prices, and I don't pretend to understand them either.

Ben Bernanke
Former Federal Reserve Board chairman
July 18, 2013

I think that, at this time, this global civilisation has gone beyond its limits . . . because it has created such a cult of money.

Pope Francis
July 26, 2013

◾ The Snowflake and the Avalanche

An avalanche is an apt metaphor of financial collapse. Indeed, it is more than a metaphor, because the systems analysis of an avalanche is identical to the analysis of how one bank collapse cascades into another.

An avalanche starts with a snowflake that perturbs other snowflakes, which, as momentum builds, tumble out of control. The snowflake is like a single bank failure, followed by sequential panic, ending in fired financiers forced to vacate the premises of ruined Wall Street firms carrying their framed photos and coffee mugs. Both the avalanche and the bank panic are examples of complex systems undergoing what physicists call a phase transition: a rapid, unforeseen transformation from a steady state to disintegration, finally coming to rest in a new state completely unlike the starting place. The dynamics are the same, as are the recursive mathematical functions used in modeling the processes. Importantly, the relationship between the frequency and severity of events as a function of systemic scale, called degree distribution, is also the same.

In assessing the risk of financial collapse, one should not only envision an avalanche but study it as well. Complexity theory, first advanced in the early 1960s, is new as the history of science goes, but it offers striking insights into how complex systems behave.

Many analysts use the words *complex* and *complicated* interchangeably, but that is inexact. A *complicated* mechanism, like the clockworks on St. Mark's Square in Venice, may have many moving parts, but it can be assembled and disassembled in straightforward ways. The parts do not adapt to one another, and the clock cannot suddenly turn into a sparrow and fly away. In contrast, *complex* systems sometimes do morph and fly away, or slide down mountains, or ruin nations. Complex systems include moving parts, called autonomous agents, but they do more than move. The agents are diverse, connected, interactive, and adaptive. Their diversity and connectivity can be modeled to a limited extent, but interaction and adaptation quickly branch into a seeming infinity of outcomes that can be modeled in theory but not in practice. To put it another way, one can know that bad things might happen yet never know exactly why.

Clocks, watches, and motors are examples of constrained systems that are complicated but not complex. Contrast these with ubiquitous complex systems, including earthquakes, hurricanes, tornadoes—and capital markets. A single human being is a complex system. One billion human beings engaged in trading stocks, bonds, and derivatives constitute an immensely complex system that defies comprehension, let alone computation. This computational challenge does not mean policy makers and risk managers should throw up their hands or use make-believe models like "value at risk." Risk management is possible with the right combination of complexity tools and another essential: humility about what is knowable.

Consider the avalanche. The climbers and skiers at risk can never know when an avalanche will start or which snowflake will cause it. But they do know that certain conditions are more dangerous than others and that precautions are possible. Snow's wetness or dryness is carefully observed, as is air temperature and wind speed. Most important, alpinists observe the snowpack size, or what physicists call systemic scale. Those in danger know that a large snowpack can unleash not just a large avalanche but an *exponentially larger* one. Sensible adaptations include locating villages away from chutes, skiing outside the slide paths, and climbing ridgelines above the snow. Alpinists can also descale the snowpack system with dynamite. One cannot predict avalanches, but one can try to stay safe.

In capital markets, regulators too often do not stay safe; rather, they increase the danger. Permitting banks to build up derivatives books is like ignoring snow accumulation. Allowing JPMorgan Chase to grow larger is like building a village directly in the avalanche path. Using value at risk to measure market danger is like building a ski lift to the unsteady snowpack with free lift tickets for all. Current financial regulatory policy is misguided because the risk-management models are unsound. More unsettling still is the fact that Wall Street executives know the models are unsound but use them anyway because the models permit higher leverage, bigger profits, and larger bonuses. The regulators suspect as much but play along, often in the hope of landing a job with the banks they regulate. Metaphorically speaking, the bankers' mansions are high on a ridgeline far from the village, while the villagers, everyday Americans and citizens around the world, are in the path of the avalanche.

Financial avalanches are goaded by greed, but greed is not a complete explanation. Bankers' parasitic behavior, the result of a cultural phase transition, is entirely characteristic of a society nearing collapse. Wealth is no longer created; it is taken from others. Parasitic behavior is not confined to bankers; it also infects high government officials, corporate executives, and the elite societal stratum.

The key to wealth preservation is to understand the complex processes and to seek shelter from the cascade. Investors are not helpless in the face of elite decadence.

■ Risk, Uncertainty, and Criticality

The prototypical explication of financial risk comes from Frank H. Knight's seminal 1921 work *Risk, Uncertainty and Profit.* Knight distinguished between *risk,* by which he meant an unknown outcome that can nevertheless be modeled with a degree of expectation or probability, and *uncertainty,* an unknown outcome that cannot be modeled at all. The poker game Texas hold'em is an example of risk as Knight used the term. When a card is about to be turned up, a player does not know in advance what it will be, but he does know with *certainty* that it will be one among fifty-two unique possibilities in one of four suits. As more cards are turned up, the certainty increases because some outcomes have been eliminated by prior play. The gambler takes risks but is not dealing with complete uncertainty.

Now imagine the same game with a player who insists on using "wild cards." In a wild card game, any card can be deemed to be any other card by any player to help her make a high hand like a full house or a straight flush. Technically, this is not complete Knightian uncertainty, but it comes close. Even the best poker players with superb computational skills cannot compute the odds of making a hand with wild cards. This is why professional poker players detest wild card games and amateurs enjoy them. The wild card is also a good proxy for complexity. Turning the two of clubs into an ace of spades on a whim is like a phase transition— unpredictable, instantaneous, and potentially catastrophic if one is on the losing side of the bet.

Knight's work came forty years before complexity theory emerged, before the advent of the computer made possible advanced research into randomness and stochastic systems. His division of the financial landscape into the black-and-white worlds of risk and uncertainty was useful at the time, but today there are more shades of gray.

Random numbers are those that cannot be predicted but can be assigned values based on a probability of occurrence over time or in a long series. Coin tosses and playing cards are familiar examples. It is impossible to know if the next coin toss will be heads or tails, and you cannot know if the next card in the deck is the ace of spades, but you can compute the odds. Stochastic models are those that describe systems based on random number inputs. Such systems are not deterministic but probabilistic, and when applied to financial markets, they allow prices and values to be assigned based on the probabilities. This was Knight's definition of *risk*. Stochastic systems may include nonlinear functions, or exponents, that cause small input changes to produce massive changes in results.

Stochastic models are supplemented by integral calculus, which measures quantity, and differential calculus, which measures change. Regressions, which are backward-looking associations of one variable to another, allow researchers to correlate certain events. This taxonomy of random numbers, stochastic systems, nonlinear functions, calculus, and regression comprises modern finance's toolkit. The application of this toolkit to derivatives pricing, value at risk, monetary policy, and economic forecasting takes practitioners to the cutting edge of economic theory.

Beyond the cutting edge is complexity theory. Complexity has not been warmly embraced by mainstream economics, in part because it reveals that much economic research for the past half-century is irrelevant or deeply flawed. Complexity is a quintessential example of new science overturning old scientific paradigms. Economists' failure to embrace the new science of complexity goes some way toward explaining why the market collapses in 1987, 1998, 2000, and 2008 were both unexpected and more severe than experts believed possible.

Complexity offers a way to understand the dynamics of feedback loops through recursive functions. These have so many instantaneous iterations that explosive results may emerge from minute causes *too small even to be observed*. An example is the atomic bomb. Physicists know that when highly enriched uranium is engineered into a *critical state* and a neutron generator is applied, a catastrophic explosion will result that can level a city; but they do *not* know precisely which subatomic particle will start the chain reaction. Modern economists spend their time looking for the subatomic particle while ignoring the critical state of the system. They are looking for snowflakes and ignoring the avalanche.

Another formal property of complex systems is that the size of the worst event that can happen is an exponential function of the system scale. This means that when a complex system's size is doubled, the systemic risk does not double; it may increase by a factor of ten or more. This is why each financial collapse comes as a "surprise" to bankers and regulators. As systemic scale is increased by derivatives, systemic risk grows exponentially.

Criticality in a system means that it is on the knife-edge of collapse. Not every complex system is in a critical state, as some may be stable or subcritical. One challenge for economists is that complex systems *not* in the critical state often behave like noncomplex systems, and their stochastic properties can appear stable and predictable right up to the instant of criticality, at which point emergent properties manifest and a catastrophe unfolds, too late to stop. Again, enriched uranium serves as an illustration. A thirty-five-pound block of uranium shaped as a cube poses no risk. It is a complex system—the subatomic particles do interact, adapt, and decay—but no catastrophe is imminent. But when the uranium block is precision engineered in two parts, one the size of a grapefruit and one like a baseball bat, and the parts are forced together by high explosives, an atomic explosion results. The system goes from subcritical to critical by engineering.

Complex systems can also go from subcritical to critical spontaneously. They morph in the same way a caterpillar turns into a butterfly, a process physicists call "self-organized criticality." Social systems including capital markets are characterized by such self-organized criticality. One day the stock market behaves well, and the next day it unexpectedly collapses. The 22.6 percent one-day stock market crash on Black Monday, October 19, 1987, and the 7 percent fifteen-minute "flash crash" on May 6, 2010, are both examples of the financial system self-organizing into the critical state; at that point, it takes one snowflake or one sell order to start the collapse. Of course, it is possible to go back after the fact and find a particular sell order that, supposedly, started the market crash (an example of hunting for snowflakes). But the sell order is irrelevant. What matters is the system state.

◼ Gold Games

Central bank gold market manipulation is an example of action in a complex system that can cause the system to reach the critical state.

That central banks intervene in gold markets is neither new nor surprising. To the extent that gold is money, and central banks control money, then central banks must control gold. Prior to gold's partial demonetization in the mid-1970s, central bank involvement in gold markets was arguably not manipulative but a matter of policy, although the policy was conducted nontransparently.

In the post–Bretton Woods era, there have been numerous well-documented central bank gold market manipulations. In 1975 Federal Reserve chairman Arthur Burns wrote a secret memorandum to President Gerald Ford that stated:

> The broad question is whether central banks and governments should be free to buy gold . . . at market-related prices. . . . The Federal Reserve is opposed. . . .
>
> Early removal of the present restraints on . . . official purchases from the private market could well release forces and induce actions that would increase the relative importance of gold in the monetary system. . . .
>
> Such freedom would provide an incentive for governments to revalue their official gold holdings at a market-related price. . . . Liquidity creation of such extraordinary magnitude would seriously endanger, perhaps even frustrate our efforts . . . to get inflation under control. . . .
>
> I have a secret understanding in writing with the Bundesbank . . . that Germany will not buy gold, either from the market or from another government, at a price above the official price of $42.22 per ounce.

Just three days after the Burns memorandum was written, President Ford sent a letter to German chancellor Helmut Schmidt incorporating the substance of Burns's advice:

THE WHITE HOUSE
WASHINGTON

JUNE 6, 1975

Dear Mr. Chancellor:

*... We ... feel strongly that some safeguards are necessary to ensure that
a tendency does not develop to place gold back in the center of the system. We
must ensure that there is no opportunity for governments to begin active
trading in gold among themselves with the purpose of creating a gold bloc or
reinstating reliance on gold as the principal international monetary medium.
In view of the world-wide inflation problem, we must also guard against
any further large increase of international liquidity. If governments were
entirely free to trade with one another at market-related prices, we would
add to our own common inflation problem. ...*

Sincerely,
Gerald R. Ford

Central bank gold market manipulation wasn't unique to the 1970s
but continued in the decades that followed. A Freedom of Information
Act (FOIA) lawsuit against the Federal Reserve System filed by an advo-
cacy group uncovered meeting notes of the secret Gold and Foreign Exchange Committee of G-10 central bank governors held at the Bank for
International Settlements on April 7, 1997. That committee is the successor to the notorious 1960s London Gold Pool price-fixing scheme. The
notes, prepared by Dino Kos of the Federal Reserve Bank of New York,
include the following:

In May 1996, the market traded the equivalent of $3 billion of gold
daily. Swap deals accounted for 75 percent of the volume. . . . Gold
had traditionally been a secretive market. . . .
  Gold leasing was also a prominent piece of the market, whose
growth central banks were very much a part of. The central banks,
in turn, had been responding to pressures that they turn a non-

earning asset into one that generates at least some positive return. . . . Central banks mostly lent gold at maturities of 3–6
months. . . . Central banks had some responsibility for the gold
leasing market since it was their activity which made that market
possible to begin with. . . . Gold does have a role as a war chest and
in the international monetary system. . . .

BIS had not sold any gold in many years. The BIS did some leasing.

[Peter] Fisher (United States) . . . noted that the price of gold . . .
had historically not trended toward the cost of production. This
seemed to suggest an ongoing supply/demand imbalance. . . . He had
the sense that the gold leasing market was an important component
in this puzzle. . . .

Mainert (Germany) asked how a big sale would affect the market.
What would happen if, say, the central banks sold 2,500 tonnes—
equivalent to one year's production. . . . Nobody took up Mainert's
challenge. . . .

[Peter] Fisher explained that U.S. gold belongs to the Treasury.
However, the Treasury had issued gold certificates to the Reserve
Banks, and so gold . . . also appears on the Federal Reserve balance
sheet. If there were to be a revaluation of gold, the certificates would
also be revalued upwards; however [to prevent the Fed's balance
sheet from expanding] this would lead to sales of government securities.

More recently, on September 17, 2009, former Federal Reserve Board
governor Kevin Warsh sent a letter to a Virginia law firm denying an
FOIA request for documentation of Fed gold swaps on the grounds that
the Fed had an exemption for "information relating to swap arrangements with foreign banks on behalf of the Federal Reserve System."
While the FOIA request was denied, Warsh's letter at least acknowledged
that central bank swaps exist.

On May 31, 2013, Eisuke Sakakibara, former vice minister of the
Japanese Ministry of Finance, cheerfully recalled how Japan's government had secretly acquired 300 tonnes of gold in the mid-1980s. This
gold acquisition does not appear in the Bank of Japan's reserve position

reported by the World Gold Council, because it was executed by the Finance Ministry rather than by the central bank:

> We bought 300 tonnes of gold in the 1980s to strike a commemorative coin for the sixtieth anniversary of the reign of Emperor Hirohito. It was a very difficult operation. We worked through JPMorgan and Citibank. We could not disclose our actions because it was a very large quantity, and we did not want the price to go up that much. So we bought gold futures, which are very liquid, and then we surprised the market by standing for delivery! Some of the bars delivered were three-nines [99.90 percent pure], but we melted them down and refined them into four-nines [99.99 percent pure] because we could only use the finest gold for the Emperor.

The gold was transported to Japan by Brinks in the upper deck of two Boeing 747s configured for cargo use. Two shipments were used not because of weight but to spread the risk. Brinks had two couriers on each flight so that the gold could be watched at all times even as one courier slept.

The foregoing documentary record is just the tip of the iceberg in terms of official gold market manipulation by central banks, finance ministries, and their respective bank agents. Still, it establishes beyond dispute that governments use a combination of gold purchases, sales, leases, swaps, futures, and political pressure to manipulate gold prices in order to achieve policy objectives, and they have done so for decades, since the end of Bretton Woods. Official gold sales that depressed gold prices were practiced extensively by Western central banks from 1975 to 2009 but came to an abrupt end in 2010, as gold prices skyrocketed and citizens questioned the wisdom of selling such a valuable asset.

The most notorious and heavily criticized case involved the sale of 395 tonnes of U.K. gold by chancellor of the exchequer Gordon Brown in a series of auctions from July 1999 to March 2002. The average price received by the U.K. was about $275 per ounce. Using $1,500 per ounce as a reference price, losses to U.K. citizens from Brown's blunder exceed $17 billion. More damaging than the lost wealth was the U.K.'s diminished standing among the ranks of global gold powers. Recently, outright gold sales by central banks as a form of price manipulation have lost their appeal as gold reserves have been depleted, prices have surged, and the United States has conspicuously refused to sell any gold of its own.

The more powerful price manipulation techniques by central banks and their private bank agents involve swaps, forwards, and futures or leases. These "paper gold" transactions permit massive leverage and exert downward pressure on gold prices, while the physical gold seldom leaves the central bank vaults.

A gold *swap* is typically conducted between two central banks as an exchange of gold for currency, with a promise to reverse the transaction in the future. In the meantime, the party receiving the currency can invest it for a return over the life of the swap.

Gold *forward* and gold *futures* transactions are conducted either between private banks and counterparties or on exchanges. These are contracts that promise gold delivery at a future date; the difference between a forward and a future is that the forward is traded over the counter with a known counterparty, while a future is traded anonymously on an exchange. Parties earn a profit or incur a loss depending on whether the gold price rises or falls between the contract date and the future delivery date.

In a *lease* arrangement, one central bank leases its gold to a private bank that sells it on a forward basis. The central bank collects a fee for the lease, like rent. When a central bank leases gold, it gives the private banks the title needed to conduct forward sales. The forward sales market is then amplified by the practice of selling *unallocated* gold. When a bank sells unallocated gold to a customer, the customer does not own specific gold bars. This allows the banks to sell multiple contracts to multiple parties using the *same* gold. In *allocated* transactions, the client has direct title to specific numbered bars in the vault.

These arrangements have one thing in common, which is that physical gold is rarely moved, and the same gold can be pledged many times to support multiple contracts. If the Federal Reserve Bank of New York leases 100 tonnes to JPMorgan in London, JPMorgan then takes legal possession under the lease, but the gold remains in the Fed's New York vault. With legal title in hand, JPMorgan can then sell the same gold ten times to different customers on an unallocated basis.

Similarly, a bank like HSBC can enter the futures market and sell 100 tonnes of gold to a buyer for delivery in three months but needs no physical gold to do so. The seller needs only to meet margin requirements in cash, which are a small fraction of the gold's value. These leveraged paper gold transactions are far more effective in manipulating market prices than outright sales, because the gold does not have to leave the central bank vaults; therefore the amount of selling power is many times greater than the gold on hand.

The easiest way for central banks to disguise their actions in the gold markets is to use bank intermediaries such as JPMorgan. The granddaddy of all bank intermediaries is the Bank for International Settlements, based in Basel, Switzerland. That the BIS acts for the central bank clients in the gold markets is not surprising; in fact, it was one reason the BIS was created in 1930. The BIS denominates its financial books and records in SDRs, as does the IMF. The BIS website states plainly, "Around 90% of customer placements are denominated in currencies, with the remainder in gold. . . . Gold deposits amounted to SDR 17.6 billion [about $27 billion] at 31 March 2013. . . . The Bank owned 115 tonnes of fine gold at 31 March 2013."

The BIS's eighty-third annual report, for the period ending March 31, 2013, states:

> The Bank transacts . . . gold on behalf of its customers, thereby providing access to a large liquidity base in the context of, for example, regular rebalancing of reserve portfolios or major changes in reserve currency allocations. . . . In addition, the Bank provides gold services such as buying and selling, sight accounts, fixed-term deposits, earmarked accounts, upgrading and refining and location exchanges.

Sight accounts in gold are unallocated, and *earmarked* accounts in gold are allocated. In finance, *sight* is an old legal term meaning "payable on demand or presentment," although there is no requirement to have the gold on hand until such demand is actually made. The BIS achieves the same leverage employed by its private bank peers using leasing, forwards, and futures.

Notably, footnote 15 of the accounting policies in the 2010 BIS annual report stated, "Gold loans comprise fixed-term gold loans *to commercial banks*." In the 2013 report, the same footnote stated, "Gold loans comprise fixed-term gold loans." Apparently by 2013 the BIS considered it wise to hide the fact that the BIS deals with private commercial banks. This deletion makes sense because the BIS is one of the main transmission channels for gold market manipulation. Central banks deposit gold with the BIS, which then leases the gold to commercial banks. Those commercial banks sell the gold on an unallocated basis, which allows ten dollars of sales or more for every one dollar of gold deposited at the BIS. Massive downward pressure is exerted on the gold market, but no physical gold ever changes hands. It is a well-honed system for gold price suppression.

While the presence of central banks in gold markets is undoubted, the exact times and places of their manipulation are not disclosed. But intriguing inferences can be made. For example, on September 18, 2009, the IMF authorized the sale of 403.3 tonnes of gold. Of that amount, 212 tonnes were sold, during October and November 2009, to the central banks of India, Mauritius, and Sri Lanka. An additional 10 tonnes were sold to the Central Bank of Bangladesh in September 2010. These sales were done by prearrangement to avoid disrupting the market. Sales of the remaining 181.3 tonnes commenced on February 17, 2010, but the buyers have never been disclosed. The IMF claimed the other sales were "on market" but also said that "initiation of on-market sales did not preclude further off-market gold sales directly to interested central banks or other official holders." In other words, the 181.3 tonnes could easily have gone to China or the BIS.

At the same time as the IMF gold sales were announced and conducted, the BIS reported a sharp spike in its own gold holdings. BIS gold increased from 154 tonnes at the end of 2009 to over 500 tonnes at the end of 2010. It is possible that the IMF transferred part of the unaccounted-for 181.3 tonnes to the BIS, and that the BIS Banking Department, controlled at the time by Günter Pleines, a former central banker from Germany, sold the gold to China. It is also possible that the large gold influx was attributable to gold swaps from desperate European banks trying to raise cash to meet obligations as their asset values imploded during the sovereign debt crisis. The answer is undisclosed, but either way the BIS stood ready to facilitate such nontransparent gold market activity as it had done for the Nazis and others since 1930.

Some of the most compelling evidence for manipulation in gold markets comes from a study conducted by the research department of one of the largest global-macro hedge funds in the world. This study involved two hypothetical investment programs over a ten-year period, from 2003 to 2013. One program would buy gold futures at the New York COMEX opening price every day and sell at the close. The other program would buy gold at the beginning of after-hours trading and sell just before the COMEX open the following day. In effect, one program would own New York hours and the other program would own the after-hours. In a non-manipulated market, these two programs should produce nearly identical results over time, albeit with daily variations. In fact, the New York program revealed catastrophic losses, while the after-hours program showed spectacular gains well in excess of the market gold price over the same period. The inescapable inference is that manipulators slam the New York close, which creates excess profit opportunities for the after-hours trader. Since the New York close is the most widely reported "price" of gold, the motivation is equally clear.

The motivation for central bank gold market manipulation is as subtle as the methods used. Central banks want inflation to reduce the real value of government debt and to transfer wealth from savers to banks. But central banks also work to suppress the price of gold. These twin goals seem difficult to reconcile. If central banks want inflation, and if a rising gold price is inflationary, why would central banks suppress the gold price?

The answer is that central banks, principally the Federal Reserve, *do* want inflation, but they want it to be *orderly* rather than disorderly. They want the inflation to come in small doses so that it goes unnoticed. Gold is highly volatile, and when it spikes up sharply, it raises inflationary expectations. The Federal Reserve and the BIS suppress gold prices not to keep them down forever, but rather to keep the increases orderly so that savers do not notice inflation. Central banks act like a nine-year-old boy who sees fifty dollars in his mom's wallet and steals one dollar thinking she won't notice. The boy knows that if he takes twenty, Mom *will* notice, and he will be punished. Inflation of 3 percent per year is barely noticed, but if it persists for twenty years, it cuts the value of the national debt almost in half. This kind of slow, steady inflation is the central banks' goal. Managing inflation expectations by manipulating gold prices downward was the rationale given by Fed chairman Arthur Burns to President Gerald Ford in the secret 1975 memo. That hasn't changed.

Since then, however, an even more ominous motive for central bank gold price manipulation has emerged. The gold price must be kept low until gold holdings are rebalanced among the major economic powers, and the rebalancing must be completed before the collapse of the international monetary system. When the world returns to a gold standard, either by choice to create inflation, or of necessity to restore confidence, it will be crucial to have support from all the world's major economic centers. A major economy that does not have sufficient gold will either be relegated to the periphery of any new Bretton Woods–style conference, or refuse to participate because it cannot benefit from gold's revaluation. As in a poker game, the United States possessed all the chips at Bretton Woods and used them aggressively to dictate the outcome. Were Bretton Woods to happen again, nations such as Russia and China would not permit the United States to impose its will; they would prefer to go their own way rather than be subordinate to U.S. financial hegemony. A more equal starting place would be required to engender a cooperative process for reforming the system.

Is there a preferred metric for rebalancing reserves? Many analysts look at the statistics for gold as a percentage of reserves. The United States has 73.3 percent of its reserves in gold; the comparable figure for China is 1.3 percent. But this metric is misleading. Most countries have reserves consisting of a combination of gold and hard currencies. But since the United States can print dollars, it has no need for large foreign currency reserves, and as a result, the U.S. reserve position is dominated by gold. China, on the other hand, has little gold but approximately $3 trillion of hard-currency reserves. Those reserves are valuable in the short run even if they are vulnerable to inflation in the future. For these reasons, the 73 percent U.S. ratio overstates U.S. strength, and the 1.3 percent ratio overstates China's weakness.

A better measure of gold's role as a monetary reserve is to divide gold's nominal market value by nominal GDP (gold-to-GDP ratio). Nominal

GDP is the total value of goods and services that an economy produces. Gold is the true monetary base, the implicit reserve asset behind the Fed's base money called M-Zero (M0). Gold is M-Subzero. The gold-to-GDP ratio reveals the true money available to support the economy and presages the relative power of a nation if a gold standard resumes. Here are recent data for a select group of economies that together comprise over 75 percent of global GDP:

Table 2. Gold-to-GDP Ratio for Selected Economies

Country	Gold (metric tonnes)	Market value of gold at $1,500/oz.	GDP	Gold/GDP ratio
Eurozone	10,783.4	$569 billion	$12.3 trillion	4.6%
United States	8,133.5	$429 billion	$15.7 trillion	2.7%
China	1,054.1	$56 billion	$8.2 trillion	0.7%
Russia	996.1	$53 billion	$2 trillion	2.7%
Japan	765.2	$40 billion	$6 trillion	0.7%
India	557.7	$29 billion	$1.8 trillion	1.6%
U.K.	310.3	$16 billion	$2.4 trillion	0.7%
Australia	79.9	$4 billion	$1.5 trillion	0.3%
Brazil	67.2	$3.5 billion	$2.4 trillion	0.1%
Canada	3.2	$0.2 billion	$1.8 trillion	0.01%
Total	22,750.6	$1,199.7 billion	$54.1 trillion	2.2%

The global gold-to-GDP ratio of 2.2 percent reveals that the global economy is leveraged to real money at a 45-to-1 ratio but with a significant skew in favor of the United States, the Eurozone, and Russia. Those three economies have ratios above the global average; the Eurozone's ratio at 4.6 percent is more than double the global average. The United States and Russia are in strategic gold parity, the result of Russia's 65 percent increase in its gold reserves since 2009. This dynamic is an eerie echo of the early 1960s "missile gap," from a time when Russia and the

United States competed for supremacy in nuclear weapons. That competition was deemed unstable and resulted in strategic arms limitations agreements in the 1970s, which have maintained nuclear stability in the forty years since. Russia has now closed the "gold gap" and stands on a par with the United States.

The conspicuous weak links are China, the U.K., and Japan, each with a 0.7 percent ratio, less than one-third the U.S.-Russia ratio and far smaller than that of the Eurozone. Other major economies, such as Brazil and Australia, stand even lower, while Canada's gold hoard is trivial compared to the size of its economy.

If gold is not money, these ratios are unimportant. If, however, there were a collapse of confidence in fiat money and a return to gold-backed money, either by design or on an emergency basis, these ratios would determine who would have the most influence in IMF or G20 negotiations to reform the international monetary system. On current form, Russia, Germany, and the United States would dominate those discussions.

■ China's Gold Deception

Once again we find ourselves looking at China. It seems absurd to posit that the international monetary system could be reformed without major participation by China, the world's second-largest economy (third if the Eurozone is viewed as a single entity). It is known, but not publicly disclosed, that China has far greater gold reserves than it states officially. If Table 2 is restated to show China with an estimated—but more accurate—4,200 tonnes of gold, then the change in ratios is dramatic.

In this revised alignment, the global ratio increases slightly from 2.2 percent to 2.5 percent, putting global gold leverage at 40 to 1. More important, China would now join the "gold club" with a 2.7 percent ratio, equivalent to Russia and the United States and comfortably above the global average.

Table 3. Impact of Chinese Stealth Acquisition on Gold-to-GDP Ratios

Country	Gold (metric tonnes)	Market value of gold at $1,500/oz.	GDP	Gold/GDP ratio
Eurozone	10,783.4	$569 billion	$12.3 trillion	4.6%
United States	8,133.5	$429 billion	$15.7 trillion	2.7%
China	**4,200.0**	**$222 billion**	**$8.2 trillion**	**2.7%**
Russia	996.1	$53 billion	$2 trillion	2.7%
Japan	765.2	$40 billion	$6 trillion	0.7%
India	557.7	$29 billion	$1.8 trillion	1.6%
U.K.	310.3	$16 billion	$2.4 trillion	0.7%
Australia	79.9	$4 billion	$1.5 trillion	0.3%
Brazil	67.2	$3.5 billion	$2.4 trillion	0.1%
Canada	3.2	$0.2 billion	$1.8 trillion	0.01%
Total	25,896.5	$1,365.7 billion	$54.1 trillion	2.5%

Although it is rarely discussed publicly by monetary elites, the increase of China's gold ratio from 0.7 percent toward 2.7 percent, as shown in the comparison of Table 2 and Table 3, has actually been occurring in recent years. When this gold rebalancing is complete, the international monetary system could move to a new equilibrium gold price without China being left behind with only paper money. The increase in China's gold reserves is designed to give China gold parity with Russia, the United States, and the Eurozone and to rebalance global gold reserves.

This rebalancing paves the way for either global inflation or gold's emergency use as a reserve currency, but the path has been complicated for China. When Europe and Japan emerged from the ashes of the Second World War, they were able to acquire gold by redeeming their dollar trade surpluses, since the dollar was freely convertible at a fixed price. U.S. gold reserves declined by 11,000 tonnes from 1950 to 1970 as Europe and Japan redeemed dollars for gold. Thirty years later China was the dominant trading nation, earning large dollar surpluses. But the gold window had been closed since 1971, and China could not swap dollars for U.S. gold at a fixed price. As a result, China was forced to acquire its gold reserves on the open market and through its domestic mines.

This market-based gold acquisition posed three dangers for China and the world. The first was that the market impact of such huge purchases meant that gold's price might skyrocket before China could complete the rebalancing. The second was that China's economy was growing so quickly that the amount of gold needed to reach strategic parity was a moving target. The third was that China could not dump its dollar reserves to buy gold because it would burden the United States with higher interest rates, which would hurt China's economy if U.S. consumers stopped buying Chinese goods in response.

The greatest risk to China in the near future is that inflation will emerge in the United States before China obtains all the gold it needs. In that case, the combination of China's faster growth and higher gold prices will make it costly to maintain its gold-to-GDP ratio. However, once China does acquire sufficient bullion, it will have a hedged position because whatever is lost to inflation will be gained in higher gold prices. At that point, China can give a green light to U.S. inflation. This move toward evenly distributed gold reserves also explains central bank efforts at price manipulation, as the United States and China have a shared interest in keeping the gold price low until China acquires its gold. The solution is for the United States and China to coordinate gold price suppression through swaps, leases, and futures. Once the rebalancing is complete, probably in 2015, there will be less reason to suppress gold's price because China will not be disadvantaged in the event of a price spike.

Evidence that the United States is accommodating China's gold reserve acquisition is not difficult to find. The most intriguing comment comes from Min Zhu, the IMF's deputy managing director. In response to a recent question concerning China's gold acquisition, he replied, "China's acquisition of gold makes sense because most global reserves have some credit element to them; they're paper money. It's a good idea to have part of your reserves in something real." The use of the term *credit* to describe reserves is consistent with the reality that all paper money is a central bank liability and therefore a form of debt. Treasury bonds purchased with paper money are likewise a form of debt. Min Zhu's distinction between *credit* reserves and *real* reserves highlights precisely the role of gold as true base money, or M-Subzero.

The reaction within the U.S. national security community to China's gold rebalancing is nonchalance. When asked about Chinese gold acquisitions, one of the highest-ranking U.S. intelligence officials shrugged and said, "Somebody's got to own it," as if gold reserves were part of a global garage sale. A senior official in the office of the secretary of defense expressed concern about the strategic implications of China's gold rebalancing but then went on to say, "The Treasury really doesn't like it when we talk about the dollar."

The Pentagon and CIA routinely defer to the Fed and the U.S. Treasury when the subject turns to gold and dollars, while Congress is mostly in the dark on this subject. Congressman James Himes, one of only four members of either party with a seat on both the House Financial Services Committee and the House Permanent Select Committee on Intelligence, said, "I never hear any discussion of gold reserve acquisition." With the military, intelligence agencies, and Congress all unconcerned or uninformed about China's acquisition of gold, the Treasury and Fed have a free hand to help the Chinese until the rebalancing is a fait accompli.

Despite the discreet and delicate handling of the global gold rebalancing, there are increasing signs that the international monetary system may collapse before a transition to gold or SDRs is complete. In the argot of chaos theorists, the system is going wobbly. Almost every "paper gold" contract has the capacity to be turned into a physical delivery through a notice and conversion provision. The vast majority of all futures contracts are rolled over into more distant settlement periods, or are closed out through an offsetting contract. But buyers of gold futures contracts have the right to request physical delivery of metal by providing notice and arranging to take delivery from designated warehouses. A gold lease can be terminated by the lessor at the end of its term. So-called unallocated gold can be turned into allocated bars, typically by paying additional fees, and the allocated gold can then be delivered to the owner on demand. Certain large gold exchange-traded fund (ETF) holders can convert to physical gold by redeeming the shares and taking gold from the ETF warehouse.

The potentially destabilizing factor is that the amount of gold subject to paper contracts is one hundred times the amount of physical gold backing those contracts. As long as holders remain in paper contracts, the system is in equilibrium. If holders in large numbers were to demand physical delivery, they could be snowflakes on an unstable mountain of paper gold. When other holders realize that the physical gold will run out before they can redeem their contracts for bullion, the slide can cascade into an avalanche, a de facto bank run, except the banks in this case are the gold warehouses that support the exchanges and ETFs. This is what happened in 1969 as European trading partners of the United States began cashing in dollars for physical gold. President Nixon shut the window on these redemptions in August 1971. If he had not done so, the U.S. gold vaults at Fort Knox would have been stripped bare by the late 1970s.

A similar dynamic commenced on October 4, 2012, when spot gold prices hit an interim peak of $1,790 per ounce. From there, gold fell over 12 percent in the next six months. Then gold crashed an additional 23.5 percent, falling to $1,200 per ounce by late June. Far from scaring off buyers, the gold crash made gold look cheap to millions of individual buyers around the world. They lined up at banks and boutiques, quickly stripping supplies. Buyers of standard 400-ounce and 1-kilo bars found there were no sellers; they had to wait almost thirty days for new bars to be produced by the refineries. The Swiss refineries Argor-Heraeus and Pamp moved to around-the-clock shifts to keep up with gold demand. Massive redemptions took place in gold ETFs, not because all investors were bearish on gold but because some wanted to obtain bullion from the ETF warehouses. COMEX warehouses holding gold for futures contract settlements saw inventories drawn down to levels last seen in the Panic of 2008. Gold futures contracts went into *backwardation,* a highly unusual condition in which gold for spot delivery is more expensive than gold for forward delivery; the opposite usually prevails because the forward seller has to pay for storage and insurance. This was another sign of acute physical shortages and high demand for immediate access to physical gold.

If a gold-buying panic were to break out today, there is no single gold window for the president to close. Instead, a multitude of contractual clauses, in fine print rarely studied by gold buyers, would be called into play. Gold futures exchanges have the ability to convert contracts to cash liquidation only and to shut off the physical delivery channels. Gold bullion banks can also settle gold forward contracts for cash and deny buyers the ability to convert to allocated gold. The "early termination" and force majeure clauses buried in contracts could be used by banks that sold more gold than they had on hand. The result would be that investors would receive a cash settlement up to the contract termination date, but not more. Investors would get some cash but no bullion and would miss the price surge sure to follow.

While physical gold was in short supply and high demand by early 2014, this did not necessarily mean that a superspike in gold prices was imminent. Not every snowslide turns into an avalanche; at times the avalanche awaits different initial conditions. Central banks still have enormous resources, including potential physical sales with which to suppress gold prices in the short run. Still, an alarm has gone off. The central banks' ability to keep a lid on gold prices has been challenged, and a new willingness of paper gold buyers to demand physical gold has emerged. As China's gold-buying operations continue apace, the entire international monetary system is tottering on the knife-edge of China's aspirations and the global demand for physical gold.

While the gold price oscillates between the forces of physical demand and central bank manipulation, another greater catastrophe is looming: the Federal Reserve is on the brink of insolvency, if not already over the brink. This conclusion comes not from a Fed critic but from Frederic S. Mishkin, one of the most eminent monetary economists in the world and mentor to Ben Bernanke and other Fed governors and economists. In his February 2013 paper "Crunch Time: Fiscal Crises and the Role of Monetary Policy," written with several colleagues, Mishkin warns that the Fed is dangerously close to the point where its independence is fatally compromised and its sole remaining purpose is to monetize deficit spending by causing inflation.

Mishkin and his coauthors make better use of complexity theory and recursive functions in their analysis than any of their peers. They point out the feedback loop in sovereign finance among larger deficits, followed by higher borrowing costs, which cause even larger deficits and still higher borrowing costs, and so on, until a death spiral begins. At that point, countries are faced with the unpalatable choice of either reducing deficits through so-called austerity measures or defaulting on the debts. Mishkin argues that austerity can hurt nominal growth, worsening the debt-to-GDP ratio, and possibly causing a debt default in the course of trying to stop one.

The alternative, in Mishkin's view, is for a central bank to keep interest rates under control by engaging in monetary ease, while politicians enact long-term deficit solutions. In the meantime, short-term deficits can be tolerated to avoid the austerity curse. Short-term monetary and fiscal ease work in tandem to keep an economy growing, while long-term fiscal reform reverses the death spiral.

Mishkin says this approach works fine in theory, but he brings us back to the real world of dysfunctional political systems that have come to rely on monetary ease to avoid hard choices on the fiscal side. Mishkin calls this condition "fiscal dominance." His paper describes the resulting crisis:

> In the extreme, unsustainable fiscal policy means that the government's intertemporal budget constraint will have to be satisfied by issuing monetary liabilities, which is known as *fiscal dominance,* or, alternatively, by a default on the government debt. Fiscal dominance forces the central bank to pursue inflationary monetary policy even if it has a strong commitment to control inflation, say with an inflation target. . . . Fiscal dominance at some point in the future forces the central bank to monetize the debt, so that despite tight monetary policy in the present, inflation will increase. . . .
>
> Ultimately, the central bank is without power to avoid the consequences of an unsustainable fiscal policy. . . . If the central bank is paying for its open-market purchases of long-term government debt with newly created reserves, . . . then ultimately all the open-market purchase does is exchange long-term government debt (in the form of the initial Treasury debt) for overnight government debt (in the form of interest-bearing reserves). It is well understood . . . that any swap of long-term for short-term debt in fact makes the government more vulnerable to . . . a self-fulfilling flight from government debt, or in the case of the U.S., to a self-fulfilling flight from the dollar. . . .

Fiscal dominance puts a central bank between a rock and a hard place. If the central bank does not monetize the debt, then interest rates on the government debt will rise sharply. . . . Hence, the central bank will in effect have little choice and will be forced to purchase the government debt and monetize it, eventually leading to a surge in inflation.

Mishkin and his coauthors point to another collapse in the making, independent of debt monetization and inflation. As the Fed buys longer-term debt with newly printed money, its balance sheet incurs large mark-to-market losses as interest rates rise. The Fed does not disclose these losses until it actually sells the bonds as part of an exit strategy, although independent analysts can estimate the size of the losses from information that is publicly available.

Monetization of debt leaves the Fed with a Hobson's choice. If the United States tips into deflation, the debt-to-GDP ratio will worsen because there is insufficient nominal growth. If the United States tips into inflation, the debt-to-GDP ratio will worsen due to higher interest rates on U.S. debt. If the Fed fights inflation by selling assets, it will recognize losses on the bond sales, and its insolvency will become apparent. This insolvency can erode confidence and cause higher interest rates on its own. Fed bond losses will also worsen the debt-to-GDP ratio since the Fed can no longer remit profits to the Treasury, which increases the deficit. There appears to be no way out of a sovereign debt crisis for the United States; the paths are all blocked. The Fed avoided a measure of pain in 2009 with its monetary exertions and market manipulations, but the pain was stored up for another day. That day is here.

Global monetary elites and the Fed, the IMF, and the BIS are playing for time. They need time for the United States to achieve long-term fiscal reform. They need time to create the global SDR market. They need time to facilitate China's acquisition of gold. The problem is that no time remains. A run on gold has begun before China has what it needs. The collapse of confidence in the dollar has begun before the SDR is ready to take its place. The Fed's insolvency is looming. As the dollar's 9/11 moment approaches, the system is blinking red.

CONCLUSION

In finance, there is no crystal ball for predicting one outcome, then proceeding on a single path. Still, it is possible to describe multiple paths and the mileposts along each one. Intelligence analysts call these mileposts "indications and warnings." Once the indications and warnings are specified, events must be observed closely, not as a passing parade of superficial headlines but as part of a dynamic systems analysis.

Investor Mohamed El-Erian of bond giant PIMCO popularized the phrase "new normal" to describe the global economy after the 2008 financial crisis. He is half right. The old normal is gone, but the new normal has not yet arrived. The global economy has fallen out of its old equilibrium but has not stabilized in a new one. The economy is in a phase transition from one state to another.

This is illustrated by applying heat to a pot of water until it boils. Water and steam are both steady states, albeit with different dynamics. In between water and steam is a stage where the water's surface is turbulent with bubbles rising, then falling back. Water is the old normal; steam is the new normal. Right now the world economy is neither—it is the turbulent surface deciding whether to fall back to water or rise to steam. Monetary policy is a matter of turning up the heat.

Certain phase transitions are irreversible. When wood burns and turns to ash, that is a phase transition, but there is no easy way to turn ash back into wood. The Federal Reserve believes that it is managing a reversible process. It believes that deflation can be turned to inflation, and then to disinflation, with the right quantity of money and the passage of time. In this, it is mistaken.

The Federal Reserve does not understand that money creation can be an irreversible process. At a certain point, confidence in money can be lost, and there is no way to reconstitute it; an entirely new system must rise in its place. A new international monetary system will rise from the ashes of the old dollar system, just as the dollar system rose from the ashes of the British Commonwealth at Bretton Woods in 1944, even before the flames of the Second World War had been extinguished.

The crux of the problem in the global financial system today is not money but debt. Money creation is being used as a means to deal with defaulted debt. By 2005 the United States, led by bankers whose self-interest blinded them to any danger, poisoned the world with excessive debt in mortgages and lines of credit to borrowers who could not repay. By itself, the mortgage problem was large but manageable. Unmanageable were the trillions of dollars in derivatives created from the underlying mortgages and trillions more in repurchase agreements, and commercial paper used to finance the mortgage-backed-securities inventories support-ing the derivatives.

When the inevitable crash came, the losses were not apportioned to those responsible—the banks and bondholders—but were passed on to the public through federal finance. From 2009 to 2012, the U.S. Treasury ran a $5 trillion cumulative deficit, and the Federal Reserve printed $1.2 trillion of new money. Similar deficit and money-printing programs were launched around the world, as derivatives creation by banks continued unabated. Only a portion of the private debt defaults were written off.

The bankers' jobs and bonuses were preserved, but nothing was achieved for the benefit of citizens. A private debt problem had been re-placed with public debt larger than the private debt had ever been. These debts are unpayable in real terms, and defaults will soon follow. The defaults by smaller nations like Greece, Cyprus, and Argentina will be through nonpayment of bonds and losses for bank depositors. Defaults for larger nations such as the United States will come from across-the-board inflation that will steal from savers, depositors, and bondholders alike.

Adding to the challenges are the warnings of a revival of an almost-forgotten phenomenon. Deflation, a condition not widely seen in advanced economies since the 1930s, has taken hold, upsetting the central bankers' inflation playbook. Deflation is rooted in depressionary psychology. Investors were shocked and frightened by events in 2008, and their immediate reaction was to stop spending, avoid risk, and move to cash. This reaction set the deflationary dynamic in motion. Much has been made about rising stock prices and housing prices since 2009, but a close examination of both shows that stock market volumes have been low, with leverage quite high. These are indications that the rising indexes are really asset bubbles, driven by professional traders and speculators, principally hedge funds, and that participation by everyday citizens has been shallow. Likewise, rising home prices have been held up not by traditional family formation but by investor pools purchasing large housing tracts with leverage, restructuring homeowner debt, or converting mortgages to rentals. Cash flows can make these pools attractive bondlike investments, but no one should mistake this financial engineering for a healthy, normalized housing market. Rising asset prices are fine for headlines and talking heads but do nothing to break the deflationary mind-set of typical investors and savers.

The fact that central banks are pursuing inflation, and cannot achieve it, is a gauge of the persistence of the underlying deflation. Money printing in the cause of defeating deflation may result in a loss of confidence in the fiat currency system. If the deflationary mind-set *is* broken, the inflationary mood may run ahead of central bank capabilities and prove impossible to contain or reverse. In the case of either persistent deflation or runaway inflation, we risk losing exactly what Paul Volcker warned was most valuable: confidence. Loss of confidence in a monetary system can rarely be restored.

Very likely, a new system will be needed, with a new foundation that can engender new confidence. The gold-backed dollar replaced sterling in stages between 1925 and 1944. The paper dollar replaced the gold-backed dollar in stages between 1971 and 1980. In each case, confidence was temporarily lost but was regained with a new store of value.

Whether the loss of confidence in the dollar results from external threats or internal neglect, investors should ask two questions: *What comes next?* and *How can wealth be preserved in the transition?*

■ Three Paths

The dollar's demise will take one of three paths. The first is world money, the SDR; the second is a gold standard; and the third is social disorder. Each of these outcomes can be foreseen, and each presents an asset-allocation strategy best able to preserve wealth.

The substitution of SDRs for dollars as the global reserve currency is already under way, and the IMF has laid out a ten-year transition plan that the United States has informally endorsed. This blueprint involves increasing the amount of SDRs in circulation and building out an infrastructure of SDR-denominated investable assets, issuers, investors, and dealers. Over time the dollar's weight in the SDR basket will be reduced in favor of the Chinese yuan.

The plan, as laid out by the IMF, exemplifies George Soros's preferred modus operandi as described by his favorite philosopher, Karl Popper. Soros and Popper call it "piecemeal engineering" and consider it their preferred form of social engineering. The Soros-Popper ideal is to make large changes in small, scarcely noticeable increments, which can be advanced or postponed, as circumstances require. Popper wrote:

> The piecemeal engineer will, accordingly, adopt the method . . . whose advocacy may easily become a means of continually postponing action until a later date, when conditions are more favourable. . . .
>
> Blueprints for piecemeal engineering are comparatively simple. They are blueprints for single institutions. . . .
>
> I do not suggest that piecemeal engineering cannot be bold, or that it must be confined to "smallish" problems.

Under the Soros-Popper method, the IMF's goal of SDR world money, initiated in 1969, could easily extend to 2025 or whenever, as Popper specified, "conditions are more favorable."

Ironically, this gradual method is *not* the most likely scenario for SDRs to replace the dollar. Instead, a financial panic in the next several years, caused by derivatives exposure and bank interconnectedness, may trigger a global liquidity crisis worse than the 1998 and 2008 crises. This time the

Fed's balance sheet, already bloated and stretched to the limit, will not be flexible enough to reliquefy the interbank market. SDRs will be pressed into service to stabilize the system as was done in 1979 and 2009. The emerging circumstances will mean the process will be carried out on a crash basis, without reference to the carefully constructed infrastructure now contemplated. Existing infrastructure from institutions such as DTCC and SWIFT will be pressed into service to facilitate the new SDR market.

Chinese acquiescence will be needed to use the SDR in this way, and in exchange for its approval, China will insist that SDRs be used not to *save* the dollar, as was done in the past, but to *replace* the dollar as quickly as possible. This process will play out in a matter of months, light speed by the standards of the international monetary system. The transition will be inflationary in dollar terms, not because of new dollar printing but because the dollar will be devalued against the SDR. From then on the U.S. economy will face severe structural adjustments as it finds it must earn its SDRs through competition in the global marketplace rather than through printing reserves at will.

In this scenario, savings in the form of bank deposits, insurance policies, annuities, and retirement benefits will be largely wiped out.

A return to a gold standard is another way out of the labyrinth of incessant money printing. This could arise from extreme inflation, where gold is needed to restore confidence, or extreme deflation, where gold is revalued by governments to raise the general price level. The gold standard will certainly not be a matter of choice but may be pursued as a matter of necessity when confidence collapses. A first approximation of an equilibrium, nondeflationary gold price is $9,000 per ounce, although higher and lower values are feasible depending on the gold standard's design specifications. The circulating currency will not be gold coins but rather dollars (if the United States takes the lead) or SDRs (if the IMF is the intermediating institution). This gold-backed SDR would be quite different from the paper SDR, but the implications for the dollar are the same. Any movement toward gold dollars or gold SDRs will be inflationary because gold will have to be revalued sharply higher in order to support world trade and finance with existing stocks of gold. As with the paper-SDR scenario, inflation resulting from the devaluation of the dollar against gold will wipe out savings of all kinds.

Social disorder is the third possible path. Social disorder involves riots, strikes, sabotage, and other dysfunctions. It is distinct from social protest because disorder involves illegality, violence, and property destruction. The disorder could be a reaction to extreme hyperinflation, which would widely and properly be seen as state-sanctioned theft. Social disorder could be a reaction to extreme deflation likely to be accompanied by bankruptcies, unemployment, and slashes in social welfare payments. Disorder could also arise in the aftermath of financial warfare or systemic collapse, when citizens realize their wealth has disappeared into a fog of hacking, manipulation, bail-ins, and confiscation.

Social disorder is impossible to predict because it is an emergent property of a complex system. Social disorder arises spontaneously from the most complex system of all—society—a system larger and more complex than the financial and digital components within it. The money riots will take the authorities by surprise. Once societal disintegration begins, it will be difficult to arrest.

If social disintegration is not predictable, the official response is. It will take the form of neofascism, the substitution of state power for liberty. This process is already well advanced in fairly calm times and will accelerate when violence erupts. As author Radley Balko has documented in *Rise of the Warrior Cop,* the state is well armed with SWAT teams, drones, armored personnel carriers, digital surveillance, tear gas, flash-bang grenades, and high-tech battering rams. Citizens will belatedly discover that every E-ZPass tollbooth in America can rapidly be converted into an interdiction point and that every traffic camera does double duty as a license plate scanner. The 2013 IRS and NSA scandals show how quickly trusted government agencies could be subverted for illegal surveillance and selective politically motivated oppression.

Republicans and Democrats are equally complicit in the rise of neofascism. Author Jonah Goldberg has documented fascism's history and shown that its origins in the early twentieth century were socialist in nature. Fascism's original exponent, Benito Mussolini, was regarded in his own time as a man of the left. Today the distinction between Left and Right as the face of fascism is less important than the distinction between those who favor state power and those who support liberty. Former New York City mayor Michael Bloomberg is a case in point. At various times he has been a Republican, a Democrat, and an independent. Throughout his tenure he exhibited what might be called the "friendly fascist" temperament. His attempted ban on large sweetened sodas in New York City was a typical state-power exercise at the expense of liberty, albeit much ridiculed. More ominous was his remark "I have my own army in the NYPD—the seventh largest army in the world."

The use of neofascist tactics to suppress political money riots would require no new legislation. The statutory authority has existed since the Trading with the Enemy Act of 1917, which was expanded and updated by the International Emergency Economic Powers Act (IEEPA) of 1977. President Franklin Roosevelt used the Trading with the Enemy Act to confiscate gold from American citizens in 1933. He did not specify who the "enemy" was; presumably it was those who owned gold. Every president since Jimmy Carter has used IEEPA to freeze and seize assets in U.S. banks. In more dire future circumstances, gold could be confiscated, bank accounts frozen, capital controls imposed, and exchanges closed. Wage and price controls could be used to suppress inflation, and modern digital surveillance could be used to disrupt black markets and incarcerate black marketeers. The money riots would be squashed quickly.

In the ontology of state power, order comes before liberty or justice.

■ Seven Signs

Investors must be alert for the indications and warnings of which path the economy is traversing. There are seven critical signs.

The first sign is *the price of gold*. Although the price of gold is manipulated by central banks, any *disorderly* price movements are a signal that the manipulation scheme is disintegrating, despite efforts at leasing, unallocated sales, and futures sales. A rapid price rise from the $1,500-per-ounce level to the $2,500-per-ounce level will not be a bubble but rather a sign that a physical buying panic has commenced and that official shorting operations are not producing the desired dampening effect. Conversely, if gold moves to the $800-per-ounce level or lower, this is a good sign of severe deflation, potentially devastating to leveraged investors in all asset classes.

Gold's continued acquisition by central banks. Purchases by China in particular are a second sign of the dollar's demise. The announcement by China in late 2014 or early 2015 that it has acquired over 4,000 tonnes of gold will be a landmark in this larger trend and a harbinger of inflation.

IMF governance reforms. This third sign will mean larger voting power for China, and U.S. legislation to convert committed U.S. lines of credit into so-called quotas at the IMF. Any changes in the SDR currency-basket composition that reduce the dollar's share will be a dollar inflation early warning. The same is true for concrete steps in the SDR infrastructure build-out. If global corporate giants such as Caterpillar and General Electric issue SDR-denominated bonds, which are acquired in portfolio by sovereign wealth funds or regional development banks, this will mark the acceleration of the baseline SDR-as-world-money plan.

The failure of regulatory reform. A fourth sign will be bank lobbyists' defeat of efforts by U.S. regulators and Congress to limit the size of big banks, reduce bank asset concentration, or curtail investment banking activities. Glass-Steagall's repeal in 1999 was the original sin that led directly to the housing market collapse in 2007 and the Panic of 2008. Efforts are under way in Congress to reinstate Glass-Steagall's main provisions. The bank lobbyists are mobilized to halt such reforms and also block derivatives regulation, higher capital requirements, and limits on banker bonuses. Bank lobbyists dominate Congress, and there is no reason to believe reform efforts will achieve more than superficial success. Absent reform, the scale and interconnectedness of bank positions will continue to grow from very high levels and at rates much faster than the real economy. The result will be another systemic and unanticipated failure, larger than the Fed's capacity to contain it. The panic's immediate impact will be highly deflationary as assets, including gold, are dumped wholesale to raise cash. This deflationary bout will be followed quickly by inflation, as the IMF pumps out SDRs to reliquefy the system.

System crashes. A fifth sign will be more frequent episodes like the May 6, 2010, flash crash in which the Dow Jones Index fell 1,000 points in minutes; the August 1, 2012, Knight Trading computer debacle, which wiped out Knight's capital; and the August 22, 2013, closure of the NAS-DAQ Stock Market. From a systems analysis perspective, these events are best understood as emergent properties of complex systems. These debacles are not the direct result of banker greed, but they are the maligned ghost in the machine of high-speed, highly automated, high-volume trading. Such events should not be dismissed as anomalies; they should be expected. An increasing tempo to such events could indicate either that trading systems are going wobbly, moving to disequilibrium, or perhaps that Chinese or Iranian army units are perfecting their cyberassault capabilities through probes and feints. In time, a glitch will spin out of control and close markets. As with the systemic risk scenario, the result is likely to be immediate deflation due to asset sales, followed by inflation as the Fed and IMF fire brigades douse the flames with a flood of new money.

The end of QE and Abenomics. The sixth sign will be a sustained reduction in U.S. or Japanese asset purchases, giving deflation a second wind, suppressing asset prices and growth. This happened in the United States when QE1 and QE2 were ended, and again in 2012 when the Bank of Japan reneged on a promised easing. However, as asset purchases are curtailed, a new increase should be expected within a year as deflationary effects develop. This would be another iteration of the stop-go monetary policies pursued by the Fed since 2008 and by the Bank of Japan since 1998. Continual flirting with deflation makes inflation harder to achieve. A more likely scenario is that money printing will continue in both nations long after 2 percent inflation is achieved. At that point, the risks are all on the side of much higher inflation as the change in expectations becomes difficult to reverse, especially in the United States.

A Chinese collapse. The seventh sign will be financial disintegration in China as the wealth-management-product Ponzi scheme collapses. China's degree of financial interconnectedness with the rest of the world is lower than that of the major U.S. and European banks, so a collapse in China would be mainly a local affair, in which the Communist Party will use reserves held by its sovereign wealth funds to assuage savers and recapitalize banks. However, the aftermath will include a resumption of Chinese efforts to cap or even devalue the yuan in foreign exchange markets to promote exports, create jobs, and restore wealth lost in the collapse. In the short run, this will prove deflationary as underpriced Chinese goods once again flood into global supply chains. In the longer run, Chinese deflation will be met with U.S. and Japanese inflation, as both countries print money to offset any appreciation in the yen or the dollar. At that point, the currency wars will be reignited, never really having gone away.

Not all of these seven signs may come to pass. The appearance of some signs may negate or delay others. They will not come in any particular order. When any one sign does appear, investors should be alert to the specific consequences described and the investment implications.

■ Five Investments

In the face of extreme inflation, extreme deflation, or a condition of social disorder, which investment portfolio is most likely to remain robust? The following assets have a proven ability to perform well in inflation *and* deflation and have stood the test of time in periods of social disorder from the Thirty Years' War to the Third Reich.

Gold. An allocation to gold of 10 to 20 percent of investable assets has much to commend it. The allocation should take physical form as coins or bullion in order to avoid the early terminations and cash settlements that are likely to affect paper gold markets in the future. Secure logistics, easily accessed by the investor, should be considered, but bank storage should be avoided, because gold stored in banks will not be accessible when most needed. An allocation above 20 percent is not recommended because gold is highly volatile and subject to manipulation, and there are other investable assets that perform the same wealth-preservation functions. A useful way to think about gold's insurance function is that a 500 percent return on 20 percent of a portfolio provides a 100 percent portfolio hedge. Gold does well in inflation, until interest rates are raised above inflation rates. In deflation, gold initially declines in nominal terms, although it may outperform other asset classes. If deflation persists, gold rises sharply as governments devalue paper currency to produce inflation by fiat. Gold offers high value for weight and is portable in the unfortunate event that social unrest requires flight.

Land. This investment includes undeveloped land in prime locations or land with agricultural potential, but it does not include land with structures. As with gold, land will perform well in an inflationary environment until nominal interest rates exceed inflation. Land's nominal value may decline in deflation, but development costs decline more rapidly. This means that the land can be developed cheaply at the bottom of a deflationary phase and provide large returns in the inflation that is likely to follow. The Empire State Building and Rockefeller Center, both in New York City, were built during the Great Depression and benefited from low labor and material costs at the time. Both projects have proved excellent investments ever since.

Fine art. This includes museum-quality paintings and drawings but is not intended to include the broader range of collectibles such as automobiles, wine, or memorabilia. Fine art offers gold's return profile in both inflation and deflation, without being subject to the manipulation that affects gold. Central banks are not concerned with disorderly price increases in the art market and do not intervene to stop them. Investors should focus on established artists, avoiding fads that may fall out of favor. Paintings are also portable and offer extremely high value for weight. A $10 million painting that weighs two pounds is worth $312,500 per ounce, over two hundred times gold's value by weight, and will not set off metal detectors. High-quality art can be acquired for more modest sums than $10 million through pooled investment vehicles that offer superb returns, although such vehicles lack the liquidity and portability of outright art ownership.

Alternative funds. This includes hedge funds and private equity funds with specified strategies. Hedge fund strategies that are robust to inflation, deflation, and disorder include long-short equity, global macro, and hard-asset strategies that target natural resources, precious metals, water, or energy. Private equity strategies should likewise involve hard assets, energy, transportation, and natural resources. Funds relying on financial stocks, emerging markets, sovereign debt, and credit instruments carry undue risk on the paths that lie ahead. Hedge funds and private equity funds offer various degrees of liquidity, although certain funds may offer no liquidity for five to seven years. Manager selection is critical and is much easier said than done. On balance, these funds should find their place in a portfolio because the benefits of diversification and talented management outweigh the lack of liquidity.

Cash. This seems a surprising choice in a world threatened with runaway inflation and crashing currencies. But cash has a place, at least for the time being, because it is an excellent deflation hedge and has embedded optionality, which gives the holder an ability to pivot into other investments on a moment's notice. A cash component in a portfolio also reduces overall portfolio volatility, the opposite of leverage. Investors searching for an ideal cash currency could consider the Singapore dollar, the Canadian dollar, the U.S. dollar, and the euro. Cash may not be the best investment *after* a calamity, but it can serve the investor well *until* the calamity emerges. The challenge, of course, is being attentive to the indications and warnings and making a timely transition to one of the alternatives already mentioned.

On the whole, a portfolio of 20 percent gold, 20 percent land, 10 percent fine art, 20 percent alternative funds, and 30 percent cash should offer an optimal combination of wealth preservation under conditions of inflation, deflation, and social unrest, while providing high risk-adjusted returns and reasonable liquidity. But no portfolio intended to achieve these goals works for the "buy-and-hold" investor. This portfolio must be actively managed. As indications and warnings become more pronounced, and as greater visibility is offered on certain outcomes, the portfolio must be modified in sensible ways. If gold reaches $9,000 per ounce, there may then come a time to sell gold and acquire more land. If inflation emerges more rapidly than expected, it may make sense to convert cash to gold. A private equity fund that performs well for five years might be redeemed without reinvestment because conditions could be more perilous by then. Precise outcomes and portfolio performance cannot be known in advance, so constant attention to the seven signs and a certain flexibility in outlook are required.

Although the scenarios described in this book are dire, they are not necessarily tomorrow's headlines. Much depends on governments and central banks, and those institutions have enormous staying power even while pursuing ultimately ruinous policies. The world has seen worse crises than financial collapse and lived to tell the tale. But when the crash comes, it will be better to be among those who have braced for the storm. We are not helpless; we can begin now to prepare to weather the inevitable outcome of the hubris of central banks.

AFTERWORD

When I wrote *Currency Wars* in 2011, I diagnosed various dangers in the financial system and prescribed concrete steps policy makers might take to mitigate those dangers. I identified ways to reverse monetary and fiscal policy blunders around the world, particularly in the United States. My tone was cautionary but hopeful. I specifically said it was late, but not too late, to undo the damage caused by bankers and restore the financial system to a sound footing that would support commerce instead of trying to siphon it dry.

In the two and a half years since I completed *Currency Wars,* conditions have indeed changed—but not for the better. Elites who in former times were self-sacrificing have become self-serving. The world has passed the point where there is much prospect of soft landings; there are no easy exits from the policy mistakes that have been committed. All that remain are hard choices.

The hoped-for mild, middling inflation that becomes self-sustaining and seems to lift all boats with money illusion is not in the cards. There is only high inflation, deflation, disorder, default, and repression on offer. Exact paths and outcomes cannot be predicted, but severe consequences can be foreseen. These consequences may play out over considerable periods of time, but the underlying processes have already commenced.

The collapse of the dollar and the collapse of the international monetary system are one and the same. Threats to the dollar are ubiquitous—lost confidence, financial war, regional hegemons, hyperinflation, and more. These threats are looming larger and may even converge as inflation erodes confidence and emboldens enemies in a feedback loop that gains energy like a hurricane on warm water. The savings of everyday citizens are in the path of the storm.

Policy makers may not be alert to the dangers surrounding the dollar, but savers and investors show much better sense. A tide in the direction of hard assets is perceptible and growing stronger.

It may be too late to save the dollar, but it is not too late to preserve wealth. We live in an ersatz monetary system that has reached its end stage. In our time, the aureate has become brazen—the golden has become brass. A return to true value based on trust is long overdue.

ACKNOWLEDGMENTS

My sincere thanks go to Melissa Flashman and Adrian Zackheim for first encouraging me to write on the challenging subject of international economics several years ago and for supporting me in this task ever since. *The Death of Money* would not exist without their help and guidance.

There is scarcely a manuscript that cannot be improved by good editing, and I was fortunate to have one of the best editorial teams around to help with *The Death of Money*. Will Rickards deftly handled the daunting burden of first-draft editing. Hugh Howard did a fine job as development editor, enlivening didactic structures. Janet Biehl's attention to detail as copy editor rivaled that of Sherlock Holmes, with felicitous results. Niki Papadopoulos, senior editor at Portfolio, was an inspiring muse and rode herd on the entire process. The quality of this book owes a lot to all of them. Any remaining errors are entirely my responsibility.

I am fortunate to have close friends among economists and market professionals, who provide me with candid advice when I need to try out new ideas or explore those of others. I have benefited greatly from their acumen, and I thank John Makin, Dave "Davos" Nolan, Peter Moran, Chris Whalen, Bob Rice, Sorin Sorescu, Benn Steil, Steve Cordasco, John Cassarini, Roger Kubarych, Steve Halliwell, Komal Sri-Kumar, Don Young, Richard Duncan, and Art Laffer for their generosity of time and spirit to help me make sense of an opaque financial landscape.

I owe a special debt to Ken Dam, who literally wrote the book on the IMF, gold, and SDRs. His 1982 classic, *The Rules of the Game,* is the indispensable source for understanding the IMF today. I follow humbly in his footsteps.

My many invitations to discuss finance in the public square of television, radio, and the Internet have helped to sharpen my analyses in ways that have contributed to this book. My sincere thanks go to Deirdre Bolton, Lauren Lyster, Adam Johnson, Vielka Todd, Max Keiser, Stacy Herbert, Kathleen Hays, Demetri Kofinas, Amanda Lang, and Annmarie Hordern for inviting me onto your programs and holding my feet to the fire through countless discussions of the euro, gold, the Fed, China, and the new depression.

Today a book on finance is as much about Washington as it is about Wall Street, and I am grateful to my friends in public policy, national security, and the media in Washington who have guided me through thickets inside the Beltway. Thank you to Taylor Griffin, Charles Duelfer, Joe Pesce, Mike Allen, and Rob Saliterman for your friendship and great advice.

Of all the research challenges I faced in writing this book, the most daunting involved the mysterious inner workings of the global gold market. I would not have been able to meet this challenge without the assistance and guidance of gold market professionals and friends Alex Stanczyk, Philip Judge, Chris Blasi, Ben Davies, John Hathaway, Ronni Stoeferle, Mark Valek, and Jan Skoyles. Thank you all.

Some of my most valuable guidance came from friends and family who read early drafts of this book, not as experts but as everyday citizens concerned about the economy and the country as a whole. I am grateful to Glen Rickards, Joan and Erv Hobson, Diane Rickards, Gwendolyn van Paasschen, and Bruce Orr for their feedback and early warnings about passages that were too dense or took too much for granted.

My immediate family was a continuous source of support and encouragement. My daughter, Ali; my son Will; my son Scott; his wife, Dominique; and their children, Thomas and Samuel, never cease to amaze me as they grow, prosper, and confront the same economic challenges I write about in this book. They are the future, and their generation gives reason for hope despite the hurdles put up by my own generation. I am deeply indebted to my wife, Ann, for her love, consolation, and endless encouragement. I'm grateful to my entire family for your immense patience during my long stretches of antisocial behavior known as writing. I love you all.

NOTES

Introduction

2 **"Suddenly Americans traveling abroad . . ."**: Janet Tavakoli, "Who Says Gold Is Money (Part Two)," *Financial Report,* Tavakoli Structured Finance, August 30, 2013, http://www.tavakolistructuredfinance.com/2013/08/tavakoli-says-gold-is -money.

Chapter 1: Prophesy

18 **"It was the most blatant case . . ."**: John Mulheren, conversation with the author, CIA Headquarters, September 26, 2003.

18 **His conviction was based on testimony . . .**: John Mulheren's 1990 conviction was overturned by the Second Circuit Court of Appeals in 1991. This complete exoneration allowed his return to the securities industry.

19 **September 5, 2001, was the day Osama bin Laden learned . . .**: Elisabeth Bumiller, "Bin Laden, on Tape, Boasts of Trade Center Attacks; U.S. Says It Proves His Guilt," *New York Times,* December 14, 2001, http://www.nytimes.com/2001/12/14/ world/nation-challenged-video-bin-laden-tape-boasts-trade-center-attacks-us -says-it.html. The September 5 reference is to the New York time zone where markets were still open. Bin Laden made the remarks in Afghanistan on September 6, 2001, local time, 9.5 hours ahead of New York.

19 **"I say the events that happened on Tuesday . . ."**: Tayser Allouni, "A Discussion on the New Crusader Wars," October 21, 2001, http://www.religioscope.com/info/ doc/jihad/ubl_int_2.htm.

20 **as well as family and friends**: National Commission on Terrorist Attacks upon the United States, *The 9/11 Commission Report* (New York: W. W. Norton, 2004), pp. 222, 237.

21 **A normal ratio of bets . . .**: For options trading data, see Allen M. Poteshman, "Unusual Option Market Activity and the Terrorist Attacks of September 11, 2001," *Journal of Business* 79, no. 4 (July 2006), pp. 1703–26, http://www.jstor.org/ stable/10.1086/503645.

21 **"Exhaustive investigations by the Securities and Exchange Commission . . ."**: National Commission on Terrorist Attacks, *9/11 Commission Report,* p. 172.

22 **the pre-9/11 options trading was based on inside information**: See Poteshman, "Unusual Option Market Activity"; Wing-Keung Wong, Howard E. Thompson, and

Kweechong Teh, "Was There Abnormal Trading in the S&P 500 Index Options Prior to the September 11 Attacks?" Social Science Research Network, April 13, 2010, http://ssrn.com/abstract=1588523; and Marc Chesney, Remo Crameri, and Loriano Mancini, "Detecting Informed Trading Activities in the Options Markets," Swiss Finance Institute Research Paper no. 11-42 (July 2012), http://ssrn.com/abstract=1522157.

22 **The leading academic study of terrorist insider trading . . . :** Poteshman, "Unusual Option Market Activity."

22 **These techniques have proved reliable . . . :** Erik Lie, "On the Timing of CEO Stock Option Awards," *Management Science* 51, no. 5 (May 2005), pp. 802–12, http://www.biz.uiowa.edu/faculty/elie/Grants-MS.pdf.

23 **"There is evidence of unusual option market activity . . .":** Poteshman, "Unusual Option Market Activity," p. 1725.

23 **"Companies like American Airlines, United Airlines . . .":** Chesney, Crameri, and Mancini, "Detecting," p. 19.

28 **"The system was blinking red":** George Tenet quoted in *9/11 Commission Report,* p. 259.

31 **"Get down to Disney World . . .":** George W. Bush quoted in Andrew J. Bacevich, "He Told Us to Go Shopping," *Washington Post,* October 5, 2008, http://articles.washingtonpost.com/2008-10-05/opinions/36929207_1_president-bush-american-consumer-congress.

39 **"CIA's Financial Spying Bags Data on Americans":** Siobhan Gorman, Devlin Barrett, and Jennifer Valentino-Devries, "CIA's Financial Spying Bags Data on Americans," *Wall Street Journal,* November 14, 2013, http://online.wsj.com/news/articles/SB10001424052702303559504579198370113163530.

Chapter 2: The War God's Face

44 **"We studied RMA exhaustively . . .":** Quoted in "The Dragon's New Teeth," *Economist,* April 7, 2012, http://www.economist.com/node/21552193.

44 **This classified plan, called "Air-Sea Battle" . . . :** Greg Jaffe, "U.S. Model for a Future War Fans Tensions with China and Inside Pentagon," *Washington Post,* August 1, 2012, http://articles.washingtonpost.com/2012-08-01/world/35492126_1_china-tensions-china-threat-pentagon.

44 **"In the near future, information warfare . . .":** Major General Wang Pufeng, "The Challenge of Information Warfare," *China Military Science,* Spring 1995, http://www.fas.org/irp/world/china/docs/iw_mg_wang.htm.

44 **The People's Liberation Army of China made this doctrine . . . :** Colonel Qiao Liang, and Colonel Wang Xiangsui, *Unrestricted Warfare* (Beijing: People's Liberation Army, 1999).

45 **"Economic prosperity that once excited . . .":** Ibid.

51 **China had been a net seller . . . :** Floyd Norris, "Data Shows Less Buying of U.S. Debt by China," *New York Times,* January 21, 2011, http://www.nytimes.com/2011/01/22/business/economy/22charts.html?_r=0.

51 **the Chinese Investment Corporation (CIC) . . . :** Andrew Ross Sorkin and David Barboza, "China to Buy $3 Billion Stake in Blackstone," *New York Times,* May 20, 2007, http://www.nytimes.com/2007/05/20/business/worldbusiness/20cnd-yuan.html?pagewanted=print.

51 **notorious for his sixtieth birthday party . . . :** James B. Stewart, "The Birthday

Party," *New Yorker,* February 11, 2008, http://www.newyorker.com/reporting/2008/02/11/080211fa_fact_stewart.

52 **"I want war, not a series . . .":** Quoted in Andrew Clark, "The Guardian Profile: Stephen Schwarzman," *Guardian,* June 15, 2007, http://www.theguardian.com/business/2007/jun/15/4.

52 **"to put its vast reserves . . .":** Sorkin and Barboza, "China to Buy."

52 **suggested mounting an attack on the Japanese . . . :** Ambrose Evans-Pritchard, "Beijing Hints at Bond Attack on Japan," *Telegraph,* September 18, 2012, http://www.telegraph.co.uk/finance/china-business/9551727/Beijing-hints-at-bond-attack-on-Japan.html.

52 **Chinese hacked the Reserve Bank of Australia . . . :** "Australia: Reserve Bank Networks Hacked," Stratfor Global Intelligence, March 11, 2013, www.stratfor.com.

53 **These combined efforts will prove useful to China . . . :** For a detailed account of China's efforts to use military intelligence to steal secrets and other intellectual property through cyberwarfare, see Mandiant, "APT1: Exposing One of China's Cyber Espionage Units," 2013, Mandiant Intelligence Center Report, http://intelreport.mandiant.com.

53 **"A highly secretive unit of the National Security Agency . . .":** Matthew M. Aid, "Inside the NSA's Ultra-Secret China Hacking Group," *Foreign Policy*, June 10, 2013, http://www.foreignpolicy.com/articles/2013/06/10/inside_the_nsa_s_ultra_secret_china_hacking_group.

54 **Quantum Dawn 2 . . . :** "Fact Sheet: Quantum Dawn 2, July 18, 2013," SIFMA, http://www.sifma.org/uploadedfiles/services/bcp/qd2-fact-sheet.pdf?n=19890.

54 **"to cause depreciation of the rial . . .":** Kasia Klimasinska and Ian Katz, "Useless Rial Is U.S. Goal in New Iran Sanctions, Treasury Says," *Bloomberg*, June 6, 2013, http://www.bloomberg.com/news/2013-06-06/useless-rial-is-u-s-goal-in-new-iran-sanctions-treasury-says.html.

55 **by dumping dollars and buying gold . . . :** Jack Farchy, "Iran Bought Gold to Cut Dollar Exposure," *Financial Times,* March 20, 2011, http://www.ft.com/cms/s/0/cc350008-5325-11e0-86e6-00144feab49a.html.

55 **an oil-for-gold swap . . . :** Dheeraj Tiwari and Rajeev Jayaswal, "India, Iran Mull over Gold-for-Oil for Now," *Economic Times,* January 8, 2011, http://articles.economictimes.indiatimes.com/2011-01-08/news/28433295_1_bilateral-issue-oil-india-imports.

55 **Turkish exports of gold to Iran . . . :** "Turkey's Gold Export to Iran Rises Again," *Hurriyet Daily News,* May 1, 2013, http://www.hurriyetdailynews.com/turkeys-gold-export-to-iran-rises-again-.aspx?pageID=238&nid=46002.

55 **a cargo plane with 1.5 tons of gold on board . . . :** "Cargo Plane with 1.5 Tons of Gold Held in Istanbul," *Hurriyet Daily News,* January 5, 2013, http://www.hurriyetdailynews.com/cargo-plane-with-15-tons-of-gold-held-in-istanbul-.aspx?pageID=238&nid=38427.

55 **Reports from the** *Voice of Russia* **speculated . . . :** "Gold Seized at Istanbul Airport Was Allegedly for Iran," *Voice of Russia,* January 6, 2013, http://voiceofrussia.com/2013_01_06/Gold-seized-at-Istanbul-airport-was-allegedly-for-Iran.

55 **"passengers flying from Kabul to the Persian Gulf . . .":** Matthew Rosenberg, "An Afghan Mystery: Why Are Large Shipments of Gold Leaving the Country?" *New York Times,* December 15, 2012, http://www.nytimes.com/2012/12/16/world/asia/as-gold-is-spirited-out-of-afghanistan-officials-wonder-why.html.

55 **strict enforcement of a prohibition on gold sales . . . :** "U.S. to Block Sale of Gold to Iran in Sanctions Clampdown," *Al Arabiya,* May 16, 2003, http://english .alarabiya.net/en/business/economy/2013/05/16/U-S-to-block-sales-of-gold -to-Iran-in-sanctions-clampdown.html.

56 **In late 2012 the United States warned Russia and China . . . :** Benoît Faucon, "U.S. Warns Russia on Iranian Bank," *Wall Street Journal,* December 11, 2012, http://online.wsj.com/news/articles/SB100014241278873233306045781450719309 69966.

57 **Iranian hackers had reportedly gained access to the software systems . . . :** Siobhan Gorman and Danny Yadron, "Iran Hacks Energy Firms, U.S. Says," *Wall Street Journal,* May 23, 2013, http://online.wsj.com/article/SB10001424127887323 336104578501601108021968.html.

57 **The Syrian government was forced to conduct business . . . :** Steve H. Hanke, "Syria's Annual Inflation Hits 200%," Cato Institute, July 1, 2013, http://www.cato .org/blog/syrias-annual-inflation-hits-200.

58 **This cat-and-mouse game . . . :** "Three Nukes for $5 billion," *Debka-Net-Weekly* 13, no. 588 (May 24, 2013), http://www.debka.com.

59 **a highly sensitive 104-page final report:** The author was a direct participant, presenter, or contributor to the Bahrain, Federation of American Scientists, Boeing, and National Defense University financial war game events described in the foregoing paragraphs.

59 **Swiss troops defended their country . . . :** Henry Samuels, "Swiss War Game Envisages Invasion by Bankrupt French," *Telegraph,* September 30, 2013, http:// www.telegraph.co.uk/news/worldnews/europe/switzerland/10344029/Swiss-war -game-envisages-invasion-by-bankrupt-French.html.

59 **Cyberattacks on U.S. infrastructure, including banks . . . :** Leading documented studies and white papers on the scope and pervasiveness of cyberattacks on U.S. systems, including financial systems, originating from various sources including China and Iran, are: "Global Energy Cyberattacks: 'Night Dragon,'" McAfee Foundstone Professional Services and McAfee Labs White Paper, February 10, 2011, http://www.mcafee.com/us/resources/white-papers/wp-global-energy-cyberattacks -night-dragon.pdf; Nicolas Falliere, Liam O. Murchu, and Eric Chien, "W.32.Stuxnet Dossier Version 1.4," Symantec, February 2011, http://www.symantec.com/content/ en/us/enterprise/media/security_response/whitepapers/w32_stuxnet_dossier.pdf; and Mandiant, "APT1: Exposing One of China's Cyber Espionage Units," 2013, Mandiant Intelligence Center Report, http://intelreport.mandiant.com.

59 **The official was Mary Shapiro . . . :** Senior SEC official, conversation with author, September 2012.

59 **the Syrian Electronic Army claimed credit . . . :** Max Fisher, "Syrian Hackers Claim AP Hack That Tipped Stock Market by $136 Billion. Is It Terrorism?" *Washington Post,* April 23, 2013, http://www.washingtonpost.com/blogs /worldviews/wp/2013/04/23/syrian-hackers-claim-ap-hack-that-tipped-stock -market-by-136-billion-is-it-terrorism.

60 **Knight Capital fiasco . . . :** Scott Patterson, Jenny Strasburg, and Jacob Bunge, "Knight Upgrade Triggered Old Trading System, Big Losses," *Wall Street Journal,* August 14, 2012, http://online.wsj.com/news/articles/SB10000872396390444318 104577589694289838100.

62 **bailout of the hedge fund Long-Term Capital Management . . . :** The author was

general counsel of Long-Term Capital Management and the principal negotiator of the 1998 bailout arranged by the Federal Reserve Bank of New York. While LTCM was a well-known trader in fixed-income and derivatives markets, the extent of its trading in equity markets was not well known. LTCM was the largest risk arbitrageur in the world, with over $15 billion in equity positions on pending deals. Upon reviewing the books and records of LTCM with the author and CEO John Meriwether on September 20, 1998, Peter R. Fisher, then head of open market operations at the Federal Reserve Bank of New York, remarked, "We knew you guys might take down the bond markets, but we had no idea you would take down the stock markets too." The Fed's effort to orchestrate a bailout commenced the next morning and was completed on September 28, 1998.

63 **the highly classified plans for continuity . . . :** Marc Ambinder, "The Day After," *National Journal,* April 11, 2011, http://www.nationaljournal.com/magazine /government-still-unprepared-for-disaster-20110411.

Chapter 3: The Ruin of Markets

70 **"The peculiar character of the problem . . .":** Friedrich A. Hayek, "The Use of Knowledge in Society," *American Economic Review* 35, no. 4 (1935), pp. 519–30, http://www.econlib.org/library/Essays/hykKnw1.html.

71 **Charles Goodhart first articulated Goodhart's Law . . . :** The paper has been reprinted in several publications. See Charles Goodhart, "Problems of Monetary Management: The U.K. Experience," in Anthony Courakis, ed., *Inflation, Depression, and Economic Policy in the West* (Lanham, Md.: Rowman and Littlefield, 1981), pp. 111–46.

73 **the wealth effect from housing prices . . . :** U.S. Congress, "Housing Wealth and Consumer Spending," Congressional Budget Office Background Paper, January 2007, http://www.cbo.gov/publication/18279.

73 **"We find . . . a positive connection . . .":** Sydney Ludvigson and Charles Steindel, "How Important Is the Stock Market Effect on Consumption?" *FRBNY Economic Policy Review,* July 1990, http://ftp.ny.frb.org/research/epr/99v05n2/9907ludv.pdf.

74 **heavily concentrated among the rich . . . :** Sherif Khalifa, Ousmane Seck, and Elwin Tobing, "Financial Wealth Effect: Evidence from Threshold Estimation," *Applied Economics Letters* 18, no. 13 (2011), http://business.fullerton.edu /economics/skhalifa/publication13.pdf.

74 **"The idea of a wealth effect . . . :** Christopher Flavelle, "Debunking the 'Wealth Effect,'" *Slate,* June 10, 2008, http://www.slate.com/articles/news_and_politics/hey _wait_a_minute/2008/06/debunking_the_wealth_effect.html.

000 **rising consumption may increase stock prices . . . :** U.S. Congress, "Housing Wealth"; and Ludvigson and Steindel, "How Important."

74 **"The issue here is not whether . . .":** Lacy H. Hunt, "The Fed's Flawed Model," Casey Research, May 28, 2013, http://www.caseyresearch.com/articles/the-feds -flawed-model.

79 **"Since wages remained soft . . .":** Ibid.

80 **the reason for this damage to SME lending . . . :** Steve H. Hanke, "The Federal Reserve vs. Small Business," Cato Institute, June 3, 2013, http://www.cato.org/blog /federal-reserve-vs-small-business-0.

81 **Federal Reserve low-interest-rate policy . . . :** Giovanni Dell'Ariccia, Luc Laeven,

and Gustavo Suarez, "Bank Leverage and Monetary Policy's Risk-Taking Channel: Evidence from the United States," IMF Working Paper no. WP/13/143, June 2013, http://www.imf.org/external/pubs/cat/longres.aspx?sk=40642.0.

82 **This is not certain to happen but is likely . . .** : This analysis is based on data and reporting in Buttonwood, "The Real Deal—Low Real Interest Rates Are Usually Bad News for Equity Markets," *Economist,* October 20, 2012, http://www.economist.com/news/finance-and-economics/21564845-low-real-interest-rates-are-usually-bad-news-equity-markets.

83 **"The Market for 'Lemons'":** George A. Akerlof, "The Market for 'Lemons': Quality Uncertainty and the Market Mechanism," *Quarterly Journal of Economics* 84, no. 3 (August 1970), pp. 488–500.

84 **"Irreversibility, Uncertainty . . .":** Ben S. Bernanke, "Irreversibility, Uncertainty, and Cyclical Investment," National Bureau of Economic Research, Cambridge, Mass., July 1980, http://www.nber.org/papers/w502.

85 **Even with huge pools of unused labor . . .** : Jason E. Taylor and Richard K. Vedder, "Stimulus by Spending Cuts: Lessons from 1946," Cato Institute, Cato Policy Report, May–June 2010, http://www.cato.org/policy-report/mayjune-2010/stimulus-spending-cuts-lessons-1946.

85 **the classic distinction between risk and uncertainty . . .** : Frank H. Knight, *Risk, Uncertainty and Profit* (1921; reprint Washington, D.C.: Beard Books, 2002).

86 **"It will pay to invest . . .":** Bernanke, "Irreversibility, Uncertainty."

86 **"It would not be difficult to recast . . .":** Ibid.

86 **the counterproductive nature of Bernanke's reasoning . . .** : Robert E. Hall, "The Routes into and out of the Zero Lower Bound," paper prepared for the Federal Reserve Bank of Kansas City Symposium, Jackson Hole, Wyo., August 13, 2013, http://www.stanford.edu/~rehall/HallJacksonHole2013.

Chapter 4: China's New Financial Warlords

90 **"Things grow and grow . . .":** *Tao Te Ching,* trans. Stephen Addis and Stanley Lombardo (Indianapolis: Hackett, 1993).

92 **the current Communist leadership's greatest fear . . .** : David T. C. Lie, eldest grandson of Zhang Xue Ming, mayor of Tianjin in the 1930s, conversation with the author, Shanghai, June 6, 2012.

94 **"The Myth of Asia's Miracle":** Paul Krugman, "The Myth of Asia's Miracle," *Foreign Affairs,* November–December 1994, p. 62, http://www.pairault.fr/documents/lecture3s2009.pdf.

95 **"China is on the eve of a demographic shift . . .":** Mitali Das and Papa N'Diaye, "Chronicle of a Decline Foretold: Has China Reached the Lewis Turning Point?" IMF Working Paper no. 13/26, January 2013, http://www.imf.org/external/pubs/cat/longres.aspx?sk=40281.0.

97 **In 2010 the ten most profitable SOEs . . .** : James McGregor, *No Ancient Wisdom, No Followers* (Westport, Conn.: Prospecta Press, 2012), p. 23.

97 **These megaprojects cover sectors . . .** : Ibid., p. 34.

101 **the interlocking interests of the political and economic elites . . .** : "Heirs of Mao's Comrades Rise as New Capitalist Nobility," *Bloomberg News,* December 26, 2012, http://www.bloomberg.com/news/2012-12-26/immortals-beget-china-capitalism-from-citic-to-godfather-of-golf.html.

103 **One report on WMP sales . . .** : Xiao Gang, "Regulating Shadow Banking,"

China Daily, October 12, 2012, p. 8, http://www.chinadaily.com.cn/opinion/2012-10/12/content_15812305.htm.

105 **"In June, a Chinese man touched down . . ."**: Alistair Macdonald, Paul Vieira, and Will Connors, "Chinese Fly Cash West, by the Suitcase," *Wall Street Journal,* January 2, 2013, p. A1, http://online.wsj.com/news/articles/SB10001424127887323635504578213933647167020.

106 **"Tackling inequality requires confronting . . ."**: Bob Davis, "China Tries to Shut Rising Income Gap," *Wall Street Journal,* December 11, 2012, p. A14, http://online.wsj.com/news/articles/SB10001424127887324640104578161493858722884.

106 **corruption, cronyism, and income inequality . . .** : Minxin Pei, "China's Troubled Bourbons," *Project Syndicate,* October 31, 2012, www.project-syndicate.org.

107 **"Investment in China may currently . . ."**: Il Houng Lee, Murtaza Syed, and Liu Xueyan, "Is China Over-Investing and Does It Matter?" IMF Working Paper no. WP/12/277, November 2012, http://www.imf.org/external/pubs/cat/longres.aspx?sk=40121.0.

108 **"Let us . . . give China five years to bring . . ."**: Michael Pettis, "The IMF on Overinvestment," *Michael Pettis' China Financial Markets,* December 28, 2012, http://www.economonitor.com/blog/2012/12.

109 **The Chinese workforce is now dominated . . .** : Houng Il Lee, Xu Qingjun, and Murtaza Syed, "China's Demography and Its Implications," IMF Working Paper no. WP/13/82, March 28, 2013, http://www.imf.org/external/pubs/cat/longres.aspx?sk=40446.0.

Chapter 5: The New German Reich

113 **"the most learned man anywhere"**: Einhard, *The Life of Charlemagne* (ninth century; reprint Kessinger, 2010).

115 **"The final step was cannibalism . . ."**: Lauro Martines, *Furies: War in Europe, 1450–1700* (New York: Bloomsbury, 2013), p. 118.

119 **"No statement about how to deal . . ."**: John Williamson, "What Washington Means by Policy Reform," Peterson Institute for International Economics, 1990, http://www.iie.com/publications/papers/paper.cfm?researchid=486.

120 **"the Beijing Consensus . . . is flexible enough . . ."**: Joshua Cooper Ramo, *The Beijing Consensus* (London, Foreign Policy Centre, 2004), p. 4.

120 **the five pillars . . .** : John Williamson, "Is the 'Beijing Consensus' Now Dominant?" *Asia Policy,* no. 13 (January 2012), pp. 1–16.

122 **six of the top ten applicants . . .** : World Intellectual Property Organization, *WIPO IP Facts and Figures 2012,* WIPO Economics and Statistics Series, http://www.wipo.int/export/sites/www/freepublications/en/statistics/943/wipo_pub_943_2012.pdf.

122 **The average European corporate tax rate . . .** : "Corporate Tax Rates Table," KPMG, http://www.kpmg.com/global/en/services/tax/tax-tools-and-resources/pages/corporate-tax-rates-table.aspx.

123 **For rail freight traffic . . .** : Leo Cendrowicz, "Switzerland Celebrates World's Longest Rail Tunnel," *Time,* October 20, 2010, http://www.time.com/time/business/article/0,8599,2026369,00.html.

124 **"So if there were really a large excess . . ."**: Paul Krugman, "Sticky Wages and the Macro Story," *New York Times,* July 22, 2012, http://krugman.blogs.nytimes.com/2012/07/22/sticky-wages-and-the-macro-story.

125 "In a currency area comprising many regions . . .": Robert A. Mundell, "A Theory of Optimum Currency Areas," *American Economic Review* 51, no. 4 (September 1961), pp. 657–65, esp. 659.

125 Europe has lagged behind the rest of the developed world . . . : Indermit Gill and Martin Raiser, "Golden Growth, Restoring the Lustre of the European Economic Model," International Bank for Reconstruction and Development, 2012, http://issuu .com/world.bank.publications/docs/9780821389652.

126 "As Chinese companies and entrepreneurs have moved . . .": Howard Schneider, "As Chinese Capital Moves Abroad, Europe Offers an Open Door," *Washington Post,* February 26, 2013, http://articles.washingtonpost.com/2013-02-26/ business/37297545_1_direct-investment-chinese-investors-rhodium-group.

126 "was an early investor in bonds . . .": Lingling Wei and Bob Davis, "China's Zhu Changhong Helps Steer Nation's Currency Reserves," *Wall Street Journal,* July 16, 2013, p. C1, http://online.wsj.com/article/SB1000142412788732366420457860630 1739504368.html.

127 the ten largest money-market funds in the United States . . . : Howard Schneider, "In a Two-Faced Euro Zone, Financial Conditions Ease and Joblessness Rises," *Washington Post,* March 1, 2013, http://articles.washingtonpost.com/2013-03-01/ business/37373712_1_euro-zone-holdings-euro-zone-17-nation-currency-zone.

129 Data for the first quarter of 1999 . . . : IMF, "Currency Composition of Official Foreign Exchange Reserves (COFER)," http://www.imf.org/external/np/sta/cofer/ eng/index.htm.

129 The cheap-dollar policy was made explicit in numerous public pronouncements . . . : Barack Obama, "Remarks by the President in State of the Union Address," January 27, 2010, http://www.whitehouse.gov/the-press-office/remarks-president -state-union-address; and Ben Bernanke, "U.S. Monetary Policy and International Implications," remarks at IMF–Bank of Japan seminar, October 14, 2012, http://www .federalreserve.gov/newsevents/speech/bernanke20121014a.htm.

131 private-sector salaries in Greece had dropped . . . : "Salaries Drop by over 10 Pct Within a Year," *ekathimerini,* July 2, 2013, http://www.ekathimerini.com/ 4dcgi/_w_articles_wsite2_1_02/07/2013_507091.

132 "Across Europe's southern rim, people recoil . . .": Marcus Walker and Alessandra Galloni, "Embattled Economies Cling to the Euro," *Wall Street Journal,* February 13, 2013, p. A1, http://online.wsj.com/news/articles/SB1000142412788732476 1004578284203099970438.

132 "Europe was not built for economic reasons . . .": Matthew Kaminski, "Guy Sorman: Why Europe Will Rise Again," *Wall Street Journal,* August 18, 2011, p. A11, http://online.wsj.com/news/articles/SB10000872396390444375104577592850 0332409044.

133 "everything from Greek real estate . . .": Stelios Bouras and Philip Pangalos, "Foreign Money Is Revisiting Greece," *Wall Street Journal,* February 25, 2013, p. C1, http://online.wsj.com/news/articles/SB10001424127887323864304578320431 435196910.

133 "The drive to improve competitiveness . . .": Hugo Dixon, "The Gloom Around Greece Is Dissipating," *New York Times,* April 21, 2013, http://www.nytimes .com/2013/04/22/business/global/the-gloom-around-greece-is-dissipating.html.

133 The fifteen-hundred-acre former Athens airport site . . . : Liz Alderman and Demitris Bounias, "Privatizing Greece, Slowly but Not Surely," *New York Times,*

November 18, 2012, http://www.nytimes.com/glogin?URI=http://www.nytimes
.com/2012/11/18/business/privatizing-greece-slowly-but-not-surely.html.

133 **"On Cosco's portion of the port . . .":** Liz Alderman, "Under Chinese, a Greek
Port Thrives," *New York Times,* October 19, 2012, http://www.nytimes
.com/2012/10/11/business/global/chinese-company-sets-new-rhythm-in-port-of
-piraeus.html?pagewanted=all.

134 **All these investment and expansion plans will have positive . . . :** Ralph Minder,
"Car Factories Offer Hope for Spanish Industry and Workers," *New York Times,*
December 28, 2012, p. B1, http://www.nytimes.com/2012/12/28/business/global
/car-factories-offer-hope-for-spanish-industry-and-workers.html?pagewanted=all;
Angeline Benoit, Manuel Baigorri, and Emma Ross-Thomas, "Rajoy Drives Spanish
Revolution with Low-Cost Manufacture," *Bloomberg,* December 19, 2012, http://
www.bloomberg.com/news/2012-12-19/rajoy-drives-spanish-revolution-with-low
-cost-manufacture.html.

134 **adverse demographics as a major hurdle . . . :** Buttonwood, "The Euro Zone
Crisis: Growth Problem," *Economist,* December 17, 2012, http://www.economist
.com/blogs/buttonwood/2012/12/euro-zone-crisis.

136 **a €60 billion bailout fund . . . :** Matina Stevis, "Euro Zone Closes In on Bank
Plans," *Wall Street Journal,* June 13, 2013, http://online.wsj.com/article/SB100014
24127887323734304578542941134353614.html.

Chapter 6: BELLs, BRICS, and Beyond

139 **The original term *BRIC* was created . . . :** Jim O'Neill, "Building Better Global
Economic BRICs," Goldman Sachs, Global Economics Paper no. 66, November 30,
2001, http://www.goldmansachs.com/our-thinking/archive/archive-pdfs/build
-better-brics.pdf.

140 **"The other members would need to recognise . . .":** Ibid., p. S11.

142 **He attributes economic success in the Baltics . . . :** Anders Åslund, "Southern
Europe Ignores Lessons from Latvia at Its Peril," Peterson Institute for International
Economics, Policy Brief no. PB12-17, June 2012, http://www.iie.com/publications
/pb/pb12-17.pdf.

143 **"The government prohibited double incomes . . .":** Ibid.

143 **"Shoppers throng Nordic design shops . . .":** Paul Ames, "Estonia Uses the Euro,
and the Economy Is Booming," CNBC, June 5, 2012, http://www.cnbc.com
/id/47691090.

144 **Estonia in particular has become a high-tech hub . . . :** Ibid.

144 **"When a credit-fueled economic boom . . .":** Andrew Higgins, "Used to Hardship, Latvia Accepts Austerity, and Its Pain Eases," *New York Times,* January 1,
2013, http://www.nytimes.com/2013/01/02/world/europe/used-to-hardship-latvia
-accepts-austerity-and-its-pain-eases.html?pagewanted=all.

144 **"While challenges remain today, you have . . .":** Christine Lagarde, "Latvia and
the Baltics—A Story of Recovery," speech delivered in Riga, Latvia, June 5, 2013,
http://www.imf.org/external/np/speeches/2012/060512.htm.

145 **"Today, Estonia's economy is the fastest-growing . . .":** Ott Ummelas, "Why
Estonia Loves the Euro," *Bloomberg Businessweek,* February 2, 2012, http://www
.businessweek.com/magazine/why-estonia-loves-the-euro-02022012.html.

146 **O'Neill has consistently downplayed the idea . . . :** Jim O'Neill, interview, CNN

Marketplace Africa, April 5, 2011, http://edition.cnn.com/2011/BUSINESS/04/05/jim.oneill.africa.bric/index.html.

148 **"We directed our Finance Ministers to examine . . .":** eThekwini Declaration, Fifth BRICS Summit, Durban, South Africa, March 27, 2013, http://www.brics5.co.za/assets/eThekwini-Declaration-and-Action-Plan-MASTER-27-MARCH-2013.pdf.

149 **"We support the reform and improvement . . .":** Ibid.

149 **a twenty-thousand-mile undersea fiber optic cable . . . :** "Brazil Plans to Go Offline from US-Centric Internet," *Hindu,* September 17, 2013, http://www.thehindu.com/news/international/world/brazil-plans-to-go-offline-from-uscentric-internet/article5137689.ece.

151 **the SCO's rejection of a U.S. application . . . :** Dilip Hiro, "Shanghai Surprise—The Summit of the Shanghai Cooperation Organisation Reveals How Power Is Shifting in the World," *Guardian,* June 16, 2006, http://www.guardian.co.uk/commentisfree/2006/jun/16/shanghaisurprise.

151 **The Prime Ministers Council of the SCO signed an agreement . . . :** "The Interbank Consortium of the Shanghai Cooperation Organisation," Shanghai Cooperation Organisation, March 16, 2009, http://www.sectsco.org/EN123/show.asp?id=51.

151 **"the Shanghai Cooperation Organisation is a good . . .":** Rick Rozoff, "The Shanghai Cooperation Organization: Prospects for a Multipolar World," Centre for Research on Globalisation, May 2009, http://www.globalresearch.ca/the-shanghai-cooperation-organization-prospects-for-a-multipolar-world.

152 **a joint Sino-Russian declaration . . . :** "China, Russia Sign Five-Point Joint Statement," Xinhua, June 18, 2009, http://news.xinhuanet.com/english/2009-06/18/content_11558133.htm.

155 **several candidates for an alternative peg . . . :** See Dr. Syed Abul Basher, "Regional Initiative in the Gulf: Search for a GCC Currency," paper presented at the International Institute for Strategic Studies Seminar, Bahrain, September 30, 2012, http://www.iiss.org/en/events/geo-economics%20seminars/geo-economics%20seminars/archive/currencies-of-power-and-the-power-of-currencies-38db.

155 **A logical extension, then, of the SDR basket approach . . . :** The author is indebted to Dr. Syed Abul Basher for the suggestion and explication of the SDR-plus-oil approach to the currency peg, ibid.

156 **the United States would continue its loose monetary policy . . . :** Ben S. Bernanke, "U.S. Monetary Policy and International Implications," remarks at IMF–Bank of Japan seminar, Tokyo, October 14, 2012, http://www.federalreserve.gov/newsevents/speech/bernanke20121014a.htm.

158 **"Today most advanced economies remain . . .":** Ben S. Bernanke, "Monetary Policy and the Global Economy," speech at the London School of Economics, London, March 25, 2013, http://www.federalreserve.gov/newsevents/speech/bernanke20130325a.htm.

160 **"The purpose of the purchases was and is . . .":** "Quantitative Easing Explained," Bank of England, http://www.bankofengland.co.uk/monetarypolicy/Pages/qe/default.aspx.

160 **"The impact on economic activity . . .":** S. Pelin Berkmen, "Bank of Japan's Quantitative and Credit Easing: Are They Now More Effective?" IMF Working Paper no. WP/12/2, January 2012, http://www.imf.org/external/pubs/ft/wp/2012/wp1202.pdf.

161 "It's very rare for monetary policy . . .": Ambrose Evans-Pritchard, "Japan's Shinzo Abe Prepares to Print Money for the Whole World," *Telegraph*, December 17, 2012, http://www.telegraph.co.uk/finance/economics/9751609/Japans-Shinzo-Abe-prepares-to-print-money-for-the-whole-world.html.

161 The BOJ pledged to purchase $1.4 trillion . . . : "Introduction to the 'Quantitative and Qualitative Monetary Easing,'" Bank of Japan, April 4, 2013, http://www.boj.or.jp/en/announcements/release_2013/k130404a.pdf.

161 "The bank will achieve . . .": Ibid.

Chapter 7: Debt, Deficits, and the Dollar

167 the contract theory of money. . . : See Eerik Lagerspetz, "Money as a Social Contract," *Theory and Decision* 17, no. 1 (July 1984), pp. 1–9. The contract theory of money has philosophical and legal roots as old as Aristotle and, in more recent centuries, John Locke and Samuel von Pufendorf. It is presented here in an updated version for the purpose of illuminating the intrinsic rather than extrinsic value of money.

168 the quantity theory of money . . . : Irving Fisher, "The Debt-Deflation Theory of Great Depressions," *Econometrica* (1933), available from the Federal Reserve Bank of St. Louis, http://fraser.stlouisfed.org/docs/meltzer/fisdeb33.pdf; and Milton Friedman, *Studies in the Quantity Theory of Money* (Chicago: University of Chicago Press, 1967).

168 the state theory of money . . . : Georg Friedrich Knapp, *The State Theory of Money* (San Diego: Simon, 2003).

168 John Maynard Keynes adopted chartalism . . . : John Maynard Keynes, *Treatise on Money*, vol. 1, *The Pure Theory of Money*, and vol. 2, *The Applied Theory of Money* (London: Macmillan, 1950).

168 acolytes of the theory of money as an arm of state power . . . : Paul McCulley and Zoltan Pozsar, "Helicopter Money: Or How I Stopped Worrying and Love Fiscal-Monetary Cooperation," GIC Global Society of Fellows, January 7, 2013, http://www.interdependence.org/wp-content/uploads/2013/01/Helicopter_Money_Final1.pdf; Stephanie A. Bell and Edward J. Nell, eds., *The State, the Market, and the Euro: Metallism versus Chartalism in the Theory of Money* (Northampton, Mass.: Edward Elgar, 2003).

168 the quantity theory of credit . . . : Richard Duncan, *The New Depression: The Breakdown of the Paper Money Economy* (Singapore: John Wiley & Sons Singapore Pte., 2012).

168 His work could properly be called *creditism* . . . : Fiona Maclachlan, "Max Weber and the State Theory of Money," working paper, http://home.manhattan.edu/~fiona.maclachlan/maclachlan26july03.htm.

170 "bet on the country": Warren Buffett, interview by Becky Quick and Joe Kernan, CNBC, November 3, 2009, http://www.cnbc.com/id/33603477.

174 Not only did this spending not produce . . . : John F. Cogan, Tobias Cwik, John B. Taylor, and Volker Wieland, "New Keynesian Versus Old Keynesian Government Spending Multipliers," National Bureau of Economic Research, Working Paper no. 14782, February 2009, http://www.nber.org/papers/w14782.pdf?new_window=1.

177 the relationship of U.S. debt and deficits . . . : John H. Makin, "Trillion-Dollar Deficits Are Sustainable for Now, Unfortunately," American Enterprise Institute,

December 13, 2012, http://www.aei.org/outloook/trillion-dollar-deficits-are
-sustainable-for-now-unfortunately.

182 **Contrary to the oft-cited . . . :** Carmen M. Reinhart and Kenneth S. Rogoff,
"Growth in a Time of Debt," National Bureau of Economic Research, Working
Paper no. 15639, January 2010, http://www.nber.org/papers/w15639.

183 **"The Liquidation of Government Debt":** Carmen M. Reinhart and M. Belen
Sbrancia, "The Liquidation of Government Debt," National Bureau of Economic
Research, Working Paper no. 16893, March 2011, http://www.nber.org/papers
/w16893.

186 **"A . . . reason why forward guidance may be needed . . .":** Michael Woodford,
"Methods of Policy Accommodation at the Interest-Rate Lower Bound," paper presented at the Federal Reserve Bank of Kansas City Symposium, Jackson Hole, Wyo.,
August 31, 2012, p. 6, emphasis in the original, http://www.kc.frb.org/publicat/
sympos/2012/mw.pdf.

186 **"In particular, the committee decided to keep . . .":** Federal Reserve, press
release, December 12, 2012, http://www.federalreserve.gov/newsevents/press/
monetary/20121212a.htm.

188 **The Fed's own staff have expressed reservations . . . :** Marco Del Negro, Marc
Giannoni, and Christina Patterson, "The Forward Guidance Puzzle," Federal Reserve Bank of New York, Staff Report no. 574, October 2012, http://newyorkfed
.org/research/staff_reports/sr574.pdf.

188 **"a thinly disguised way of aiming . . .":** Charles Goodhart, "Central Banks Walk
Inflation's Razor Edge," *Financial Times,* January 30, 2013, http://www.ft.com/intl
/cms/s/0/744e4a96-661c-11e2-b967-00144feab49a.html.

188 **a highly detailed critique of the Fed's easy-money policy . . . :** Jeremy C. Stein,
"Overheating in Credit Markets: Origins, Measurement, and Policy Responses,"
Federal Reserve Bank of St. Louis Research Symposium, February 7, 2013, http://
www.federalreserve.gov/newsevents/speech/stein20130207a.htm.

Chapter 8: Central Bank of the World

190 **To meet Dr. Min Zhu . . . :** The profile in this chapter is based on Dr. Min Zhu,
conversation with the author, New York City, November 8, 2012; Dr. Min Zhu,
lecture at the Watson Institute, Brown University, Providence, R.I., March 29, 2013.

193 **a China–western hemisphere supply-chain cluster . . . :** Riordan Roett and Gua-
dalupe Paz, eds., *China's Expansion into the Western Hemisphere: Implications for
Latin America and the United States* (Washington, D.C.: Brookings Institution
Press, 2008).

195 **After being vetted and groomed in midlevel positions . . . :** See William D. Co-
han, "Rethinking Robert Rubin," *Bloomberg Businessweek,* September 30, 2012,
http://www.businessweek.com/articles/2012-09-19/rethinking-robert-rubin; and
Jonathan Stempel and Dan Wilchins, "Robert Rubin Quits Citigroup amid Criticism," Reuters, January 9, 2009, http://www.reuters.com/article/2009/01/09/us
-citigroup-rubin-idUSN0930738020090109.

197 **Min Zhu believes the world . . . :** Min Zhu, conversation with the author.

198 **"Central bankers like to say . . . ":** Ibid.

198 **IMF economists such as José Viñals . . . :** IMF Monetary and Capital Markets
Department, "Macrofinancial Stress Testing—Principles and Practices," August 22,
2012, http://www.imf.org/external/np/pp/eng/2012/082212.pdf.

199 "Each member shall deal with the Fund . . .": IMF Articles of Agreement, Article V, Section 1, http://www.imf.org/external/pubs/ft/aa/index.htm.

200 Today the IMF website touts loans . . . : "IMF Lending Arrangements as of May 13, 2013," International Monetary Fund, http://www.imf.org/external/np/fin/tad/extarr11.aspx?memberKey1=ZZZZ&date1key=2020-02-28.

201 the SDR-to-dollar exchange rate . . . : This analysis uses an exchange rate of one U.S. dollar to 0.667 SDRs. Updates to the exchange rate are available at "Exchange Rate Archives by Month," International Monetary Fund, http://www.imf.org/external/np/fin/data/param_rms_mth.aspx.

202 President Obama sent letters to the congressional leadership . . . : "Letters from the President to the Bipartisan Leadership on NAB Fund," Office of the Press Secretary, White House, April 20, 2009, http://www.whitehouse.gov/the-press-office/letters-president-bipartisan-leadership-nab-fund.

203 The president's letter said: Ibid.

204 "significant step forward": "IMF Managing Director Dominique Strauss-Kahn Welcomes U.S. Congressional Approval of IMF-Related Legislation, Including U.S. Financial Commitment of up to US$100 Billion," International Monetary Fund, Press Release no. 09/220, June 18, 2009, http://www.imf.org/external/np/sec/pr/2009/pr09220.htm.

205 "Why Is the U.S. Bankrolling . . .": John Gizzi, "Why Is the U.S. Bankrolling IMF's Bailouts in Europe?" Human Events, April 25, 2011, http://www.humanevents.com/2011/05/02/why-is-the-us-bankrolling-imfs-bailouts-in-europe.

205 "We will miss them": Sandrine Rastello and Timothy R. Homan, "Lagarde Boosting China IMF Clout Requires New Allies," Bloomberg, April 10, 2013, http://www.bloomberg.com/news/2013-04-10/lagarde-boosting-china-imf-clout-requires-new-allies.html.

206 However, President Obama did not include the new requests in his 2012 or 2013 budgets . . . : Lesley Wroughton and David Lawder, "Senate Rebuffs Obama Request to Shift Fund for IMF," Reuters, March 12, 2013, http://www.reuters.com/article/2013/03/12/us-usa-imf-reforms-idUSBRE92B04K20130312.

206 "I am here with my little bag . . .": Pan Pylas, "Christine Lagarde at Davos 2012: 'I Am Here with My Little Bag, to Collect a Bit of Money,'" Huffington Post, January 28, 2012, http://www.huffingtonpost.com/2012/01/28/christine-lagarde-davos-2012_n_1239050.html.

206 "We have been able to significantly increase . . .": Howard Schneider, "Q & A with IMF Director Christine Lagarde," Washington Post, June 29, 2013, http://articles.washingtonpost.com/2013-06-29/business/40269400_1_christine-lagarde-imf-former-french-finance-minister.

207 object to the use of the term money . . . : "Easy Money: Consequences of the Global Liquidity Glut," Milken Institute 2012 Global Conference, May 1, 2012, http://www.milkeninstitute.org/events/gcprogram.taf?function=detail&EvID=3353&eventid=GC12.

207 "The SDR may be allocated by the IMF . . .": International Monetary Fund, Annual Report 2012, Appendix VI: Financial Statements for FY 2012, Independent Auditors' Report on the Special Drawing Rights Department, June 21, 2012, p. 31, http://www.imf.org/external/pubs/ft/ar/2012/eng/pdf/a6.pdf; emphasis added.

210 "The SDR differed from nearly all prior proposals . . .": Kenneth W. Dam, The Rules of the Game: Reform and Evolution in the International Monetary System (Chicago: University of Chicago Press, 1982), pp. 151–52.

211 **the Price-adjusted Broad Dollar Index . . . :** This index is available as part of the statistical series published by the board of governors of the Federal Reserve System and available as part of the Foreign Exchange Rates H.10 data series at http://www .federalreserve.gov/releases/h10/summary/indexbc_m.htm.

212 **a multiyear, multistep plan . . . :** IMF Strategy, Policy, and Review Department, "Enhancing International Monetary Stability—A Role for the SDR?" January 7, 2011, http://www.imf.org/external/np/pp/eng/2011/010711.pdf.

212 **Beyond the SDR bond market creation . . . :** Ibid. See also IMF Finance and Strategy, Policy, and Review Departments, "Criteria for Broadening the SDR Currency Basket," September 23, 2011, http://www.imf.org/external/np/pp/eng /2011/092311.pdf.

212 **"If there were political willingness to do so . . .":** IMF Strategy, Policy, and Review Department, "Enhancing International Monetary Stability—A Role for the SDR?"

213 **"non-members . . . and other official entities":** IMF Articles of Agreement, Article XVII, Section 3(i), http://www.imf.org/external/pubs/ft/aa/index.htm#a5s1.

213 **The BIS is notorious for facilitating Nazi gold swaps . . . :** Adam Lebor, *Tower of Basel: The Shadowy History of the Secret Bank That Runs the World* (New York: Public Affairs, 2013), chap. 3.

213 **China had acquired the equivalent of $1.24 billion . . . :** Annual Report 2012, International Monetary Fund, Appendix VI: Financial Statements for FY 2012, Independent Auditors' Report on the Special Drawing Rights Department, June 21, 2012, Schedule 2, http://www.imf.org/external/pubs/ft/ar/2012/eng/pdf/a6.pdf. The IMF also records the positions of those members whose holdings of SDRs are less than their allocations because they have swapped SDRs for convertible currencies with other members. Such members are subject to a requirement of "reconstitution" in accordance with Article XIX, Section 6(a) of the IMF Articles of Agreement, which means that the shortfall in SDRs must be made up at some future date, presumably through repurchases of SDRs with convertible currency earned subsequent to the liquidity crisis that gave rise to the initial issuance. However, the IMF Articles of Agreement are extremely flexible with regard to how the reconstitution requirement will be applied, and Article XIX, Section 6(b) allows the rules to be changed at any time. The United States does not have effective veto power with respect to proposed changes of this kind.

213 **"They are fake money . . .":** Min Zhu, conversation with the author.

213 **"In all its decisions with respect to the allocation . . .":** IMF Articles of Agreement, Article XVIII, Section 1(a), http://www.imf.org/external/pubs/ft/aa/index .htm.

Chapter 9: Gold Redux

216 *paranoid, fear-based* . . . : Nouriel Roubini, "After the Gold Rush," *Project Syndicate,* June 1, 2013, http://www.project-syndicate.org/commentary/the-end-of -the-gold-bubble-by-nouriel-roubini.

216 **"I only know of two men who . . .":** Quoted in Gary Dorsch, "What's Behind the Global Flight into Gold?" *Financial Sense Observations,* June 30, 2010, http:// www.financialsensearchive.com/Market/dorsch/2010/0630.html.

220 **"Money is gold, and nothing else":** J. P. Morgan, *Testimony of J. P. Morgan Before the Bank and Currency Committee of the House of Representatives at Wash-*

ington, D.C., December 18–19, 1912, http://memory.loc.gov/service/gdc/scd0001/2006/20060517001te/20060517001te.pdf.

220 President Nixon ended U.S. dollar convertibility into gold . . . : For a learned review of the workings of the Committee for Reform of the International Monetary System, the "Committee of 20," its recommendations, and the eventual entry into force of the Second Amendment to the IMF Articles of Agreement in 1978, see Kenneth W. Dam, *The Rules of the Game: Reform and Evolution in the International Monetary System* (Chicago: University of Chicago Press, 1982), pp. 211–90.

220 the United States dumped 412 tons of gold on the market . . . : Ibid., p. 273n92.

221 The total gold supply in the world today . . . : This measure of total gold and all further reference to specific gold quantities in this chapter are as of July 2013 and are available from the World Gold Council, www.gold.org.

221 money supplies of the ECB, the Bank of Japan, . . . : These figures are taken from the websites of the Federal Reserve System, http://www.federalreserve.gov; the European Central Bank, http://www.ecb.int/home/html/index.en.html; the Bank of Japan, http://www.boj.or.jp/en; and the People's Bank of China, http://www.pbc.gov.cn/publish/english/955/2013/20130313140427964275661/2013031314042796 4275661_.html, as of July 11, 2013. Japanese yen were converted to U.S. dollars at 100 to 1; euros at 0.77 to 1; yuan at 6.1 to 1.

223 chose to return sterling to gold at the prewar rate. . . : For an extended analysis of this topic, from which this section is partly drawn, see Murray N. Rothbard, *What Has Government Done to Our Money?* part 4, "The Monetary Breakdown of the West, 3. Phase III: The Gold Exchange Standard (Britain and the United States) 1926–1931," at Ludwig von Mises Institute, http://mises.org/money/4s3.asp.

224 he recites it *ad nauseam* . . . : See, for example, Paul Krugman, "Golden Instability," *New York Times,* August 26, 2012, http://krugman.blogs.nytimes .com/2012/08/26/golden-instability.

225 The facts speak for themselves . . . : Statistics on gold production, gold demand, and gold supply in this section are from the World Gold Council, www.gold.org.

227 No such prearranged central bank or IMF sales to China have been reported . . . : The closest correspondence to potential prearrangement appears in the fourth quarter of 2002, when China's reported gold reserves *increased* 99.84 tonnes and Switzerland's *declined* 70.4 tonnes at the same time; see World Gold Council, www.gold .org. However, no evidence of prearrangement between Switzerland and China has been found. If a Switzerland-to-China trade were prearranged, it would likely have been handled through the facilities of the Bank for International Settlements (BIS) in Basel. The central bank of Switzerland, the Swiss National Bank, has been a member of the BIS since its inception in 1930; see the Swiss National Bank website at http://www.snb.ch/en/iabout/internat and UN treaty archives at http://treaties .un.org/Pages/showDetails.aspx?objid=0800000280167c31.

227 The agents are principally located . . . : Senior bankers and asset managers with firsthand knowledge of China's global gold-buying operations, conversations with the author, Hong Kong, September 2012.

227 In a masterpiece of market savvy . . . : China's gold purchasing agents, conversations with the author, New York City, August 7, 2013; Perth Mint, e-mail to the author, dated September 25, 2013.

227 Partly as a result of these large-scale covert operations . . . : Brendan Conway, "China: Soon to Be World's Biggest Gold Importer, If It Isn't Already," *Barron's,*

February 6, 2013, http://blogs.barrons.com/focusonfunds/2013/02/06/china-soon
-to-be-worlds-biggest-gold-importer-if-it-isnt-already.

228 **By 2012, China was producing over 370 tonnes per year . . . :** See U.S. Geolog-
ical Survey, "Gold," Mineral Commodity Summaries, January 2013, http://minerals
.usgs.gov/minerals/pubs/commodity/gold/mcs-2013-gold.pdf.

229 **Russia is the world's fourth-largest gold producer:** Ibid.

230 **The Federal Reserve vaults hold approximately 6,400 tonnes . . . :** See Scott
Mayerowitz, "Welcome to the World's Largest Gold Vault," ABC News, September
19, 2009, http://abcnews.go.com/Business/story?id=5835433&page=1; and Mike
Hanlon, "The Big Picture: This Vast Vault of Gold Under the Bank of England
Should Weather Credit Crunch," *Daily Mail,* October 22, 2008, http://forums
.canadiancontent.net/news/78369-vast-vault-gold-under-bank.html. Since the *Daily
Mail* report, which cites a figure of 4,600 tonnes, approximately 100 tonnes have
been repatriated to Venezuela.

231 **an eight-year plan to repatriate all the gold . . . :** "Deutsche Bundesbank's New
Storage Plan for Germany's Gold Reserves," Deutsche Bundesbank, press notice,
January 16, 2013, http://www.bundesbank.de/Redaktion/EN/Pressemitteilungen/
BBK/2013/2013_01_16_storage_plan_gold_reserve.htm.

232 **an initiative that requires all Swiss gold . . . :** Luzi Stamm, "'Gold Initiative': A
Swiss Initiative to Secure the Swiss National Bank's Gold Reserves," Volksinitiative
Rettet unser Schweizer Gold, press release, September 20, 2011, http://www
.goldinitiative.ch/downloads/goldinitiative-english.pdf.

233 **"I don't know . . .":** Katharina Bart and Albert Schmieder, "Swiss Right-Wing
Forces Referendum on Banning SNB Gold Sales," Reuters, March 20, 2013, http://
www.reuters.com/article/2013/03/20/us-swiss-gold-idUSBRE92J0Z320130320.

233 **The remainder is divided . . . :** Jaco Schipper, "90% of Dutch Gold Reserve Is
Held Abroad," *Market Update,* January 7, 2012, http://www.marketupdate.nl
/nieuws/valutacrisis/90-of-dutch-gold-reserve-is-held-abroad.

235 **The international monetary debate . . . :** For a scholarly, in-depth study of efforts
at reform of the international monetary system including the C-20, the Jamaica
Meeting, and the Second Amendment to the IMF Articles of Agreement, see Kenneth
W. Dam, *The Rules of the Game: Reform and Evolution in the International Monetary System* (Chicago: University of Chicago Press, 1982).

236 **"You are . . . asking this to someone . . .":** Mario Draghi, lecture at the John F.
Kennedy Jr. Forum at the Institute of Politics, Harvard University, Cambridge,
Mass., October 9, 2013, https://forum.iop.harvard.edu/content/public-address
-mario-draghi.

Chapter 10: Crossroads

244 **"a chronic condition of sub-normal activity . . .":** John Maynard Keynes, *The
General Theory of Employment, Interest, and Money* (San Diego: Harcourt, 1964),
p. 249.

245 **Based on duration if not strength . . . :** John H. Makin, "Third Time Unlucky:
Recession in 2014?" American Enterprise Institute, July 30, 2013, http://www.aei
.org/outlook/economics/monetary-policy/third-time-unlucky-recession-in-2014.

245 **Despite cheerleading in late 2013 . . :** Daniel Alpert, "The New Sick-onomy?
Examining the Entrails of the U.S. Employment Situation," *EconoMonitor,* July 24,

2013, http://www.economonitor.com/danalperts2cents/2013/07/24/the-new-sick
-onomy-examining-the-entrails-of-the-u-s-employment-situation.

247 **By August 2013, total student loans backed . . . :** "The Rolling Student Loan
Bailout," *Wall Street Journal,* August 9, 2013, http://online.wsj.com/article/SB1000
14241278873239687045786522291680883634.html.

252 **"the test of a first-rate intelligence . . .":** F. Scott Fitzgerald, *The Crack-Up* (1936;
reprint New York: New Directions, 2009).

254 **The bitcoin phenomenon began in 2008 . . . :** Satoshi Nakamoto, "Bitcoin: A
Peer-to-Peer Electronic Cash System," November 1, 2008, http://bitcoin.org/bitcoin
.pdf.

255 **the history of barter is mostly a myth:** David Graeber, *Debt: The First 5,000
Years* (Brooklyn, N.Y.: Melville House, 2011), pp. 21–41.

256 **"Sept. 11 was not a failure of intelligence or coordination . . .":** Thomas L.
Friedman, "A Failure to Imagine," *New York Times,* May 19, 2002, http://www
.nytimes.com/2002/05/19/opinion/a-failure-to-imagine.html.

Chapter 11: Maelstrom

271 **"The broad question is whether central banks . . .":** Arthur F. Burns, memorandum to President Gerald R. Ford, June 3, 1975, U.S. Department of State, Office of
the Historian, http://history.state.gov/historicaldocuments/frus1969-76v31/d86.

272 **"We . . . feel strongly that some safeguards . . .":** President Gerald R. Ford to
Chancellor Helmut Schmidt, June 6, 1975, Gerald R. Ford Library, Ann Arbor,
Mich., http://www.fordlibrarymuseum.gov/library/document/0351/1555807.pdf.

272 **the secret Gold and Foreign Exchange Committee . . . :** Adam Lebor, *Tower of
Basel: The Shadowy History of the Secret Bank That Runs the World* (New York:
Public Affairs, 2013), p. 189.

272 **"In May 1996, the market traded the equivalent . . .":** Dino Kos, Gold and
Foreign Exchange Committee Discussion on Gold Market, April 7, 1997, http://
www.gata.org/files/FedMemoG-10Gold&FXCommittee-4-29-1997.pdf.

273 **"information relating to swap arrangements . . .":** Kevin M. Warsh, Board of
Governors of the Federal Reserve System, to William J. Olson, September 17, 2009,
http://www.gata.org/files/GATAFedResponse-09-17-2009.pdf.

274 **"We bought 300 tonnes of gold . . .":** Eisuke Sakakibara, conversation with the
author, Seoul, South Korea, May 31, 2013.

274 **The gold was transported to Japan . . . :** Retired official of Brinks, conversation
with the author, Hickory, N.C., November 10, 2013.

274 **The most notorious and heavily criticized case . . . :** Holly Watt and Robert
Winnett, "Goldfinger Brown's £2 Billion Blunder in the Bullion Market," *Sunday
Times,* April 15, 2007, http://www.thesundaytimes.co.uk/sto/Test/politics/
article63170.ece.

276 **"Around 90% of customer placements . . .":** Bank for International Settlements,
Financial Statements, updated June 24, 2013 , http://www.bis.org/banking/balsheet
.htm (accessed July 21, 2013).

276 **"The Bank transacts . . . gold on behalf of its customers . . .":** Bank for International Settlements, 83rd Annual Report, March 31, 2013, p. 110, http://www.bis
.org/publ/arpdf/ar2013e7.pdf#page=44.

277 **"Gold loans comprise fixed-term gold loans *to commercial banks*":** Bank for

International Settlements, 80th Annual Report, March 31, 2010, p. 158n15, http://www.bis.org/publ/arpdf/ar2010e8.htm; emphasis added.

277 "Gold loans comprise fixed-term gold loans": Bank for International Settlements, 83rd Annual Report, June 23, 2013, p. 133n15, http://www.bis.org/publ/arpdf/ar2013e7.pdf.

277 on September 18, 2009, the IMF authorized the sale of 403.3 tonnes . . . : Information in this extended analysis of IMF gold sales comes from "Questions and Answers, IMF Gold Sales," International Monetary Fund, updated May 16, 2013, http://www.imf.org/external/np/exr/faq/goldfaqs.htm.

283 "China's acquisition of gold makes sense . . .": Dr. Min Zhu, conversation with the author, New York City, November 8, 2012.

284 "Somebody's got to own it . . .": High-ranking intelligence official, conversation with the author, McLean, Va., December 13, 2012.

284 "I never hear any discussion . . .": James Himes, conversation with the author, Southport, Conn., July 15, 2013.

286 Mishkin warns that the Fed is dangerously close . . . : David Greenlaw, James D. Hamilton, Peter Hooper, and Frederic S. Mishkin, "Crunch Time: Fiscal Crises and the Role of Monetary Policy," U.S. Monetary Policy Forum, February 22, 2013, rev. July 29, 2013, http://dss.ucsd.edu/~jhamilto/USMPF13_final.pdf.

287 "In the extreme, unsustainable fiscal policy . . .": Ibid., pp. 61–62.

Conclusion

292 "The piecemeal engineer will, accordingly . . .": Karl Popper, *The Open Society and Its Enemies* (Princeton, N.J.: Princeton University Press, 1971), pp. 157–59. Popper is quoted in George Soros, "How to Save the Euro from the EU Crisis—The Speech in Full," *Guardian*, April 9, 2013, http://www.guardian.co.uk/business/2013/apr/09/george-soros-save-eu-from-euro-crisis-speech.

294 the state is well armed with SWAT teams . . . : Radley Balko, *Rise of the Warrior Cop: The Militarization of America's Police Forces* (New York: Public Affairs, 2013).

290 Author Jonah Goldberg has documented fascism's history . . . : Jonah Goldberg, *Liberal Fascism: The Secret History of the American Left from Mussolini to the Politics of Meaning* (New York: Doubleday, 2008).

295 More ominous was his remark . . . : Quoted in Balko, *Warrior Cop*, p. 333.

SELECTED SOURCES

ARTICLES

Akerlof, George A. "The Market for 'Lemons': Quality Uncertainty and the Market Mechanism." *Quarterly Journal of Economics* 84, no. 3 (August 1970), pp. 488–500.

Alderman, Liz. "Under Chinese, a Greek Port Thrives." *New York Times,* October 19, 2012, http://www.nytimes.com/2012/10/11/business/global/chinese -company-sets-new-rhythm-in-port-of-piraeus.html.

Alderman, Liz, and Demitris Bounias. "Privatizing Greece, Slowly but Not Surely." *New York Times*, November 18, 2012, www.nytimes.com/glogin?URI=http:// www.nytimes.com/2012/11/18/business/privatizing-greece-slowly-but-not-surely .html.

Allouni, Tayser. "A Discussion on the New Crusader Wars," October 21, 2001, http://www.religioscope.com/info/doc/jihad/abl_int_2.htm.

Ambinder, Marc. "The Day After." *National Journal,* April 11, 2011, http://www. nationaljournal.com/magazine/government-still-unprepared-for -disaster-20110411.

Åslund, Anders. "Southern Europe Ignores Lessons from Latvia at Its Peril," Peterson Institute for International Economics, Policy Brief no. PB12-17, June 2012, http://www.iie.com/publications/pb/pb12-17.pdf.

———. "Paul Krugman's Baltic Problem," *Foreign Policy,* September 13, 2012, http://www.foreignpolicy.com/articles/2012/09/13/paul_krugmans_baltic_ problem.

Bak, Per. "The Devil's Staircase." *Physics Today* 39, no. 12 (1986), pp. 38–45.

———. "Catastrophes and Self-Organized Criticality." *Computers in Physics*, no. 5 (1991), pp. 430–33.

Barnett, Lionel, Joseph T. Lizier, Michael Harré, Anil K. Seth, and Terry Bossomaier. "Information Flow in a Kinetic Ising Model Peaks in the Disordered Phase." *Physical Review Letters* 111, no. 17 (2013), pp. 177203-1–177203-3, http://prl.aps.org/abstract/PRL/v111/i17/e177203.

Barro, Robert J. "Are Government Bonds Net Wealth?" *Journal of Political Economy* 82 (1974), pp. 1095–117.

Barro, Robert J., and Charles J. Redlick. "Macroeconomic Effects from Government Purchases and Taxes." National Bureau of Economic Research, Working Paper no. 15369, September 2009, http://www.nber.org/papers/w15369.

Barsky, Robert B., and Lawrence H. Summers. "Gibson's Paradox and the Gold Standard." *Journal of Political Economy* 96 (1988), pp. 528–50.

Basher, Dr. Syed Abul. "Regional Initiative in the Gulf: Search for a GCC Currency." Paper presented at the International Institute for Strategic Studies Seminar, Bahrain, September 30, 2012, http://www.iiss.org/en/events/geo-economics%20seminars/geo-economics%20seminars/archive/currencies-of-power-and-the-power-of-currencies-38db.

Benoit, Angeline, Manuel Baigorri, and Emma Ross-Thomas. "Rajoy Drives Spanish Revolution with Low-Cost Manufacture." *Bloomberg,* December 19, 2012, http://www.bloomberg.com/news/2012-12-19/rajoy-drives-spanish-revolution-with-low-cost-manufacture.html.

Berkmen, S. Pelin. "Bank of Japan's Quantitative and Credit Easing: Are They Now More Effective?" IMF Working Paper no. WP/12/2, January 2012, http://www.imf.org/external/pubs/ft/wp/2012/wp1202.pdf.

Bernanke, Ben S. "Irreversibility, Uncertainty, and Cyclical Investment." National Bureau of Economic Research, Working Paper no. 502, July 1980, http://www.nber.org/papers/w502.

———. "The Macroeconomics of the Great Depression: A Comparative Approach." *Journal of Money, Credit and Banking* 27 (1995), pp. 1–28.

———. "Deflation: Making Sure 'It' Doesn't Happen Here." Address to the National Economists Club, Washington, D.C., November 21, 2002, http://www.federalreserve.gov/boarddocs/speeches/2002/20021121/default.htm.

———. "U.S. Monetary Policy and International Implications." Remarks at IMF–Bank of Japan seminar, Tokyo, October 14, 2012, http://www.federalreserve.gov/newsevents/speech/bernanke20121014a.htm.

———. "Monetary Policy and the Global Economy." Speech at the London School of Economics, London, March 25, 2013, http://www.federalreserve.gov/newsevents/speech/bernanke20130325a.htm.

Blanchard, Oliver, and Roberto Perotti. "An Empirical Characterization of the Dynamic Effects of Changes in Government Spending and Taxes on Output." *Quarterly Journal of Economics* (2002), pp. 1329–68.

Bouras, Stelios, and Philip Pangalos. "Foreign Money Is Revisiting Greece." *Wall Street Journal,* February 25, 2013, p. C1, http://online.wsj.com/news/articles/SB10001424127887323864304578320431435196910.

Bumiller, Elisabeth. "Bin Laden, on Tape, Boasts of Trade Center Attacks; U.S. Says It Proves His Guilt." *New York Times,* December 14, 2001, http://www.nytimes.com/2001/12/14/world/nation-challenged-video-bin-laden-tape-boasts-trade-center-attacks-us-says-it.html.

Buttonwood. "The Real Deal—Low Real Interest Rates Are Usually Bad New for Equity Markets." *Economist,* October 20, 2012, http://www.economist.com/news/finance-and-economics/21564845-low-real-interest-rates-are-usually-bad-news-equity-markets.

———. "The Euro Zone Crisis: Growth Problem." *Economist,* December 17, 2012, http://www.economist.com/blogs/buttonwood/2012/12/euro-zone-crisis.

"Cargo Plane with 1.5 Tons of Gold Held in Istanbul." *Hurriyet Daily News,* January 5, 2013, http://www.hurriyetdailynews.com/cargo-plane-with-15-tons-of -gold-held-in-istanbul-.aspx?pageID=238&nid=38427.

Cendrowicz, Leo. "Switzerland Celebrates World's Longest Rail Tunnel." *Time,* October 20, 2010, http://www.time.com/time/business/article/ 0,8599,2026369,00.html.

Chesney, Marc, Remo Crameri, and Loriano Mancini. "Detecting Informed Trading Activities in the Options Markets." Swiss Finance Institute Research Paper no. 11-42 (July 2012), http://ssrn.com/abstract=1522157.

"China, Russia Sign Five-Point Joint Statement," Xinhua, June 18, 2009, http:// news.xinhuanet.com/english/2009-06/18/content_11558133.htm.

Christ, Carl F. "A Short-Run Aggregate-Demand Model of the Interdependence and Effects of Monetary and Fiscal Policies with Keynesian and Classical Interest Elasticities." *American Economic Review* 57, no. 2 (May 1967).

Clark, Andrew. "The *Guardian* Profile: Stephen Schwarzman." *Guardian,* June 15, 2007, http://www.theguardian.com/business/2007/jun/15/4.

Cogan, John F., Tobias Cwik, John B. Taylor, and Volker Wieland. "New Keynesian Versus Old Keynesian Government Spending Multipliers." National Bureau of Economic Research, Working Paper no. 14782, March 2009, http://www.nber .org/papers/w14782.

Cogan, John F., and John B. Taylor. "The Obama Stimulus Impact? Zero." *Wall Street Journal,* December 9, 2010, http://online.wsj.com/news/articles/ SB10001424052748704679204575646603792267296.

Das, Mitali, and Papa N'Diaye. "Chronicle of a Decline Foretold: Has China Reached the Lewis Turning Point?" IMF Working Paper no. WP/13/26, January 2013, http://www.imf.org/external/pubs/cat/longres.aspx?sk=40281.0.

Davis, Bob. "China Tries to Shut Rising Income Gap." *Wall Street Journal,* December 11, 2012, p. A14, http://online.wsj.com/news/articles/ SB10001424127887324640104578161493858722884.

Del Negro, Marco, Marc Giannoni, and Christina Patterson. "The Forward Guidance Puzzle." Federal Reserve Bank of New York, Staff Report no. 574, October 2012, http://newyorkfed.org/research/staff_reports/sr574.pdf.

Dell'Ariccia, Giovanni, Luc Laeven, and Gustavo Suarez. "Bank Leverage and Monetary Policy's Risk-Taking Channel: Evidence from the United States." IMF Working Paper no. WP/13/143, June 2013, http://www.imf.org/external/pubs/ cat/longres.aspx?sk=40642.0.

Dixon, Hugo. "The Gloom Around Greece Is Dissipating." *New York Times,* April 21, 2013, http://www.nytimes.com/2013/04/22/business/global/the-gloom -around-greece-is-dissipating.html.

Eichengreen, Barry. "The Dollar Dilemma: The World's Top Currency Faces Competition." *Foreign Affairs,* September–October 2009, pp. 53–68.

Eichengreen, Barry, and Marc Flandreau. "The Rise and Fall of the Dollar, Or When Did the Dollar Replace Sterling as the Leading Reserve Currency?" National

Bureau of Economic Research, Working Paper no. 14154, July 2008, http://www.nber.org/papers/w14154.

Eichengreen, Barry, and Douglas A. Irwin. "The Slide to Protectionism in the Great Depression: Who Succumbed and Why?" National Bureau of Economic Research, Working Paper no. 15142, July 2009, http://www.nber.org/papers/w15142.

eThekwini Declaration. Fifth BRICS Summit, Durban, South Africa, March 27, 2013, http://www.brics5.co.za/assets/eThekwini-Declaration-and-Action-Plan-MASTER-27-MARCH-2013.pdf.

Evans-Pritchard, Ambrose. "Beijing Hints at Bond Attack on Japan." *Telegraph,* September 18, 2012, http://www.telegraph.co.uk/finance/china-business/9551727/Beijing-hints-at-bond-attack-on-Japan.html.

———. "Japan's Shinzo Abe Prepares to Print Money for the Whole World." *Telegraph,* December 17, 2012, http://www.telegraph.co.uk/finance/economics/9751609/Japans-Shinzo-Abe-prepares-to-print-money-for-the-whole-world.html.

Falliere, Nicolas, Liam O. Murchu, and Eric Chien. "W.32.Stuxnet Dossier Version 1.4," Symantec, February 2011, http://www.symantec.com/content/en/us/enterprise/media/security_response/whitepapers/w32_stuxnet_dossier.pdf.

Farchy, Jack. "Iran Bought Gold to Cut Dollar Exposure." *Financial Times,* March 20, 2011, http://www.ft.com/cms/s/0/cc350008-5325-11e0-86e6-00144feab49a.html.

Farchy, Jack, and Roula Khalaf. "Gold Key to Financing Gaddafi Struggle." *Financial Times,* March 21, 2011, http://www.ft.com/intl/cms/s/0/588ce75a-53e4-11e0-8bd7-00144feab49a.html.

Faucon, Benoît. "U.S. Warns Russia on Iranian Bank." *Wall Street Journal,* December 11, 2012, http://online.wsj.com/news/articles/SB10001424127887323330604578145071930969966.

Ferguson, Niall. "Complexity and Collapse: Empires on the Edge of Chaos." *Foreign Affairs,* March–April 2010, http://www.foreignaffairs.com/articles/65987/niall-ferguson/complexity-and-collapse.

Fisher, Irving. "The Debt-Deflation Theory of Great Depressions." *Econometrica* (1933), available from the Federal Reserve Bank of St. Louis, http://fraser.stlouisfed.org/docs/meltzer/fisdeb33.pdf.

Fisher, Max. "Syrian Hackers Claim AP Hack That Tipped Stock Market by $136 Billion. Is It Terrorism?" *Washington Post,* April 23, 2013, http://www.washingtonpost.com/blogs/worldviews/wp/2013/04/23/syrian-hackers-claim-ap-hack-that-tipped-stock-market-by-136-billion-is-it-terrorism.

Flavelle, Christopher. "Debunking the 'Wealth Effect.'" *Slate,* June 10, 2008, http://www.slate.com/articles/news_and_politics/hey_wait_a_minute/2008/06/debunking_the_wealth_effect.html.

Forbes, Kristin. "Why Do Foreigners Invest in the United States?" National Bureau of Economic Research, Working Paper no. 13908, April 2008, http://www.nber.org/papers/w13908.

Gang, Xiao. "Regulating Shadow Banking." *China Daily,* October 12, 2012, http://www.chinadaily.com.cn/opinion/2012-10/12/content_15812305.htm.

Gelb, Leslie H. "GDP Now Matters More Than Force: A U.S. Policy for the Age of

Economic Power." *Foreign Affairs*, November–December 2010, http://www.foreignaffairs.com/articles/66858/leslie-h-gelb/gdp-now-matters-more-than-force.

Gill, Indermit, and Martin Raiser. "Golden Growth: Restoring the Lustre of the European Economic Model." International Bank for Reconstruction and Development, 2012, http://issuu.com/world.bank.publications/docs/9780821389652.

"Gold Seized at Istanbul Airport Was Allegedly for Iran." *Voice of Russia,* January 6, 2013, http://voiceofrussia.com/2013_01_06/Gold-seized-at-Istanbul-airport-was-allegedly-for-Iran.

Goodhart, Charles. "Central Banks Walk Inflation's Razor Edge." *Financial Times,* January 30, 2013, http://www.ft.com/intl/cms/s/0/744e4a96-661c-11e2-b967-00144feab49a.html.

Hanemann, Thilo, and Daniel H. Rosen. "China Invests in Europe, Patterns, Impacts and Policy Implications." Rhodium Group, June 2012, http://download.www.arte.tv/permanent/u1/Quand-la-Chine/RHG_ChinaInvestsInEurope_June2012[1].pdf.

Hanke, Steve H. "The Federal Reserve vs. Small Business." Cato Institute, June 3, 2013, http://www.cato.org/blog/federal-reserve-vs-small-business-0.

———. "Syria's Annual Inflation Hits 200%." Cato Institute, July 1, 2013, http://www.cato.org/blog/syrias-annual-inflation-hits-200.

Hayek, Friedrich. "The Use of Knowledge in Society." *American Economic Review* 35, no. 4 (September 1945), pp. 519–30, http://www.econlib.org/library/Essays/hykKnw1.html.

"Heirs of Mao's Comrades Rise as New Capitalist Nobility." *Bloomberg News,* December 26, 2012, http://www.bloomberg.com/news/2012-12-26/immortals-beget-china-capitalism-from-citic-to-godfather-of-golf.html.

Hetzel, Robert L. "Monetary Policy in the 2008–2009 Recession." *Economic Quarterly* 95 (2009), pp. 201–33.

Higgins, Andrew. "Used to Hardship, Latvia Accepts Austerity, and Its Pain Eases." *New York Times,* January 1, 2013, http://www.nytimes.com/2013/01/02/world/europe/used-to-hardship-latvia-accepts-austerity-and-its-pain-eases.html?pagewanted=all.

Hiro, Dilip. "Shanghai Surprise—The Summit of the Shanghai Cooperation Organisation Reveals How Power Is Shifting in the World." *Guardian*, June 16, 2006, http://www.guardian.co.uk/commentisfree/2006/jun/16/shanghaisurprise.

Hunt, Lacy H. "The Fed's Flawed Model." Casey Research, May 28, 2013, http://www.caseyresearch.com/articles/the-feds-flawed-model.

International Monetary Fund. "Currency Composition of Official Foreign Exchange Reserves (COFER)," http://www.imf.org/external/np/sta/cofer/eng/index.htm.

———. "Proposal for a General Allocation of SDRs." Report, June 9, 2009, http://www.imf.org/external/np/pp/eng/2009/060909.pdf.

———. "A Framework for the Fund's Issuance of Notes to the Official Sector," June 17, 2009, http://www.imf.org/external/np/pp/eng/2009/063009.pdf.

———. "IMF to Begin On-Market Sales of Gold." Press Release no. 10/44, February 17, 2010, http://www.imf.org/external/np/sec/pr/2010/pr1044.htm.

———. "Systematic Risk and the Redesign of Financial Regulation." Global Financial Stability Report, April 2010, http://www.imf.org/external/pubs/ft/gfsr/2010/01/pdf/chap2.pdf.

———. "The IMF-FSB Early Warning Exercise: Design and Methodological Toolkit." September 2010, http://www.imf.org/external/np/pp/eng/2010/090110.pdf.

———. "IMF Determines New Currency Weights for SDR Valuation Basket." Press Release no. 10/434, November 15, 2010, http://www.imf.org/external/np/sec/pr/2010/pr10434.htm.

Jaffe, Greg. "U.S. Model for a Future War Fans Tensions with China and Inside Pentagon." *Washington Post,* August 1, 2012, http://articles.washingtonpost.com/2012-08-01/world/35492126_1_china-tensions-china-threat-pentagon.

Kaminski, Matthew. "Guy Sorman: Why Europe Will Rise Again." *Wall Street Journal,* August 18, 2011, p. A11, http://online.wsj.com/news/articles/SB10000872396390444375104577592850332409044.

———. "Trying to Save Europe, 'Step by Step.'" *Wall Street Journal,* December 4, 2012, p. A17, http://online.wsj.com/news/articles/SB10001424127887323901604578157282337844170.

Kannan, Prakash, and Fritzi Köhler-Geib. "The Uncertainty Channel of Contagion." IMF Working Paper no. WP/09/219, October 2009, http://www.imf.org/external/pubs/ft/wp/2009/wp09219.pdf.

"Kazakhstan—Two Decades of Global Initiatives." *First Magazine,* http://www.firstmagazine.com/DownloadSpecialReportDetail.1225.ashx.

Khalifa, Sherif, Ousmane Seck, and Elwin Tobing. "Financial Wealth Effect: Evidence from Threshold Estimation." *Applied Economics Letters* 18, no. 13 (2011), http://business.fullerton.edu/economics/skhalifa/publication13.pdf.

King, Mervyn. "Do We Need an International Monetary System?" Speech given at Stanford Institute for Economic Policy Research, March 11, 2011, http://www.bankofengland.co.uk/publications/Documents/speeches/2011/speech480.pdf.

Krugman, Paul. "The Myth of Asia's Miracle." *Foreign Affairs,* November–December 1994, p. 62, http://www.pairault.fr/documents/lecture3s2009.pdf.

———. "Sticky Wages and the Macro Story." *New York Times,* July 22, 2012, http://krugman.blogs.nytimes.com/2012/07/22/sticky-wages-and-the-macro-story.

Lagerspetz, Eerik. "Money as a Social Contract." *Theory and Decision* 17, no. 1 (July 1984), pp. 1–9.

Lee, Il Houng, Murtaza Syed, and Liu Xueyan. "Is China Over-Investing and Does It Matter?" IMF Working Paper no. WP/12/277, November 2012, http://www.imf.org/external/pubs/cat/longres.aspx?sk=40121.0.

Lee, Il Houng, Xu Qingjun, and Murtaza Syed. "China's Demography and Its Implications." IMF Working Paper no. WP/13/82, March 28, 2013, http://www.imf.org/external/pubs/cat/longres.aspx?sk=40446.0.

Lie, Eric. "On the Timing of CEO Stock Option Awards." *Management Science* 51, no. 5 (May 2005).

Ludvigson, Sydney, and Charles Steindel. "How Important Is the Stock Market Effect on Consumption?" *FRBNY Economic Policy Review,* July 1990, http://ftp.ny.frb.org/research/epr/99v05n2/9907ludv.pdf.

McAfee Roundstone Professional Services and McAfee Labs. "Global Energy Cyberattacks: 'Night Dragon,'" February 10, 2011, http://www.mcafee.com/us/resources/white-papers/wp-global-energy-cyberattacks-night-dragon.pdf.

McCulley, Paul, and Zoltan Pozsar. "Helicopter Money: Or How I Stopped Worrying and Love Fiscal-Monetary Cooperation." GIC Global Society of Fellows, January 7, 2013, http://www.interdependence.org/wp-content/uploads/2013/01/Helicopter_Money_Final1.pdf.

Macdonald, Alistair, Paul Vieira, and Will Connors. "Chinese Fly Cash West, by the Suitcase." *Wall Street Journal,* January 2, 2013, http://online.wsj.com/news/articles/SB10001424127887323635504578213933647167020.

McGregor, James. "China's Drive for 'Indigenous Innovation': A Web of Industrial Policies," July 28, 2010, http://www.uschamber.com/sites/default/files/reports/100728chinareport_0.pdf.

Maclachlan, Fiona. "Max Weber and the State Theory of Money." Working paper, http://home.manhattan.edu/~fiona.maclachlan/maclachlan26july03.htm.

Makin, John H. "Inflation Is Better Than Deflation." American Enterprise Institute, March 2009, http://www.aei.org/article/economics/fiscal-policy/inflation-is-better-than-deflation.

———. "Trillion-Dollar Deficits Are Sustainable for Now, Unfortunately." American Enterprise Institute, December 13, 2012, http://www.aei.org/outloook/trillion-dollar-deficits-are-sustainable-for-now-unfortunately.

Mandiant. "APT1 Exposing One of China's Cyber Espionage Units," 2013, Mandiant Intelligence Center Report, http://intelreport.mandiant.com.

Martin, Michael F. "China's Sovereign Wealth Fund." Congressional Research Service, January 22, 2008, http://www.fas.org/sgp/crs/row/RL34337.pdf.

Merton, Robert K. "The Self-Fulfilling Prophecy." *Antioch Review* 8, no. 2 (Summer 1948), pp. 193–210.

Milgram, Stanley. "Behavioral Study of Obedience." *Journal of Abnormal Social Psychology* (1963).

Minder, Ralph. "Car Factories Offer Hope for Spanish Industry and Workers." *New York Times*, December 28, 2012, p. B1, http://www.nytimes.com/2012/12/28/business/global/car-factories-offer-hope-for-spanish-industry-and-workers.html?pagewanted=all.

"Money: DeGaulle v. the Dollar." *Time*, February 12, 1965, http://content.time.com/time/magazine/article/0,9171,840572,00.html.

Mundell, Robert A. "A Theory of Optimum Currency Areas." *American Economic Review* 51, no. 4 (September 1961), pp. 657–65, esp. 659.

Newman, Mark. "Power Laws, Pareto Distributions and Zipf's Law." *Contemporary Physics* 46 (September 2005), pp. 323–51.

Nixon, Richard M. Address to the Nation Outlining a New Economic Policy, August 15, 1971, http://www.presidency.ucsb.edu/ws/index.php?pid=3115#axzz1LXd02JEK.

O'Neill, Jim. "Building Better Global Economic BRICs." Goldman Sachs, Global Economics Paper no. 66, November 30, 2001, http://www.goldmansachs.com/our-thinking/archive/archive-pdfs/build-better-brics.pdf.

Patterson, Scott, Jenny Strasburg, and Jacob Bunge. "Knight Upgrade Triggered Old Trading System, Big Losses." *Wall Street Journal,* August 14, 2012, http://online .wsj.com/news/articles/SB10000872396390444318104577589694289838100.

Pei, Minxin. "China's Troubled Bourbons." *Project Syndicate,* October 31, 2012, www.project-syndicate.org.

Pettis, Michael. "The IMF on Overinvestment." *EconoMonitor,* December 28, 2012, http://www.economonitor.com/blog/2012/12/the-imf-on-overinvestment/.

Poteshman, Allen M. "Unusual Option Market Activity and the Terrorist Attacks of September 11, 2001." *Journal of Business* 79, no. 4 (July 2006), http:// econpapers.repec.org/article/ucpjnlbus/v_3a79_3ay_3a2006_3ai_3a4_3ap_3a1703 -1726.htm.

Pufeng, Major General Wang. "The Challenge of Information Warfare." *China Military Science,* Spring 1995, http://www.fas.org/irp/world/china/docs/iw_mg_ wang.htm.

Reinhart, Carmen M., and Kenneth S. Rogoff. "Growth in a Time of Debt." National Bureau of Economic Research, Working Paper no. 15639, January 2010, http://www.nber.org/papers/w15639.

Reinhart, Carmen M., and M. Belen Sbrancia. "The Liquidation of Government Debt." National Bureau of Economic Research, Working Paper no. 16893, March 2011, http://www.nber.org/papers/w16893.

Rickards, James G. "A New Risk Management Model for Wall Street." *Journal of Enterprise Risk Management* (March 2009), pp. 20–24.

———. "Keynesianism, Monetarism and Complexity." *Reuters Rolfe Winkler Capital Jungle Blog,* January 7, 2010, http://blogs.reuters.com/rolfe-winkler /2010/01/07/keynesianism-monetarism-and-complexity.

Romer, Christina A. "The Debate That's Muting the Fed's Response." *New York Times,* February 26, 2011, http://www.nytimes.com/2011/02/27/business/27view .html.

Romer, Christina A., and Jared Bernstein. "The Job Impact of the American Recovery and Reinvestment Plan." Council of Economic Advisers, January 9, 2009.

Rosenberg, Matthew. "An Afghan Mystery: Why Are Large Shipments of Gold Leaving the Country?" *New York Times,* December 15, 2012, http://www.nytimes .com/2012/12/16/world/asia/as-gold-is-spirited-out-of-afghanistan-officials -wonder-why.html.

Scheinkman, José A., and Michael Woodford. "Self-Organized Criticality and Economic Fluctuations." *American Economic Review* 84, no. 2 (May 1994), pp. 417–21.

Schneider, Howard. "As Chinese Capital Moves Abroad, Europe Offers an Open Door." *Washington Post,* February 26, 2013, http://articles.washingtonpost .com/2013-02-26/business/37297545_1_direct-investment-chinese-investors -rhodium-group.

———. "In a Two-Faced Euro Zone, Financial Conditions Ease and Joblessness Rises." *Washington Post,* March 1, 2013, http://articles.washingtonpost .com/2013-03-01/business/37373712_1_euro-zone-holdings-euro-zone-17 -nation-currency-zone.

Singh, Manmohan, and James Aitken. "The (Sizable) Role of Rehypothecation in the Shadow Banking System." IMF Working Paper no. WP/10/172, July 2010, http://www.imf.org/external/pubs/ft/wp/2010/wp10172.pdf.

Sornette, Didier. "Critical Market Crashes." *Physics Reports* 378 (2003), pp. 1–98.

———. "Dragon-Kings, Black Swans and the Prediction of Crises." *International Journal of Terraspace Science and Engineering* (December 2009), http://arxiv.org/pdf/0907.4290.pdf.

Sornette, Didier, and Ryan Woodard. "Financial Bubbles, Real Estate Bubbles, Derivative Bubbles, and the Financial and Economic Crisis." Proceedings of Applications of Physics and Financial Analysis Conference Series, May 2, 2009, http://arxiv.org/pdf/0905.0220.pdf.

Stein, Jeremy C. "Overheating in Credit Markets: Origins, Measurement, and Policy Responses." Federal Reserve Bank of St. Louis Research Symposium, February 7, 2013, http://www.federalreserve.gov/newsevents/speech/stein20130207a.htm.

Stevis, Matina. "Euro Zone Closes in on Bank Plans." *Wall Street Journal,* June 13, 2013, online.wsj.com/article/SB10001424127887323734304578542941134353614.html.

Stewart, James B. "The Birthday Party." *New Yorker,* February 11, 2008, http://www.newyorker.com/reporting/2008/02/11/080211fa_fact_stewart.

Subbotin, Alexander. "A Multi-Horizon Scale for Volatility." Centre d'Economie de la Sorbonne, working paper, March 3, 2008.

Swensson, Lars E. O. "The Zero Bound in an Open Economy: A Foolproof Way of Escaping from a Liquidity Trap." National Bureau of Economic Research, Working Paper no. 7957, October 2000, http://www.nber.org/papers/w7957.

———. "Escaping from a Liquidity Trap and Deflation: The Foolproof Way and Others." National Bureau of Economic Research, Working Paper no. 10195, December 2003, http://www.nber.org/papers/w10195.

Taylor, Jason E., and Richard K. Vedder. "Stimulus by Spending Cuts: Lessons from 1946." Cato Institute, Cato Policy Report, May–June 2010, http://www.cato.org/policy-report/mayjune-2010/stimulus-spending-cuts-lessons-1946.

Taylor, John B. "Discretion Versus Policy Rules in Practice." Carnegie-Rochester Conference Series on Public Policy (1993), pp. 195–214, http://www.stanford.edu/~johntayl/Papers/Discretion.PDF.

———. "Evaluating the TARP." Testimony for the Committee on Banking, Housing and Urban Affairs, U.S. Senate, March 17, 2011, http://www.stanford.edu/~johntayl/Taylor%20TARP%20Testimony.pdf.

Tiwari, Dheeraj, and Rajeev Jayaswal. "India, Iran Mull over Gold-for-Oil for Now." *Financial Times,* January 8, 2011, http://articles.economictimes.indiatimes.com/2011-01-08/news/28433295_1_bilateral-issue-oil-india-imports.

Tsirel, Sergey V., et al. "Log-Periodic Oscillation Analysis and Possible Burst of the 'Gold Bubble' in April–June 2011," http://arxiv.org/pdf/1012.4118.pdf.

Ummelas, Ott. "Why Estonia Loves the Euro." *Bloomberg Businessweek,* February 2, 2012, http://www.businessweek.com/magazine/why-estonia-loves-the-euro-02022012.html.

UN Conference on Trade and Development. "Reform of the International Monetary and Financial System." Chap. 4 in *Trade and Development Report, 2009.* New

York and Geneva: United Nations, 2009, http://unctad.org/en/docs/tdr2009 _en.pdf.

UN Department of Economic and Social Affairs. "Reforming the International Financial Architecture." Chap. 5 in *World Economic and Social Survey 2010: Retooling Global Development*. New York: United Nations, 2010, http://www .un.org/esa/analysis/wess/wess2010files/wess2010.pdf.

U.S. Congress. "Housing Wealth and Consumer Spending." Congressional Budget Office Background Paper, January 2007, http://www.cbo.gov/publication/18279.

U.S. Government Accountability Office. "Iran Sanctions: Impact in Furthering U.S. Objectives Is Unclear and Should Be Reviewed," December 2007, http://www .gao.gov/new.items/d0858.pdf.

Walker, Marcus, and Alessandra Galloni. "Embattled Economies Cling to the Euro." *Wall Street Journal*, February 13, 2013, p. A1, http://online.wsj.com/news/ articles/SB10001424127887324761004578284203099970438.

Williamson, John. "What Washington Means by Policy Reform." Peterson Institute for International Economics, April 1990, http://www.iie.com/publications/ papers/paper.cfm?researchid=486.

———. "Is the 'Beijing Consensus' Now Dominant?" *Asia Policy*, no. 13 (January 2012), pp. 1–16.

Wong, Wing-Keung, Howard E. Thompson, and Kweechong Teh. "Was There Abnormal Trading in the S&P 500 Index Options Prior to the September 11 Attacks?" Social Science Research Network, April 13, 2010, http://ssrn.com/ abstract=1588523.

Woodford, Michael. "Convergence in Macroeconomics: Elements of the New Synthesis." Paper prepared for the annual meeting of the American Economics Association, New Orleans, January 4, 2008, http://www.columbia.edu/~mw2230/ Convergence_AEJ.pdf.

———. "Simple Analytics of the Government Expenditure Multiplier." National Bureau of Economic Research, Working Paper no. 15714, January 2010, http:// www.nber.org/papers/w15714.

———. "Methods of Policy Accommodation at the Interest-Rate Lower Bound." Paper presented at the Federal Reserve Bank of Kansas City Symposium, Jackson Hole, Wyo., August 31, 2012, http://www.kc.frb.org/publicat/sympos/2012/ mw.pdf.

World Economic Forum. "More Credit with Fewer Crises: Responsibly Meeting the World's Growing Demand for Credit." Report in Collaboration with McKinsey, January 2010, http://www3.weforum.org/docs/WEF_NR_More_credit_fewer _crises_2011.pdf.

World Gold Council. "Gold: A Commodity like No Other," April 2011, http://www .exchangetradedgold.com/media/ETG/file/Gold_a_commodity_like_no_other .pdf.

World Intellectual Property Organization. *WIPO IP Facts and Figures 2012*. WIPO Economics and Statistics Series, http://www.wipo.int/export/sites/www/ freepublications/en/statistics/943/wipo_pub_943_2012.pdf.

"World Money: A More Equal System." *Time*, January 3, 1972.

Yellen, Janet L. "Improving the International Monetary and Financial System." Remarks delivered at the Banque de France International Symposium, Paris, March 4, 2011, http://www.federalreserve.gov/newsevents/speech/yellen20110304a.htm.

BOOKS

Acemoglu, Daron, and James A. Robinson. *Why Nations Fail: The Origins of Power, Prosperity, and Poverty.* New York: Crown Business, 2012.

Admati, Anat, and Martin Hellwig. *The Banker's New Clothes.* Princeton, N.J.: Princeton University Press, 2013.

Alperovitz, Gar. *America Beyond Capitalism: Reclaiming Our Wealth, Our Liberty, and Our Democracy.* Hoboken, N.J.: John Wiley & Sons, 2005.

Anderson, Benjamin M. *Economics and the Public Welfare: A Financial and Economic History of the United States, 1914–1946.* Indianapolis: Liberty Press, 1979.

Authers, John. *The Fearful Rise of Markets.* Upper Saddle River, N.J.: FT Press, 2010.

Babbin, Jed, and Edward Timberlake. *Showdown: Why China Wants War with the United States.* Washington, D.C.: Regnery, 2006.

Bagehot, Walter. *Lombard Street: A Description of the Money Market.* New York: Scribner, Armstrong, 1873.

Bak, Per. *How Nature Works: The Science of Self-Organized Criticality.* New York: Copernicus, 1996.

Balko, Radley. *Rise of the Warrior Cop: The Militarization of America's Police Forces.* New York: Public Affairs, 2013.

Barabasi, Albert-Laszlo. *Linked.* New York: Plume, 2003.

Barbero, Alessandro. *Charlemagne: Father of a Continent.* Berkeley: University of California Press, 2004.

Beinhocker, Eric D. *Origin of Wealth: Evolution, Complexity, and the Radical Remaking of Economics.* Cambridge, Mass.: Harvard University Press, 2007.

Bell, Stephanie A., and Edward J. Nell, eds. *The State, the Market, and the Euro: Metallism versus Chartalism in the Theory of Money.* Northampton, Mass.: Edward Elgar, 2003.

Bergman, Ronen. *The Secret War with Iran.* New York: Free Press, 2008

Bernanke, Ben S. *Essays on the Great Depression.* Princeton, N.J.: Princeton University Press, 2000.

Bernstein, Peter L. *Capital Ideas: The Improbable Origins of Modern Wall Street.* Hoboken, N.J.: John Wiley & Sons, 2005.

———. *A Primer on Money, Banking and Gold.* New York: John Wiley & Sons, 2008.

Bookstaber, Richard. *A Demon of Our Own Design: Markets, Hedge Funds, and the Perils of Financial Innovation.* Hoboken, N.J.: John Wiley & Sons, 2007.

Bordo, Michael David. *The Classical Gold Standard: Some Lessons for Today.* Federal Reserve Bank of St. Louis, May 1981.

Brown, Cynthia Stokes. *Big History: From the Big Bang to the Present.* New York: New Press, 2007.

Buchanan, Mark. *Ubiquity: The Science of History . . . or Why the World Is Simpler Than We Think*. New York: Crown, 2001.

Casey, Michael J. *The Unfair Trade: How Our Broken Global Financial System Destroys the Middle Class*. New York: Crown Business, 2012.

Casti, John. *X-Events: The Collapse of Everything*. New York: William Morrow, 2012.

Chaisson, Eric J. *Cosmic Evolution: The Rise of Complexity in Nature*. Cambridge, Mass.: Harvard University Press, 2001.

Chernow, Ron. *The House of Morgan: An American Banking Dynasty and the Rise of Modern Finance*. New York: Simon and Schuster, 1999.

Christian, David. *Maps of Time: An Introduction to Big History*. Berkeley: University of California Press, 2004.

Coggen, Philip. *Paper Promises: Debt, Money and the New World Order*. New York: Public Affairs, 2012.

Conrad, Edward. *Unintended Consequences: Why Everything You've Been Told About the Economy Is Wrong*. New York: Portfolio/Penguin, 2012.

Courakis, Anthony, ed. *Inflation, Depression, and Economic Policy in the West*. Lanham, Md.: Rowman and Littlefield, 1981.

Dam, Kenneth W. *The Rules of the Game: Reform and Evolution in the International Monetary System*. Chicago: University of Chicago Press, 1982.

Duncan, Richard. *The New Depression: The Breakdown of the Paper Money Economy*. Singapore: John Wiley & Sons Singapore Pte., 2012.

Easley, David, and Jon Kleinberg. *Networks, Crowds and Markets*. Cambridge, U.K.: Cambridge University Press, 2010.

Eichengreen, Barry. *Golden Fetters: The Gold Standard and the Great Depression, 1919–1939*. New York: Oxford University Press, 1995.

———. *Global Imbalances and the Lessons of Bretton Woods*. Cambridge, Mass.: MIT Press, 2007.

———. *Globalizing Capital: A History of the International Monetary System*, 2nd ed. Princeton, N.J.: Princeton University Press, 2008.

———. *Exorbitant Privilege: The Rise and Fall of the Dollar and the Future of the International Monetary System*. Oxford: Oxford University Press, 2011.

Einhard. *The Life of Charlemagne*. Ninth century; reprint Kessinger Publishing, 2010.

Eisen, Sara, ed. *Currencies After the Crash: The Uncertain Future of the Global Paper-Based Currency System*. New York: McGraw-Hill, 2013.

Fenby, Jonathan. *Tiger Head, Snake Tails: China Today, How It Got There and Where It Is Heading*. New York: Overlook Press, 2012.

Fergusson, Adam. *When Money Dies: The Nightmare of Deficit Spending, Devaluation, and Hyperinflation in Weimar Germany*. New York: Public Affairs, 2010.

Financial Crisis Inquiry Commission. *The Financial Crisis Inquiry Report: Final Report on the National Commission on the Causes of the Financial and Economic Crisis in the United States*. New York: Public Affairs, 2011.

Fleming, Ian. *Goldfinger*. New York: Avenel Books, 1988.

Freeland, Chrystia. *Plutocrats: The Rise of the New Global Super-Rich and the Fall of Everyone Else*. New York: Penguin Press, 2012.

Friedman, Milton. *Studies in the Quantity Theory of Money*. Chicago: University of Chicago Press, 1967.

Friedman, Milton, and Anna Jacobson Schwartz. *A Monetary History of the United States, 1867–1960*. Princeton, N.J.: Princeton University Press, 1963.

Gallarotti, Giulio M. *The Anatomy of an International Monetary Regime: The Classical Gold Standard, 1880–1914*. New York: Oxford University Press, 1995.

Gleick, James. *The Information*. New York: Pantheon, 2011.

Goldberg, Jonah. *Liberal Fascism: The Secret History of the American Left from Mussolini to the Politics of Meaning*. New York: Doubleday, 2008.

Goodhart, C. A. E. *The New York Money Market and the Finance of Trade, 1900–1913*. Cambridge, Mass.: Harvard University Press, 1969.

Graeber, David. *Debt: The First 5,000 Years*. Brooklyn, N.Y.: Melville House, 2011.

Guangqian, Peng, and Yao Youzhi, eds. *The Science of Military Strategy*. Beijing: Military Science Publishing House, 2005.

Guillén, Mauro F., and Emilio Ontiveros. *Global Turning Points: Understanding the Challenges for Business in the 21st Century*. Cambridge, U.K.: Cambridge University Press, 2012.

Hahn, Frank. *Money and Inflation*. 1982; reprint Cambridge, Mass.: MIT Press, 1985.

Hahn, Frank, and F. P. R. Brechling, eds. *The Theory of Interest Rates*. London: Macmillan, 1965.

Hahn, Robert W., and Paul C. Tetlock, eds. *Information Markets: A New Way of Making Decisions*. Washington, D.C.: AEI Press, 2006.

Hamilton, Alexander. *Writings*. New York: Literary Classics of the United States, 2001.

Hapler, Stefan. *The Beijing Consensus: How China's Authoritarian Model Will Dominate the Twenty-First Century*. New York: Basic Books, 2010.

Hayek, Friedrich A. *The Fortunes of Liberalism: Essays on Austrian Economics and the Ideal of Freedom*. Edited by Peter G. Klein. Indianapolis: Liberty Fund, 1992.

———. *Good Money*. Edited by Stephen Kresge. 2 parts. Indianapolis: Liberty Fund, 1999.

Jensen, Henrik Jeldtoft. *Self-Organized Critically: Emergent Complex Behavior in Physical and Biological Systems*. New York: Cambridge University Press, 1998.

Johnson, Clark H. *Gold, France, and the Great Depression, 1919–1932*. New Haven, Conn.: Yale University Press, 1997.

Kahneman, Daniel, Paul Slovic, and Amos Tversky, eds. *Judgment Under Uncertainty: Heuristics and Biases*. Cambridge, U.K.: Cambridge University Press, 1982.

Kahneman, Daniel, and Amos Tversky, eds. *Choices, Values, and Frames*. Cambridge, U.K.: Cambridge University Press, 2000.

Keen, Steve. *Debunking Economics: The Naked Emperor Dethroned?* London: Zed Books, 2011.

Keynes, John Maynard. *The Economic Consequences of the Peace*. London: Macmillan, 1920.

———. *A Tract on Monetary Reform*. 1923; reprint LaVergne, Tenn.: BN Publishing, 2008.

———. *Treatise on Money*. 2 vols. 1930; reprint London: Macmillan, 1950.

———. *The General Theory of Employment, Interest, and Money*. 1936; reprint San Diego: Harcourt, 1964.

Kindleberger, Charles P. *The World in Depression, 1929–1939*. Berkeley: University of California Press, 1986.

———. *Maniacs, Panics, and Crashes: A History of Financial Crises,* rev. ed. New York: Basic Books, 1989.

Kindleberger, Charles P., and Robert Aliber. *Maniacs, Panics, and Crashes: A History of Financial Crises*. Hoboken, N.J.: John Wiley & Sons, 2005.

Knapp, Georg Friedrich. *The State Theory of Money*. First German edition 1924; reprint San Diego: Simon, 2003.

Knight, Frank H. *Risk, Uncertainty and Profit*. 1921; reprint Washington, D.C.: Beard Books, 2002.

Krugman, Paul. *Pop Internationalism*. Cambridge, Mass.: MIT Press, 1997.

———. *The Accidental Theorist and Other Dispatches from the Dismal Science*. New York: W. W. Norton, 1998.

———. *End This Depression Now*. New York: W. W. Norton, 2012.

Kuhn, Thomas S. *The Structure of Scientific Revolutions*. 1962; reprint Chicago: University of Chicago Press, 1996.

Lam, Lui. *Nonlinear Physics for Beginners*. Singapore: World Scientific, 1998.

Lao-Tze. *Tao Te Ching*. Translated by Stephen Addis and Stanley Lombardo. Indianapolis: Hackett, 2013.

Lebor, Adam. *Tower of Basel: The Shadowy History of the Secret Bank That Runs the World*. New York: Public Affairs, 2013.

Lehrman, Lewis E. *Paper Money or the True Gold Standard: A Monetary Reform Plan Without Official Reserve Currencies*. 2nd ed. Greenville, N.Y.: Lehrman Institute, 2012.

Lind, Michael. *Land of Promise: An Economic History of the United States*. New York: Harper, 2012.

Litan, Robert E., and Benn Steill. *Financial Statecraft: The Role of Financial Markets in American Foreign Policy*. New Haven, Conn.: Yale University Press, 2006.

Lowenstein, Roger. *When Genius Failed: The Rise and Fall of Long-Term Capital Management*. New York: Random House, 2000.

Luman, Ronald R., ed. *Unrestricted Warfare Symposium*. 3 vols. Laurel, Md.: Johns Hopkins University Applied Physics Laboratory, 2007–9.

McGregor, James. *No Ancient Wisdom, No Followers*. Westport, Conn.: Prospecta Press, 2012.

Mackay, Charles. *Extraordinary Popular Delusions and the Madness of Crowds*. New York: Farrar, Straus and Giroux, 1932.

McKinnon, Ronald I. *The Unloved Dollar Standard: From Bretton Woods to the Rise of China*. Oxford: Oxford University Press, 2013.

Mandelbrot, Benoit. *The Fractal Geometry of Nature*. New York: W. H. Freeman, 1983.

Mandelbrot, Benoit, and Richard L. Hudson. *The (Mis)Behavior of Markets: A Fractal View of Risk, Ruin, and Reward*. New York: Basic Books, 2004.

Martines, Lauro. *Furies: War in Europe, 1450–1700*. New York: Bloomsbury, 2013.

Marx, Karl. *Selected Writings*. Edited by David McLellan. Oxford: Oxford University Press, 1977.

Mead, Walter Russell. *God and Gold: Britain, America, and the Making of the Modern World*. New York: Random House. 2007.

Meltzer, Allan H. *A History of the Federal Reserve*, vol. 1, *1913–1951*. Chicago: University of Chicago Press, 2003.

———. *Why Capitalism?* Oxford: Oxford University Press, 2012.

Milgram, Stanley. *The Individual in a Social World: Essays and Experiments*, 2nd ed. New York: McGraw-Hill, 1992.

Mill, John Stuart. *On Liberty*. Indianapolis: Hackett, 1978.

Miller, Edward S. *Bankrupting the Enemy: The U.S. Financial Siege of Japan Before Pearl Harbor*. Annapolis, Md.: Naval Institute Press, 2007.

Miller, Tom. *China's Urban Billion: The Story Behind the Biggest Migration in Human History*. London: Zed Books, 2012

Mills, C. Wright. *The Power Elite*. Oxford: Oxford University Press, 1956.

Mitchell, Melanie. *Complexity: A Guided Tour*. New York: Oxford University Press, 2009.

National Commission on Terrorist Attacks upon the United States. *The 9/11 Commission Report*. New York: W. W. Norton, 2004.

Newman, Mark, Albert-Laszol Barabasi, and Duncan J. Watts. *The Structure and Dynamics of Networks*. Princeton, N.J.: Princeton University Press, 2006.

Noah, Timothy. *The Great Divergence, America's Growing Inequality Crisis and What We Can Do About It*. New York: Bloomsbury, 2011.

Palley, Thomas, I. *From Financial Crisis to Stagnation: The Destruction of Shared Prosperity and the Role of Economics*. Cambridge, U.K.: Cambridge University Press, 2012.

Pettis, Michael. *The Great Rebalancing: Trade, Conflict, and the Perilous Road Ahead for the World Economy*. Princeton, N.J.: Princeton University Press, 2013.

Phillips, Chester Arthur, and Thomas Francis McManus. *Banking and the Business Cycle: A Study of the Great Depression in the United States*. New York: Macmillan, 1937.

Popper, Karl R. *The Open Society and Its Enemies*. Princeton, N.J.: Princeton University Press, 1971.

Qiao Liang, Colonel, and Colonel Wang Xiangsui. *Unrestricted Warfare*. 1999; reprint Panama City: Pan American, 2002.

Ramo, Joshua Cooper. *The Beijing Consensus*. London: Foreign Policy Centre, 2004.

———. *The Age of the Unthinkable: Why the New World Disorder Constantly Surprises Us and What We Can Do About It*. New York: Little, Brown, 2009.

Ray, Christina. *Extreme Risk Management: Revolutionary Approaches to Evaluating and Measuring Risk*. New York: McGraw-Hill, 2010.

Reinhart, Carmen M., and Kenneth S. Rogoff. *This Time Is Different: Eight Centuries of Financial Folly*. Princeton, N.J.: Princeton University Press, 2009.

Roett, Riordan, and Guadalupe Paz, eds. *China's Expansion into the Western Hemisphere: Implications for Latin America and the United States*. Washington, D.C.: Brookings Institution Press, 2008.

Schelling, Thomas. *Micromotives and Macrobehavior*. New York: W. W. Norton, 1978.

———. *The Strategy of Conflict*. Cambridge, Mass.: Harvard University Press, 1980.

Schleifer, Andrei. *Inefficient Markets: An Introduction to Behavioral Finance*. Oxford: Oxford University Press, 2000.

Schumpeter, Joseph A. *Capitalism, Socialism and Democracy*. London: George Allen and Unwin, 1976.

Shales, Amity. *The Forgotten Man: A New History of the Great Depression*. New York: HarperCollins, 2007.

Shilling, A. Gary. *Deflation: How to Survive and Thrive in the Coming Wave of Deflation*. New York: McGraw-Hill, 1999.

———. *The Age of Deleveraging: Investment Strategies for a Decade of Slow Growth and Deflation*. Hoboken, N.J.: John Wiley & Sons, 2011.

Silver, Nate. *The Signal and the Noise: Why So Many Predictions Fail—But Some Don't*. New York: Penguin Press, 2012.

Sims, Jennifer E., and Burton Gerber, eds. *Transforming U.S. Intelligence*. Washington, D.C.: Georgetown University Press, 2005.

Smith, Adam. *The Theory of Moral Sentiments*. Lexington, Ky.: Private Reprint Edition, 2013.

Sorman, Guy. *The Empire of Lies: The Truth About China in the Twenty-First Century*. New York: Encounter Books, 2008.

Steil, Benn. *The Battle of Bretton Woods: John Maynard Keynes, Harry Dexter White, and the Making of New World Order*. Princeton, N.J.: Princeton University Press, 2013.

Steil, Benn, and Manuel Hinds. *Money, Markets and Sovereignty*. New Haven, Conn.: Yale University Press, 2009.

Steil, Benn, and Robert E. Litan. *Financial Statecraft: The Role of Financial Markets in American Policy*. New Haven, Conn.: Yale University Press, 2006.

Stewart, Bruce H., and J. M. Thompson. *Nonlinear Dynamics and Chaos*, 2nd ed. John Wiley & Sons, 2002.

Strogatz, Steven. *Sync: The Emerging Science of Spontaneous Order*. New York: Hyperion, 2003.

Tainter, Joseph A. *The Collapse of Complex Societies*. Cambridge, U.K.: Cambridge University Press, 1988

Takeyh, Ray. *Hidden Iran: Paradox and Power in the Islamic Republic*. New York: Henry Holt, 2006.

Taleb, Nassim Nicholas. *Fooled by Randomness: The Hidden Role of Chance in the Markets and in Life*. New York: Texere, 2001.

———. *The Black Swan: The Impact of the Highly Improbable.* New York: Random House, 2007.

Taylor, John B. *Getting Off Track: How Government Actions and Interventions Caused, Prolonged, and Worsened the Financial Crisis.* Stanford, Calif.: Hoover Institution Press, 2009.

Thompson, J. M. T., and H. B. Stewart. *Nonlinear Dynamics and Chaos,* 2nd ed. New York: John Wiley & Sons, 2002.

Tilden, Freeman. *A World in Debt.* Toronto: Friedberg Commodity Management, 1983.

Von Mises, Ludwig. *The Theory of Money and Credit.* Indianapolis: Liberty Fund, 1980.

Von Mises, Ludwig, et al. *The Austrian Theory of the Trade Cycle and Other Essays.* Compiled by Richard M. Ebeling. Auburn, Ala.: Ludwig von Mises Institute, 1996.

Von Neumann, John, and Oskar Morgenstern. *The Theory of Games and Economic Behavior.* Princeton, N.J.: Princeton University Press, 1944.

Waldrop, Mitchell. *Complexity: The Emerging Science at the Edge of Order and Chaos.* New York: Simon and Schuster, 1992.

Watts, Duncan J. *Six Degrees: The Science of a Connected Age.* New York: W. W. Norton, 2003.

———. *Everything Is Obvious, Once You Know the Answer.* New York: Crown Business, 2011.

Wolfram, Stephen. *A New Kind of Science.* Champaign, Ill.: Wolfram Media, 2002.

Woodward, Bob. *Maestro: Greenspan's Fed and the American Boom.* New York: Simon and Schuster, 2000.

Wriston, Walter B. *The Twilight of Sovereignty: How the Information Revolution Is Transforming Our World.* New York: Charles Scribner's Sons, 1992.

Yergen, Daniel, and Joseph Stanislaw. *The Commanding Heights: The Battle Between Government and the Marketplace That Is Remaking the Modern World.* New York: Simon and Schuster, 1998.

Zijlstra, Jelle. *Dr. Jelle Zijlstra: Gesprekken en geschriften.* Naarden, Netherlands: Strengholt, 1978.

———. *Per slot van rekening, memoires.* Den Haag, Netherlands: CIP-Gegevens Koninklijke Bibliotheek, 1992.

INDEX